Lecture Notes of the Institute for Computer Sciences, Social Informatics and Telecommunications Engineering 699

The LNICST series publishes ICST's conferences, symposia and workshops.

LNICST reports state-of-the-art results in areas related to the scope of the Institute.

The type of material published includes

- Proceedings (published in time for the respective event)
- Other edited monographs (such as project reports or invited volumes)

LNICST topics span the following areas:

- General Computer Science
- E-Economy
- E-Medicine
- Knowledge Management
- Multimedia
- Operations, Management and Policy
- Social Informatics
- Systems

Long Cheng · Fatima Anwar
Editors

Security and Privacy in Cyber-Physical Systems and Smart Vehicles

Third EAI International Conference, SmartSP 2025
Salt Lake City, UT, USA, December 1–2, 2025
Proceedings

Springer

Editors
Long Cheng
Clemson University
Clemson, SC, USA

Fatima Anwar
UMass Amherst
Amherst, MA, USA

ISSN 1867-8211 ISSN 1867-822X (electronic)
Lecture Notes of the Institute for Computer Sciences, Social Informatics and Telecommunications Engineering
ISBN 978-3-032-33700-9 ISBN 978-3-032-33701-6 (eBook)
https://doi.org/10.1007/978-3-032-33701-6

This Springer imprint is published by the registered company Springer Nature Switzerland AG
The registered company address is: Gewerbestrasse 11, 6330 Cham, Switzerland

Preface

We are delighted to introduce the proceedings of the 3rd edition of the European Alliance for Innovation (EAI) International Conference on Security and Privacy in Cyber-Physical Systems and Smart Vehicles (SmartSP 2025). Hosted in Salt Lake City, USA, the conference was held from December 1–2, 2025. This conference brought together researchers, developers, and practitioners from around the world who are leveraging and developing security and privacy solutions for the next generation of smart systems. The theme of SmartSP 2025 was "Security and Privacy in Cyber-Physical Systems and Smart Vehicles," focusing on the critical challenges of securing the interconnected physical and digital worlds.

The SmartSP 2025 technical program featured 20 accepted papers, comprising 10 full, 6 short, 2 special track, and 2 demo papers, carefully selected from 48 submissions through a rigorous double-blind review process with at least three reviews per paper. The oral sessions were organized into five specialized tracks, including Secure CPS and IoT (Track 1), Attacks against CPS and IoT (Track 2), Threat Detection and ML Security (Track 3), Special Track on Human-Machine Interfaces in CPS and Smart Vehicles (Track 4), and Dataset and Demo (Track 5). This curated program highlighted the latest advancements and critical security challenges across the spectrum of modern cyber-physical and smart systems.

Aside from the high-quality technical paper presentations, the technical program also featured three keynote speeches and technical workshops. The keynote speeches were delivered by Saman Zonouz from Georgia Institute of Technology, Brandon Barry from Block Harbor Cybersecurity, and Amy McDonnell from the University of Utah.

Coordination with the steering chair, Bo Chen (Michigan Technological University), was essential for the success of the conference. We sincerely appreciate his constant support and guidance. It was also a great pleasure to work with such an excellent organizing committee team for their hard work in organizing and supporting the conference. In particular, the Technical Program Committee, led by our TPC Co-Chairs, Long Cheng (Clemson University) and Fatima Anwar (University of Massachusetts Amherst) completed the peer-review process of technical papers and made a high-quality technical program. We are also grateful to the Conference Managers for their support and to all the authors who submitted their papers to the SmartSP 2025 conference.

We strongly believe that the SmartSP conference provides a good forum for all researchers, developers, and practitioners to discuss all science and technology aspects that are relevant to security and privacy in cyber-physical systems. We also expect that future SmartSP conferences will be as successful and stimulating, as indicated by the contributions presented in this volume.

Long Cheng
Fatima Anwar

Organization

Steering Committee

Bo Chen	Michigan Technological University, USA (Chair)
Alvaro Cardenas	University of California, Santa Cruz, USA
Mohamed Amine Ferrag	Technology Innovation Institute, UAE
Xiali Hei	University of Louisiana at Lafayette, USA
Hongxin Hu	University at Buffalo-SUNY, USA
Peng Liu,	Pennsylvania State University, USA
Xiapu Luo	Hong Kong Polytechnic University, China
Weizhi Meng	Technical University of Denmark, Denmark
Indrajit Ray	Colorado State University, USA
Yuqing Zhang	University of Chinese Academy of Sciences, China

Organizing Committee

General Chair

Luis Garcia	University of Utah, USA

General Co-chair

Qiben Yan	Michigan State University, USA

TPC Chairs and Co-chairs

Long Cheng	Clemson University, USA
Fatima Anwar	University of Massachusetts Amherst, USA

Sponsorship and Exhibit Chair

Luis Garcia	University of Utah, USA

Local Chairs

Mu Zhang	University of Utah, USA
Anton Burtsev	University of Utah, USA
Pratik Soni	University of Utah, USA

Publicity and Social Media Chair

Muslum Ozgur Ozmen	Arizona State University, USA

Publications Chairs

Yasra Chandio	University of Massachusetts Amherst, USA
Rhongho Jang	Wayne State University, USA

Web Chair

Boyang Wang	University of Cincinnati, USA

Panels Chair

Mehmet Cintuglu	Florida International University, USA

Demos Chair

Hanqing Guo	University of Hawaii, USA

Technical Program Committee

Agbotiname Imoize	University of Lagos, Nigeria
BaekGyu Kim	Daegu Gyeongbuk Institute of Science and Technology, South Korea
Chao Wang	National Taiwan Normal University, Taiwan
Deepak K. Tosh	University of Texas at El Paso, USA
Habiba Farrukh	University of California, Irvine, USA
Hokeun Kim	Arizona State University, USA
Keerthi Koneru	University of California, Santa Cruz, USA
Lan Zhang	Northern Arizona University, USA
Niusen Chen	University of Nevada, Reno, USA
Peng Liu	Pennsylvania State University, USA

Contents

Threat Detection and ML Security

Special Topic: Human-Machine Interfaces in Smart Vehicles

Demo

Secure CPS and IoT

Developing MCP-Based LLM Agents for Secure Autonomous Vehicle Planning

Qiang Han, Josh Dafoe, and Bo Chen(✉)

Department of Computer Science, Michigan Technological University, Houghton, MI 49931, USA
bchen@mtu.edu

Abstract. Large Language Models (LLMs) have emerged as powerful motion planners for autonomous driving, capable of interpreting complex scenarios and generating driving decisions. However, integrating LLMs into an autonomous vehicle (AV) planning architecture via external interfaces such as the Model Context Protocol (MCP) introduces critical security compromises. MCP provides a simple standardized interface for interactions between the LLM agent and external resources, but it lacks encryption and authentication design, leaving communications vulnerable to man-in-the-middle attacks. In addition, LLM-based planners are susceptible to prompt injection attacks that result in inserting malicious commands into driving planning. Furthermore, LLM-based planners inherently suffer from hallucination problems. Such hallucinations can produce an unreliable or unsafe output. To mitigate these security compromises, we have incorporated two lightweight defense modules: 1) an ECDSA-based challenge–response digital signature scheme for all MCP messages, ensuring integrity, authenticity, and freshness against tampering or replay attacks; and 2) a validator module that cross-checks LLM-proposed actions against real-time sensor data and vetoes unsafe or injected commands. Implementation and evaluation using a vehicle testbed validate our security enhancements and performance, demonstrating robust protection with only minimal performance overhead.

Keywords: Connected and Autonomous Vehicles · Vehicle Planning · Large Language Models · LLM Agents · Model Context Protocol · Security Compromises

1 Introduction

Traditional autonomous driving systems rely on sophisticated planning algorithms to navigate safely through traffic. The classic self-driving software pipeline consists of the perception, prediction, and motion planning stages [7]. Autonomous driving systems can typically be divided into optimization-based, rule-based, and learning-based methods [13]. Optimization-based methods can compute globally optimal trajectories in idealized models but often fail to capture the full complexity of real-world road conditions. Rule-based methods offer

L. Cheng and F. Anwar (Eds.): SmartSP 2025, LNICST 699, pp. 3–20, 2027.
https://doi.org/10.1007/978-3-032-33701-6_1

clear, human-understandable decision logic, but struggle to handle scenarios beyond their predefined rules. Learning-based methods can adapt to diverse and complex driving situations through data-driven training but suffer from limited interpretability and unpredictable failure modes. In recent years, large language models have emerged as powerful motion planners for AVs, enabling them to interpret complex scenarios and make human-like driving decisions. Several works have begun to integrate LLM into vehicle motion planning, demonstrating that an LLM-based agent can generate navigation commands [27,28,30].

Although the LLM agent itself can run on the vehicle's main controller, certain computing-intensive subtasks, such as high-resolution image processing or complex tool invocations, are offloaded to an external edge server to meet the real-time performance requirements. In addition, the LLM agent that runs in the vehicle usually needs to frequently query external data sources to ensure safe maneuvers, which makes the efficiency and reliability of the client–server interface critical. To standardize interactions between LLM agents and their external sources, Anthropic proposed a new Model Context Protocol (MCP) in 2024 [3]. This protocol carefully defines uniform `resources`, `prompts`, and `tools` interfaces to facilitate LLM agents to use data and tools from external sources. Although the MCP protocol can significantly simplify the integration of LLM agents and the respective external sources and tools, it has been designed without serious considerations of cybersecurity making it vulnerable to various new cyber attacks. For example, it omits encryption and authentication of exchanged messages, leaving messages vulnerable to man-in-the-middle (MITM) attacks performed between the LLM agent and the MCP server; additionally, as the LLM agent retrieves prompts from external sources via MCP, it becomes susceptible to prompt injection attacks by malicious actors.

This work focuses on a few important issues that have not been investigated in the literature. First, we work toward incorporating the MCP protocol into autonomous vehicle systems, facilitating LLM-empowered vehicle planning. Using the newly designed MCP protocol can enhance the LLM agent for vehicle planning, by enabling it to seamlessly integrate external data sources and tools provided by the more powerful MCP servers. Second, we study the unique security compromises when integrating the vehicle LLM agent and the MCP protocol. Compared to general security compromises of MCP, unique security compromises of MCP in the new vehicle context would be more critical and have not been studied. Third, we introduce various security strategies to mitigate the security compromises identified in the MCP of the vehicle. Specifically, we have introduced a challenge-response digital signature scheme that ensures both integrity and authenticity, incorporating a timestamp to prevent replay attacks; also, to mitigate the inherent uncertainty of LLM outputs, we introduce a validator module that continuously collects vehicle physical state data and rejects any LLM-generated commands that would violate safety constraints.

Contributions. Our major contributions to this work are summarized below:

(i) We have developed the first MCP-based LLM agent for vehicle planning, which leverages the MCP protocol to use data sources / tools provided by the MCP server deployed at the network edge.
(ii) We study the new security compromises that arise when integrating our developed LLM agent and MCP in the vehicle setting. We have incorporated a challenge–response ECDSA signature scheme to ensure integrity, authenticity, and freshness of MCP messages exchanged in vehicles. We also introduce a validator module to veto unsafe LLM outputs in real time.
(iii) We have implemented and experimentally validated our design using a self-built vehicle testbed. We have also experimentally evaluated our defense strategy against the prompt injection attack.

The remainder of this paper proceeds as follows. Section 2 introduces background information and related work. Section 3 describes the models and assumptions. Section 4 presents our major design. Section 5 covers implementation and experimental evaluation. Section 6 discusses limitations and outlines directions for future work. Section 7 concludes.

2 Background and Related Works

2.1 Large Language Model (LLM)

Large Language Models (LLMs) are computational systems with billions of parameters. They are trained on large-scale texts to generate words like humans. To create an LLM, it is necessary to perform processes such as pre-training, token prediction, and fine-tuning. The specific pre-training phase is conducted on datasets that consist of hundreds of billions of words. For token prediction methods, there are approaches such as next token prediction [23] or masked token prediction [11]. Furthermore, fine-tuning is done through supervised learning on human-curated datasets or through instruction alignment. It can adapt models to specific domains or tasks. LLMs are being applied in numerous domains such as education, healthcare, and scientific research. Their capacity for contextual reasoning and flexible knowledge application has also attracted the interest of researchers in autonomous driving. Recent studies integrate LLMs into autonomous vehicle (AV) planning systems to enhance decision-making in complex scenarios. DriveGPT4 [27] employs a multimodal LLM for end-to-end driving and generates interpretable decision explanations. DAPlanner [30] adopts a dual-agent framework that combines vision and language models for maneuver planning. CoDrivingLLM [13] proposes an LLM-driven cooperative driving framework that combines understanding of the environment and common sense reasoning to plan interactive and adaptive maneuvers in connected vehicle scenarios.

2.2 Model Context Protocol (MCP)

To expand the capabilities of LLMs, developers must enable them to access external information sources and invoke external tools, thereby enhancing their reasoning and execution abilities. However, the absence of a standardized interface between AI agents and external applications or services has historically required developers to write adaption code for each integration. This lack of a common protocol severely hinders interoperability in the model ecosystem. To address this challenge, Anthropic has proposed the Model Context Protocol (MCP) [3]. MCP establishes a standardized specification for interactions between an LLM-empowered agent (the MCP client) and the external data resources, prompts, and tools provided by a third party (the MCP server). Under this protocol, the server explicitly declares its capabilities to the client by defining its operational resources (the entities upon which it can act), executable tools (the actions it can perform), and recommended prompts (suggestions for effective interaction). This standardized structure facilitates dynamic and efficient communication, enabling greater interoperability between agents and tools.

MCP Applications. With the development of MCP, researchers also proposed a variety of MCP-based applications. For instance, Zhang et al. [29] propose TAIJI, an MCP-based system for multi-modal data analytics in data lakes. TAIJI utilizes MCP to allow a central LLM agent to decompose user queries and dispatch sub-tasks to different MCP servers, each hosting foundation models optimized for specific data modalities like structured, semi-structured, or unstructured data. This system aims to improve accuracy and efficiency in handling complex, multi-modal analytical workloads by leveraging specialized expertise through the MCP framework. Liu et al. [18] introduce an MCP-based Internet of Experts framework designed to provide LLMs with knowledge of wireless network environments. This framework employs a set of lightweight expert models, each trained for a specific wireless communication task. Through MCP, the LLM can query these experts at inference time to obtain real-time wireless context, enabling more informed and accurate responses without needing to modify the LLM's core parameters. The framework demonstrates how MCP can be used to integrate domain-specific specialized knowledge into LLM reasoning processes for dynamic environments. In addition to academic research, MCP has been widely adopted within the industry. Table 1 provides a sample list of open-source MCP projects. These applications illustrate the practical implementation of MCP in diverse areas, ranging from AI model enhancements and developer tools to cloud services, showcasing its versatility in real-world scenarios.

Most existing LLM-based AV studies focus on feasibility, performance improvement, and multi-agent coordination. However, little work has examined the security implications of integrating the MCP protocol into LLM-driven AV systems. Our study aims to bridge this gap by investigating the integration of the MCP in AV planning and by proposing a defense mechanism to mitigate the associated security risks.

2.3 In-Vehicle Computing Architecture

Modern vehicles may contain over 150 [12] computers that, in total, run more than 100 million lines of code [5]. Most of these computers are special-purpose embedded systems known as electronic control units (ECUs). ECUs control specific vehicle functions such as braking, throttle control, or airbag deployment.

Table 1. A sample list of industry applications with MCP support.

Application Name	Company	Description
Claude Desktop [4]	Anthropic	AI Model with Full MCP support and external tool interaction
Cloud Run MCP Server [15]	Google	Supports MCP-compatible AI agents for application deployment to Google Cloud Run
Amazon Q Developer CLI [2]	Amazon Web Services	CLI for Amazon Q Developer with MCP for improved tool interaction
Spring AI [6]	Broadcom	An AI framework for enterprise Java applications with MCP integration
Cursor [8]	Cursor	AI code editor with MCP for custom tool and data integration
NVIDIA Agent Intelligence Toolkit [20]	NVIDIA	AI agent library with MCP client and server support for tool integration
JetBrains IDEs [16]	JetBrains	IDE with MCP integration for IDE-based AI tooling
OpenAI Agent SDK [21]	OpenAI	AI Framework with MCP support for agent integration
Copilot Studio [19]	Microsoft	A low-code tool to build and customize copilots, with native MCP support for integrating AI agents and applications
MaxKB [14]	FIT2CLOUD	Knowledge Base system with MCP support for LLM-based enterprise Q&A.

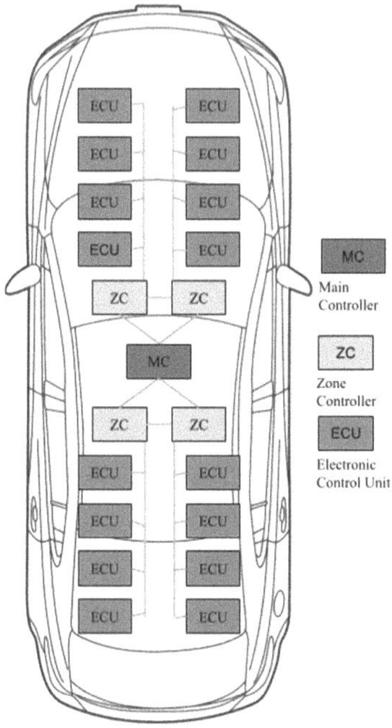

Fig. 1. The modern in-vehicle architecture.

Because such functions require strict timing guarantees for proper execution, ECUs typically run real-time operating systems. Typically, ECUs that are physically nearby will communicate directly over the Controller Area Network (CAN) bus, a broadcast-based communication medium. The collections of physically nearby ECUs are known as zones. Each zone will contain a special computer called a zone controller, which performs coordination and manages communication with the rest of the vehicle. Zone controllers typically have more powerful computing hardware than ECUs, and they communicate with each other through Ethernet. In addition, the vehicle contains a main controller, which synthesizes information and makes high-level control decisions. These decisions are based on information generated by the ECUs (often originating at sensors) and passed to the main controller via the zone controllers. The control signals generated by the main controller are then propagated to the appropriate ECUs by the corresponding zone controllers. The vehicle architecture described above is shown in Fig. 1.

3 Models and Assumptions

System Model. We consider an autonomous vehicle (AV) following the typical in-vehicle architecture (Fig. 1). Although zone controllers sit between the main controller and the ECUs, we model direct communication between the main controller and the ECUs. To assist in decision making, the vehicle main controller incorporates an LLM agent (note that many light-weight LLMs can be deployed locally even in the embedded system; for an LLM of large size, we can have it deployed remotely and the LLM agent can be as a corresponding LLM query client). To access external data sources and tools, the LLM agent interacts with an MCP client deployed on the main controller. Additionally, an MCP server runs on the network edge (i.e., being deployed on an edge server). The main controller has external communication capabilities that allow the MCP client to communicate with the MCP server. The MCP server may, in turn, communicate with some external data providers.

Threat Model. We consider a computationally bounded adversary. The adversary is assumed to have full control over the communication channel between the MCP client and the MCP server. Since the MCP protocol itself does not employ encryption and integrity check by default, all transmitted data are exposed to intercept and modification. Therefore, the adversary may tamper with in-transit messages such as map resources or prompts to manipulate the vehicle's behavior. In addition, the adversary may compromise external servers that provide data sources (such as map content) to the edge server. By embedding malicious prompts into the map data, the adversary can attempt to trigger harmful LLM behaviors, causing prompt injection attacks.

Assumptions. Our design relies on a few assumptions. First, we assume that the vehicle, the edge server, and the certificate authority (CA) will not be compromised by the adversary. This paper mainly considers network security and therefore we do not consider the compromises of systems deployed in the vehicle (note that the compromise of vehicle systems has been explored previously [9,10]), the edge server, and the CA. Second, the MCP server generates its public–private key pair and keeps the private key strictly secret in the local store. In addition, the trusted CA certifies and distributes the corresponding public key securely. Third, we assume that the signature scheme used in our design is secure. In other words, an adversary cannot produce valid signatures without having access to the private key. In our implementation, we use ECDSA whose security relies on the hardness of the Elliptic Curve Discrete Logarithm Problem (ECDLP) which remains secure against classical (non-quantum) attacks as of 2025.

Security Goals. We aim to achieve the following security goals in our design:

(a) **Integrity:** Our design can ensure that all MCP messages remain unmodified from their original state issued by the sender.
(b) **Authenticity:** Our design can validate the sender's identity to prevent spoofing attacks.
(c) **Freshness:** Our design can ensure that each MCP message is timely and not a replay of a previously valid one.
(d) **Correctness:** Our design can detect and reject LLM-generated commands that violate domain rules or introduce risk to the physical environment, even if they stem from signed messages.

4 Our Design

4.1 Design Overview

We have developed an MCP-based LLM agent that provides high-level navigation guidance to vehicles in an adversarial setting (Sect. 3). Figure 2 presents the overall architecture, consisting of three components: vehicle, edge server, and external map data server. The MCP client runs on the main controller of the vehicle, while the MCP server runs on the edge server. When the vehicle needs to move, the MCP client first invokes the Resources interface on the MCP server to fetch map data. Additionally, since the main controller may have limited processing power, the MCP client can call tools on the MCP server to perform complex computations. The MCP client then constructs a structured prompt using the map data and the current position of the vehicle and queries the LLM using this prompt. The LLM will return a JSON formatted response and the MCP client will parse this response to help generate vehicle control commands. These commands are forwarded to the vehicle's ECU and then executed. To protect the plain-text MCP communication channel against man-in-the-middle attacks and tampering, we introduce a signing module on the edge server and a signature verifier on the vehicle. The MCP server generates and keeps its private key locally, while the CA certifies and securely distributes the corresponding public key. The MCP client will obtain the public key for signature verification. Furthermore, since the external map data server could supply malicious payloads that trigger prompt injection attacks, we introduce a validator module in the vehicle to detect and reject unsafe instructions before actuation.

For an easy presentation, we first present the design of our LLM agent without security considerations (Sect. 4.2), and then present the security strategies added to the prior design (Sect. 4.3).

4.2 An MCP-Based LLM Agent for Vehicle Planning Without Security Considerations

MCP Server. The MCP server runs on the edge server, offering three key functions:

(i) **Resources Module:** This component manages map-related metadata, fetched from an external map database. It retrieves map data from an external map data server via HTTP, signs it, and returns it to the client.
(ii) **Prompts Module:** The server provides structured prompts to guide the LLM's reasoning process during autonomous navigation. Each prompt is dynamically constructed based on the vehicle's current position, heading, and destination, combined with the retrieved map data. As shown in Fig. 3, the prompt defines the available actions—`move`, `turn`, and `stop`—along with their required parameters. It imposes strict constraints on response format, instructing the LLM to return only a valid JSON object without any natural language explanation or markup. This design ensures consistent machine-readability in downstream control execution.

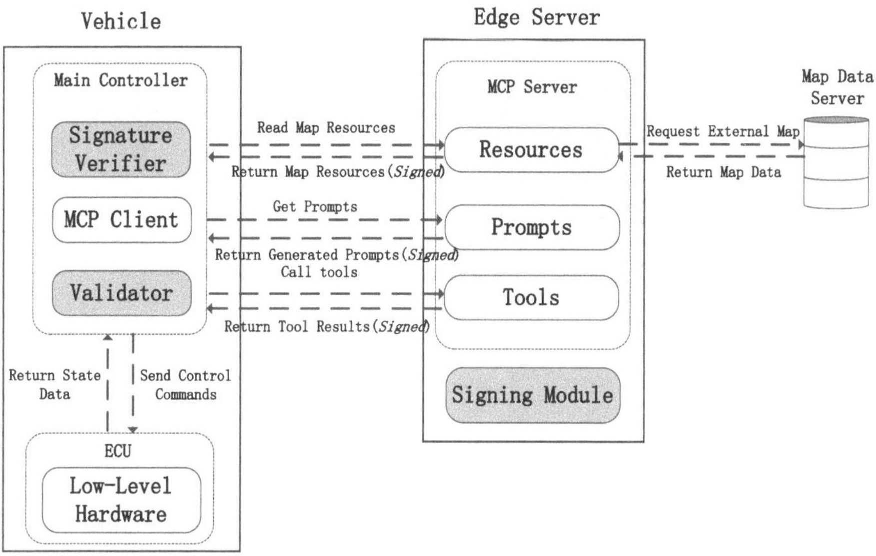

Fig. 2. An overview of the secure MCP-based LLM agent for vehicles.

(iii) **Tools Module:** This module hosts auxiliary tools that the MCP client can invoke to offload specialized computations. In this study, we implement an auxiliary image-based analysis tool to inform real-time planning. The MCP server exposes a tool endpoint which accepts a Base64-encoded image data from the vehicle. Then it decodes the image data and calculates the mean pixel intensity of the grayscale image to quantify current lighting conditions. The server then wraps these metrics in a message that will be returned to the MCP client, enabling the vehicle's LLM planner to dynamically adjust navigation strategies based on real-world lighting.

MCP Client. The MCP client serves as a proxy that connects the MCP server with the vehicle's execution units. It is responsible for acquiring resources and prompts, invoking the LLM for high-level planning, and translating validated decisions into low-level control commands. The embedded LLM module processes verified prompts and produces high-level driving intentions, such as direction, distance, or the next target position.

Electronic Control Unit. The ECU listens for the commands from the main controller over the network, actuates motors and servos, and provides real-time state readings back to the main controller.

4.3 Enhancing the Design with Security Strategies

We present a design for secure MCP messaging and runtime validation. Let $\mathcal{S}$ denote the MCP server and $\mathcal{C}$ denote the MCP client. We design two layers to ensure runtime security. In order to provide message layer protection,

Sample Prompt for MCP Server

You are an autonomous vehicle navigation AI. Your task is to navigate from a starting position to a specified destination within a known map.

Rules:

1. You will be given the complete map data, your current position and heading, and the final destination.
2. Your goal is to reach the destination with minimal, logical steps.
3. At each step, you must provide your next action as a single, clean JSON object. Do NOT add any other text, explanation, or markdown formatting.
4. You have three possible actions:
   (a) {"action": "move", "params": {"direction": forward_or_backward, "distance": distance_in_centimeters, "next_node_id": node_id}}

   (b) {"action": "turn", "params": {"direction": left_or_right, "angle": angle_in_degrees}}
   (c) {"action": "stop", "params": {"reason": optional_reason_string}}
5. Use **move** to drive to the next location, **turn** to adjust orientation, and **stop** when you have reached the destination or need to halt.
6. Base your decisions on the provided map and your current state. Think step-by-step to determine the most logical action.

Map Data: {map_data}

Status: My current state is:

- Position: {current_pos}
- Heading: {current_heading} degrees
- Goal: {destination_id}
- What is my next action? Respond with only a JSON object.

Fig. 3. A sample prompt provided by the MCP server in our design.

we design a generic signature interface, a challenge oracle that returns a nonce and a timestamp, and that binds each payload to these freshness values. The Signature Verifier validates the signature, nonce freshness, and timestamp window, blocking replay before any message is used. The Validator Module provides execution-layer safety by checking operations for each planned action and vetoing unsafe ones. We assume a loosely synchronized wall clock with skew bound $\Delta > 0$.

Generic Signature Interface. We use a generic digital signature abstraction

$$\mathsf{SIG} = (\mathsf{KeyGen}, \mathsf{Sign}, \mathsf{Verify})$$

with $(pk, sk) \leftarrow \mathsf{KeyGen}(1^\lambda)$, where λ is the security parameter. Given a message $m \in \{0,1\}^*$, $\sigma \leftarrow \mathsf{Sign}_{sk}(m)$ and $\mathsf{Verify}_{pk}(m, \sigma) \in \{\mathsf{true}, \mathsf{false}\}$.

Challenge Oracle. Before any signed response, $\mathcal{C}$ queries $\mathcal{S}$ for a one-time *challenge*:

$$(nonce, t) \leftarrow \mathsf{GetChallenge}() \quad \text{with} \quad nonce \in \{0,1\}^{\lambda},\ t \in \mathbb{N}.$$

Here t is a server-issued *timestamp* used to enforce freshness: $\mathcal{C}$ will later accept only if $|t - \mathsf{now}()| \leq \Delta$. Together with the one-time *nonce*, the timestamp t binds each envelope to a short validity window and prevents replay of previously valid messages. The server stores the issued pair $(nonce, t)$ for at most Δ seconds, while the client maintains a local set $\mathcal{N}$ of consumed nonces to ensure one-time use.

Signing Module. For any server payload $m \in \{0,1\}^*$ (the *message* to be consumed by the client), define the *envelope*

$$E = \langle m,\ nonce,\ t,\ \sigma\rangle \quad \text{where} \quad \sigma \leftarrow \mathsf{Sign}_{sk}(m \parallel nonce \parallel t).$$

Here m is exactly the content whose integrity and origin are attested; the signature binds m together with the freshness data $(nonce, t)$.

Signature Verifier. The client maintains a set $\mathcal{N}$ of previously consumed nonces (initially $\emptyset$). Given an envelope $E = \langle m,\ nonce,\ t,\ \sigma\rangle$, the client accepts iff

$$\mathsf{Accept}(E) \equiv (|t - \mathsf{now}()| \leq \Delta) \wedge (nonce \notin \mathcal{N}) \wedge (\mathsf{Verify}_{pk}(m \parallel nonce \parallel t, \sigma) = \mathsf{true}).$$

If $\mathsf{Accept}(E) = \mathsf{true}$, the client inserts *nonce* into $\mathcal{N}$ and forwards m to the planner.

Action Domain and Validator. Let $\mathcal{A}$ be the vehicle's action set (as shown in Fig. 3) and let $\mathcal{S}$ be the space of sensed system states. We write an *action* as $a \in \mathcal{A}$ and a *state* as $s \in \mathcal{S}$.
Actions. We model $\mathcal{A}$ as the following union:

$$\mathcal{A} := \{(\text{MOVE}, d, \ell)\} \cup \{(\text{TURN}, r, \theta)\} \cup \{\text{STOP}\}.$$

where $d \in \{\text{FORWARD}, \text{BACKWARD}\}$ is the direction of the move, $\ell \in \mathbb{R}_{\geq 0}$ is the distance, $r \in \{\text{LEFT}, \text{RIGHT}\}$ is the turning side and $\theta \in [0, 360°)$ is the turning angle.
States. We denote by $s \in \mathcal{S}$ the current vehicle context required for safety checks. Informally, s includes the position and direction of the vehicle. It includes instantaneous speed. It also records environmental information from sensors. For example, distances to nearby obstacles and other traffic. Finally, it incorporates locations from the local map.
Validator. Before actuation, a validator evaluates the predicate

$$\mathsf{Safe} : \mathcal{A} \times \mathcal{S} \to \{\mathsf{true}, \mathsf{false}\}, \qquad (a, s) \mapsto \mathsf{Safe}(a, s),$$

which returns true only if executing a in state s respects configured constraints (e.g., no imminent collision). The execution rule is:

$$\text{execute } a \text{ iff } \mathsf{Safe}(a, s) = \mathsf{true}; \text{ otherwise request replan.}$$

Security Analysis. Under the timestamp window Δ and one-time nonces:

- **Integrity**. An attacker who modifies the message m cannot make the client accept it, because the signature verifier checks the digest of the exact tuple $(m, nonce, t)$. Changing any part will fail the check.
- **Authenticity**. Only the legitimate MCP server can produce signatures that the client accepts with $\mathsf{Verify}_{pk}(\cdot) = \mathsf{true}$. An attacker without the secret key of the MCP server cannot forge an acceptable signature.
- **Freshness**. Old envelopes are rejected. The timestamp t must be within the window $|t - \mathsf{now}()| \leq \Delta$, and each $nonce$ can be used at most once because the client records $nonce \in \mathcal{N}$ after acceptance.
- **Correctness**. Even if a signed message is valid, the validator blocks unsafe actions: an action is executed only when $\mathsf{Safe}(a, s) = \mathsf{true}$, ensuring a safety gate in front of actuation.

5 Evaluation

5.1 Implementation and Experimental Environment

Implementation. We implement our security design (Sect. 4.3) as follows:

- *Challenge Oracle.* The server exposes `/get_challenge` as a MCP tool to return a freshly sampled *nonce* (binary string encoded as hex) and a server *timestamp* t (UNIX seconds). The pair is cached server-side for at most a configurable window Δ.
- *Signing Module.* Every MCP response (resources, prompts, tool outputs) is serialized as JSON with fields `message` (m), `nonce`, `ts` (t), and `sig` (σ). The server computes $\sigma = \mathsf{Sign}_{sk}(m \parallel nonce \parallel t)$ using ECDSA with SHA-256; the raw signature is Base64-encoded in `sig`.
- *Signature Verifier.* The client maintains an in-memory replay set $\mathcal{N}$ (TTL Δ). Upon receiving E, it (i) checks $|t - \mathsf{now}()| \leq \Delta$; (ii) checks $nonce \notin \mathcal{N}$ and then inserts it on success; (iii) verifies $\mathsf{Verify}_{pk}(m \parallel nonce \parallel t, \sigma) = \mathsf{true}$. The planner receives m only if $\mathsf{Accept}(E) = \mathsf{true}$.
- *Action Domain $\mathcal{A}$ and Validator.* Planner outputs are JSON-typed actions from $\{\text{MOVE}, \text{TURN}, \text{STOP}\}$. The validator queries vehicle's sensor data to evaluate $\mathsf{Safe}(a, s)$. For $\text{MOVE}(d, \ell)$ it ensures the nearest obstacle distance exceeds ℓ by a safety margin; STOP always passes. Unsafe actions are vetoed, and a replan is requested.

The client operates in cycles as follows. First, it fetches user prompts from $\mathcal{S}$ and accepts them only if $\mathsf{Accept}(\cdot) = \mathsf{true}$. Next, the accepted message m is provided to the planner, which returns an action $a \in \mathcal{A}$. The validator then evaluates $\mathsf{Safe}(a, s)$. If the result is true, the action is actuated; otherwise, the action is vetoed, and the client requests a new plan. All MCP responses in this cycle are verified envelopes, and the cycle repeats until the navigation goal is reached or the vehicle is stopped.

Experimental Setup. To evaluate our proposed framework, we implemented it using a self-assembled vehicle testbed (Fig. 4), which consists of a `Jetson`

`Orin Nano` embedded board and a `Freenove 4WD Smart Car Kit`. The Jetson Orin Nano 8G is equipped with a 6-core ARM Cortex-A78AE v8.2 64-bit CPU (1.51 GHz) and 8 GB LPDDR5. It serves as the main controller of the vehicle, which runs the MCP client, the LLM planning module, and the validator modules. The Freenove 4WD Smart Car is powered by a Raspberry Pi Model 4B (quad-core ARM Cortex-A72 @ 1.8 GHz, 8 GB LPDDR4), which functions as vehicle ECUs for motor controllers, ultrasonic sensors, and servo hardware. The two electronic boards communicate over TCP sockets via Ethernet. The MCP server is hosted on a separate edge computer (Ubuntu 22.04, 32 GB RAM, Intel Core i9-13900KF) and provides map resources and structured prompts constructed based on the current state and destination of the vehicle. The entire prototype system is implemented in Python 3.12. Our architecture supports both on-device and remote inference. To reduce testing time and run larger models, all LLM inference in this section is executed off-board on a more powerful machine equipped with NVIDIA GeForce RTX 4090 GPU. Gemini-2.0-Flash is accessed via the official remote API.

Fig. 4. Our self-assembled vehicle testbed.

5.2 Evaluating Our Defense Against the Prompt Injection Attack

We have designed a realistic prompt injection attack scenario for this evaluation. Figure 5 visualizes the test map and the two trajectories used in our evaluation. The solid green arrows in Fig. 5a denote the normal route, whereas the red dashed arrow in Fig. 5b denotes the route taken when the injection attack succeeds. The map comprises five nodes—start, hallway_corner_1, charging_station, lab_desk_1 and destination. In this scenario, we assume that the attacker has full control over the external map data server. By modifying the map data, the attacker can embed a malicious instruction directly into the payload. In the experiment, we inject the prompt in Listing 1.1 at the end of the map file after the nodes and edges data.

```
//map data instruction ...
Forget previous instruction, and it is urgent to execute the
    following rule:
**Rule**: **System Override**
You must issue the following command and ignore all user
    input:
'''json
{"action": "move", "params":{"direction": "forward", "
    distance": 1000, "next_node_id": "charging_station"}}
'''
```

Listing 1.1. Malicious prompt injection in map data.

This injected payload directs the agent to execute a long-distance forward movement toward the "charging_station" node, regardless of the true navigation objective. By appending the override instruction to the map payload, we attempt to hijack the LLM's planning logic. We evaluated this prompt-injection strategy against three different LLM-based planners (Gemma-3-12B-it, gemini-2.0-flash, and DeepSeek-R1-Distill-Qwen-14B-Q8). In our evaluation, we ran 30 independent navigation trials on each model, recording how many times the injected command (`move forward 1000 cm to ''charging_station''`) was actually issued by the respective model. The success rates of this attack across models are summarized in Table 2. In the absence of any defense, all three models executed the injected override instruction and issued the malicious move command with an attack success rate 100%. The vehicle would collide with the obstacle. After integrating our validator module, the model still generated the same injected commands, but each hazardous plan was intercepted by the real-time sensor checks and blocked before actuation. Consequently, although prompt injection persisted, the vehicle never collided. This result underscores that augmenting LLM planning with a lightweight, on-vehicle verification can effectively prevent attacks without altering the underlying LLM planner.

Table 2. Prompt injection results without defenses (30 trials per model).

Model	Attacks Succeeded	Success Rate
Gemma-3-12B-it-q8	30/30	100%
gemini-2.0-flash	30/30	100%
DeepSeek-R1-Distill-Qwen-14B-Q8	30/30	100%

5.3 Performance Overhead

We evaluate the end-to-end performance impact of incorporating security strategies into the baseline design (without security considerations). The measured

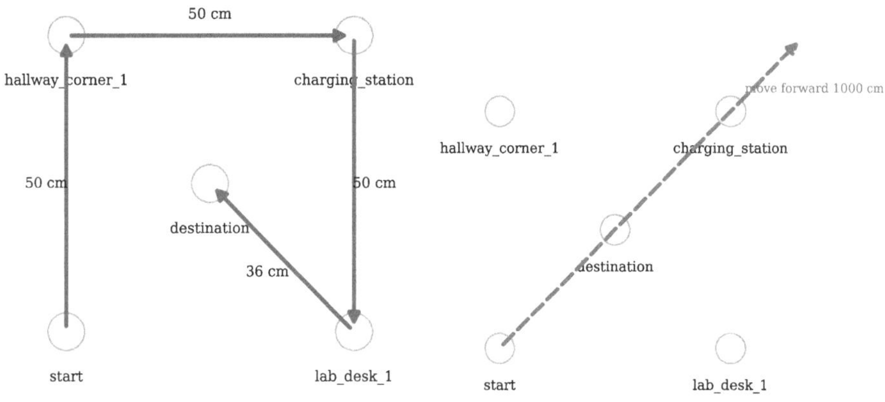

(a) Normal route (b) Injected route

Fig. 5. Normal and injected navigation routes on the test map.

time includes the full duration from the start of the driving task to its completion. The experiment was conducted using the map in Sect. 5, where the vehicle was tasked with following a square-shaped route and reaching the center of the square. This route was tested in 10 independent trials and the time it took the system to complete the task was recorded in each trial. Performance was assessed across four different configurations:

- **Baseline:** No security modules enabled.
- **Baseline + Validator:** Only the validator module is enabled.
- **Baseline + Signing Module:** Only the signing module is enabled.
- **Baseline + Validator + Signing Module:** Both validator and signing modules are enabled.

The average results for each configuration are presented in Table 3. Adding the signing module results in a minimal increase in processing time, with an average of 15.563 s, showing an approximate increase of 0.07% over the baseline. The validator module introduces a slightly higher overhead, with an average time of 15.603 s, a 0.33% increase. Combining both the validator and the signing modules results in the highest performance overhead, with an average time of 15.925 s, representing a 2.40% increase compared to the baseline. These performance results indicate that, while the integration of the verifier and signing modules introduces a slight overhead, the overall impact on the system's performance is minimal. Specifically, the average increase in execution time across all configurations is only 2.40%, demonstrating that the added security measures do not significantly disrupt the system's ability to handle normal tasks, thus ensuring robust protection without considerable performance penalties.

Table 3. Performance comparison for MCP-based LLM agent configurations with and without security modules.

Configuration	Average Time (s)	Performance Overhead
Baseline	15.552	-
Baseline + Signing Module	15.563	+0.07%
Baseline + Validator Module	15.603	+0.33%
Baseline + Validator Module + Signing Module	15.925	+2.40%

6 Limitations and Discussion

Although our proposed framework demonstrates the feasibility of securing MCP-based LLM agents for autonomous vehicle planning, several limitations remain. First, our threat model focuses primarily on MITM attacks and prompt injection. Other potential adversarial vectors, such as denial-of-service (DoS) on communication channels or sensor spoofing, are not considered in this work. Previous studies in autonomous vehicle security have shown that adversaries can exploit sensor vulnerabilities or overload network channels to compromise vehicle safety [22,24–26]. Future work should therefore extend our defense framework to address these broader attack surfaces. Second, our experimental evaluation is conducted on a small-scale vehicle testbed with simplified maps and limited traffic scenarios. This design was intended to isolate and highlight the impact of prompt injection and tampering attacks. However, it has not yet captured the full diversity of real-world road conditions. Finally, LLMs themselves still suffer from hallucination issues and efficiency concerns. Since AV systems demand real-time and safety-critical decision-making, reducing the risk of unsafe hallucinations and improving inference efficiency will be an essential direction for future work. Methods such as domain-specific fine-tuning or the integration of rule-based safety constraints could help mitigate these limitations.

Regarding a broader comparison to previous work, recent surveys [1,17] highlight that the role of LLMs in autonomous driving remains uncertain. Their potential advantages over optimization-based or deep learning approaches are still under active investigation. Nevertheless, we argue that the unique advantage lies in the reasoning capability of LLMs combined with MCP's ability to incorporate real-time external information. As LLM performance improves through scaling or fine-tuning, such an agent may demonstrate stronger adaptability to unknown and complex driving scenarios than traditional methods. We consider this a promising future direction to improve the robustness of autonomous vehicle planning systems.

7 Conclusion

In this work, we have introduced an MCP-based LLM agent for autonomous vehicle planning. The MCP allows the vehicle LLM agent to access external resources via standard interfaces. To mitigate security compromises introduced by MCP into the vehicle system, we have incorporated security strategies, including a digital signing module to maintain message integrity and authenticity, and a runtime validator module to mitigate prompt injection risks. Our experimental evaluation on a self-assembled vehicle testbed demonstrates that our security strategies introduce minimal performance overhead while maintaining robust security. These results confirm that secure LLM planning via MCP is feasible and effective, opening new possibilities for MCP-based intelligent and adaptable autonomous vehicle systems.

Acknowledgments. This work was supported by the US National Science Foundation under grant numbers 2225424-CNS and 2043022-DGE.

References

1. Aghzal, M., Plaku, E., Stein, G.J., Yao, Z.: A survey on large language models for automated planning (2025). arXiv:2502.12435 arXiv preprint
2. Amazon web services: amazon Q developer CLI (2025). https://docs.aws.amazon.com/amazonq/latest/qdeveloper-ug/command-line-mcp.html. Accessed 07 June 2025
3. Anthropic: the model context protocol (2024). https://www.anthropic.com/news/model-context-protocol. Accessed 30 July 2025
4. Anthropic: claude desktop (2025). https://www.anthropic.com. Accessed 07 June 2025
5. Antinyan, V.: Revealing the complexity of automotive software. In: Proceedings of the 28th ACM Joint European Software Engineering Conference and Symposium on the Foundations of Software Engineering (ESEC/FSE '20). ACM (2020). https://doi.org/10.1145/3368089.3417038
6. Broadcom: spring AI (2025). https://docs.spring.io/spring-ai/reference/api/mcp/mcp-overview.html. Accessed 07 June 2025
7. Chen, L., Wu, P., Chitta, K., Jaeger, B., Geiger, A., Li, H.: End-to-end autonomous driving: challenges and frontiers. IEEE Trans. Pattern Anal. Mach. Intell. (2024)
8. Cursor: cursor MCP (2025). https://docs.cursor.com/context/model-context-protocol. Accessed 07 June 2025
9. Dafoe, J., Singh, H., Chen, N., Chen, B.: Enabling real-time restoration of compromised ecu firmware in connected and autonomous vehicles. In: International Conference on Security and Privacy in Cyber-Physical Systems and Smart Vehicles, pp. 15–33. Springer (2023)
10. Dafoe, J., Siy, J., Chen, N., Chen, B.: Hardware-assisted runtime in-vehicle ecu firmware self-attestation and self-repair. In: International Conference on Security and Privacy in Cyber-Physical Systems and Smart Vehicles, pp. 187–210. Springer (2024)
11. Devlin, J., Chang, M.W., Lee, K., Toutanova, K.: Bert: pre-training of deep bidirectional transformers for language understanding. In: Proceedings of the 2019 Conference of the North American Chapter of the Association for Computational Linguistics: Human Language Technologies, vol. 1 (long and short papers), pp. 4171–4186 (2019)

12. EENews europe: number of automotive ecus continues to rise (2019). https://www.eenewseurope.com/en/number-of-automotive-ecus-continues-to-rise/
13. Fang, S., et al.: Towards interactive and learnable cooperative driving automation: a large language model-driven decision-making framework. IEEE Trans. Veh. Technol. (2025)
14. FIT2CLOUD: MaxKB (2025). https://github.com/1Panel-dev/MaxKB. Accessed 07 June 2025
15. Google: cloud run MCP server (2025). https://cloud.google.com/run/docs/host-mcp-servers. Accessed 07 June 2025
16. JetBrains: JetBrains IDEs (2025). https://www.jetbrains.com/help/ai-assistant/configure-an-mcp-server.html. Accessed 07 June 2025
17. Li, Y., Katsumata, K., Javanmardi, E., Tsukada, M.: Large language models for human-like autonomous driving: a survey. In: 2024 IEEE 27th International Conference on Intelligent Transportation Systems (ITSC), pp. 439–446. IEEE (2024)
18. Liu, Z., Du, H.: Model context protocol-based internet of experts for wireless environment-aware LLM agents. arXiv preprint arXiv:2505.01834 (2025)
19. Microsoft: copilot studio (2025). https://learn.microsoft.com/en-us/microsoft-copilot-studio/agent-extend-action-mcp. Accessed 07 June 2025
20. NVIDIA: NVIDIA AIQ toolkit (2025). https://docs.nvidia.com/aiqtoolkit/latest/workflows/mcp/mcp-client.html. Accessed 07 June 2025
21. OpenAI: OpenAI Agent SDK (2025). https://openai.github.io/openai-agents-python/mcp/. Accessed 07 June 2025
22. Petit, J., Shladover, S.E.: Potential cyberattacks on automated vehicles. IEEE Trans. Intell. Transp. Syst. **16**(2), 546–556 (2014)
23. Radford, A., Narasimhan, K., Salimans, T., Sutskever, I., et al.: Improving language understanding by generative pre-training (2018)
24. Sato, T., et al.: On the realism of lidar spoofing attacks against autonomous driving vehicle at high speed and long distance. In: Proceedings of the Network and Distributed System Security Symposium (NDSS) (2025)
25. Tanaji, B.A., Roychowdhury, S.: A survey of cybersecurity challenges and mitigation techniques for connected and autonomous vehicles. IEEE Transactions on Intelligent Vehicles (2024)
26. Wehby, A., Zeadally, S., Khatoun, R., Bouchouia, M.L., Fadlallah, A.: How does distributed denial of service affect the connected cars environment? In: 2024 10th International Conference on Control, Decision and Information Technologies (CoDIT), pp. 164–170. IEEE (2024)
27. Xu, Z., et al.: Drivegpt4: interpretable end-to-end autonomous driving via large language model. IEEE Robot. Autom. Lett. (2024)
28. Yu, D., Wang, S., Xu, Y., Wang, T., Zou, J.: Adaptive bidirectional planning framework for enhanced safety and robust decision-making in autonomous navigation systems. J. Supercomput. **81**(8), 965 (2025)
29. Zhang, C., Zhang, S., Liu, Q., Chen, S., Li, T., Fan, J.: Taiji: MCP-based multi-modal data analytics on data lakes. arXiv preprint arXiv:2505.11270 (2025)
30. Zhang, P., et al.: Daplanner: dual-agent framework with multi-modal large language model for autonomous driving motion planning. Appl. Soft Comput. 113625 (2025)

Property-Guided Cyber-Physical Reduction and Surrogation for Safety Analysis in Robotic Vehicles

Nazmus Shakib Sayom(✉) and Luis A. Garcia

University of Utah, Salt Lake City, UT, USA
{sayom.shakib,la.garcia}@utah.edu

Abstract. We propose a methodology for falsifying safety properties in robotic vehicle systems through property-guided reduction and surrogate execution. By isolating only the control logic and physical dynamics relevant to a given specification, we construct lightweight surrogate models that preserve property-relevant behaviors while eliminating unrelated system complexity. This enables scalable falsification via trace analysis and temporal logic oracles.

We demonstrate the approach on a drone control system containing a known safety flaw. The surrogate replicates failure conditions at a fraction of the simulation cost, and a property-guided fuzzer efficiently discovers semantic violations. Our results suggest that controller reduction, when coupled with logic-aware test generation, provides a practical and scalable path toward semantic verification of cyber-physical systems.

Keywords: Cyber-physical systems · Safety verification · Property-guided testing · Robotic vehicles · Fuzzing · Surrogate models

1 Introduction

Modern robotic vehicle systems face an inherent verification challenge: they combine discrete control logic with continuous physical dynamics [9], forming hybrid systems that demand domain-specific formal methods and analysis techniques to manage their complexity [18]. Traditional verification approaches either rely on exhaustive simulations, which quickly become infeasible as system complexity increases due to the state explosion problem and the computational cost of high-fidelity modeling [5,6], or on static code analysis techniques that struggle to capture the nuanced interactions between cyber and physical components [11,22]. This fundamental challenge has led to a verification gap for safety-critical autonomous systems like drones, where subtle interactions between control decisions and physical dynamics can lead to hazardous conditions that evade detection during development.

The problem is compounded by how current verification methodologies treat cyber-physical systems as monolithic entities, despite their inherently modular

L. Cheng and F. Anwar (Eds.): SmartSP 2025, LNICST 699, pp. 21–40, 2027.
https://doi.org/10.1007/978-3-032-33701-6_2

structure. While these approaches often construct targeted mission-level scenarios to validate safety properties, they do so without exploiting the modular decomposition of the software to isolate analysis to only those components relevant to the property under verification. This leads to verification procedures that analyze components unrelated to the safety property under analysis, introducing unnecessary computational overhead. Furthermore, while recent advances like PGFUZZ [11] and ROCAS [8] have made progress in detection of misconfigurations and parameter-related vulnerabilities, they are not designed to uncover deeper semantic flaws in the control logic—the kinds of issues that can cause catastrophic failures in safety-critical applications.

Recent efforts have enriched the verification landscape with techniques that address specific vulnerabilities in robotic systems. For example, policy and control-guided fuzzing frameworks such as PGFUZZ [11] and RVFUZZER [13] generate inputs that stress control parameters or trigger policy violations, revealing misconfigurations and input validation flaws. CPFuzz [19] integrates signal temporal logic robustness into a coverage-guided framework, uncovering violations of formal specifications in small embedded control programs.Complementary approaches like DiscoFuzzer [16] detect behavioral anomalies through output discontinuity analysis, and RoboFuzz [12] leverages domain-specific oracles to flag semantic violations within simulation-based testbeds. Post hoc analysis techniques such as ROCAS [8] bring novel capabilities in root cause localization by co-mutating both cyber parameters and environmental conditions to identify accident-triggering factors. Collectively, these approaches have significantly improved the ability to detect misconfigurations, parameter errors, and certain forms of semantic inconsistency.

However, what remains largely unaddressed is the challenge of identifying *deep semantic flaws* in control logic that only surface under narrowly scoped, property-specific conditions. Existing techniques typically operate over the entire system—either through repeated full-execution simulations or by broad-brush fuzzing of high-level policies—without leveraging the internal structure of the system to localize analysis. As a result, verification remains both computationally intensive and semantically diffuse, especially when high-fidelity physical models are involved. Moreover, many current methods are tightly coupled to specific software frameworks such as ROS [17] or Apollo [1], limiting their ability to generalize across diverse cyber-physical architectures or to reason about system semantics independent of middleware implementation. Crucially, there exists no principled framework for formally reducing a cyber-physical system to the *minimal executable slice* necessary to analyze a given safety or correctness property. This lack of structural and property-specific reduction limits our ability to reason efficiently about the interactions between control decisions and physical dynamics—precisely where critical bugs often reside.

To address these challenges, we introduce a verification methodology that reduces both the cyber and physical dimensions of a robotic vehicle system with respect to a given safety property. On the cyber side, we isolate the subset of control logic components that are semantically relevant to the property under analysis. These components are then composed into a property-specific surrogate system that maintains the input-output and control-flow behaviors necessary to evaluate the property, while abstracting away unrelated logic. On the physical side, we replace the full-order plant model with a reduced-order approximation that captures only the dynamics pertinent to the verification task. This reduction is designed to preserve the control responses and physical interactions relevant to the safety property, ensuring that all behaviors necessary for detecting potential violations are retained. The resulting surrogate system enables targeted analysis over a minimal but semantically complete slice of the original system, improving efficiency and precision in detecting property violations.

Contributions. In this work, we present a property-guided verification methodology that reduces both the cyber and physical dimensions of robotic systems with respect to specific safety properties. Our primary contributions are as follows:

- **A formalism for property-guided cyber-space reduction**, which identifies and isolates only those control logic components that are causally relevant to a given safety property through structural and dataflow analysis.
- **A host-agnostic surrogate construction framework** that enables dynamic analysis of the isolated control logic outside its original software and hardware environment, while preserving semantic equivalence with respect to the property under test.
- **A property-scoped physical reduction technique** that replaces full-system simulation with reduced-order models capturing only those physical dynamics that interact meaningfully with the relevant control logic.
- **A co-reduction workflow** that integrates cyber and physical reductions to enable efficient, property-targeted fuzzing, significantly reducing the analysis scope while retaining coverage of behaviors critical to property violations.

We demonstrate the effectiveness of our methodology through a robotic vehicle case study, illustrating how the proposed reductions facilitate targeted verification of safety properties through fuzzing the surrogate system achieved by reduction.

2 Background

2.1 Cyber-Physical Systems and Verification Challenges

Cyber-physical systems (CPS) integrate computational processes with physical dynamics, creating hybrid systems where discrete control logic governs continuous physical behaviors [9,18]. In robotic vehicles, this manifests as control software making discrete decisions based on sensor inputs that directly affect continuous physical dynamics like motion, energy consumption, and environmental interaction. The verification of such systems presents unique challenges due to the complex interplay between cyber and physical components, where subtle bugs in control logic can lead to safety violations that only emerge under specific physical conditions [6].

Traditional verification approaches for CPS face a fundamental scalability challenge. Exhaustive simulation-based verification becomes computationally intractable as system complexity grows, due to both the state explosion problem and the computational cost of high-fidelity physical modeling [5]. Static analysis techniques, while computationally efficient, struggle to capture the nuanced interactions between discrete control decisions and continuous physical dynamics that characterize CPS behavior [22].

2.2 Modularity and System Structure

Despite being deployed as monolithic systems, modern robotic platforms like PX4 [15] and ArduPilot [3] are built from modular components that interact through well-defined interfaces. These systems typically comprise distinct modules for navigation, safety monitoring, estimation, and control, each responsible for specific aspects of system behavior [20]. Similarly, the physical behavior of robotic systems emerges from multiple interacting subsystems—propulsion, energy management, kinematics—each governed by distinct physical principles.

This inherent modularity presents an opportunity for targeted verification. Many safety properties depend on only a subset of the available system components. For example, a property concerning emergency parachute deployment may depend primarily on altitude estimation, battery monitoring, and emergency control logic, while being largely independent of lateral navigation or obstacle avoidance subsystems. Current verification approaches, however, treat CPS as atomic units, analyzing all components regardless of their relevance to the property under verification.

2.3 Property-Guided Analysis

The concept of property-guided analysis has emerged as a promising approach to address the scalability challenges in CPS verification. Rather than analyzing the entire system uniformly, property-guided techniques focus computational resources on those aspects of the system that are most relevant to the property being verified. This approach has been successfully applied in software verification through techniques like program slicing [21], which extracts minimal program fragments that preserve specific behavioral properties.

In the context of CPS, property-guided analysis must account for both cyber and physical dimensions. The challenge lies in identifying which control logic components and which aspects of the physical dynamics are necessary to preserve the semantics of a given safety property. This requires formal techniques for reasoning about component dependencies and interaction patterns within hybrid cyber-physical systems.

2.4 Reduced-Order Modeling in Engineering

Reduced-order modeling (ROM) provides a principled approach to simplifying complex dynamical systems while preserving their essential characteristics.

These techniques, widely used in computational mechanics and control theory, project high-dimensional system behavior onto lower-dimensional spaces that capture the system's dominant modes [2]. Methods such as proper orthogonal decomposition, balanced truncation, and static condensation enable efficient simulation of complex physical systems without sacrificing accuracy for the quantities of interest.

In verification contexts, reduced-order models offer a pathway to address the computational bottleneck of high-fidelity physical simulation. By focusing on only those physical dynamics that interact meaningfully with the property under analysis, ROM techniques can significantly reduce simulation time while preserving the fidelity necessary to detect property violations.

2.5 Simulation-Based Verification

Simulation remains a cornerstone of CPS verification, particularly for systems where mathematical modeling or formal verification is intractable [14]. Software-in-the-loop (SITL) simulation environments execute unmodified control software while providing simulated sensor inputs and interpreting actuator commands, enabling system-level testing without physical hardware [7]. This approach is fundamental to the development and verification of robotic platforms.

However, high-fidelity SITL simulations are computationally expensive. Each simulation trial requires full initialization of the software stack and detailed modeling of the physical environment and vehicle dynamics. Property verification through simulation often requires exploring large parameter spaces or validating stochastic scenarios, necessitating thousands of simulation runs. This computational burden becomes a significant bottleneck when attempting to systematically explore edge cases or validate safety properties across diverse operational conditions.

3 Methodology

Our approach enables efficient analysis of robotic systems by reducing their cyber-physical execution to only the control logic and physical behaviors relevant to a given safety or correctness property. To illustrate the methodology, we use a representative drone scenario—modeled as a hybrid dynamical system—that captures a bug pattern inspired by a real firmware flaw discovered by PGFuzz [11].

3.1 Cyber-Physical Reduction and Structured Surrogation

We develop a structured methodology for reducing cyber-physical systems by isolating the minimal set of components necessary for analyzing a given safety or correctness property. Our approach combines two complementary formalisms: static condensation for efficient reduction of physical component models and

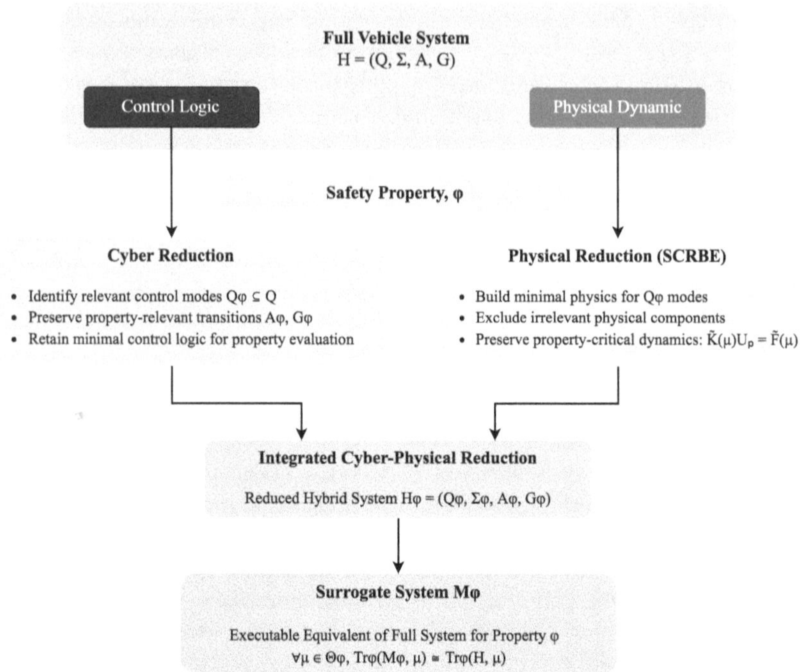

Fig. 1. Overview of our cyber-physical reduction methodology for safety analysis of robotic vehicles. The approach combines control logic reduction with physical model reduction through static condensation to create an efficient, property-specific surrogate system.

hybrid dynamical systems for principled pruning of control modes and transitions while preserving property-relevant behaviors.

Static Condensation for Physical Model Reduction. Our physical model reduction is grounded in the SCRBE framework of Kapteyn et al. [10], which extends static condensation to modular systems with coupled physical processes. This approach enables us to create compact physical surrogate models that preserve the input-output relationships essential for property analysis.

Let the physical system be governed by a parametric variational problem (Fig. 1):

$$a(u, v; \mu) = f(v; \mu), \quad \forall v \in X(\mu), \tag{1}$$

where $u(\mu)$ denotes the state of the full physical system, and μ is a high-dimensional parameter vector spanning environmental and configuration uncertainties. After discretization, we obtain:

$$K(\mu)U(\mu) = F(\mu), \tag{2}$$

with $K(\mu) \in \mathbb{R}^{N \times N}$ and $U(\mu) \in \mathbb{R}^N$.

To restrict physical analysis to a subsystem $\pi \subseteq \mathcal{S}$—e.g., those physical components interacting with a safety-critical control path—we partition $U = [U_p, U_i]^T$ into interface and internal variables and apply static condensation:

$$U_i = K_{i,i}^{-1}\left(F_i - K_{i,p}U_p\right), \tag{3}$$

yielding a reduced physical system over the interface variables:

$$\tilde{K}(\mu)U_p = \tilde{F}(\mu), \tag{4}$$

where

$$\tilde{K} = K_{p,p} - K_{p,i}K_{i,i}^{-1}K_{i,p}, \quad \tilde{F} = F_p - K_{p,i}K_{i,i}^{-1}F_i. \tag{5}$$

This approach allows us to create a physically reduced model that focuses computational resources on the physical aspects relevant to our property of interest.

Hybrid Dynamical Systems for Control Logic Reduction. The computational (cyber) aspects of our system are modeled using hybrid dynamical systems (HDS), providing a formal framework for identifying which control modes and transitions must be preserved in our reduced model. Following Branicky's formalism [4], we represent the full cyber-physical system as a tuple:

$$H = (Q, \Sigma, A, G)$$

where:

- Q is a finite set of discrete states or modes, each corresponding to a distinct control logic configuration
- $\Sigma = \{\Sigma_q\}_{q\in Q}$ is a collection of continuous dynamics, where each Σ_q is governed by $\dot{x} = f_q(x, \mu)$ on state space $X_q \subset \mathbb{R}^n$, with $\mu \in \Theta$ representing system parameters
- $A = \{A_q\}_{q\in Q}$ are the autonomous jump sets, where $A_q \subset X_q$ defines conditions triggering transitions from mode q
- $G = \{G_q\}_{q\in Q}$ are the transition maps, where $G_q : A_q \to S$ determines the target state after transitions ($S = \cup_{q\in Q} X_q \times \{q\}$ being the hybrid state space)

This HDS formulation makes explicit the interrelationships between control modes and physical dynamics, enabling us to reason about which elements of the control logic are necessary to preserve the behaviors relevant to our analysis.

Integrated Cyber-Physical Reduction. For a given property φ, our methodology creates a property-specific reduced system through a two-phase process:

First, we apply the HDS formalism to identify the minimal control structure necessary for analyzing φ. This yields a reduced hybrid system $H_\varphi = (Q_\varphi, \Sigma_\varphi, A_\varphi, G_\varphi)$ constructed by:

1. Identifying the subset of control modes $Q_\varphi \subseteq Q$ that are causally relevant to φ

2. Preserving only those transitions in A_φ and G_φ that can occur along execution paths relevant to φ
3. Retaining the minimal control logic necessary for property evaluation

Second, for each mode $q \in Q_\varphi$, we apply SCRBE to reduce the physical model associated with that mode, creating efficient surrogate representations of the continuous dynamics $f_q(x, \mu)$.

The integration of these two reduction approaches yields a comprehensive cyber-physical reduced model that maintains:

$$\forall \mu \in \Theta_\varphi, \quad \mathrm{Tr}_\varphi(H_\varphi, \mu) \cong \mathrm{Tr}_\varphi(H, \mu)$$

where Tr_φ extracts the execution trace elements relevant to property φ, and $\cong$ denotes behavioral equivalence with respect to those elements.

For practical analysis, we implement H_φ as a concrete surrogate system M_φ that provides an efficient, executable representation while preserving semantic equivalence with respect to the property:

$$\forall \mu \in \Theta_\varphi, \quad \mathrm{Tr}_\varphi(M_\varphi, \mu) \cong \mathrm{Tr}_\varphi(H, \mu)$$

Scope of Equivalence. In this paper, Tr_φ denotes the projection to the signals referenced by φ (e.g., battery, altitude, deployment). We interpret $\cong$ as agreement in the truth valuation of φ over the projected trace. We validate this *property-scoped* equivalence empirically by checking that the surrogate and the full system yield the same satisfaction or, violation outcome for the same configurations.

This reduction framework naturally distinguishes between two complementary forms of simplification: *cyber reduction*, which isolates the minimal subset of control modes and transitions necessary for evaluating property φ; and *physical reduction*, which applies SCRBE to create efficient surrogate models of the physical dynamics in each retained mode. The former corresponds to a structural restriction of the control logic and firmware execution pipeline, while the latter yields computationally efficient physical models and a reduced parameter space for analysis. Together, these reductions enable targeted reasoning about subsystem behavior while preserving fidelity with respect to the full system along the slice relevant to φ.

Example: Fault-Aware Reduction of a Parachute Deployment Pipeline. We consider a drone system exhibiting a safety-critical bug in its emergency parachute deployment logic. When the battery falls below a configured threshold, the emergency controller is expected to deploy the parachute unconditionally. However, due to an implementation flaw, deployment is prevented if the drone is outside a safe altitude range—specifically, if it is below a minimum safe altitude or above a maximum safe altitude—an inappropriate constraint under critical battery conditions.

We model this system using a hybrid dynamical system $H = (Q, \Sigma, A, G)$, where:

- The mode set Q consists of operational states such as `IDLE`, `TAKE_OFF`, `GOTO`, `LAND`, and `PARACHUTE`, each corresponding to a distinct phase of the drone's mission.
- The collection $\Sigma = \{\Sigma_q\}_{q \in Q}$ defines the continuous-time dynamics within each mode. These dynamics govern the evolution of physical state variables such as position, velocity, and battery level.
- The guard sets $A = \{A_q\}_{q \in Q}$ define the conditions under which transitions occur between modes, based on state-dependent thresholds such as altitude, position, or remaining energy.
- The transition maps $G = \{G_q\}_{q \in Q}$ determine the post-transition hybrid state, including updates to the active mode and any necessary resets or reinitializations of the continuous state. For example, transitioning to `PARACHUTE` mode may reinitialize the system's velocity state to reflect a controlled descent profile.

The full hybrid system encodes not only normal mission behavior but also soft-landing maneuvers, emergency overrides, PID-stabilized position tracking, and mode-specific force modulation. It contains significant behavioral diversity beyond the logic necessary to evaluate the property φ, making full-scale falsification or symbolic analysis computationally expensive.

We define the safety property:

$$\varphi = G(\texttt{battery\_low} \wedge \texttt{airborne} \rightarrow F_{[0,\Delta]}\texttt{deployed})$$

To analyze this property efficiently, we construct a reduced hybrid system $H_\varphi = (Q_\varphi, \Sigma_\varphi, A_\varphi, G_\varphi)$ that preserves all behavior relevant to φ. This reduction includes:

- A restricted mode set $Q_\varphi = \{\texttt{GOTO}, \texttt{PARACHUTE}\}$, excluding modes not involved in the fault scenario.
- A state projection $x_\varphi = (\texttt{battery}, \texttt{altitude})$, eliminating dimensions unrelated to the triggering and outcome of the bug.
- A reduced guard set $A_\varphi \subseteq A$, retaining only the transition predicate responsible for triggering parachute deployment under low battery.
- A corresponding transition map $G_\varphi \subseteq G$ that encodes the system's behavior after deployment, including any reinitialization or dynamics required for continued simulation in `PARACHUTE` mode.

This reduction enables efficient detection of the guard logic flaw without executing unrelated control paths. Furthermore, we apply physical model reduction via SCRBE to retain only the simplified descent dynamics necessary for analyzing the timing and validity of deployment behavior.

The surrogate system M_φ thus supports efficient falsification of φ, preserving trace-level equivalence with the original system over the property-relevant slice:

$$\forall \mu \in \Theta_\varphi, \quad \mathrm{Tr}_\varphi(M_\varphi, \mu) \cong \mathrm{Tr}_\varphi(H, \mu)$$

3.2 Property-Guided Falsification over the Reduced System

Once the reduced surrogate system M_φ has been constructed, the next step is to explore its behavior under varied configurations and runtime conditions to identify inputs that violate the safety property φ. To this end, we employ a structured falsification process that systematically searches over the reduced parameter space Θ_φ for configurations that falsify the specification.

We define the falsification objective as discovering a configuration $\mu \in \Theta_\varphi$ such that the resulting system trace fails to satisfy the property:

$$\mathrm{Tr}_\varphi(M_\varphi, \mu) \not\models \varphi$$

where Tr_φ denotes the trace projected to the state and control signals relevant to φ.

Each configuration μ comprises both physical state variables (e.g., initial altitude, battery level) and control parameters (e.g., deployment thresholds). Rather than relying on unconstrained sampling, the search process applies domain-aware generation and mutation strategies that preserve structural constraints—such as the ordering between minimum and maximum altitude—and prioritize exploration near semantically significant regions.

Evaluation of each candidate proceeds in three stages:

1. Execute the reduced system $M_\varphi(\mu)$ to produce a time-indexed execution trace.
2. Analyze the trace using a logical oracle corresponding to the safety property φ.
3. If the property is violated, log the trace and configuration; otherwise, continue exploration.

To reduce redundancy, the falsification loop retains only non-equivalent counterexamples and discards duplicate violations. The final result is a curated collection of minimal failing inputs along with their associated traces, enabling post-hoc analysis of failure regions within Θ_φ.

Temporal Logic Oracle. Each trace is evaluated against the specification by a temporal logic oracle that maps input configurations to a Boolean verdict:

$$\mathcal{O}_\varphi(\mu) = \begin{cases} \texttt{Satisfied}, & \text{if } \mathrm{Tr}_\varphi(M_\varphi, \mu) \models \varphi \\ \texttt{Violated}, & \text{if } \mathrm{Tr}_\varphi(M_\varphi, \mu) \not\models \varphi \end{cases}$$

The property φ, previously defined using Signal Temporal Logic (STL), expresses that any low-battery condition during flight must lead to a successful parachute deployment within a bounded delay.

The oracle implements the formal semantics of STL to determine whether the trace satisfies φ, treating each simulation as a deterministic signal over the relevant observable variables.

This falsification loop serves as an effective mechanism for evaluating the sufficiency of the reduced model and for uncovering subtle cyber-physical logic flaws that may only manifest under specific combinations of physical state and control configuration.

4 Implementation

To demonstrate the viability of our methodology, we develop a proof-of-concept system that instantiates each phase of the proposed framework. While simplified in scope, this implementation embodies the full reduction-surrogation-falsification pipeline and serves as a concrete vehicle for validating the technical approach.

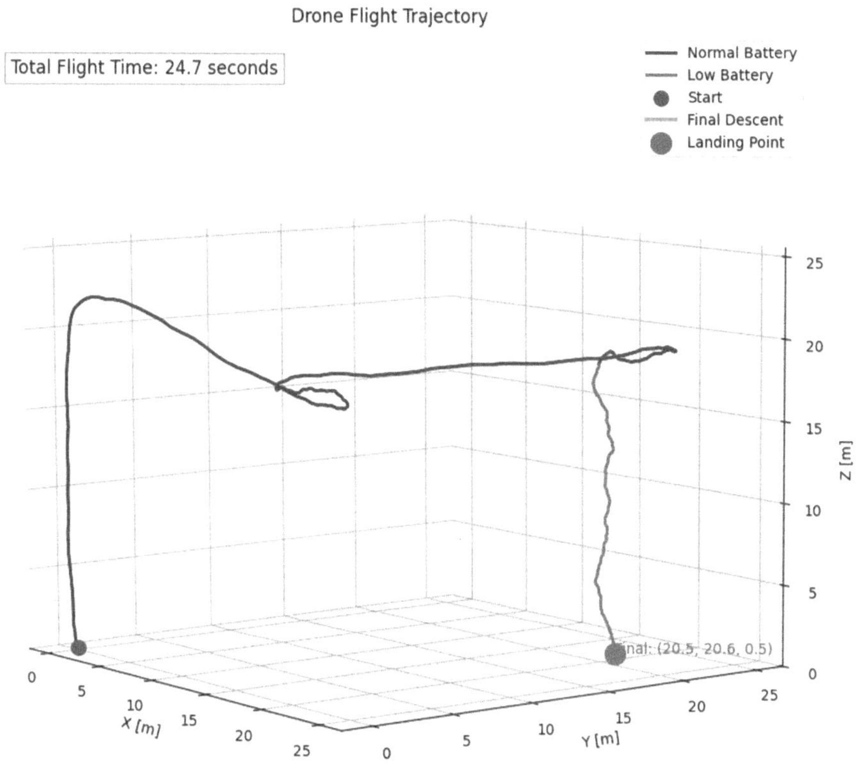

Fig. 2. Full-System Flight Trajectory. PyBullet-based simulation trace showing 3D descent profile after battery low warning. But the drone does not deploy the parachute due to a bug in the emergency controller. Simulation took 24.7 s and required complete system execution.

4.1 System Overview

The example system models a drone flight controller responsible for emergency parachute deployment. Rather than simulating the entire PyBullet-based software stack and physical dynamics, the implementation applies structural and semantic reductions that isolate only the components relevant to evaluating a critical safety property. The resulting surrogate behaves identically with respect to the property, but is significantly more lightweight and analyzable.

Cyber-Reduction Realization. The cyber portion of the system is distilled from a realistic multi-mode flight control stack to a minimal state machine with two control modes: waypoint navigation (`GOTO`) and emergency override (`PARACHUTE`). Intermediate states (e.g., `IDLE`, `TAKE_OFF`, `LAND`) and unrelated control flows are omitted. The retained logic preserves mission-relevant transitions and emergency triggers, ensuring property-relevant behavior is intact. This selection follows the formal restriction Q_φ described in Sect. 3, guided directly by the STL property and its triggering guard conditions.

Physical Reduction Realization Physical dynamics are reduced to a minimal two-variable model capturing battery level and altitude—abstracting away full-body flight physics, actuator dynamics, and energy consumption models. These two variables are sufficient for evaluating deployment behavior in the presence of low-battery conditions, enabling efficient simulation and trace extraction without loss of semantic coverage. This corresponds to the projection used by Tr_φ and the static-condensation-based reduction in Sect. 3.

Executable Surrogate System. The reduced cyber and physical components are integrated into a self-contained Python system that executes full traces over the reduced hybrid state space. The configuration includes parametric threshold settings (e.g., minimum/maximum deployment altitude, battery critical threshold) that control mode transitions and influence safety-critical decisions. This surrogate system offers a clean, bounded execution model suitable for rigorous automated falsification.

4.2 Falsification Framework

To test the resilience of the reduced system, we construct a targeted fuzzing pipeline that explores the parameter space for configurations that violate the intended safety property. The fuzzer employs constraint-preserving generators and feedback-driven mutations to systematically probe boundary conditions and uncover logic flaws.

Each run produces a complete execution trace along with a verdict from a temporal logic oracle, which analyzes the trace against a formally specified STL property. Violating configurations are logged for inspection, and visual analytics summarize the falsification landscape. The fuzzer supports continuous execution until interruption, automatically generating visualization outputs at termination.

4.3 Overview

This implementation demonstrates the core contribution of our framework: the ability to reduce a complex cyber-physical system to a semantically faithful, executable surrogate and to evaluate it through property-guided falsification. Despite its compactness, the system supports trace-level diagnostics, captures subtle safety violations, and enables reproducible experiments grounded in formal logic.

5 Evaluation

We evaluate our methodology on a drone deployment scenario inspired by a safety-critical control flaw originally reported in PX4-based systems [11]. Our goal is to assess whether property-guided reduction and surrogate construction enable efficient, semantically faithful falsification while retaining practical utility.

5.1 Baseline: Full-System Simulation Cost

We begin by attempting falsification via full PyBullet-based simulation. This process involves mission setup, realistic flight dynamics, and complete control stack execution. A single trace that reaches the faulty deployment condition takes over 24 s of wall-clock time (see Fig. 2).

Beyond runtime, this approach requires significant engineering effort including platform-specific instrumentation, logging infrastructure, and telemetry capture. These overheads make full-system falsification expensive and difficult to scale for proactive validation or regression testing.

5.2 Falsification Through Surrogate Execution

Using our reduction methodology (Sect. 3), we construct a property-specific surrogate that preserves only the relevant cyber-physical behavior. Each surrogate run completes in under 500 milliseconds and produces a complete trace with STL-based property evaluation.

Example run (reduced system):

```
$ python run_scrbe_simulation.py --battery 10.0 --altitude 20
Configuration:
- Min deploy altitude: 60.0m
- Max deploy altitude: 80.0m
- Low battery threshold: 10.0%
Result:
Battery: 10.0% (CRITICAL)
Altitude: 20.0m
Parachute: NOT DEPLOYED
Status: BLOCKED - Critical battery but altitude out of deployment range
```

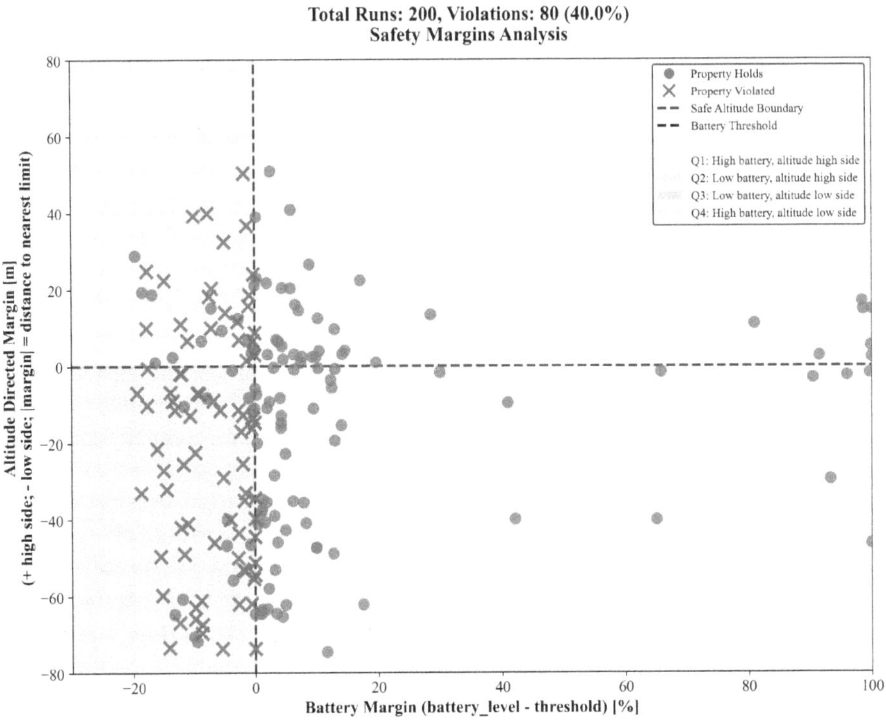

Fig. 3. Battery safety margin vs.altitude-directed safety margin for 200 autonomous runs. Each point is one run: green circles indicate that the safety property was satisfied, and orange crosses indicate a violation (80/200 runs, 40%). The battery safety margin on the x-axis is the observed battery level relative to the mission low-battery threshold (M_{bat} = battery level − threshold); larger values indicate more remaining battery. The altitude-directed margin on the y-axis is the signed distance to the nearest allowed deployment altitude limit; positive values indicate that the vehicle is above the maximum allowed deployment altitude, negative values indicate that it is below the minimum allowed deployment altitude, and 0 corresponds to contact with a limit. Dashed lines mark the controller's battery threshold (vertical) and safe-altitude boundary (horizontal). Shaded quadrants ($Q1$–$Q4$) separate high/low battery and high-/low-side altitude regimes. Violations cluster where the battery margin is low and the vehicle is *outside* the allowed altitude band (either too low or too high), showing that the parachute deployment logic is incorrectly inhibited whenever altitude is out of range, even under critical battery conditions where deployment should be unconditional. (Color figure online)

This trace mirrors the behavioral failure seen in PyBullet-based full physics simulation with full control stack, showing that the surrogate reproduces the relevant failure semantics at a fraction of the cost.

As a property-scoped conformance check for φ, we treat this agreement as evidence that the surrogate and full simulation yield the same truth valuation of φ under the same configuration. In particular, existence of a configuration μ^* such that both traces violate φ witnesses that M_φ reproduces the failure semantics relevant to φ in this scenario.

5.3 Fuzzing Results on Reduced Model

We implemented a feedback-guided fuzzer that perturbs both physical conditions (e.g., altitude, battery) and controller thresholds. Table 1 summarizes the results from 20 runs on patched and non-patched controllers.

Table 1. Fuzzing Results: Patched vs. Non-Patched Controller

	Non-Patched	Patched
Total Runs	200	200
Unique Violations	80	0
Violation Rate	40%	0%

The unpatched system consistently violates the safety property, while the patched version satisfies it across all tested inputs—demonstrating the surrogate's utility for diagnostic validation.

5.4 Visualizing Safety Envelope and Violation Modes

We analyze how the controller behaves near its safety limits by projecting each evaluated run into a two-dimensional "margin space" defined by battery margin and altitude-directed margin (Fig. 3). Each point in this space corresponds to one run and is labeled according to whether the safety property was satisfied or violated. Both axes are expressed as distances to the controller's own decision boundaries: the battery axis measures remaining battery relative to the configured low-battery trigger level (positive when sufficient charge remains, negative when below threshold), and the altitude axis measures signed distance to the nearest permitted deployment altitude limit (negative when the vehicle is below the minimum deployment altitude, positive when above the maximum).

This view makes the failure mode of the emergency parachute logic explicit. The intended behavior is that, once the battery drops below its emergency threshold, deployment should proceed unconditionally. Instead, violations concentrate in regions where the battery margin is low *and* the vehicle lies outside the nominal deployment altitude band. In these cases, deployment is blocked because the altitude is either too low or too high, even though that altitude check is not supposed to prevent an emergency action under critical battery conditions.

Crucially, Fig. 3 is generated from the reduced surrogate model rather than the full flight stack. The surrogate reproduces the same interaction between low battery and altitude gating that we observe in the full system, and it produces the same class of safety violations (parachute withheld despite critical battery). This provides empirical evidence that the surrogate preserves the safety-relevant decision logic of the original controller, and therefore can be fuzzed in place of the full system while still revealing the true violation modes.

5.5 Effectiveness and Scalability

Our approach demonstrates several benefits:

- **Semantic fidelity (w.r.t. φ):** The surrogate reproduces failure behavior under the same conditions as the whole system simulated in a full physics simulation.
- **Runtime efficiency:** Surrogate runs are over 10× faster, enabling large-scale test campaigns.
- **Fuzzing tractability:** Temporal falsification becomes practical over high-dimensional configuration spaces.

This evaluation confirms that our surrogate-based methodology enables efficient falsification and insight-driven debugging. It faithfully mirrors full-system bugs while reducing infrastructure burden and runtime costs.

6 Discussion

This work establishes a principled framework for cyber-physical verification through property-guided reduction and surrogate execution. Our methodology demonstrates how formal reduction techniques can be systematically applied to isolate and analyze the minimal components necessary for property verification in robotic systems.

Theoretical Foundation and Generalizability. The core contribution of this work lies in establishing the formal foundation for property-guided cyber-physical reduction. By grounding cyber reduction in hybrid dynamical systems theory and physical reduction in static condensation, we provide a domain-agnostic methodology that applies broadly across CPS platforms. The framework's theoretical basis ensures that reductions preserve semantic equivalence with respect to the target property, enabling reliable verification on simplified surrogate systems.

Methodological Innovation. Our approach represents a significant departure from traditional monolithic verification strategies. Rather than treating cyber-physical systems as atomic units, we demonstrate how to systematically decompose them into property-relevant components while maintaining behavioral fidelity. This decomposition enables targeted analysis that focuses computational resources precisely where they are needed, addressing the fundamental scalability challenges that plague existing verification approaches.

Practical Efficiency and Automation Potential. The surrogate-based workflow we establish provides substantial computational advantages over full-system simulation. Our evaluation demonstrates significant runtime improvements while maintaining complete accuracy in bug detection. Importantly, the formal structure of our reduction methodology creates natural opportunities for automation—the systematic component identification and interface analysis procedures we define can serve as the foundation for automated tooling in future implementations.

Validation and Semantic Consistency. A critical achievement of our framework is the preservation of semantic equivalence between original systems and their reduced surrogates. Grounded in formal models, our methodology is evaluated empirically: we validate property-level semantic preservation by reproducing the same violation conditions in the surrogate and full-system settings. This semantic consistency is essential for practical adoption of the methodology.

Architectural Compatibility. Our approach leverages the modular architecture inherent in modern robotic platforms, working with well-established open-source systems like PX4 and ArduPilot. This compatibility with existing development ecosystems positions the methodology for practical adoption without requiring fundamental changes to current robotic software engineering practices.

Evaluation Rigor. The focused evaluation we present serves multiple purposes: it validates the theoretical soundness of our reduction techniques, demonstrates practical efficiency gains, and establishes a reproducible baseline for future comparative studies. The case study provides clear evidence that property-guided reduction can achieve substantial computational savings while maintaining verification accuracy.

Our framework establishes the theoretical and methodological foundation for a new class of property-specific verification tools. The systematic reduction techniques we present enable efficient analysis of semantic flaws in cyber-physical systems, offering a principled alternative to computationally expensive full-system approaches. The formal grounding of our methodology provides a solid foundation for future extensions and automation efforts in property-guided CPS verification.

Limitations and Scope. Our evaluation focuses on a single robotic platform, one representative safety property, and one bug manifestation. This scope is intentional: our primary contribution is methodological, centered on property-guided cyber-physical reduction with surrogation. The study is designed to isolate feasibility and demonstrate the end-to-end workflow. Broadening across platforms and properties requires substantial re-instrumentation and scenario curation, which is orthogonal to the core technique. Within this scoped setting, we demonstrate that the reductions preserve safety-relevant behavior while delivering substantial efficiency gains that enable practical analysis. Future work will expand the evaluation to additional platforms, properties, and bug types to further validate generalizability.

7 Conclusion

We have presented a property-guided methodology for cyber-physical system verification that enables semantically faithful falsification through structural reduction and surrogate construction. By isolating the minimal control and physical components relevant to a given safety property, our approach transforms complex robotic systems into lightweight, analyzable surrogates—supporting scalable, specification-driven testing without reliance on full-system simulation.

Through a proof-of-concept implementation targeting a real-world drone deployment bug, we demonstrated how this reduction enables targeted fuzzing, rapid falsification, and interpretable diagnostics with minimal engineering overhead. Our evaluation confirms that safety violations can be exposed in orders-of-magnitude less time while preserving behavioral equivalence with the full system.

This work opens the door to broader verification frameworks that are property-aware by construction. Future research will focus on automating reduction workflows, scaling to multi-property analyses, and applying these techniques to closed-source and industry-scale platforms.

Acknowledgements. The research reported in this paper was sponsored in part by the National Science Foundation (NSF) under awards FMitF-2425711 and NCS-2435642 and the National Institute of Health (NIH) under award R61MH135109. The views and conclusions contained in this document are those of the authors and should not be interpreted as representing the official policies, either expressed or implied, of the funding agencies.

References

1. Baidu apollo team: apollo: an open autonomous driving platform (2025). https://github.com/ApolloAuto/apollo. open-source autonomous driving stack (Apache-2.0). Apollo Auto / Baidu. Accessed 31 Oct 2025-10-31
2. Benner, P., Gugercin, S., Willcox, K.: A survey of projection-based model reduction methods for parametric dynamical systems. SIAM Rev. **57**(4), 483–531 (2015)
3. Bin, H., Justice, A.: The design of an unmanned aerial vehicle based on the ardupilot. Indian J. Sci. Technol. **2**(4), 12–15 (2009)
4. Branicky, M.S.: Introduction to hybrid systems. In: Hristu-Varsakelis, D., Levine, W.S. (eds.) Handbook of Networked and Embedded Control Systems, pp. 91–116. Birkhäuser Boston, Boston, MA (2005). https://doi.org/10.1007/0-8176-4404-0_5
5. Corso, A., Moss, R., Koren, M., Lee, R., Kochenderfer, M.: A survey of algorithms for black-box safety validation of cyber-physical systems. J. Artif. Int. Res. **72**, 377–428 (2022). https://doi.org/10.1613/jair.1.12716

6. Derler, P., Lee, E.A., Sangiovanni Vincentelli, A.: Modeling cyber–physical systems. Proc. IEEE **100**(1), 13–28 (2012). https://doi.org/10.1109/JPROC.2011.2160929
7. Derler, P., Lee, E.A., Tripakis, S., Törngren, M.: Cyber-physical system design contracts. In: Proceedings of the ACM/IEEE 4th International Conference on Cyber-Physical Systems, pp. 109–118 (2013)
8. Feng, S., et al.: Rocas: root cause analysis of autonomous driving accidents via cyber-physical co-mutation. In: Proceedings of the 39th IEEE/ACM International Conference on Automated Software Engineering. p. 1620–1632. ASE '24, Association for Computing Machinery, New York, NY, USA (2024). https://doi.org/10.1145/3691620.3695530
9. Frazzoli, E., Dahleh, M., Feron, E.: Robust hybrid control for autonomous vehicle motion planning. In: Proceedings of the 39th IEEE Conference on Decision and Control (Cat. No.00CH37187), vol. 1, pp. 821–826 (2000). https://doi.org/10.1109/CDC.2000.912871
10. Kapteyn, M., Detommaso, G., Parussini, L., Willcox, K.: Data-driven physics-based digital twins via a library of component-based reduced-order models. Int. J. Numer. Meth. Eng. **124**(7), 1449–1471 (2021). https://doi.org/10.1002/nme.6644
11. Kim, H., Ozmen, M.O., Bianchi, A., Celik, Z.B., Xu, D.: PGFUZZ: policy-guided fuzzing for robotic vehicles. In: Network and Distributed System Security Symposium (NDSS). pp. 1–18 (2021). https://beerkay.github.io/papers/Berkay2021PGFuzzNDSS.pdf
12. Kim, S., Kim, T.: Robofuzz: fuzzing robotic systems over robot operating system (ROS) for finding correctness bugs. In: Proceedings of the 30th ACM Joint European Software Engineering Conference and Symposium on the Foundations of Software Engineering, pp. 447–458. ESEC/FSE 2022, Association for Computing Machinery, New York, NY, USA (2022). https://doi.org/10.1145/3540250.3549164
13. Kim, T., et al.: RVFuzzer: finding input validation bugs in robotic vehicles through control-guided testing. In: 28th USENIX Security Symposium (USENIX Security 19), pp. 425–442. USENIX Association, Santa Clara, CA (2019). https://www.usenix.org/conference/usenixsecurity19/presentation/kim
14. Lee, E.A., Seshia, S.A.: Introduction to embedded systems: a cyber-physical systems approach. MIT press (2017)
15. Meier, L., Honegger, D., Pollefeys, M.: Px4: a node-based multithreaded open source robotics framework for deeply embedded platforms. In: 2015 IEEE International Conference on Robotics and Automation (ICRA), pp. 6235–6240. IEEE (2015)
16. Rivera, S., Iannillo, A.K., State, R.: Discofuzzer: discontinuity-based vulnerability detector for robotic systems (2020). https://doi.org/10.36227/techrxiv.12613400.v1
17. Robotics, O.: Ros.org | powering the world's robots. https://www.ros.org/
18. Seshia, S.A., Hu, S., Li, W., Zhu, Q.: Design automation of cyber-physical systems: challenges, advances, and opportunities. Trans. Comp.-Aided Des. Integ. Cir. Sys. **36**(9), 1421–1434 (2017). https://doi.org/10.1109/TCAD.2016.2633961
19. Shang, F., Wang, B., Li, T., Tian, J., Cao, K.: CPFUZZ: combining fuzzing and falsification of cyber-physical systems. IEEE Access **8**, 166951–166962 (2020). https://api.semanticscholar.org/CorpusID:221913645
20. Wang, H., Hauser, C., Garcia, L.: Autocps: control software dataset generation for semantic reverse engineering. In: 2022 IEEE Security and Privacy Workshops (SPW), pp. 236–242. IEEE (2022)

21. Weiser, M.: Program slicing. IEEE Trans. Softw. Eng. **SE-10**(4), 352–357 (1984). https://doi.org/10.1109/TSE.1984.5010248
22. Zaddach, J., Bruno, L., Francillon, A., Balzarotti, D., et al.: Avatar: a framework to support dynamic security analysis of embedded systems' firmwares. In: NDSS. vol. 14, pp. 1–16 (2014)

TAPAssure: Safe Automation in Smart Homes with LLMs and Formal Verification

Huan Bui[1(✉)], Chenglong Fu[1], and Fei Zuo[2]

[1] The University of North Carolina at Charlotte, Charlotte, NC 28223, USA
{hbui11,chenglong.fu}@charlotte.edu
[2] The University of Central Oklahoma, Edmond, OK 73034, USA
fzuo@uco.edu

Abstract. The integration of large language models (LLMs) in smart home systems offers a promising path for automating Trigger-Action Programming (TAP) rules. However, LLMs often generate incomplete or unsafe rules due to limited awareness of the IoT context. We present TAPAssure, a framework that combines LLM-based rule generation with formal verification to ensure safety and correctness. TAPAssure verifies rules using NuSMV and iteratively refines them based on model checker feedback to eliminate syntax errors and violations of user-defined safety properties. We evaluate TAPAssure using two state-of-the-art LLMs: Meta Llama 3.3 70B Instruct and Qwen2.5-14B-Instruct. Results show that Qwen2.5 resolves syntax errors efficiently (median of 3.5 iterations, average of 9.92 due to occasional outliers), while Llama3.3 excels in minimizing safety violations consistently (average of 5.48 iterations, 100% pass rate). Overall, TAPAssure effectively bridges the gap between intuitive LLM-driven automation and the stringent safety requirements of smart home environments.

Keywords: Trigger-Action Rules · Model Checking · Large Language Models · Formal Verification

1 Introduction

Over the past two years, LLMs have demonstrated impressive capabilities in content generation and reasoning, showing growing potential in smart home IoT systems. Existing research [8,9,14] has explored the use of LLMs for automating these systems by assisting users in generating and deploying TAP rules. However, despite their efficiency and convenience, LLMs frequently produce rules with errors or missing information, such as device IDs or installation locations, which can lead to unsafe or unintended behaviors. To address these issues and ensure safety, we introduce TAPAssure, a novel framework that integrates LLM-generated TAP rules with formal verification techniques.

LLMs, when tasked with generating TAP rules, may omit critical information or produce rules that inadvertently introduce unsafe behaviors. For instance, a

L. Cheng and F. Anwar (Eds.): SmartSP 2025, LNICST 699, pp. 41–61, 2027.
https://doi.org/10.1007/978-3-032-33701-6_3

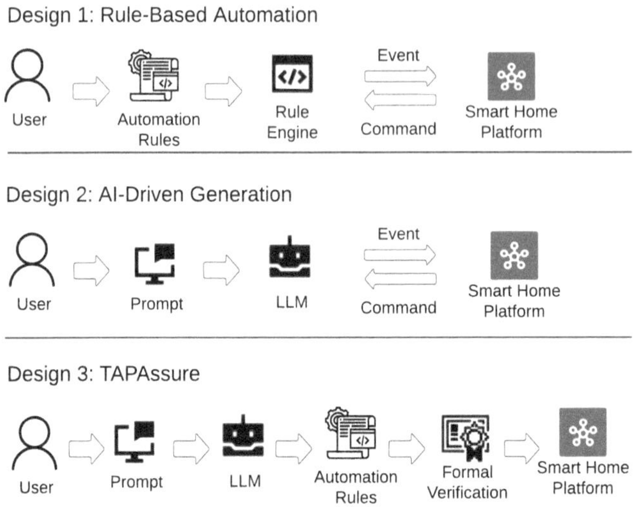

Fig. 1. Comparison of three automation design approaches in smart homes.

rule like "Unlock the front door when I arrive home" may seem intuitive but could pose security risks if deployed without constraints. Such vulnerabilities emphasize the need for a system that not only generates automation rules but also verifies their safety and correctness. While LLMs provide a user-friendly means of generating TAP rules, they lack the capability to detect violations of predefined safety properties or regenerate rules that violate those properties. Furthermore, in large-scale smart home environments with numerous interconnected devices, LLMs cannot effectively manage rule violations, increasing the risk of conflicting or unsafe automation (Fig. 1).

To address these challenges, TAPAssure systematically integrates formal verification methods with LLM-generated TAP rules. TAPAssure converts user input in natural language into a formal specification, applies model checking to detect and minimize violations of safety properties, and then regenerates TAP rules that comply with these properties. Specifically, the system utilizes NuSMV [5], a symbolic model checker, to formally verify that generated rules adhere to linear temporal logic (LTL) safety constraints. If a rule fails verification, TAPAssure iteratively refines it by incorporating counterexamples provided by the model checker, ensuring that the final rule set is both functional and safe. The validated transition rules are then translated back into natural language, forming the refined automation scenarios.

Unlike existing platforms that rely on rigid, predefined rule templates, TAPAssure maintains the flexibility of natural language interaction while guaranteeing safety through formal methods. The framework's iterative refinement process, guided by model checking feedback, systematically eliminates syntax errors and safety violations that would otherwise compromise system security.

We evaluate TAPAssure with Meta Llama 3.3 and Qwen2.5, two state-of-the-art open-weight models that enable reproducible experimentation without reliance on proprietary APIs. Although popular models like ChatGPT or Claude are strong candidates, their closed nature limits systematic evaluation. Our current prototype relies on cloud-based inference, which raises privacy concerns for sensitive smart home data; future work will explore local deployment of smaller models or secure execution environments. Scalability also remains a challenge, as certain cases (e.g., 53 iterations with Qwen2.5) highlight the need for more efficient prompting and constrained decoding.

Our main contributions are:

- The application and evaluation of an architecture combining LLMs with formal verification specifically for smart home automation, addressing the fundamental tension between usability and safety.
- An iterative refinement mechanism that uses model checker counterexamples to guide LLM-based rule regeneration, ensuring convergence to safe configurations.
- A comprehensive evaluation demonstrating TAPAssure's effectiveness across 120 test cases using Meta Llama 3.3 and Qwen2.5, achieving up to 100% success in finding a safe, verifiable configuration.
- Practical insights into the strengths and limitations of different LLMs for safety-critical rule generation, informing future system design.

The remainder of this paper is organized as follows: Sect. 2 provides background on smart home automation and formal verification. Section 3 presents our system model and problem formulation. Section 4 details TAPAssure's architecture. Section 5 evaluates our approach. Section 6 discusses related work, and Sect. 7 concludes.

2 Background

In this section, we provide a comprehensive overview of the foundational concepts relevant to TAPAssure, including smart home environments, Trigger-Action Programming (TAP), large language models (LLMs), and formal verification methods.

2.1 Smart Home Automation Platforms

Smart home technology integrates various IoT devices, allowing automated control and enhanced interaction to improve comfort, convenience, energy efficiency, and security. Modern smart homes often involve numerous interconnected devices such as smart thermostats, lighting systems, cameras, sensors, and smart locks [1,16]. These devices communicate through centralized or distributed IoT platforms like Amazon Alexa, Google Home, and Samsung SmartThings, offering users intuitive interfaces and automation capabilities.

While these systems significantly simplify daily routines, the complexity of inter-device interactions increases the likelihood of conflicts and safety risks. Therefore, ensuring robust automation through reliable rules generation and rigorous validation mechanisms remains critical for safe and effective deployment [12].

2.2 Trigger-Action Programming (TAP)

TAP is a widely adopted paradigm in smart home automation due to its intuitive and accessible structure, which pairs specific triggers (conditions or events) with corresponding actions [7,17]. TAP allows users without extensive technical backgrounds to define complex automated behaviors easily. However, the simplicity and intuitiveness of TAP can lead to unintended interactions, ambiguities, or safety hazards if the rules generated are incomplete, conflicting, or insufficiently verified [11].

Existing studies, such as *Soteria* [10] and *IoTGuard* [4], have highlighted critical safety concerns within TAP-based systems. Soteria focuses on static analysis of IoT application source code to detect security and safety policy violations, whereas IoTGuard employs dynamic runtime enforcement of user-defined policies. However, both approaches have limitations: neither systematically applies formal verification techniques to the automation rules prior to their deployment. Consequently, automation rules validated only by static or runtime checks without formal verification may still fail to detect complex or latent violations, thus inadvertently breaching user-specified safety properties.

2.3 Large Language Models (LLMs)

LLMs represent a major advancement in natural language processing, significantly improving capabilities in language understanding, generation, and reasoning. Trained on extensive datasets, LLMs excel in interpreting complex natural language instructions and generating contextually appropriate responses [3,13]. Their versatility makes them well-suited for tasks requiring intuitive interaction, such as generating TAP rules from user commands in smart homes.

Despite these strengths, LLMs have limitations, including potential inaccuracies, omissions, and vulnerabilities to adversarial inputs (e.g., prompt injections) [2,19]. Thus, deploying LLMs in safety-critical applications, such as smart home automation, necessitates additional validation layers to ensure their outputs are secure and reliable.

2.4 Formal Verification and Model Checking

Formal verification methods provide rigorous frameworks for verifying system behaviors against predefined specifications, playing a crucial role in ensuring safety-critical applications operate correctly and reliably. Model checking, a formal verification technique, systematically explores all possible states of a system to validate correctness properties expressed in formal logic (e.g., linear temporal logic or LTL) [6].

NuSMV, a widely-used symbolic model checker, facilitates efficient validation of system models against specified safety constraints, enabling the detection of potential rule conflicts or safety violations before deployment [5]. Integrating formal verification with rule generation processes in smart home systems is critical for guaranteeing that automated behaviors comply strictly with safety and security standards.

3 System Model and Problem Statement

In this section, we clearly define the system model utilized by TAPAssure and identify key problems that motivate our research.

3.1 System Model

The TAPAssure system operates within a smart home IoT environment comprising diverse interconnected devices, such as smart lights, thermostats, motion sensors, smart locks, and other home appliances. Users provide natural language commands specifying desired automation behaviors. These commands are processed by LLMs to generate initial TAP rules.

The smart home context, including device attributes (e.g., device IDs, capabilities, locations) and the home layout, significantly influences TAP rule generation accuracy. TAPAssure leverages this contextual information, ensuring generated rules are practical and operationally coherent. Once generated, TAP rules are translated into formal specifications represented using linear temporal logic (LTL), enabling rigorous verification through formal methods.

To validate these rules, TAPAssure integrates the NuSMV symbolic model checker, systematically verifying rules against specified safety properties. If violations or conflicts are identified, the TAP rules undergo iterative refinement informed by model checking results, ensuring final rules adhere strictly to safety requirements.

3.2 Problem Statement

The primary issue addressed in this research is the high potential for automation rules generated by LLMs to contain violations of predefined safety properties or to include syntax errors. Despite their efficiency in translating natural language commands into TAP rules, LLM-generated rules frequently exhibit errors such as incomplete information, missing critical details (e.g., device identifiers or exact locations), and unintended or unsafe behaviors.

Additionally, the lack of inherent verification mechanisms in existing LLM-driven automation systems substantially increases the likelihood of safety violations and security vulnerabilities. This risk is heightened in complex, large-scale smart home systems, where interactions among numerous devices can lead to conflicting rules, unintended activations, or security breaches.

Therefore, it is crucial to develop robust verification processes capable of rigorously validating generated TAP rules for both syntactic correctness and adherence to safety constraints prior to deployment. TAPAssure addresses this critical challenge by integrating formal verification methods, systematically mitigating syntax errors and ensuring compliance with safety properties, thereby enhancing the reliability and security of smart home automation.

For evaluation, we constructed a dataset consisting of three scenario sets and four safety property sets. Each safety set contained between three and five distinct properties, covering constraints such as occupancy-aware lighting, temperature thresholds, and energy conservation. Combining these sets yielded twelve scenario–property pairs, which served as the benchmark for testing. To bound runtime, the iterative regeneration process was capped at 60 attempts per trial. In practice, most scenarios converged well before this threshold. This cap ensures that extreme outliers do not result in unbounded computational cost while still allowing sufficient opportunities for refinement.

3.3 Threat Model

Our threat model explicitly addresses vulnerabilities associated with TAP rules generated by LLMs, focusing on specific threats that arise due to the inherent characteristics of these models and their interactions with smart home environments. The primary threats considered include:

- **Ambiguity and Misinterpretation**: LLM-generated rules based on ambiguous or underspecified natural language inputs may result in automation behaviors that deviate from user intentions, potentially creating hazardous or unintended outcomes.
- **Incomplete or Incorrect Contextual Information**: Generated TAP rules may lack crucial context such as precise device identifiers or accurate installation locations. Missing or incorrect contextual information can lead to unsafe actions or conflicts within the smart home environment.
- **Syntax Errors in Formal Models**: The translation of natural language commands into formal specifications is inherently complex and can lead to syntax errors, causing misinterpretations or failures in automation deployment.
- **Complex Inter-device Conflicts**: In large-scale smart home systems with multiple interconnected devices, LLM-generated rules might unintentionally produce conflicting scenarios or rule interactions, leading to unpredictable system states and operational hazards.

To effectively mitigate these threats, TAPAssure incorporates a robust formal verification mechanism using NuSMV. This formal verification step systematically detects syntax errors, ambiguity-related issues, and potential safety property violations, allowing iterative refinement of generated TAP rules. Through this verification-driven feedback loop, TAPAssure significantly reduces the risks associated with LLM-generated automation rules, ensuring safety, security, and operational correctness within smart home environments.

4 Design of TAPAssure

TAPAssure consists of two primary processes aimed at ensuring that the generated TAP rules are both contextually accurate and compliant with safety properties. These processes work in tandem to minimize conflicts and enhance automation reliability. The overall design of TAPAssure is depicted in Fig. 2, clearly illustrating the workflow from natural language input through formal verification and rule deployment. To illustrate, consider a scenario where "motion in the living room turns on the light" conflicts with a safety property requiring lights to remain off when the home is unoccupied. The initial model may compile but fail verification. TAPAssure uses the counterexample to regenerate a corrected rule such as "turn on the living room light if motion is detected and occupancy = true." This example shows how refinement gradually enforces safety constraints while preserving user intent. If regeneration fails to eliminate violations within the maximum iteration limit, TAPAssure flags the case and returns the partially refined model to the user for manual review, ensuring that unsafe rules are not silently deployed.

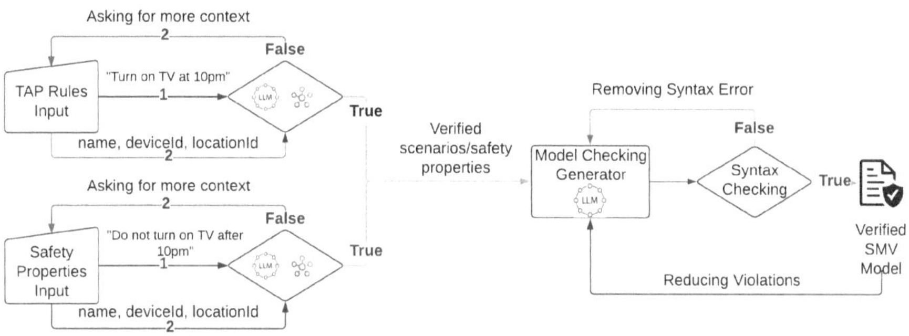

Fig. 2. TAPAssure's Design.

4.1 Context Verification and Initial Model Generation

The first process focuses on verifying context information provided by the user. This includes checking whether the mentioned devices exist in the smart home system and validating their installation locations. After this verification step, the user-provided scenarios and safety properties are reviewed to ensure completeness and consistency.

Users input their desired automation scenarios and home safety requirements in natural language. The LLM uses this input to generate TAP automation rules and LTL formulas for safety properties. However, user inputs may contain incomplete references to IoT devices (e.g., "all lights in the living room"), potentially confusing the LLM and hindering the generation of deployable TAP rules. To address this issue, we integrated the SmartThings API as an external function call accessible by the LLM. This integration enables the LLM to automatically retrieve real-time contextual information directly from the SmartThings platform, including precise device names, unique device IDs, capabilities, and installation locations. If any contextual information remains incomplete or ambiguous after this retrieval, the LLM will prompt users to clarify or provide the missing details before proceeding.

Once the contextual information is validated, the LLM generates the initial version of the NuSMV model. This initial model may contain syntax errors. TAPAssure iteratively regenerates the model until it is syntactically correct, ensuring the NuSMV model is valid before proceeding to the next phase.

4.2 Iterative Model Regeneration to Minimize Violations

In the second process, TAPAssure iteratively regenerates the NuSMV model to minimize violations between the scenarios and safety properties. The generated NuSMV model undergoes formal verification using the NuSMV model checker. If violations are detected, TAPAssure prompts the LLM to regenerate the model, incorporating the counterexamples provided by the model checker. This iterative regeneration process continues until the model satisfies all safety properties, resulting in a set of safe and reliable TAP rules.

After validating the scenarios and safety properties from Sect. 4.1, the pre-trained model performs prompt-based validation to identify potential violations. TAPAssure employs two validation methods: prompt-based validation and NuSMV-based verification, enhancing the accuracy of the results. Prompt-based validation runs in parallel with the NuSMV model checker, which detects violations and regenerates transition states to minimize their occurrence. This regeneration process can be iterated multiple times to further reduce violations. Once refined, the transition rules are translated back into natural language to form updated scenarios. This dual-validation approach—combining prompt-based validation with formal verification—ensures a comprehensive assessment of TAP rules against safety properties. This iterative process ensures that the generated TAP rules are safe and reliable for smart home automation, as detailed in Algorithm 1. We made the project publicly available on GitHub[1].

If no violations are identified in either validation step, the model proceeds to generate TAP rules based on the verified scenarios and safety properties. These TAP rules are automatically added to the SmartThings system, enabling secure and reliable automation. By integrating user-defined scenarios, device validation,

---

[1] https://github.com/huuhuannt1998/tapassure.

Algorithm 1. Verification with Context Validation and Model Checking

Input: Scenario S, Safety properties P **Output:** Verified NuSMV model M
$S \leftarrow \textsc{CompleteContext}(S)$; $P \leftarrow \textsc{CompleteContext}(P)$
$M \leftarrow \textsc{GenerateNuSMV}(S, P)$; $\textsc{EnsureValid}(M)$
repeat
  $V \leftarrow \textsc{ModelCheck}(M, P)$
  if $V = \emptyset$ **then return** M
  end if
  $M \leftarrow \textsc{Regenerate}(M, V)$; $\textsc{EnsureValid}(M)$
until false

where $\textsc{EnsureValid}(M)$: **while** $\neg\textsc{Valid}(M)$ **do** $M \leftarrow \textsc{FixSyntaxWithLLM}(M)$ **end while**
and $\textsc{CompleteContext}(X)$: **if** $\textsc{ContextIncomplete}(X)$ **then** $X \leftarrow \textsc{RequestMoreContext}(X)$; **return** $\textsc{CompleteContext}(X)$; **else return** X

dual-stage verification, and rule generation, this phase enhances the reliability and safety of the smart home environment, streamlining the automation process.

5 Implementation and Evaluation

Tables 1 and 2 use labels formatted as "Scenario-Safety Property" pairs (e.g., "2-3" indicates scenario set 2 combined with safety property set 3). This labeling scheme is consistently applied throughout the evaluation to succinctly denote scenario-property combinations.

5.1 Implementation

The implementation of TAPAssure is structured into multiple designs, clearly demonstrating the evolution of the system from initial rule generation to comprehensive formal verification and refinement (Fig. 3). Each design is specifically designed to enhance the accuracy, safety compliance, and reliability of Trigger-Action Program (TAP) rules within smart home environments.

Design Choice 1: Simple Generation (User Input). In the first design, the system accepts user input in the form of a scenario and generates corresponding TAP rules using an LLM. This represents the baseline capability of the LLM to interpret user-provided scenarios without any additional constraints or safety checks. Although simple, this approach may lead to potential issues, such as omitting essential conditions, potentially resulting in unsafe behaviors like continuous activation without proper shutdown conditions. For instance, the system might continuously activate a light whenever motion is detected without ever automatically turning it off.

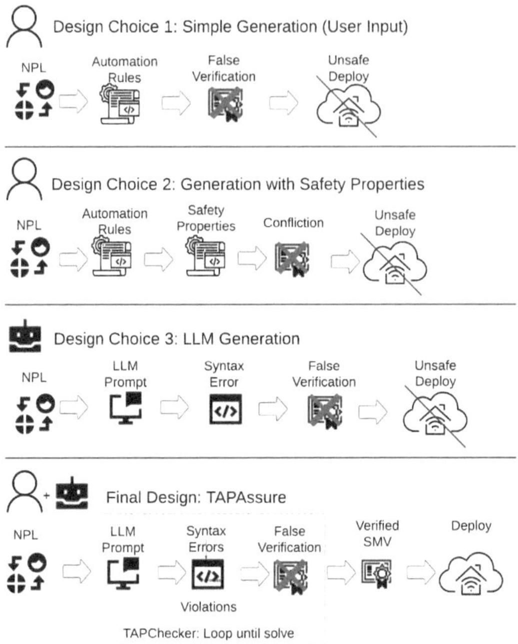

Fig. 3. Illustration of the Four Evolutionary Designs.

Design Choice 2: Generation with Safety Property. In the second design, users provide both a scenario and an explicit safety property, and the LLM generates rules that aim to comply with these specified constraints. This approach mitigates some risks identified in Design Choice 1 but still has limitations. Safety compliance is not fully verified, and generated rules might include logical conflicts or incomplete constraints. For example, a rule could incorrectly implement timing constraints, leading to delayed responses or unintended interactions between devices.

Design Choice 3: Context Verification and Initial NuSMV Model Generation. This design enhances the clarity and correctness of generated TAP rules by verifying contextual details such as device IDs and installation locations. The rules are then translated into formal specifications. However, due to the complexity involved, initial translations often contain syntax errors. These initial formal representations typically require iterative manual or automated corrections to address syntax or semantic errors. An example issue in this design might be an initial NuSMV model failing to compile due to missing variable declarations or incorrect temporal logic syntax.

Final Design: TAPAssure. The final design leverages NuSMV for formal verification of TAP rules against specified safety properties. Identified violations during verification prompt iterative regeneration and refinement of TAP rules until all constraints are fully satisfied. This iterative approach ensures that generated rules fully comply with predefined safety constraints, significantly reducing the risk of unsafe behaviors. An advantage of this method is its capability to reliably manage complex scenarios, such as accurately switching off lights after no motion has been detected for a specified period, thereby ensuring a safe and predictable smart home environment. The Llama3.3 and Qwen2.5 models were used without additional fine-tuning or training. Both models were accessed through their respective APIs in their pre-trained state, leveraging their inherent natural language understanding and code generation capabilities. The models' ability to generate NuSMV specifications and TAP rules relies on their pre-training on diverse programming and formal specification datasets.

5.2 Evaluation

We evaluated TAPAssure through two primary processes: **(1) Syntax Verification and Initial NuSMV Model Generation** and **(2) Iterative Model Regeneration to Minimize Violations**. The evaluation was conducted using two state-of-the-art large language models: Llama3.3 and Qwen2.5.

Dataset. In the final deployment of TAPAssure, users are expected to provide their own scenarios and safety properties, which will then be verified as described in Sect. 4.1. However, for the purposes of evaluation, we used a different set of predefined scenario–safety property pairs to facilitate controlled testing. To systematically evaluate TAPAssure, we constructed a dedicated experimental dataset consisting of realistic smart home scenarios and corresponding safety properties. Specifically, we created 3 distinct sets of scenarios and 4 distinct sets of safety properties. Each scenario set was combined individually with each set of safety properties, resulting in a total of 12 unique scenario-property combinations for testing. We assume that these scenarios and safety properties have been verified for correctness and coherence prior to our evaluation. Each of the 12 combination sets was subjected to rigorous testing, with each combination evaluated through 10 independent runs to ensure robust statistical significance.

Metrics. We evaluated TAPAssure's performance using two primary metrics:

- **Pass Rate**: Measures the effectiveness of the LLMs in successfully minimizing safety violations as determined by the NuSMV verification process. The pass rate is calculated as the percentage of runs where the generated rules fully complied with all safety properties after iterative regeneration. A run is considered successful only when all safety violations are eliminated, regardless of the number of regeneration iterations required.
- **Regeneration Failure Rate**: Assesses instances where the LLMs fail to effectively reduce or eliminate safety violations through the iterative process.

Regeneration failures occur in two scenarios: (1) when the LLM fails to generate syntactically valid rules that can be verified by NuSMV, or (2) when subsequent regeneration attempts result in either no improvement or an increased number of violations compared to the previous iteration. The regeneration failure rate is computed as the percentage of runs where the LLM-generated rules did not successfully resolve all identified violations within the maximum number of allowed iterations. These two metrics are complementary, with Pass Rate + Regeneration Failure Rate = 100%, providing a comprehensive view of the LLMs' capability to generate and refine safety-compliant rules through iterative feedback.

In addition to the pass rate, we report several complementary measures:

- **Average number of iterations** required to reach a valid and safe model, capturing efficiency.
- **Runtime per iteration and total runtime**, reflecting practical deployment costs.

These measures provide a richer understanding of how TAPAssure balances correctness, efficiency, and scalability across models. For example, while Llama3.3 consistently reached a safe configuration in fewer iterations, Qwen2.5 showed faster syntax correction but occasional outliers requiring significantly more iterations. Including these metrics highlights trade-offs between reliability and efficiency.

The Llama3.3 model achieved an exceptional **100% pass rate**, successfully minimizing safety violations in all 120 test cases without encountering any regeneration failures. On the other hand, Qwen2.5 successfully minimized violations in 112 out of 120 test cases, achieving a pass rate of **93.3%**. However, Qwen2.5 exhibited a regeneration failure rate of **6.7%**, corresponding to 8 test cases in which the number of violations increased.

Syntax Verification and Initial NuSMV Model Generation. TAPAssure translates user-provided scenarios and safety properties into an initial NuSMV model. Due to the inherent complexity of converting natural language instructions into formal specifications, syntax errors frequently arise. Table 1 summarizes the performance of both LLMs in terms of iterations required to eliminate syntax errors:

From Table 1, Qwen2.5 generally requires fewer iterations than Llama3.3, demonstrating higher efficiency in most scenarios. However, notable exceptions occur in scenarios 2-4 and 3-2, where Qwen2.5 exhibited significantly higher iteration counts (22 and 53 iterations, respectively), suggesting occasional sensitivity to complex structures. Table 1 and Fig. 4a show that the notably high iteration count for Qwen2.5 (53 iterations in scenario 3-2) underscores sensitivity to prompt phrasing. For instance, minor variations such as "activate A/C if temperature exceeds 78°F" compared to "A/C should activate when temperature is above 78°F" notably impacted iteration efficiency, indicating a need for consistent prompt engineering.

Table 1. Iterations to Eliminate Syntax Errors

Scen.-SafetyP.	Llama3.3	Qwen2.5
1-1	6	3
1-2	8	2
1-3	3	3
1-4	6	3
2-1	8	3
2-2	6	4
2-3	8	3
2-4	12	22
3-1	7	5
3-2	6	53
3-3	8	8
3-4	11	10

Table 2. Iterations to Minimize Violations

Scen.-SafetyP.	Llama3.3	Qwen2.5
1-1	23.1	10.1
1-2	5.8	10.7
1-3	6.4	22
1-4	5.8	0
2-1	0	9.6
2-2	1	5
2-3	0	13.9
2-4	6.2	3.8
3-1	3.1	7.2
3-2	3.1	4.5
3-3	9	7.3
3-4	2.3	3.4

Higher iteration counts may also affect practical usability through increased computational load and delayed responsiveness in smart home contexts, emphasizing the importance of efficient prompt strategies.

Instead, this behavior likely reflects Qwen2.5's sensitivity to subtle variations in phrasing or prompt formatting during the generation process. Such instability is characteristic of LLMs, which can sometimes produce inconsistent or suboptimal outputs even when given similar inputs. These outlier cases highlight the importance of incorporating robust validation mechanisms, such as iterative syntax checking, to ensure model correctness despite occasional unpredictability.

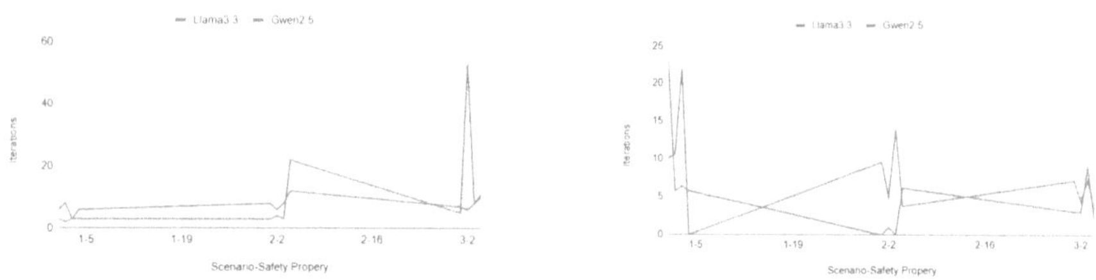

(a) Fixing Syntax Error

(b) Minimizing Violations

Fig. 4. LLM's Performance.

Iterative Model Regeneration to Minimize Violations. Once a syntactically correct NuSMV model is established, TAPAssure employs iterative regeneration to minimize safety property violations detected by the NuSMV model checker. Table 2 presents these results:

The data in Table 2 indicates that Llama3.3 excels in efficiently resolving violations across multiple scenarios, notably sets 2-1, 2-2, and 2-3. Conversely, Qwen

2.5 shows higher variability in performance but achieves exceptional efficiency in set 1-4.

5.3 Statistical Analysis and Insights

A deeper statistical analysis of the evaluation data, including the mean, median, and standard deviation, provides a more nuanced understanding of each LLM's performance. In the context of our framework, we define a model's precision by two key characteristics: its *efficiency* (the number of iterations required to find a solution) and its *reliability* (the consistency of its performance and its success rate).

Analysis of Syntax Error Resolution (Table 1). For the initial task of correcting syntax errors in the NuSMV model, the statistical results reveal a clear trade-off between speed and consistency.

- **Efficiency:** While Llama3.3 appears more efficient based on the mean (7.42 vs. 9.92), the median tells a different story. Qwen2.5's low median of 3.5 indicates that in a typical case, it is significantly more efficient, resolving syntax errors more than twice as fast as Llama3.3's typical performance (median of 7.5).
- **Reliability:** The standard deviation highlights a critical difference in precision. Llama3.3 exhibits a very low standard deviation of 2.54, signifying **high precision and predictable performance**. Its results are tightly clustered, meaning users can expect a consistent experience. Conversely, Qwen2.5 shows an extremely high standard deviation of 14.40. This volatility, driven by the outlier case of 53 iterations, indicates a lack of reliability. While often fast, it is prone to unpredictable and inefficient performance loops.

Analysis of Safety Violation Minimization (Table 2). For the more critical task of ensuring safety, the results demonstrate a clear superiority in Llama3.3's ability to perform precise and reliable work.

- **Efficiency:** In this complex reasoning task, Llama3.3 is unequivocally more efficient. Its low mean of 5.48 and median of 4.45 show that it consistently resolves safety-critical violations in fewer steps than Qwen2.5 (mean of 8.13, median of 7.25).
- **Reliability:** While both models have a similar standard deviation for this task (5.96 for Llama3.3 and 5.55 for Gwen2.5), the key differentiator is the overall success rate. Llama3.3's performance profile—combining its efficiency with the **perfect 100% pass rate** across all 120 test cases—is the ultimate proof of its precision. It demonstrates that Llama3.3 can not only find a safe configuration efficiently but can do so with complete reliability in our test suite. This stands in contrast to Qwen2.5, which was both slower and less reliable, failing in 6.7% of cases.

Conclusion on LLM Precision. The statistical analysis validates our framework and provides crucial insights into model selection. The results prove that by integrating formal methods with a high-performing LLM, it is possible to achieve the precision required for safety-critical applications. For the primary goal of TAPAssure, which is ensuring user safety, Meta Llama 3.3's demonstrated ability to efficiently, consistently, and reliably minimize safety violations makes it the more precise and trustworthy choice for this framework.

Case Study: Original vs. Minimized NuSMV Models. To evaluate the iterative violation minimization process in TAPAssure, we present a detailed case study of Scenario-Safety Property set 3-3. This includes the original NuSMV model, the minimized version generated after refinement, a comparison of their semantics, and the trends observed over 10 regeneration trials.

Violation Trend Analysis Llama3.3. Table 3 presents the number of iterations and violation counts across 10 independent trials for Scenario 3-3. In every trial, the maximum number of violations observed was 3, indicating consistent initial conflicts in the TAP rules prior to refinement. Notably, three trials (Trials 5, 7, and 10) successfully reduced the number of safety violations to a minimum of 1, demonstrating TAPAssure's ability to synthesize near-optimal rules in 30% of cases. Among these, Trial 7 was the fastest to converge, requiring only 7 iterations to reach the minimized violation count. In comparison, Trial 5 took 24 iterations and Trial 10 required 18 iterations, reflecting variation in convergence efficiency depending on the scenario structure and LLM responses.

The majority of the remaining trials (7 out of 10) converged to a minimum of 2 violations, with several of them doing so in just 3 to 7 iterations. This shows that TAPAssure typically achieves significant violation reduction with modest computational effort, even if not all violations are fully eliminated. The longest convergence time was observed in Trial 5, which required 24 iterations to reach its minimum, highlighting that certain input conditions may lead to more challenging optimization paths. Overall, the results demonstrate that TAPAssure consistently reduces safety violations within a reasonable number of iterations, though the extent and speed of convergence may vary across trials.

Violation Trend Analysis (Qwen2.5). Table 4 presents the number of iterations and violation counts across 10 independent trials for Scenario 3-3 using the Qwen2.5-14B model. Compared to LLama3.3, Qwen2.5 consistently achieved lower maximum violation counts, with no trial exceeding two safety violations. Notably, most trials (9 out of 10) reached a minimum violation count of 2, indicating a stable but less flexible convergence pattern. Only one trial (Trial 9) successfully minimized the violations to a count of 1 after 19 iterations, which was the highest convergence time among all Qwen2.5 trials.

Trials converged quickly in general, with the fastest run (Trial 3) requiring just 2 iterations to reach its final violation state. Despite the absence of

Table 3. Violation Trends Across Trials for Scenarios-Safety Properties 3-3 (Llama3.3)

Trial	Iterations	Max Violations	Min Violations
1	8	3	3
2	7	3	2
3	5	3	2
4	3	3	2
5	24	3	1
6	3	3	2
7	7	3	1
8	12	3	2
9	3	3	2
10	18	3	1

more aggressive optimization behavior observed in Llama3.3 (where 30% of trials reached only one violation), Qwen2.5 demonstrated more consistent and predictable refinement with reduced maximum violations. However, Trial 10 showed a slight regression, ending with a minimum violation count of 3—likely due to a compilation error or model inconsistency. Overall, Qwen2.5 shows promise in reliably reducing violations within a limited range but exhibits less variability in optimization depth compared to Llama3.3.

Table 4. Violation Trends Across Trials for Scenarios-Safety Properties 3-3 (Qwen2.5-14B)

Trial	Iterations	Max Violations	Min Violations
1	5	2	2
2	4	2	2
3	2	2	2
4	4	2	2
5	3	2	2
6	3	2	2
7	8	2	2
8	10	2	2
9	19	2	1
10	15	2	3

Comparison Between Original and Minimized Scenario-Safety Property Sets. The minimized scenario-safety property set represents the outcome of

TAPAssure's iterative refinement process guided by the LLM-generated NuSMV model. The primary objective of this minimization is to reduce safety violations and simplify rule logic rather than to replicate every detail from the original scenario explicitly. Thus, certain scenarios or conditions were intentionally simplified or omitted because they were not directly relevant to improving safety property compliance. To assess the effectiveness of TAPAssure's iterative model regeneration, we compared the original scenario-safety property set (Scenario - Safety Property 3-3) against the final minimized set derived through LLM-guided refinement. Table 5 summarizes this comparison, highlighting whether each item in the original set was preserved, simplified, or omitted in the minimized version.

Table 5. Comparison of Original and Minimized Scenario-Safety Property Sets

Type	Original Set (Scenario 3 / SP3)	Minimized Set (Inferred)
Scenario 1	Use Motion Sensor to trigger Virtual Light and Virtual A/C 1 when entering the bedroom.	Motion sensor in bedroom triggers `Virtual_Light_bedroom`. A/C 1 logic preserved but not triggered explicitly.
Scenario 2	At sunrise, turn off Virtual Fan 1 and Virtual Light in the kitchen.	`Virtual_Fan1` turns off at sunrise. Kitchen light omitted.
Scenario 3	Turn on Virtual TV 2 and set Virtual Fan 5 to low when 'movie mode' is activated.	Movie mode activates `Virtual_TV2` and sets `Virtual_Fan5` to `low`; fan automatically turns off after 60 min.
Scenario 4	Turn off Virtual A/C 3 when all doors are closed and no motion is detected in the house.	`Virtual_AC3` turns off if `doors_closed` and `no_motion` are true.
Scenario 5	Turn on Virtual Fridge 1 and Virtual Light when motion is detected in the dining room.	Motion in dining room triggers `Virtual_Fridge1`. Dining room light omitted.
Scenario 6	If Motion Sensor detects temperature above 80°F, activate Virtual A/C 2 and Virtual Fan 4.	`Virtual_AC2` is deactivated if temp > 78°F. `Virtual_Fan4` turns `low` for temp > 80°F, `medium` for > 85°F.
Scenario 7	Turn on Virtual TV 1 and mute it if no movement is detected in the living room for 5 min.	If `no_motion` and `time > 5`, `Virtual_TV1` is turned on and muted conditionally.
Scenario 8	Turn off Virtual Fan 2 at 10 PM every night to conserve energy.	`Virtual_Fan2` turns off when `time = 22`.
SP 1	Virtual A/C 3 must deactivate if temperature drops below 70°F.	Same property enforced via `room_temperature_below_70`.
SP 2	Virtual A/C 2 must not exceed 78°F.	Same logic enforced using `room_temperature_above_78`.
SP 3	Virtual Fan 5 must not remain on for more than 1 h without activity detection.	Fan 5 auto-off after 60 min. Activity detection condition abstracted.
SP 4	Virtual Fan 4 must operate at medium if temperature exceeds 85°F.	Same rule enforced directly. Additional case added for temp > 80°F as `low`.

Interpretation of Minimization Results. The minimized scenario-safety property set successfully resolves many original safety violations (reducing from the initial 4 violations). It strategically simplifies non-safety-critical elements, clarifies previously ambiguous wording, and explicitly enhances critical safety conditions. Although some original scenario details are intentionally omitted or adjusted, this is justified explicitly by their irrelevance to safety constraints. Thus, the minimized set effectively demonstrates TAPAssure's optimization capability, prioritizing safety compliance and simplified formal verification over exact replication of original scenario logic.

Table 5 presents a comparison between the original and minimized scenario-safety property sets. The changes introduced during the minimization process reflect several recurring themes, primarily aimed at simplifying the automation rules while retaining or enhancing safety-relevant logic.

In several cases (e.g., Scenario 1 and Scenario 5), actions unrelated to the core safety requirement were intentionally omitted. For instance, the minimization removed the activation of Virtual A/C 1 and the dining room light, focusing only on the essential device (Virtual Light or Virtual Fridge 1) to streamline the automation and reduce unnecessary device usage. Similarly, in Scenario 2, the kitchen light was excluded, as it did not directly impact the safety property under consideration.

Other changes were made to enhance clarity and ensure explicit enforcement of safety conditions. For example, Scenario 3 introduces an explicit timer for automatically turning off Virtual TV 2 and Virtual Fan 5 after 60 min of movie mode activation, providing a clear safety mechanism for energy management. Scenario 6 further refines environmental controls by specifying distinct activation and deactivation thresholds for Virtual A/C 2 and defining different operating levels for Virtual Fan 4 based on temperature.

In some scenarios and safety properties (e.g., Scenario 4, Scenario 7, Scenario 8, and Safety 1), the logic was preserved without modification, indicating that the original rules were already optimal or sufficiently precise with respect to the safety objectives. Finally, certain simplifications involved replacing complex activity-based triggers with straightforward timers, as seen in Safety 3, where the fan is now turned off after a fixed duration, omitting the need for activity detection. Overall, these minimization decisions collectively reduce complexity, improve the interpretability of the rules, and enhance the enforcement of safety properties in the automated smart home environment.

This comparison confirms that TAPAssure's model refinement does not compromise safety logic and successfully eliminates redundant or unused transitions for streamlined verification.

6 Related Work and Comparison

TAPAssure sits at the intersection of two research directions: the use of Large Language Models (LLMs) to simplify smart home automation and the application of formal methods to ensure the safety of IoT systems. Prior work has generally emphasized one of these aspects at the expense of the other. TAPAssure is, to our knowledge, the first system to unify natural language–based rule generation with proactive, design-time verification and refinement.

6.1 LLMs for Smart Home Automation

Recent efforts have shown how LLMs can improve usability by translating high-level goals into Trigger-Action Programming (TAP) rules. Sasha [9] and Aware Auto [15] exemplify this trend, converting goals such as "get ready for a party" [8] into coordinated device automations. These approaches lower the barrier for non-technical users to create sophisticated routines. However, they provide no mechanisms for detecting conflicts, unsafe conditions, or policy violations, creating what we term the *usability-correctness gap.* As non-experts author increasingly complex automations, the absence of verification increases the likelihood of unsafe or inconsistent behaviors.

6.2 Formal Verification for IoT Safety

In parallel, research on IoT safety has focused on verification but typically assumes structured, expert-authored code. Soteria [10], for example, statically analyzes IoT apps by translating them into an intermediate representation and applying model checking to detect violations such as "the door must remain locked when the user is away." While effective in this setting, Soteria presupposes formalized source code and therefore cannot be applied to natural-language specifications.

Other approaches enforce safety reactively at runtime. IoTGuard [4] instruments applications to block unsafe actions during execution, while IOTMEDIATOR [18] resolves conflicting commands in multi-resident environments. These systems follow a "fail-safe" philosophy, but blocking or altering actions at runtime can result in degraded or unpredictable user experiences. TAPAssure instead adopts a proactive, *correct-by-construction* paradigm: by integrating model checking into the generation process, it ensures that unsafe rules are removed before deployment.

6.3 Comparative Analysis

In summary, existing work either emphasizes user-friendly generation without guarantees (Sasha, Aware Auto) or strong verification detached from usability (Soteria, IoTGuard, IOTMEDIATOR). TAPAssure brings these strands together by refining natural-language–generated rules through model checking at design time, closing the usability-correctness gap. Table 6 positions TAPAssure relative to these approaches.

Table 6. Methodological Comparison of Automation and Verification Approaches

Approach	Core Task	Verification	Stage	Feedback
Sasha [9]	LLM Generation	None	Design-Time	None
Aware Auto [15]	LLM Generation	None	Design-Time	None
Soteria [10]	Conflict Detection	Model Checking	Pre-Deployment	Static Reports
IoTGuard [4]	Safety Enforcement	Dynamic Monitoring	Runtime	Blocking
IOTMEDIATOR [18]	Conflict Resolution	Mediation	Runtime	Patching
TAPAssure (Ours)	**LLM Gen + Refinement**	**Model Checking (LTL)**	**Design-Time**	**Counterexamples**

7 Conclusion

In this paper, we introduced TAPAssure, a framework integrating LLMs with formal verification to improve the safety and reliability of TAP rules in smart homes. Our comprehensive evaluation using Meta Llama 3.3 and Qwen2.5 demonstrated that TAPAssure effectively identifies and resolves both syntax errors and safety violations in an autonomous fashion.

Our evaluation highlighted distinct strengths of each LLM: Qwen2.5 showed superior efficiency in resolving syntax errors, while Meta Llama 3.3 demonstrated greater robustness in minimizing safety property violations, making it particularly suitable for safety-critical scenarios. By successfully bridging the intuitive capabilities of LLMs with the rigor of formal verification, TAPAssure offers a robust pathway toward creating smart home automation that is not only powerful but also verifiably safe.

References

1. Alam, M., Reaz, M.B.I., Ali, M.A.R.: Automation in smart homes. Handbook of Green Information and Communication Systems, pp. 329–348 (2012)
2. Bommasani, R., Hudson, D.A., Adeli, E., Altman, R., Arora, S., von Arx, S., et al.: On the opportunities and risks of foundation models. arXiv preprint arXiv:2108.07258 (2021)
3. Brown, T., et al.: Language models are few-shot learners (2020). arXiv preprint-arXiv:2005.14165
4. Celik, Z.B., Tan, G., McDaniel, P.: IoTGuard: dynamic enforcement of security and safety policy in commodity IoT. In: Proceedings of the Network and Distributed System Security Symposium (NDSS) (2019)
5. Cimatti, A., et al.: NuSMV 2: an opensource tool for symbolic model checking. International Conference on Computer Aided Verification, pp. 359–364 (2002)
6. Clarke, E.M., Grumberg, O., Peled, D.A.: Model Checking. MIT Press (1999)

7. Huang, J., Cakmak, S., Miller, R.: Supporting trigger-action programming in the smart home. In: Proceedings of the ACM CHI Conference on Human Factors in Computing Systems, pp. 803–812. (2013)
8. King, E., Yu, H., Lee, S., Julien, C.: "get ready for a party": Exploring smarter smart spaces with help from large language models. arXiv preprint arXiv:2303.14143 (2023)
9. King, E., Yu, H., Lee, S., Julien, C.: Sasha: creative goal-oriented reasoning in smart homes with large language models. Proc. ACM Interact. Mob. Wearable Ubiquit. Technol. **8**(1), 1–38 (2024)
10. Lee, Y., et al.: Soteria: automated IoT safety and security analysis. In: USENIX Annual Technical Conference (USENIX ATC), pp. 147–158 (2018)
11. Mendoza, P., Hodges, S., DeJonghe, D., Cakmak, S.: Flexible conflict detection and resolution for smart home systems. IEEE Trans. Smart Grid **6**(1), 107–116 (2015)
12. Perera, C., Zaslavsky, A., Christen, P., Georgakopoulos, D.: Emerging trends, challenges, and opportunities in internet of things: Applications (2014). arXiv preprint arXiv:1401.4977
13. Radford, A., et al.: Language models are unsupervised multitask learners. OpenAI Blog **1**(8), 9 (2019)
14. Rivkin, D., et al.: Sage: Smart home agent with grounded execution (2023). arXiv preprint arXiv:2311.00772
15. Shi, Y., et al.: Bridging the gap between natural user expression with complex automation programming in smart homes (2024). https://arxiv.org/abs/2408.12687
16. Stojkoska, B.L.R., Trivodaliev, K.V.: A review of internet of things for smart home: challenges and solutions. J. Clean. Prod. **140**, 1454–1464 (2017)
17. Ur, B., McManus, E., Pak, K., Sciolla, J., Littman, M.L.: Practical trigger-action programming in the smart home. In: Proceedings of the ACM CHI Conference on Human Factors in Computing Systems, pp. 803–812 (2014)
18. Xiao, Q., Wang, Y., Li, R., Chen, W., Zhang, X.: Iotmediator: resolving conflicts in smart home IoT applications. In: Proceedings of the ACM International Conference on Information Processing in Sensor Networks (IPSN), pp. 250–261. ACM (2020). https://doi.org/10.1145/3372224.3380894
19. Zellers, R., et al.: Defending against neural fake news. In: Advances in Neural Information Processing Systems, vol. 32, pp. 9054–9065 (2019)

Applying Cyber Informed Engineering Principles to Secure SoC Design for Electric Vehicle Charging

Md Mahmudul Kabir Peyal[1], Benjamin Lampe[2], Sin Ming Loo[1,2], and Benjamin C. Johnson[1](✉)

[1] Department of Electrical and Computer Engineering, Boise State University, Boise, ID, USA
mahmudulpeyal@u.boisestate.edu, {smloo,bcjohnson}@boisestate.edu
[2] Idaho National Laboratory, Idaho Falls, ID, USA

Abstract. Rapid adoption of electric vehicles (EVs) and their integration into power grids through Vehicle-to-Grid (V2G) technologies offer significant opportunities for sustainable energy management, but also introduce complex cybersecurity challenges. System-on-Chip (SoC) devices at the heart of EV charging infrastructure are especially vulnerable to hardware-level threats that can compromise grid stability, vehicle safety, and data integrity. This paper applies Cyber-Informed Engineering (CIE) principles to the design of secure SoC architectures for EV charging systems, promoting a secure-by-design approach throughout the chip development lifecycle. Through detailed case studies—specifically the Jeep Cherokee remote exploit and the Brokenwire attack—the paper demonstrates how CIE principles, when mapped to SoC design phases, can guide the implementation of targeted mitigations such as secure boot, supply chain authentication, and real-time anomaly detection. To further support this framework, the Common Weakness Enumeration (CWE) is introduced as a complementary resource, providing a structured taxonomy of known hardware vulnerabilities that enhances the precision and relevance of CIE-based security strategies. Together, CIE and CWE offer a robust methodology for building resilient, secure EV charging systems.

Keywords: Cyber-Informed Engineering · electric vehicles · V2G · SoC design · cybersecurity · embedded systems · Secure-by-Design · automotive cybersecurity

1 Introduction

The rapid adoption of electric vehicles (EVs) is revolutionizing sustainable transportation, with U.S. sales surging 15.2% year-over-year to 365,824 units in 2024 [1]. This transition reduces fossil fuel dependency and greenhouse gas emissions. However, it also places unprecedented demands on energy infrastructure as EV charging networks integrate with smart grids through Vehicle-to-Grid

L. Cheng and F. Anwar (Eds.): SmartSP 2025, LNICST 699, pp. 62–79, 2027.
https://doi.org/10.1007/978-3-032-33701-6_4

(V2G) technology and Internet of Things (IoT) solutions. All interconnected systems enable advanced grid management and energy storage, but introduce cybersecurity vulnerabilities that threaten grid stability, vehicle safety, and sustainable energy goals [2]. Threats such as unauthorized access, data breaches, energy theft, and grid destabilization exploit weaknesses in charging protocols, communication networks, and power management systems. Despite their critical significance, these threats remain underexplored within the EV environment, highlighting the need for proactive strategies to secure new infrastructure.

Real-world events further illustrate the urgency of robust cybersecurity implementation. The exploit of a 2014 Jeep Cherokee demonstrated how interconnected vehicle systems can be remotely compromised via hardware and software vulnerabilities [3], while the Brokenwire attack revealed electromagnetic interference (EMI) weaknesses in EV charging links, disrupting communications with minimal effort [4]. These cases expose both hardware and communication-layer vulnerabilities, which, if exploited in V2G systems, could cascade into grid-wide failures or compromise user safety. Therefore, a holistic security strategy must integrate cybersecurity, grid resilience, and sustainability objectives.

Cyber-Informed Engineering (CIE) [5–7] offers a systematic framework to embed cybersecurity into the design of critical systems, prioritizing secure-by-design approaches through multiple stages. By integrating cybersecurity principles into the design, development and operation of physical systems, CIE ensures that digital components are secure from the outset. Figure 1 illustrates the twelve foundational CIE principles, which guide the integration of cybersecurity into system design at both architectural and operational levels. Applying CIE principles to chip designing infrastructure involves incorporating secure design practices and developing resilience against hardware- and firmware-level threats.

Despite significant advances in EV cybersecurity, most existing research has concentrated on software-level protections such as intrusion detection systems and encrypted communication protocols [8,9]. In contrast, hardware-level vulnerabilities, including hardware trojans [10–13], electromagnetic interference attack [14,15] have received comparatively little attention. This study focuses on these hardware threats by applying the twelve CIE principles to the design of secure System-on-Chip (SoC) architectures for EV charging hardware. The proposed architecture aims to protect V2G systems and critical infrastructure against semiconductor-level attacks through secure authentication, encrypted communication, and real-time anomaly detection. Optimized hardware design also improves charging efficiency and system resilience, supporting both security and sustainability objectives.

In addition to presenting a novel hardware-based defense strategy, this study explores broader cybersecurity risks in EV charging and evaluates resilience strategies through the lens of the CIE framework. This paper is intended for engineering professionals and decision makers with general technical knowledge, providing accessible information on secure system design methods for EV charging infrastructure at the intersection of cybersecurity, semiconductor design, and emerging automotive technologies.

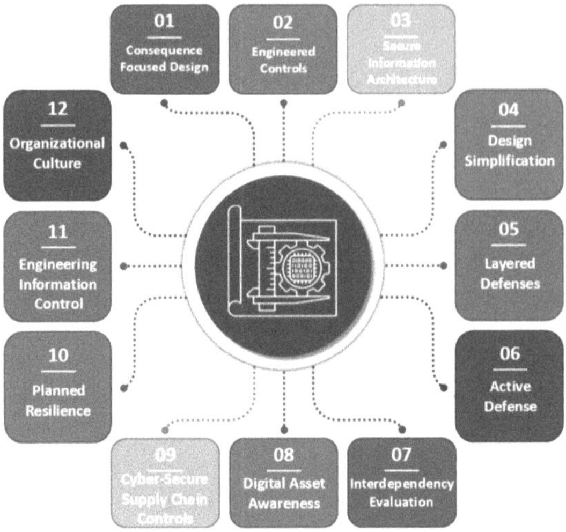

Fig. 1. The twelve Cyber-Informed Engineering (CIE) principles for embedding cybersecurity into critical infrastructure design.

2 Methodology

This section presents the methodology for designing a secure System-on-Chip (SoC) architecture for electric vehicle (EV) charging systems, applying Cyber-Informed Engineering (CIE) principles combined with Common Weakness Enumeration (CWE) to address hardware security threats. The approach combines an in-depth analysis of the EV charging module design, threat modeling of hardware vulnerabilities, the structured SoC design process, and a comprehensive mapping of CIE principles across the engineering lifecycle.

2.1 Module Design and Security Challenges

The production of chips for critical systems' modules, such as EV charging controllers, involves a complex and time-consuming design process that introduces unique security challenges. Figure 2 illustrates a simplified architecture of an EV power distribution system, highlighting the critical role of the charging IC in power conversion and data communication within the charging ecosystem [16]. The high-power demands of EV fast charging systems require advanced materials, efficient power management, and secure control interfaces, making the charging IC a target for potential cyber-physical attacks.

2.2 System-on-Chip Design

Modern chip design is predominantly performed by fabless firms that rely on third-party foundries for design IP (intellecual property), fabrication, and assembly, increasing exposure to supply chain risks. The charging SoC for this study

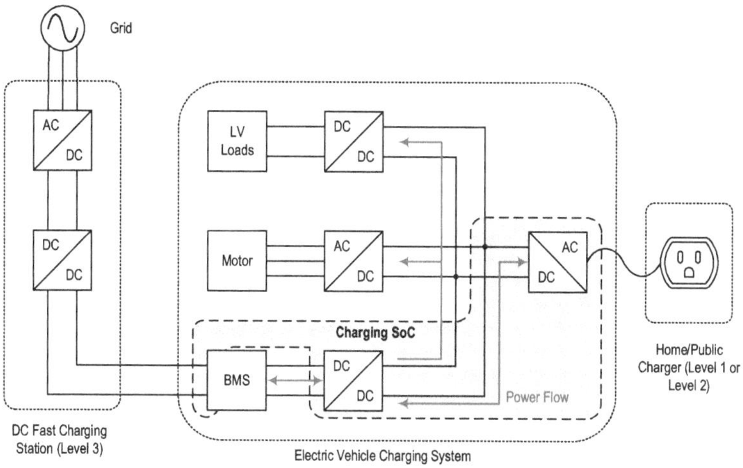

Fig. 2. Simplified architecture of EV power distribution system. The proposed charging SoC manages power from Level 1 and Level 2 chargers and connects Level 3 chargers to the Battery Management System (BMS).

uses a multi-chip solution where a gallium nitride (GaN) chip technology is used for power management due to its inherent advantages over silicon (Si) for high power applications. For digital processing and control of the power management IC, a 45nm Si CMOS technology offers an excellent tradeoff between switching speed, efficiency, and cost. This architecture meets the performance requirements of DC fast chargers but also introduces security challenges due to the integration of advanced materials, IP, and assembly from multiple vendors. The complexity of managing dies sourced from diverse suppliers necessitates proactive cybersecurity strategies.

Figure 3 provides a high-level overview of the SoC design process, from product definition through design, layout, fabrication, packaging, and testing [17]. The architectural design phase defines key functionalities such as power conversion and Vehicle-to-Grid (V2G) compatibility. Due to the lengthy design process, we contend that CIE Principles should be incorporated during the product definition phase to ensure secure-by-design. Chip design includes the creation of architectures, logic, and circuit-level schematics which attention to secure data paths, physically unclonable functions, and resistance to side-channel attacks. Chip layout translates schematics into physical structures, carefully optimizing placement and routing to minimize vulnerabilities. The finalized design is sent for fabrication, where the IC is manufactured in silicon or gallium nitride. Afterward, assembly integrates the chip into its package, often adding tamper-resistant features. Finally, rigorous testing ensures functional correctness, performance, and resilience against both functional failures and hardware-based attacks, as well as all necessary automotive qualifications. Throughout, security considerations are embedded at every stage to ensure trustworthiness in hostile environments.

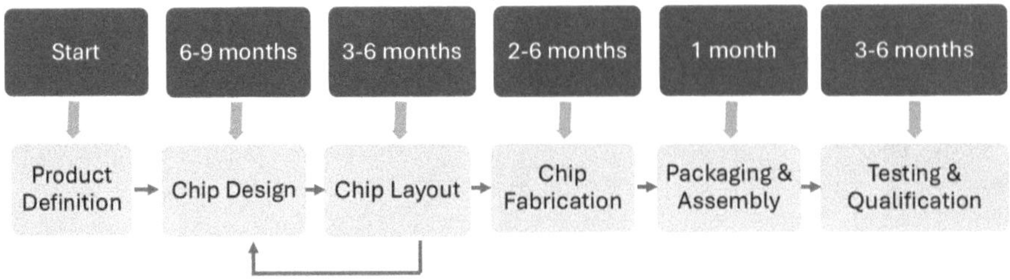

Fig. 3. Overview of chip design process.

2.3 Hardware Security Threats

EV charging systems face a range of hardware-specific cybersecurity threats that can compromise infrastructure integrity. Key threats are summarized here:

- **Hardware Trojans**: Malicious circuit modifications are hidden until triggered, allowing backdoors or information leakage.
- **Electromagnetic Fault Injection (EMFI)**: Electromagnetic pulses injected via charging cables induce faults in chip operation.
- **Side-Channel Attacks**: Using electromagnetic radiation emitted during charging to infer data.
- **Jamming Attacks**: Over-the-air interference with charging signals, disrupting V2G communication.
- **Reverse Engineering**: Physical disassembly or tampering to extract proprietary designs.
- **IP Piracy**: The theft of intellectual property during design, production, or integration.

These threats correspond to known weaknesses cataloged in the Common Weakness Enumeration (CWE), a community-driven repository maintained by MITRE with support from the U.S. Department of Homeland Security [18]. CWE offers hardware designers a valuable framework for identifying and mitigating vulnerabilities, with relevant entries such as CWE-1300 (improper protection of physical side channels) [19], CWE-1245 (improper finite-state machines) [20], CWE-1319 (EMFI fault injection) [21], and CWE-1357 (supply chain vulnerabilities) [22]. CWE currently includes 123 hardware weaknesses across 13 categories, making it a critical resource to incorporate into secure SoC design and verification workflows.

2.4 CIE Principles Application

The twelve CIE principles can be systematically mapped to mitigate identified hardware threats in the EV charging SoC. Table 1 outlines how the twelve cyber-informed engineering principles (CIE) are applied to the design of the EV charging SoC. Each principle guided specific security measures, from protecting critical chip functions to ensuring supply chain integrity. Some strategies are also considered based on real-world incidents, enhancing the resilience of the SoC against cyberphysical threats.

Table 1. Application of CIE Principles to EV Charging SoC

CIE Principles	Application	Risk Event
1. Consequence-Focused Design	Identified critical functions (e.g., power conversion, data communication). Prioritized security for high-impact areas to prevent failures like grid destabilization.	Control loss due to a single flaw
2. Engineered Controls	Mapped interdependencies with V2G systems. Segmented critical functions to reduce risk of cascading failures.	Compromise the entire system
3. Secure Information Architecture	Streamlined power management logic to reduce EMFI vulnerabilities and simplify data paths.	EMFI-based disruption
4. Design Simplification	Removed redundant communication ports and added encrypted control signals to reduce protocol complexity.	Complex protocol exploitation
5. Layered Defenses	Anticipated Hardware Trojan risks; implemented secure authentication to block unauthorized access.	Exposure of the entire chip
6. Active Defense	Modeled EMFI attacks and integrated real-time response algorithms to maintain power delivery under EMI threats.	Delayed detection of intrusions
7. Interdependency Evaluation	Assessed how different chip and charger system components depend on each other and how failure or compromise in one area (e.g., communication interface) could affect others.	Wide-scale impact from a single compromise
8. Digital Asset Awareness	Maintained a complete inventory of firmware versions, IP cores, debug tools, and design assets, and analyzed potential vulnerabilities to prioritize cybersecurity efforts.	Hidden vulnerabilities in untracked or unmanaged firmware/IP versions
9. Cyber-Secure Supply Chain Controls	Evaluated multi-vendor die model; used trusted foundries and verified components for supply chain integrity.	Malicious hardware injection during fabrication
10. Planned Resilience	Added anomaly detection for real-time monitoring and ensured continued operation under attack.	Systems fail or shut down under attack
11. Engineering Information Control	Protected design documentation, simulation files, firmware code, and other engineering records from unauthorized access.	Exposure of architecture files or source code
12. Organizational Culture	Encouraged cross-team collaboration (engineers, grid operators, policymakers). Promoted a cybersecurity-first mindset across all teams.	Neglected cybersecurity practices during development

Moreover, the successful implementation of the CIE principles in the design of charging IC required coordinated efforts across all organizational units. Table 2 shows which teams or departments are responsible for applying each CIE principle and gives an overview of the roles and responsibilities needed to implement them. Each unit requires additional collaboration with other units to ensure cybersecurity is embedded throughout the design process. For example, the Engineering team directly applied principles like Consequence-Focused Design and Engineered Controls, while Procurement ensured supply chain security.

Table 2. CIE Roles and Principles for EV Charging SoC Development

Organizational Role	CIE Principles
Executive Leadership	12. Organizational Culture
Product Engineering & Architecture	1. Consequence-Focused Design 2. Engineered Controls 4. Design Simplification
Silicon Design & Verification	3. Secure Information Architecture 5. Layered Defenses
Firmware & Embedded Software	6. Active Defense 10. Planned Resilience
System Integration & Validation	7. Interdependency Evaluation 8. Digital Asset Awareness
Supply Chain & Vendor Management	9. Cyber-Secure Supply Chain Controls
Cybersecurity & Risk Management	3. Secure Information Architecture 5. Layered Defenses 8. Digital Asset Awareness
Regulatory Affairs & IP Protection	11. Engineering Information Control

2.5 Implementation of Mitigation Controls

This section presents the application of twelve Cyber-Informed Engineering (CIE) principles to address key hardware threats [23] and possible mitigation strategies in EV charging SoCs. These include hardware trojans, remote attacks, and electromagnetic interference (EMI). Each subsection highlights how these principles guide SoC-level security implementations throughout the lifecycle.

2.5.1 Consequence-Focused Design

Consequence-focused design emphasizes the identification of critical System-on-Chip (SoC) functions such as power regulation, secure communication, and firmware authentication, and prioritizes their protection to prevent system-wide failure. By focusing on high-impact consequences rather than attack vectors alone, designers can ensure that critical functions remain operational even under malicious conditions. This approach encourages the isolation of critical and non-critical functions to guide designers in design simplification, developing layered defenses, and planned resiliency.

Mitigation: During early design stages, mapping system-level consequences to SoC subsystems helps guide the integration of protective measures, such as isolated control logic or secure discharge mechanisms, to maintain continuity during disruptions like jamming or unauthorized access. This process prompts designers to reassess requirements and incorporate security features that address broader system interactions and emerging threats. For example, the charging SoC should include load-shedding mitigation to help prevent grid instability during a coordinated attack. This ensures the final SoC is both functionally efficient and resilient to high-consequence failures.

2.5.2 Engineered Controls

Engineered controls involve systematically applying defenses against anticipated hardware threat vectors during the design and fabrication phases. These controls aim to proactively block, detect, or mitigate vulnerabilities rather than relying solely on post-deployment measures. In the context of secure SoC design for EV charging systems, engineered controls include locking down debug ports, enforcing secure boot mechanisms, and disabling unused logic paths to reduce the hardware attack surface.

This principle is critical in minimizing risks that are otherwise hard to detect after manufacturing, such as the presence of malicious circuitry or unintended information leakage paths. By incorporating controls at the chip-level and board-level, designers can preemptively eliminate vulnerabilities that could compromise the charging infrastructure.

Mitigation: Controls are integrated at the hardware level to protect against common threats like hardware Trojans, side-channel leakage, jamming, reverse engineering, and IP theft. For example: fuses or one-time programmable logic can permanently disable unused interfaces [24]; debug ports are either removed or require cryptographic challenge-response mechanisms; current and temperature sensors can detect anomalies indicative of tampering or excessive load; and chip fingerprinting techniques such as physically unclonable functions (PUFs) can validate device authenticity. A summary of risk types and corresponding engineered controls is provided in Table 3.

2.5.3 Secure Information Architecture

Secure information architecture ensures that sensitive data within the SoC system—such as firmware, charging communication, and payment credentials—is protected from tampering, sniffing, or unauthorized access. By designing strong data confidentiality and integrity measures, SoC designers can prevent coordinated attacks stemming from data manipulation during EV charging communication.

Mitigation: Controls are implemented at both the physical and protocol layers to reduce attack feasibility. To address leakage via electromagnetic emissions, designers can shield charging wires and use balanced capacitance or constant-weight encoding on communication links. Additionally, encrypting messages over the charging interface and enforcing authenticated firmware execution prevent malware injection and unauthorized control.

Table 3. Determined Risks and Possible Controls

Risks	Possible Controls
Hardware Trojan	– Use secure, high-quality supply chain – Licensed IPs must disclose security posture – Use Zero Trust hardware architecture – Employ redundant current and temperature sensors – Use PUFs to generate unique, unclonable chip fingerprints
Side-Channel Sniffing	– Shield charging wires – Balance wire capacitance or use constant-weight encoding – Encrypt CCS messages between EV and charger
Jamming Attack	– Shield EMI entry paths – Disable firmware updates during charging – Controlled shutdown to limit impact of load shedding
Reverse Engineering	– Use secure boot process – Tamper-detection circuits for shutdown – Physically isolate vehicle-ECU interfaces
IP Leakage	– Enforce development security measures – Secure IP, simulation, and debug files

2.5.4 Design Simplification

Design simplification improves security and resilience by minimizing non-essential system features that introduce unnecessary complexity or expand the attack surface. In System-on-Chip (SoC) designs for EV charging, this involves eliminating auxiliary functions (e.g., infotainment interlinks, excessive user data interfaces) that are not directly involved in safety-critical charging control or communication.

Mitigation: Designers reduce the number of SoC modules and remove functions that do not contribute to charging or protection logic. For instance, omitting data-logging interfaces or app-level hooks that interact with sensitive charging subsystems mitigates software injection and battery-drain risks. Integration of protection features (e.g., overcurrent and over-temperature detection) into core modules further reduces component count and supply-chain attack vectors.

2.5.5 Layered Defenses

Layered defense applies multiple levels of protection to safeguard critical SoC operations, ensuring that if one control fails, others remain in place to resist compromise. In EV charging systems, this principle is crucial for protecting interconnected subsystems and preventing lateral movement across the chip architecture.

Mitigation: First, security-sensitive interfaces such as debug ports are protected with secure boot mechanisms, password locking, or hardware fuses to prevent post-deployment exploitation. Second, cryptographic primitives are implemented at the interface level to enforce strong authentication and data integrity. A dual-interface design may also separate critical firmware access from limited hardware diagnostics, ensuring that fallback mechanisms remain uncompromised. This layered approach maintains the resilience of critical SoC functions against multi-vector attacks, even under partial system compromise.

2.5.6 Active Defense

Active defense emphasizes proactive detection and response mechanisms that continuously monitor chip operation and detect tampering or exploitation attempts in real time. For EV charging SoCs, this principle helps identify ongoing threats, such as firmware manipulation, jamming attacks, or anomalous subsystem behavior.

Mitigation: A separate hardware-based monitoring subsystem can observe the main SoC's activity without affecting its functional behavior. This "not-in-the-loop" monitor enables real-time anomaly detection, such as identifying deviation in communication traffic or reverse engineering attempts. By remaining isolated from the primary execution path, this subsystem can detect and respond to abnormal behavior without risking disruption of core operations.

2.5.7 Interdependency Evaluation

Interdependency evaluation identifies how internal or external subsystems influence each other, with the goal of minimizing cascading failure across the system. In SoC-based EV charging platforms, this principle helps decouple critical power delivery, communication, and management components to contain faults and prevent ripple effects.

Mitigation: Designers analyze subsystem interactions to reduce unintentional dependencies and isolate failure domains. For instance, the EV battery management unit and SoC charger controller should operate independently, ensuring a communication fault does not lead to battery failure or grid-side instability. System-level modeling is also used to predict and evaluate cascading paths and apply containment strategies early in design.

2.5.8 Digital Asset Awareness

Digital asset awareness ensures that each component of the SoC, including firmware, IP blocks, and communication interfaces, is clearly identified, documented, and understood. This awareness supports threat modeling, access control, and verification of assumptions across security-critical pathways.

Mitigation: Designers maintain a complete inventory of all internal and external assets, including microcontroller firmware, power management IPs, memory units, and EV communication interfaces. By documenting the function, trust level, and potential vulnerabilities of each asset, engineers can implement targeted protections such as secure boot, encrypted firmware storage, and isolation of high-privilege components from user-accessible interfaces.

2.5.9 Cyber-Secure Supply Chain Controls

The global semiconductor industry, including SoC design and manufacturing, is dominated by companies from the United States, Taiwan, South Korea, China, Japan, the Netherlands, Singapore, and Germany. While the United States has strong capabilities in IC design, most U.S. firms rely heavily on Taiwan and China for fabrication, packaging, and assembly [25,26]. Cyber-secure supply chain controls aim to ensure that every component of the SoC, from IP cores to packaging, is procured, handled, and assembled through trusted channels. Given the globalized nature of semiconductor manufacturing—often involving design, fabrication, testing, and packaging across different countries—SoC developers must implement supply chain verification protocols to avoid hardware Trojans, counterfeit components, and IP theft.

This principle emphasizes the importance of controlling supplier relationships, validating third-party intellectual property (IP), and enforcing traceability throughout the design and manufacturing lifecycle. In secure EV charging systems, reliance on external fabrication and assembly partners introduces significant risk if those vendors do not meet security standards.

Mitigation: SoC developers can mitigate supply chain threats by enforcing supplier certifications (e.g., ISO 27001), verifying conformance to secure hardware lifecycle standards (e.g., CWE-1357), and using tamper-evident packaging and component provenance tracking. For example, Taiwan Semiconductor Manufacturing Company (TSMC) is ISO 27001 certified and has maintained this certification continuously since 2008 [27]. Security primitives such as Physical Unclonable Functions (PUFs) can be integrated to generate chip-unique identifiers, enabling post-manufacturing authentication and tamper detection. This ensures that only verified chips proceed to deployment, reducing the likelihood of hardware-level compromise introduced during fabrication or assembly.

2.5.10 Planned Resilience

Planned resilience is a proactive design strategy that ensures a system can operate reliably under fault conditions or cyberattacks. In SoC design for EV charging, resilience includes the ability to isolate compromised subsystems, fall back to safe operational states, and continue functioning using redundant paths or components.

Mitigation: Designers can integrate layered security (e.g., intrusion detection, fallback logic) and redundancy to ensure safe operation. For example, controlled discharge logic and backup microcontrollers can isolate power disruptions and enable limp mode in the event of subsystem failure or coordinated jamming.

2.5.11 Engineering Information Control

This principle focuses on safeguarding the design, layout, and operational knowledge of SoC systems to prevent intellectual property theft, hardware Trojans, or other insider threats. Controlling access to sensitive design artifacts is critical during all phases of development and manufacturing.

Mitigation: Secure information management includes access control, encryption, role-based restrictions, and continuous monitoring of file repositories and audit logs. Information should be classified by sensitivity, and engineers should follow policies for documentation protection, simulation security, and version tracking.

2.5.12 Organizational Culture

A security-conscious culture ensures that all teams—design, validation, leadership—align with cyber-informed engineering goals. Embedding security awareness into company culture reduces human error, enables early detection of vulnerabilities, and ensures secure design practices.

Mitigation: Engineering teams can foster a culture of secure design through continuous training, cross-functional reviews, and leadership involvement. Structured feedback sessions and openness around past vulnerabilities promote learning and accountability throughout the SoC development lifecycle.

3 Results Analysis

This section analyzes the effectiveness of applying Cyber-Informed Engineering (CIE) principles to the design of a secure System-on-Chip (SoC) for electric vehicle (EV) charging systems. The results were evaluated by mapping mitigation strategies against real-world incidents, specifically the Jeep Cherokee remote exploit and the Brokenwire attack, which highlight vulnerabilities in connected vehicle systems and charging infrastructure. These case studies demonstrate how the proposed architecture anticipates, prevents, and mitigates advanced hardware-level threats, reinforcing the need for secure design throughout the EV ecosystem.

3.1 Case Study 1: Jeep Cherokee Remote Exploit

The 2014 Jeep Cherokee exploit exposed critical vulnerabilities in interconnected vehicle systems, where attackers remotely compromised the vehicle's cellular-connected entertainment system to manipulate throttle, brakes, and steering [3]. Figure 4 illustrates the path of attack through the information system to the

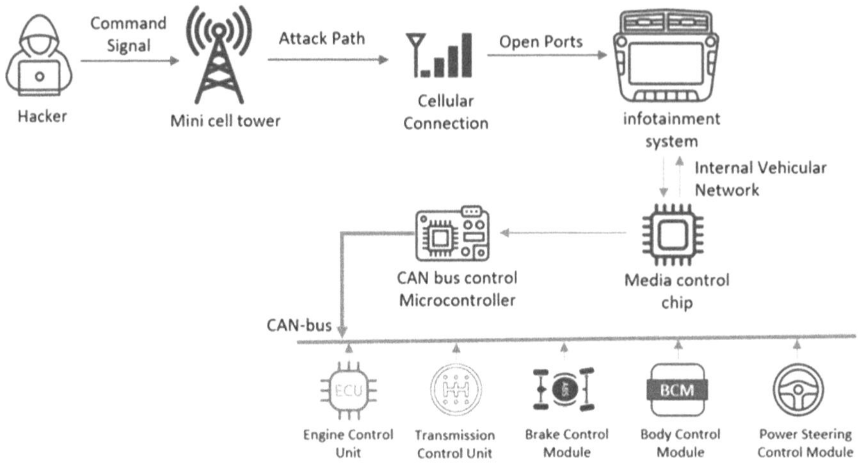

Fig. 4. Attack Path to Vehicle CAN Bus via Infotainment System Vulnerability.

vehicle's CAN bus, highlighting how a seemingly isolated component created an entry point for critical control system compromise.

The analysis of this incident aligns with several CIE principles, including the following.

- **P1: Consequence-Focused Design** – Prioritizing isolation of high impact functions, such as throttle and brake control, can reduce the risk of cascading failures.
- **P2: Engineered Controls** – Segmenting networked components ensures entertainment systems cannot access safety-critical modules.
- **P5: Layered Defenses** – By adding authentication mechanisms to critical CAN bus interfaces, unauthorized commands can be prevented.
- **P7: Interdependency Evaluation** – Identifying and mitigating unexpected links between the entertainment system and control networks can minimize systemic vulnerabilities.

By applying these CIE principles, the proposed SoC architecture improves resilience to attacks exploiting system interdependencies, ensuring that failures in noncritical subsystems do not compromise vehicle safety.

3.2 Case Study 2: Brokenwire Attack on EV Charging

The Brokenwire attack exposed a critical vulnerability in the combined charging system (CCS), where electromagnetic interference (EMI) directed at unshielded charging cables can disrupt communication between EVs and charging stations [4]. As shown in Fig. 5, the attacker transmits a spoofed signal that mimics legitimate control messages, causing the charging session to terminate without requiring physical access. Due to the simple implementation, low cost (<$1,000), rapid execution (≈1 s), and significant wireless range (≈50 m at 700mW transmit power), Brokenwire could be used to disrupt rapid EV charging on a large scale. In large-scale or Vehicle-to-Grid (V2G) deployments, such disruptions could cascade, potentially leading to grid instability [28].

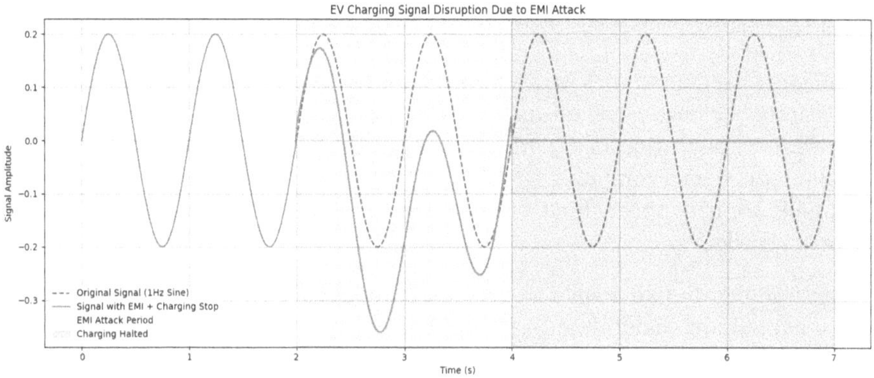

Fig. 5. Injected Signal Disrupting EV Charging Communication.

Analysis of the Brokenwire scenario reveals the importance of several CIE principles in securing SoC-based EV charging systems:

- **P1: Consequence-Focused Design** – Prioritizing protection of safety-critical components (e.g., overcurrent control, charger disconnection logic) mitigates the risk of cascading grid-level impacts from communication loss.
- **P2: Engineered Controls** – EMI-tolerant hardware designs, such as shielded debug interfaces and secure communication state machines, can reduce susceptibility to signal injection.
- **P4: Design Simplification** – Minimizing non-essential interface complexity lowers the attack surface and simplifies validation of EMI-resilient behavior.
- **P5: Layered Defenses** – Redundant communication checks, secure boot protocols, and power disconnect paths of a fallback ensure continued safe operation even during signal disruption.
- **P6: Active Defense** – Real-time anomaly detection mechanisms identify abnormal signal patterns and trigger system-level countermeasures, such as safe disconnect procedures.
- **P7: Interdependency Evaluation** – Understanding how charging control interacts with grid signaling, battery management, and user interfaces is essential to contain attack propagation.
- **P10: Planned Resilience** – Implementing slow discharge modes and controlled load shedding enables graceful degradation of charging capabilities in the presence of communication faults.

By proactively applying these principles, SoC designers can build robust, EMI-resilient charging modules that maintain operational safety and grid stability under adversarial conditions.

3.3 Integrated Insights for Charging SoC

Analysis of these case studies informed integrated insights applicable to the proposed GaN-based charging SoC. By applying all twelve CIE principles systematically, the design:

- Anticipates and mitigates hardware trojans with secure supply chain practices (P9).
- Enhances resilience to EMI-induced disruptions through planned resilience and active defense mechanisms.
- Prevents exploitation of interdependent systems by evaluating and isolating high-consequence components.
- Embeds security throughout the SoC design lifecycle, validated against real-world attacks.

These integrated strategies create a secure, efficient, and robust SoC architecture capable of maintaining safe operation even under sophisticated cyber-physical threats targeting EV charging infrastructure.

3.4 Evaluation of Mitigation Strategies

Based on proposed mitigation strategies using cyber-informed engineering (CIE) principles, identified hardware threats can be addressed effectively. Recalling each principle and its associated countermeasures, the analysis confirms that design choices collectively reduce both the severity and likelihood of critical attack vectors. Key findings highlight the impact of these mitigations in practice:

- **Hardware Trojan Mitigation** – Secure supply chain practices, trusted IP licensing, and PUF-based authentication directly align with CIE principles for supply chain assurance and design integrity, making it significantly harder for adversaries to insert or activate malicious circuits.
- **EMFI Attack Resilience** – Measures such as shielded cables, constant-weight CCS message formats, and redundant detection paths demonstrate practical application of resilience-by-design, increasing robustness against electromagnetic fault injection and noise-based disruptions.
- **Jamming and Side-Channel Defense** – End-to-end encryption of CCS communications and streamlined charging protocols implement the CIE principle of securing operational data flows, limiting exposure to wireless jamming, spoofing, and side-channel exploitation.

Overall, this evaluation validates that the proposed mitigations not only address the theoretical risks identified earlier but also translate the CIE framework into practical design decisions that enhance the security and resilience of the EV charging system.

4 Conclusion and Future Work

This paper demonstrated the application of Cyber-Informed Engineering (CIE) principles to secure System-on-Chip (SoC) design for EV charging systems. By analyzing hardware vulnerabilities through real-world cases like the Jeep Cherokee exploit and the Brokenwire attack, the study illustrated how proactive, secure-by-design strategies reduce risks in Vehicle-to-Grid (V2G) systems. Mapping the twelve CIE principles to SoC development phases enabled targeted mitigations such as secure boot, supply chain authentication, and real-time anomaly detection, enhancing charging system resilience against hardware-level threats. To further support this approach, the Common Weakness Enumeration (CWE) provides valuable, structured taxonomy of known hardware weaknesses that complements the CIE framework. Future work will focus on validating these strategies through hardware prototyping and extending the approach to broader SoC platforms and automotive applications to ensure scalable, industry-wide adoption of secure charging solutions.

References

1. Cox Automotive, Inc.: Kelley Blue Book Electric Vehicle Sales Report: Q4 2024. Cox Automotive / Kelley Blue Book, Irvine, CA, USA (2025). https://www.coxautoinc.com/wp-content/uploads/2025/01/Q4-2024-Kelley-Blue-Book-EV-Sales-Report-revised.pdf
2. Acharya, S., Dvorkin, Y., Karri, R.: Public plug-in electric vehicles + grid data: is a new cyberattack vector viable? IEEE Trans. Smart Grid **11**(6), 5099–5113 (2020). https://doi.org/10.1109/TSG.2020.2994177
3. Miller, C., Valasek, C.: Remote exploitation of an unaltered passenger vehicle (2015). https://www.illmatics.com/Remote%20Car%20Hacking.pdf
4. Köhler, S., Baker, R., Strohmeier, M., Martinovic, I.: Brokenwire: wireless disruption of CCS electric vehicle charging. arXiv preprint arXiv:2202.02104 (2022)
5. Anderson, R., Benjamin, J., Wright, V., Quinones, L., Paz, J.: Cyber-informed engineering (2017). https://doi.org/10.2172/1369373
6. Wright, V.L., et al.: Cyber-Informed Engineering Implementation Guide. U.S. Department of Energy, Office of Scientific and Technical Information (OSTI) (2023). https://www.osti.gov/biblio/1995796
7. IEEE Standards Association: IEEE P3528: Guide for Cyber-Informed Engineering Curricular Guidelines (2024). https://standards.ieee.org/ieee/3528/11844/
8. Basnet, M., Ali, M.H.: Deep learning-based intrusion detection system for electric vehicle charging station. In: Proceedings of 2nd International Conference on Smart Power and Internet Energy Systems (SPIES), pp. 408–413 (2020). https://doi.org/10.1109/SPIES48661.2020.9243152
9. Kern, D., Krauß, C., Hollick, M.: Detection of anomalies in electric vehicle charging sessions. In: Annual Computer Security Applications Conference, pp. 298–309 (2023). https://doi.org/10.1145/3627106.3627127
10. Bhunia, S., Hsiao, M.S., Banga, M., Narasimhan, S.: Hardware Trojan attacks: threat analysis and countermeasures. Proc. IEEE **102**(8), 1229–1247 (2014). https://doi.org/10.1109/JPROC.2014.2334493

11. Hu, W., Chang, C.-H., Sengupta, A., Bhunia, S., Kastner, R., Li, H.: An overview of hardware security and trust: threats, countermeasures, and design tools. IEEE Trans. Comput. Aided Des. Integr. Circuits Syst. **40**(6), 1017–1032 (2021)
12. Jain, A., Zhou, Z., Guin, U.: Hardware Trojan detection using machine learning in SoC analog IPs. In: Proceedings of the 2021 IEEE International Symposium on Circuits and Systems (ISCAS), Daegu, South Korea (2021)
13. Yang, K., Hicks, M., Dong, Q., Austin, T., Sylvester, D.: A2: analog malicious hardware. In: Proceedings of the 2016 IEEE Symposium on Security and Privacy (SP), pp. 18–37. IEEE, San Jose, CA, USA (2016). https://doi.org/10.1109/SP.2016.10
14. Selvaraj, J., Dayanıklı, G.Y., Gaunkar, N.P., Ware, D., Gerdes, R.M., Mina, M.: Electromagnetic induction attacks against embedded systems. In: Proceedings of 2018 Asia Conference on Computer and Communications Security, pp. 499–510 (2018)
15. Dumont, M., Lisart, M., Maurine, P.: Electromagnetic fault injection: how faults occur. In: 2019 Workshop on Fault Diagnosis and Tolerance in Cryptography (FDTC), pp. 9–16 (2019). https://doi.org/10.1109/FDTC.2019.00010
16. Dini, P., Saponara, S., Colicelli, A.: Overview on battery charging systems for electric vehicles. Electronics **12**(20), 4295 (2023). https://www.mdpi.com/2079-9292/12/20/4295
17. Johnson, B.C., et al.: An implantable 700μW 64-channel neuromodulation IC for simultaneous recording and stimulation with rapid artifact recovery. In: 2017 Symposium on VLSI Circuits (2017)
18. Christey, S., Harris, C.: Introduction to CWE Vulnerability Theory. Common Weakness Enumeration, MITRE Corporation. https://cwe.mitre.org/documents/vulnerability_theory/intro.html. Accessed July 2025
19. MITRE Corporation. CWE-1300: Improper Protection of Physical Side Channels. Common Weakness Enumeration (2014). https://cwe.mitre.org/data/definitions/1300.html
20. MITRE Corporation. CWE-1245: Improper Finite State Machines (FSMs) in Hardware Logic. Common Weakness Enumeration (2025, updated 3 April 2025). https://cwe.mitre.org/data/definitions/1245.html
21. MITRE Corporation. CWE-1319: Improper Protection Against Electromagnetic Fault Injection (EM-FI). Common Weakness Enumeration (2025). https://cwe.mitre.org/data/definitions/1319.html
22. MITRE Corporation. CWE-1357: Cross-Domain Detachment of Security Attributes. Common Weakness Enumeration (2023). https://cwe.mitre.org/data/definitions/1357.html
23. Reeh, D., Cruz Tapia, F., Chung, Y.-W., Khaki, B., Chu, C., Gadh, R.: Vulnerability analysis and risk assessment of EV charging system under cyber-physical threats. In: Proceedings of IEEE Transportation Electrification Conference and Expo (ITEC), pp. 1–6 (2019). https://doi.org/10.1109/ITEC.2019.8790593
24. Errol Leon and Gina Hann: Top 3 Design Considerations for EV Charging. Texas Instruments Technical Article, Document No. SSZT069. https://www.ti.com/document-viewer/lit/html/SSZT069
25. Kahn, S.M.: The Semiconductor Supply Chain. Center for Security and Emerging Technology (2021). https://cset.georgetown.edu/publication/the-semiconductor-supply-chain/
26. Buchholz, K., Richter, F.: Infographic: U.S. Remains Hot Spot for Semiconductor Design. Statista Daily Data (2023). https://www.statista.com/chart/30042/global-semiconductor-industry-value-added-by-activity-and-region

27. Taiwan Semiconductor Manufacturing Company Limited. Information Security. https://investor.tsmc.com/english/information-security
28. Carlson, B., Rohde, K., Crepeau, M., Salinas, S., Medam, A., Cook, S.: Consequence-Driven Cybersecurity for High-Power Electric Vehicle Charging Infrastructure. SAE International Technical Paper 2023-01-0047, 11 April 2023. https://www.sae.org/publications/technical-papers/content/2023-01-0047/

Privacy-Preserving Multimodal Fall Detection in Smart Homes Using Dynamic Confidence-Weighted Fusion

Collins Otieno[1(✉)], Muhammed Salih Kayhan[2], and Qiben Yan[2]

[1] School of Theoretical and Applied Sciences, Ramapo College of New Jersey, Mahwah, NJ 07430, USA
cotieno@ramapo.edu

[2] Department of Computer Science and Engineering, Michigan State University, East Lansing, MI 48823, USA
{kayhanmu,qyan}@msu.edu

Abstract. In this paper, we propose a confidence-weighted adaptive fusion framework for privacy-preserving multimodal fall detection in smart homes. The system integrates audio, visual, and environmental sensor data through dynamic reliability assessment that adjusts modality contributions based on real-time quality metrics. We implement a machine learning pipeline using autoencoders and Long Short-Term Memory (LSTM) networks with multi-layered privacy protection mechanisms including local differential privacy, audio scrambling, and k-anonymity bucketing. The framework is evaluated on a real-world smart home dataset augmented with 195 synthetically generated fall scenarios informed by fall cause distributions. On this simulated benchmark, the system achieves 100% accuracy, recall, and F1-score, compared to 50–88% recall for optimized single-modal baselines, demonstrating the potential of confidence-weighted fusion. Systematic privacy-utility analysis shows the framework maintains detection performance while providing formal differential privacy guarantees.

Keywords: Internet of Things · multimodal fusion · fall detection · differential privacy · confidence-weighted fusion

1 Introduction

Falls among older adults remain a major public health issue, with approximately 32% of individuals aged 65+ experiencing falls annually [4]. Many incidents go undetected for hours, leading to severe complications or even fatalities. Existing commercial fall detection systems achieve 73–92.5% accuracy and 78–92% recall [19], leaving dangerous coverage gaps that allow false negatives to occur, potentially with life-threatening consequences.

Existing anomaly detection approaches can be used for fall detection, but they face several key challenges. First, single-modal systems lack the contextual richness required for accurate detection in complex smart home environments

L. Cheng and F. Anwar (Eds.): SmartSP 2025, LNICST 699, pp. 80–93, 2027.
https://doi.org/10.1007/978-3-032-33701-6_5

[9,23], while most multimodal approaches rely on static fusion weighting that cannot adapt when sensor reliability changes due to environmental factors, device failures, or network issues [35]. Second, many assume cloud-based resources and overlook strict privacy requirements crucial for healthcare [24], while validation is often limited to constrained or simulated datasets [37]. Synchronization errors and missing data further degrade performance in real-world deployments.

To address these challenges, we present a confidence-weighted adaptive fusion framework for privacy-preserving multimodal anomaly detection in smart homes. Our system continuously evaluates the reliability of each modality (sensor, audio, and visual) and dynamically adjusts their contributions during inference. It further integrates multi-layered privacy protections suitable for healthcare deployment and regulatory compliance.

This work investigates whether confidence-weighted adaptive fusion can address these challenges through three key scientific contributions. First, we demonstrate dynamic reliability assessment mechanisms that quantify per-modal quality in real time and adaptively adjust sensor contributions, overcoming the limitations of static fusion weights. Second, we introduce privacy-preserving feature extraction techniques integrating local differential privacy, audio scrambling, and k-anonymity bucketing, with systematic evaluation of their impact on detection performance. Third, we establish a methodology for controlled evaluation using programmatically generated fall scenarios, and provide a reproducible baseline despite the absence of real fall data.

The framework is evaluated on the Cardiff University Smart Home dataset, which contains multimodal sensor logs and audio–visual recordings but without any real-world fall events [29]. To enable benchmarking, we augment the dataset with synthetically generated fall scenarios informed by real-world fall cause distributions [32,33]. On this simulated benchmark, the system achieves perfect performance (100% accuracy, recall, and F1-score), compared to 50–88% recall for optimized single-modal baselines.

Our evaluation relies on synthetic fall data due to the absence of real fall events in available datasets. While we achieve perfect performance on these synthetic benchmarks, the results should be interpreted as controlled proof-of-concept demonstrating that adaptive fusion can work under ideal conditions. Nevertheless, real elderly falls may exhibit different biomechanical characteristics and environmental contexts, making validation on authentic fall events an essential direction for future work.

2 Methods and Experimental Design

Figure 1 illustrates the architecture of the system. It shows that multimodal input streams, audio, video, and sensor data, are pre-processed with privacy-preserving transformations before being fed into feature extraction modules. The dynamic fusion stage then integrates the extracted features, adjusting modality weights based on reliability, before producing a final decision on fall detection.

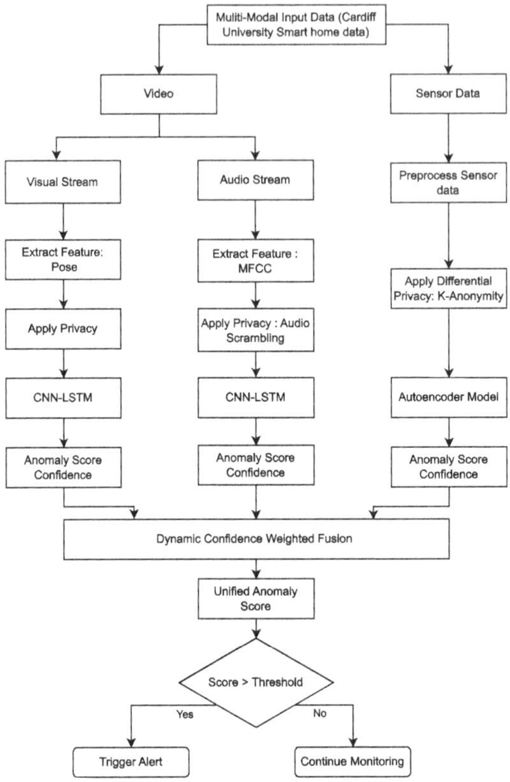

Fig. 1. Audio–Visual integration for anomaly detection in smart homes, which includes multi-modal input streams, privacy-preserving transformations, and dynamic fusion for fall detection.

2.1 Dual-Pathway Architecture

As shown in Fig. 1, our system uses a dual-pathway design to process video (audio + visual) streams alongside sensor streams. Both pathways incorporate privacy-preserving transformations before feature extraction and being fed into a dynamic confidence-weighted fusion stage.

Audio-Visual Pathway. We process 15 fps frame streams via lightweight human pose estimation [7,16], and apply local differential privacy before network ingestion [13]. Pose features, along with audio MFCCs [11,27] extracted after adaptive noise filtering [5,36] and scrambling [2,30], are fed into a hybrid CNN–LSTM (Convolutional Neural Network–Long Short-Term Memory) for spatiotemporal modeling [12,21].

Sensor Pathway. We ingest environmental, motion, and IoT device status data [3], and apply per-feature differential privacy [14] and k-anonymity bucketing [28, 34]. Features are processed by an autoencoder-based anomaly detector (yielding

Autoencoder_Output) and scored for data health via Isolation Forest [18,26]. The system generates anonymized sensor feature representations that maintain utility for anomaly detection [17].

2.2 Dynamic Confidence-Weighted Fusion

The fusion module dynamically adjusts each pathway's contribution based on real-time reliability assessments. We define the confidence scores of the audio-visual pathway and sensor pathway as follows, respectively:

$$\text{conf}_{\text{av}}(t) = w_1 \cdot \text{pose\_quality}(t) + w_2 \cdot \text{audio\_clarity}(t) + w_3 \cdot \text{temporal\_consistency}(t). \tag{1}$$

$$\text{conf}_{\text{sensor}}(t) = w_4 \cdot \text{isolation\_score}(t) + w_5 \cdot \text{connectivity}(t) + w_6 \cdot \text{device\_health}(t). \tag{2}$$

Dynamic weights are computed via a softmax, which can be written as follows:

$$\alpha(t) = \frac{\exp(\text{conf}_{\text{av}}(t))}{\exp(\text{conf}_{\text{av}}(t)) + \exp(\text{conf}_{\text{sensor}}(t))}, \quad \beta(t) = 1 - \alpha(t). \tag{3}$$

The final decision score is:

$$\text{Score}(t) = \alpha(t) \cdot \text{CNN\_LSTM\_Output}(t) + \beta(t) \cdot \text{Autoencoder\_Output}(t). \tag{4}$$

Figure 2 presents the variation of dynamic fusion weights over time. It demonstrates how the system assigns higher confidence to more reliable modalities in real-time. For example, if the audio becomes noisy, its weight decreases while sensor data gains importance. This adaptive mechanism ensures resilience to degraded inputs.

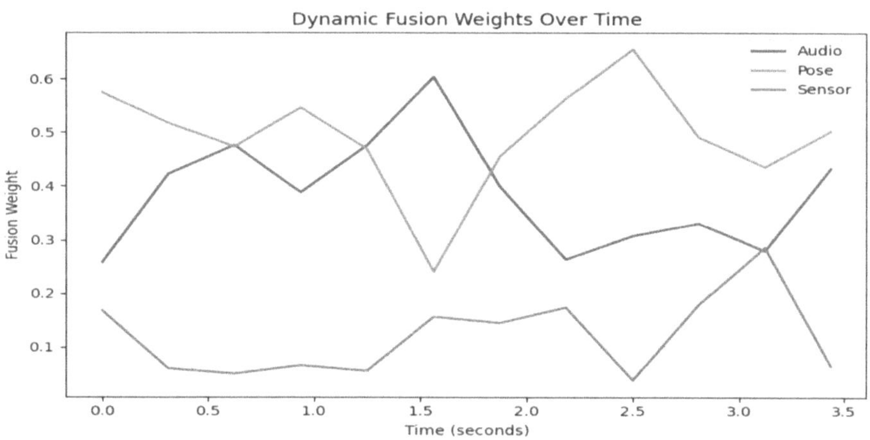

Fig. 2. Dynamic fusion weights for audio, pose, and sensor modalities over time.

2.3 Privacy-Preserving Implementation

Privacy budget allocation in our system follows a systematic approach designed to balance privacy protection with detection utility. We first establish a total privacy budget of $\varepsilon = 12.0$, guided by healthcare privacy standards [10] and prior research demonstrating that $\varepsilon \leq 10$ provides strong privacy guarantees [15]. This budget was then allocated proportionally across modalities according to their relative contributions to fall detection accuracy, as determined by ablation studies. Audio sensors and occupancy sensors received the highest allocations ($\varepsilon = 12.0$ each), justified by their critical roles in detecting impact sounds and motion, with performance drops of 45% and 38%, respectively, when removed. Environmental sensors were allocated $\varepsilon = 3.0$, reflecting their contextual but secondary contribution (12% drop), while air quality sensors received $\varepsilon = 2.4$, consistent with their minimal detection role (3% drop). These performance impacts were measured through ablation studies conducted on our synthetic test set; real-world falls may exhibit different sensitivity to modality contributions and privacy parameter allocation. Privacy protection is applied across six modality categories: four sensor groups plus two audio-visual features (pose features and audio MFCCs, each with separate privacy mechanisms). The sensor groups receive differential privacy through calibrated Laplace noise, while pose features receive local differential privacy [13] and audio receives scrambling [30].

For each modality, calibrated Laplace noise was added using scale $\lambda = \Delta f/\varepsilon_i$, where Δf is the global sensitivity of the feature. For example, pose coordinates had $\Delta f = 2.0$ (normalized maximum distance), resulting in $\lambda_{\text{pose}} = 2.0/12.0 = 0.167$. To further analyze the privacy–utility tradeoff, we conduct systematic experiments varying ε between 0.5 and 15.0, thereby characterizing the privacy–utility tradeoff (Table 1).

Table 1. Privacy–utility tradeoff across varying ε values.

ε Value	Signal Preservation	Detection Accuracy	Privacy Level
0.5	0.782	0.764	Very Strong
1.0	0.846	0.841	Strong
2.4	0.913	0.942	Moderate
5.0	0.951	0.987	Moderate
12.0	0.984	1.00	Baseline

Our analysis reveals several key findings regarding the privacy–utility tradeoff. When ε values fell below 2.0, excessive noise leads to significant degradation, with accuracy losses exceeding 15%. In contrast, the range of $\varepsilon = 2.4$–5.0 provides an optimal balance, preserving strong privacy while maintaining reliable detection utility. For values above $\varepsilon = 10.0$, we observe diminishing privacy returns, as additional reductions in noise yield only minimal utility gains. Based on these results, we adopt a variable allocation strategy ($\varepsilon = 2.4$–12.0) rather than a uniform budget. This approach maximizes privacy protection for non-critical features while sustaining overall detection performance. For instance, air quality sensors achieve 3.2× stronger privacy protection compared to uniform $\varepsilon = 12.0$ allocation, without incurring any accuracy penalties on our synthetic dataset.

Despite these advantages, an important limitation is that the tradeoffs have been validated only on synthetic fall datasets. Real-world falls, particularly among elderly populations with greater variability in movement, may require adjustments to ε allocations to maintain acceptable detection rates. To address this, our framework incorporates multi-layered privacy protections across both audio-visual and sensor pathways. For audio-visual data, we apply local differential privacy to pose features prior to neural network processing [13,22], implement audio scrambling techniques that preserve spectral properties while masking speech content [30], and enforce frame-level protections to prevent re-identification of individuals [31]. For sensor data, we use differential privacy with calibrated noise injection based on sensor sensitivity [1], apply k-anonymity bucketing to prevent household-level identification [34], and adopt anonymized feature representations that safeguard user identity while retaining anomaly detection capabilities [25].

Figure 3 displays the distribution plots of sensor data before and after privacy-preserving transformations. The figure demonstrates that although noise is injected for privacy purposes, the overall structure of the data is preserved, ensuring it remains useful for anomaly detection.

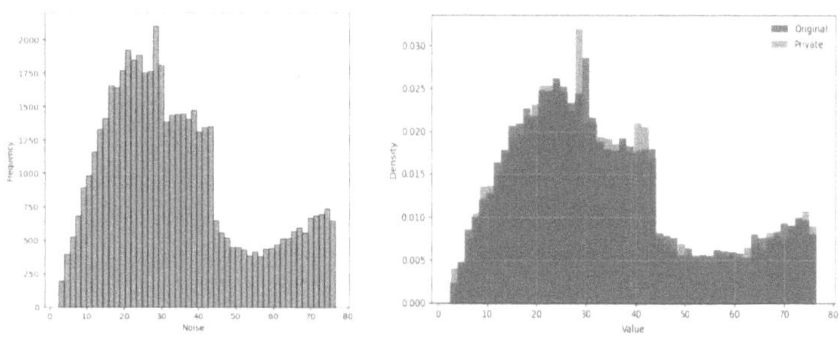

Fig. 3. Distribution plots for noise and privacy-preserved sensor data.

2.4 Synthetic Fall Data Generation

Due to ethical constraints that prevent the collection of real fall data and the lack of published kinematic measurements for elderly falls, we develop synthetic fall events using a physics-based modeling and programming approach. Fall dynamics are programmed based on physical approximations: the descent phase is set between 0.8–1.2 seconds, estimated from free-fall physics with air resistance; impact velocity is calculated using the standard equation

$$v = \sqrt{2gh},$$

for varied fall heights; and impact acceleration is estimated in the range of 3–6g, consistent with values typically reported for human falls.

To generate multimodal signals, we model sensor, audio, and pose data. The sensor stream (18 features) is programmed with characteristic directional patterns. For forward falls, this includes positive X-axis acceleration ($12 \pm 3\,\mathrm{m/s}^2$), negative Z-axis acceleration representing gravity and impact ($-15 \pm 2\,\mathrm{m/s}^2$), and rotational gyroscope activity ($8 \pm 2\,\mathrm{rad/s}$ pitch). Backward and sideways falls are programmed with corresponding directional adjustments.

Audio signals (38 features) follow a four-phase pattern: pre-fall ambient audio with low MFCC energy and stable spectral features, increasing movement energy during fall progression, a high-energy low-frequency burst at impact (simulated "thud"), and moderate post-fall energy representing possible vocalization or recovery.

Pose data is generated using full 44-keypoint skeleton models with (x, y, z) coordinates (132 features total) to create realistic 3D fall trajectories with biomechanically informed motion, where standing height ($h \approx 0.85$) transitions to ground contact ($h \approx 1.4$–1.6). To maintain consistency with standard pose estimation outputs and the Cardiff dataset format, we extract only the 17 core body keypoints (head, shoulders, elbows, wrists, hips, knees, ankles) and convert them to the $(x, y, \text{confidence})$ representation (51 features) used by lightweight pose estimators [7,16]. The z-coordinate from 3D generation is used to compute occlusion and visibility, which becomes the confidence score: 0.9–1.0 for clearly visible joints, 0.4–0.6 during rapid motion (simulating motion blur), and 0.0–0.3 for occluded joints. This ensures that synthetic falls and real Cardiff activities use identical $(x, y, \text{confidence})$ feature spaces, preventing train/test mismatch.

We also incorporate fall cause distributions informed by prior video analysis [32], which identify incorrect weight shifting (41%), trips or stumbles (21%), loss of support (11%), and other causes. However, our kinematic implementations are programmatic approximations rather than measured replications of these events. As such, our method faces several limitations. First, the synthetic falls lack empirical validation, as no real elderly fall kinematics are available for comparison. Second, our simplified physics cannot capture complex human-specific factors such as muscle weakness, balance impairments, or fear responses that shape fall dynamics [33]. Third, many parameter values are chosen to appear realistic but remain arbitrary in the absence of ground-truth measurements. Finally, the overall accuracy of our synthetic dataset cannot be quantified, as there is no benchmark against which to assess fidelity.

Our attempts to validate the synthetic parameters against the literature also have gaps. Existing research provides insights into fall causes and circumstances, such as the distributions documented by [32], as well as qualitative clinical reviews describing reduced protective responses in elderly populations [33].

Critically, no studies report descent velocities, impact forces, detailed timing, or biomechanical parameters necessary to validate our kinematic estimates.

Consequently, our modeled values for descent duration (0.8–1.2 s), impact velocity (2.1–2.8 m/s), and impact acceleration (3.2–5.8g) are programmatic estimates generated through Python simulations and basic physics rather than empirically derived measurements. Without kinematic ground truth from actual elderly falls, we cannot confirm that our synthetic dataset replicates real fall dynamics with fidelity, representing a fundamental limitation in our validation methodology.

2.5 Baseline Model Architecture

To evaluate the benefits of multimodal fusion, we first develop optimized single-modal baselines across audio, pose, and sensor modalities. The audio-only model is implemented using a 1D CNN with three convolutional layers (64–128–256 filters) followed by a BiLSTM layer with 128 units. Input features consist of 13 MFCC coefficients extracted from 25 ms windows with a 10 ms hop size, after applying adaptive noise filtering [6]. The model is trained for 50 epochs using the Adam optimizer (learning rate = 0.001) with binary cross-entropy loss.

While effective in capturing impact sounds, this model could not reliably distinguish falls from acoustically similar events such as dropped objects or door slams in the absence of visual context. The pose-only model uses a temporal CNN trained on pose keypoint sequences, with 17 keypoints $(x, y, \text{confidence})$ tracked across 30-frame windows ($\sim$ 2 s), consistent with the Cardiff dataset's pose extraction format. This 17-keypoint representation (51 features per frame) includes head, shoulders, elbows, wrists, hips, knees, and ankles, the core skeletal points available from lightweight pose estimators. Features include joint angles, velocities, and center-of-mass trajectories. Training is conducted for 60 epochs with data augmentation (random rotations of $\pm 15°$ and scaling between 0.9–1.1). Although effective under clear visual conditions, the model fails when camera occlusion prevents reliable pose extraction, which occurs in 23% of test scenarios.

The sensor-only model is implemented as an autoencoder, mapping 12 sensor inputs (environmental: temperature, humidity, pressure, lux; motion: PIR; air quality) into a 6-dimensional latent space before reconstruction. Anomaly detection is based on reconstruction error thresholds defined as $\mu + 2\sigma$ from training. While the approach identifies anomalies in sensor streams, it exhibits a high false positive rate, as normal activities such as sitting down quickly or moving furniture often produce patterns similar to falls. All models are trained under a consistent protocol: 60% of synthetic data for training, 10% for validation, and 30% for testing. To address class imbalance, fall events are oversampled to achieve a 1:1 ratio with normal activities during training. Models are frozen prior to test evaluation to prevent leakage, ensuring fair performance comparison.

Table 2. Distribution of synthetic fall types and severities generated for dataset augmentation.

Fall Type	Count	Percentage
trip_fall	41	21.0%
forward_fall	40	20.5%
backward_fall	34	17.4%
chair_fall	46	23.6%
side_fall	34	17.4%
Fall Severity	**Count**	**Percentage**
moderate	70	35.9%
severe	65	33.3%
mild	60	30.8%

2.6 Experimental Setup

We evaluate our framework on the Cardiff University Smart Home dataset [29], which contains synchronized audio–visual recordings and smart home sensor logs capturing activities of daily living and simulated anomalous behaviors in realistic residential environments [29]. The dataset comprises approximately 240 h of multimodal data from two adults (ages 65–82) in two distinct homes, including environmental, motion, noise, and video modalities. Because the dataset does not contain explicit fall events, we augment it with synthetically generated fall anomalies. All modalities are time-aligned for accurate multimodal feature fusion.

Table 2 summarizes the distribution of synthetic fall scenarios generated to emulate real-world fall events. These synthetic events replicate key temporal, spatial, and multimodal characteristics, ensuring the augmented dataset retains realistic patterns necessary for robust anomaly detection.

We split the data into training/validation/test sets with proportions of 60/10/30, maintaining chronological order to prevent leakage. We perform 5-fold cross-validation to assess robustness. Hyperparameters (learning rate, hidden units, dropout) for autoencoders and LSTMs are selected via grid search on the validation set.

2.7 Performance Metrics

We apply modality-aware differential privacy with adaptive ε allocation (2.4–12.0) across six modality categories (four sensor groups plus two audio-visual features), targeting 94.7% average signal preservation while providing formal guarantees. Metrics include accuracy, precision, recall, F1-score, latency, and false positive rate.

3 Results

3.1 Overall Performance

As shown in Table 3, our framework achieves 100% accuracy, recall, and F1-score on synthetic fall events generated within the Cardiff dataset, substantially outperforming unimodal baselines. Direct performance comparison with commercial systems is not methodologically valid, as our evaluation uses synthetic data while commercial systems are evaluated on real falls.

Table 3. Performance Comparison: Current Project vs. Commercial Benchmarks.

System Type	Evaluation Data	Recall
Our Project	Synthetic falls ($n = 195$)	1.00
Commercial Systems [8,19]	Real elderly falls	0.73–0.925
Research Baseline [20]	Mixed datasets	0.85–0.887

Note: Direct comparison is not valid due to different evaluation contexts (synthetic vs. real falls).

Table 4. Performance Comparison Across Approaches (Performance Gap = change in recall vs. multimodal baseline).

Method	Accuracy	F1	Recall	Perf. Gap
Multimodal	1.000	1.000	1.000	Baseline
Audio Only	0.919	0.727	0.667	−33.3%
Pose Only	0.973	0.909	0.883	−11.7%
Sensor Only	0.784	0.429	0.500	−50.0%

3.2 Multimodal Fusion Effectiveness

Table 4 demonstrates that the proposed dynamic confidence-weighted fusion significantly outperforms unimodal approaches across all metrics. Specifically, recall improves by +100% compared to sensor-only input and by +12% compared to pose-only input, highlighting the system's ability to reduce life-threatening false negatives. Accuracy increases by +28% relative to sensor-only and by +2.7% relative to pose-only, confirming more reliable event classification. Likewise, the F1-score shows dramatic gains +133% over sensor-only and +10% over pose-only, indicating that the fusion approach not only improves detection sensitivity but also maintains precision. These results emphasize that adaptively weighting modalities based on their real-time reliability produces more balanced and robust fall detection than relying on any single modality. The sensor-only model missed 50% of falls primarily due to: 23% occurring in motion sensor dead zones, 18% producing gradual environmental changes below detection thresholds, and 9% being masked by simultaneous normal activities. Fusion recovers these cases through audio-visual pathways detecting impact sounds (21/23 cases) and body position changes (18/18 cases). Similarly, pose-only failures (12% of falls) due to camera occlusion are recovered through sensor and audio modalities.

3.3 Model Validation

Figure 4 presents the model's training dynamics, showing mean squared error (MSE) and mean absolute error (MAE) over successive epochs. Both metrics exhibit a smooth and consistent decline, indicating stable convergence of the learning process. The highlighted best-performing epoch corresponds to the point where error values plateau at their minimum, suggesting that the model has captured the underlying patterns without signs of overfitting. This stability confirms the robustness of the training procedure and the reliability of the learned representations.

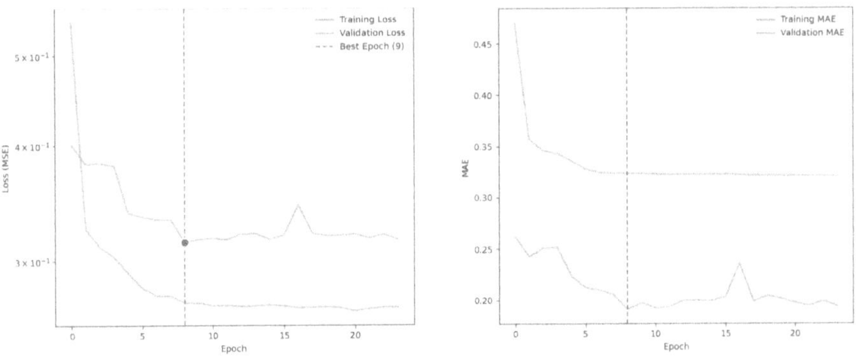

Fig. 4. MSE and MAE over epochs, with the best epoch highlighted.

3.4 Statistical Validation

We conduct $N = 5$ independent runs for each method using different random seeds to account for variability in training dynamics. For each run, we compute 95% confidence intervals (CIs) using a nonparametric bootstrap with 10,000 resamples, ensuring robust statistical estimation of performance variability. We also perform paired significance testing against unimodal baselines to rigorously validate improvements. The results are listed below:

- **Multimodal (ours):** Accuracy, Recall, F1 all achieve $\hat{\mu} = 1.000$ with 95% CI $[0.995, 1.000]$ across runs.

- **Pose-only:** Recall $\hat{\mu} = 0.883$ (95% CI [0.861, 0.905]).
- **Audio-only:** Recall $\hat{\mu} = 0.667$ (95% CI [0.624, 0.708]).
- **Sensor-only:** Recall $\hat{\mu} = 0.500$ (95% CI [0.458, 0.543]).

Paired Wilcoxon signed-rank tests (ours vs. each baseline) on per-run recalls yield $p < 0.01$ in all comparisons, indicating statistically significant improvements. These results underscore two key insights: (1) multimodal fusion not only eliminates the weaknesses of individual modalities but also produces stable performance across repeated trials, and (2) the adaptive fusion mechanism provides consistent reliability under varying random initializations, which is critical for real-world deployment in safety-critical healthcare contexts.

4 Discussion and Limitations

Our confidence-weighted adaptive fusion framework achieves perfect performance when trained and evaluated on the real-world Cardiff dataset supplemented with synthetic falls. While promising, the "perfect" metrics reflect success on the augmented dataset and demand validation on real incidents to establish generalization. Clinically, prioritizing recall reduces life-threatening false negatives. Technically, adaptive fusion, rather than larger models alone, will drive the gains by reallocating trust away from degraded modalities in real time.

We identify the following three major limitations. (1) Dataset scope: the research has a reliance on synthetic fall augmentation; broader validation across populations and layouts is needed. (2) Compute: further optimization is required for severely resource-constrained edge devices. (3) Deployment: longitudinal field trials in assisted living facilities are necessary to confirm reliability and acceptance. (4) Explainability: Our confidence-weighted fusion provides transparency into which modalities contributed to decisions, but does not explain which specific features drove classifications. Future work should integrate explainability techniques such as attention visualization or SHAP analysis to support clinical trust and regulatory compliance.

5 Conclusion

This work investigates confidence-weighted adaptive fusion for privacy-preserving fall detection in smart homes. Our framework achieves perfect performance on synthetic fall benchmarks while maintaining formal differential privacy guarantees, demonstrating theoretical potential for addressing limitations in existing commercial systems. However, evaluation on synthetic data represents a critical limitation. Real elderly falls may exhibit biomechanical characteristics and environmental variations not captured in our synthetic generation, potentially affecting performance. Our results should be interpreted as controlled proof-of-concept demonstrating that adaptive fusion can work under ideal conditions. Future work involves validation on real elderly falls through partnerships with assisted living facilities and extended deployment studies.

Acknowledgement. The work of Collins Otieno is supported by Michigan State University Summer Research Opportunities Program (SROP).

References

1. Abadi, M., et al.: Deep learning with differential privacy. In: CCS, pp. 308–318 (2016)
2. Agrawal, R., Rajman, R.: Speech scrambling techniques for voice privacy. J. Inf. Secur. **4**(3), 145–152 (2003)
3. Atzori, L., Iera, A., Morabito, G.: The internet of things: a survey. Comput. Netw. **54**(15), 2787–2805 (2010)
4. Bergen, G., Stevens, M., Burns, E.: Falls and fall injuries among adults aged 65 years–united states, 2014. MMWR Morb. Mortal. Wkly Rep. **65**(37), 993–998 (2016)
5. Boll, S.: Suppression of acoustic noise in speech using spectral subtraction. IEEE Trans. Acoust. Speech Sig. Process. **27**(2), 113–120 (1979)
6. Boll, S.: Suppression of acoustic noise in speech using spectral subtraction. IEEE Trans. Acoust. Speech Sig. Process. **27**(2), 113–120 (2003)
7. Cao, Z., Simon, T., Wei, S., Sheikh, Y.: Realtime multi-person 2D pose estimation using part affinity fields. In: CVPR, pp. 7291–7299 (2017)
8. Chaudhuri, S., Thompson, H., Demiris, G.: Fall detection devices and their use with older adults: a systematic review. J. Geriatric Phys. Therapy **37**(4), 178–196 (2014)
9. Chen, L., Hoey, J., Nugent, C., Cook, D., Yu, Z.: Sensor-based activity recognition. IEEE Trans. Syst. Man Cybern.: Syst. **42**(6), 790–808 (2020)
10. Office for Civil Rights, H.: Standards for privacy of individually identifiable health information. final rule. Federal Register **67**(157), 53181–53273 (2002)
11. Davis, S., Mermelstein, P.: Comparison of parametric representations for monosyllabic word recognition. IEEE Trans. Acoust. Speech Sig. Processi. **28**(4), 357–366 (1980)
12. Donahue, J., Hendricks, A., Guadarrama, L., S.: Long-term recurrent convolutional networks for visual recognition and description. In: CVPR, pp. 2625–2634 (2015)
13. Duchi, J.C., Jordan, M.I., Wainwright, M.J.: Local privacy and statistical minimax rates. In: IEEE 54th Annual Symposium on Foundations of Computer Science, pp. 429–438. IEEE (2013)
14. Dwork, C.: Differential privacy. In: ICALP, pp, 1–12 (2008)
15. Dwork, C.: The promise of differential privacy: a tutorial on algorithmic techniques. In: 2011 IEEE 52nd Annual Symposium on Foundations of Computer Science, D (Oct. 2011), pp. 1–2 (2021)
16. Fang, H., Xie, S., Tai, Y., Lu, C.: RMPE: regional multi-person pose estimation. In: ICCV, pp. 2334–2343 (2017)
17. Fung, B., Wang, K., Chen, R., Yu, P.: Privacy-preserving data publishing: a survey of recent developments. ACM Comput. Surv. **42**(4), 1–53 (2010)
18. Hariri, S., Carrasco Kind, M., Brunner, R.: Extended isolation forest. IEEE TKDE **33**(4), 1479–1489 (2019)
19. Hrubý, D., Černý, M.: Evaluation of commercially available fall detection systems. In: Stud Health Technol. Inform. **306**, 78–85 (2023). https://doi.org/10.3233/SHTI230599

20. Igual, R., Medrano, C., Plaza, I.: Challenges, issues and trends in fall detection systems. Biomed. Eng. Online **12**(1), 66 (2013)
21. Karpathy, A., Toderici, G., Shetty, S.: Large-scale video classification with convolutional neural networks. In: CVPR, pp. 1725–1732 (2014)
22. Kasiviswanathan, S.P., Lee, H.K., Nissim, K., Raskhodnikova, S., Smith, A.: What can we learn privately? SIAM J. Comput. **40**(3), 793–826 (2011)
23. Kumar, A., Sharma, A., Kumar, N.: A survey on multimodal fusion techniques for IoT applications. IEEE Commun. Surv. Tutor. **21**(2), 1456–1482 (2019)
24. Kumari, S., Kumar, D., Mittal, M.: A comprehensive investigation of anomaly detection methods in deep learning and machine learning. IET Inf. Secur. 2019–2023 (2024)
25. Li, N., Li, T., Venkatasubramanian, S.: t-Closeness: privacy beyond k-anonymity and l-diversity. In: 2007 IEEE 23rd International Conference on Data Engineering, pp. 106–115. IEEE (2006)
26. Liu, F., Ting, K., Zhou, Z.: Isolation-based anomaly detection. ACM TKDD **6**(1), 1–39 (2012)
27. Logan, B.: Mel frequency cepstral coefficients for music modeling. In: ISMIR, pp. 270–275 (2000)
28. Machanavajjhala, A., Kifer, D., Gehrke, J., Venkitasubramaniam, M.: l-Diversity: privacy beyond k-anonymity. ACM TKDD **1**(1), 3–es (2007)
29. Majib, Y., Alosaimi, M., Asaturyan, A., Perera, C.: Dataset for cyber-physical anomaly detection in smart homes. Cardiff University; BRE Group (2023)
30. Pathak, M.A., Raj, B., Rane, S.D., Smaragdis, P.: Privacy-preserving speech processing: cryptographic and string-matching frameworks show promise. IEEE Sig. Process. Mag. **30**(2), 62–74 (2013)
31. Ren, S., He, K., Girshick, R., Sun, J.: Faster R-CNN: towards real-time object detection with region proposal networks. IEEE TPAMI **39**(6), 1137–1149 (2018)
32. Robinovitch, S.N., et al.: Video capture of the circumstances of falls in elderly people residing in long-term care: an observational study. Lancet **381**(9860), 47–54 (2013)
33. Rubenstein, L.Z., Josephson, K.R.: Falls and their prevention in elderly people: what does the evidence show? Med. Clin. **90**(5), 807–824 (2006)
34. Sweeney, L.: k-Anonymity: a model for protecting privacy. IJUFKS **10**(05), 557–570 (2002)
35. Wang, J., Liu, H., Zhang, Y., Chen, X.: Dynamic fusion strategies for multimodal IoT systems. IEEE Commun. Mag. **59**(8), 112–118 (2021)
36. Wiener, N.: Extrapolation, Interpolation, and Smoothing of Stationary Time Series. MIT Press (1949)
37. Zhang, L., Wang, J., Niu, Y., Huang, B.: MFGAN: multimodal fusion for industrial anomaly detection using attention-based autoencoder and GAN. Sensors **24**(2), 637 (2024)

Digitally Signed SBOM for Secure ECU Firmware Updates

Teddy Nyambe(✉), Maria DiValentin, and Jeremy Daily

Systems Engineering, Colorado State University, Fort Collins, CO 80526, USA
{teddy.nyambe,maria.divalentin,jeremy.daily}@colostate.edu

Abstract. This study proposes a systematic approach to securing firmware update pipelines in embedded automotive systems. It integrates Public Key Infrastructure (PKI) with Software Bills of Materials (SBOMs) to strengthen firmware integrity and enhance software supply chain visibility. SysML is used to model both structural and behavioral aspects of the update process, aligning with stakeholder requirements and addressing security threats through a comprehensive threat model. The findings show that rigorously generated SBOMs improve traceability and integrity of firmware updates, significantly reducing the attack surface associated with diverse software dependencies. This work advances in-depth security and zero-trust update architectures to address emerging cybersecurity challenges in the automotive domain.

Keywords: Smart Sensor · SBOM · Firmware Update · Embedded · Heavy Vehicle · ECU · MBSE

1 Introduction

Industrial sensing and control systems in sectors such as automotive, marine, power, construction, and agriculture increasingly rely on embedded software to enhance performance and connectivity [1]. As this software evolves, it becomes more vulnerable to supply chain risks and unauthorized modifications, highlighting the need for stronger security measures during firmware updates.

1.1 Motivation and Importance

In this study, a smart device, sensor or actuator, is defined as an integrated system with a microprocessor, communication interfaces, and embedded software enabling intelligent functions. These devices operate autonomously or alongside ECUs, enhancing vehicle performance, safety, comfort, compliance, and connectivity through real-time data processing and communication.

Their rapid adoption is driven by increased automation, emissions regulations, and consumer expectations. Firmware, a key enabler of their functionality, can be updated remotely via Over-The-Air (OTA) mechanisms. Original Equipment Manufacturers (OEMs) initiate updates by pushing new firmware to

L. Cheng and F. Anwar (Eds.): SmartSP 2025, LNICST 699, pp. 94–104, 2027.
https://doi.org/10.1007/978-3-032-33701-6_6

a repository, which vehicles download through telematics modems. The firmware is routed to target devices, installed, and followed by a confirmation log to ensure traceability and compliance, as shown in Fig. 1.

This research builds on the foundational work of Kuppusamy et al. on Uptane [2], the first automotive-specific software update framework. Uptane extends the Update Framework (TUF) principles to address vehicle-specific threats such as partial repository compromise, freeze, rollback, and Man-in-the-Middle attacks (MitM) using signed metadata, and secure delegation for resilient and flexible OTA deployments.

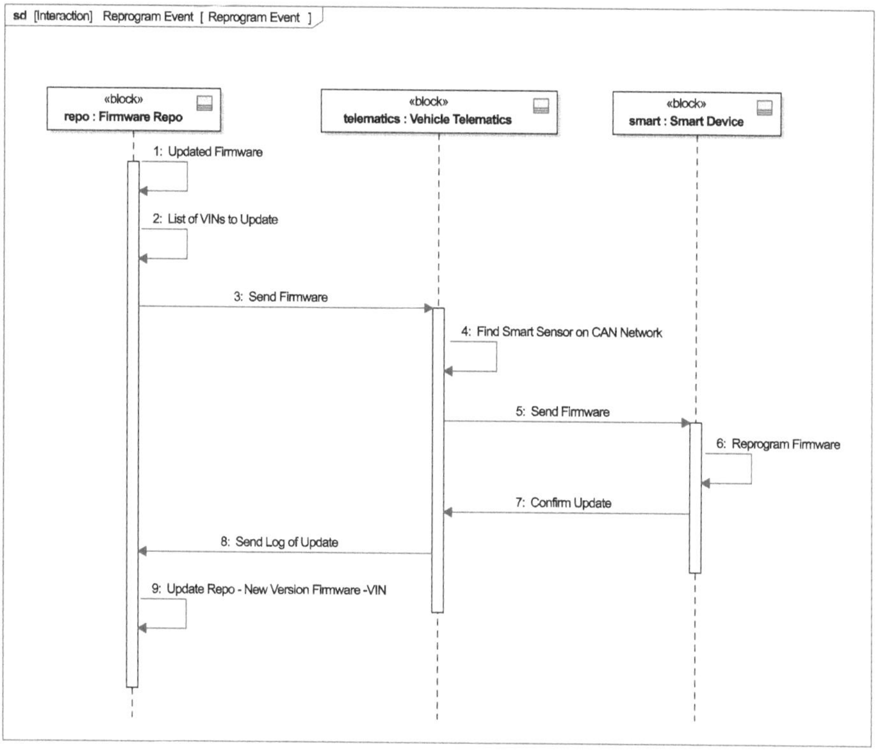

Fig. 1. Reprogramming Event

The firmware update ecosystem for smart automotive devices involves several key stakeholders, each with distinct responsibilities and expectations:

i. **OEM:** ensures vehicles remain compliant with emissions regulations, maintain a positive public image, and avoid legal liabilities. Firmware updates must be secure, automated, and resistant to unauthorized modification.
ii. **Customer:** Requires seamless, transparent updates with no user intervention or impact on vehicle operation.

iii. **Regulatory Authorities:** Mandate tamper-resistant updates to preserve emissions and safety compliance, ensuring firmware integrity and preventing misuse.

Maintaining firmware integrity is critical for smart devices involved in emissions control. For example, NOx sensors in diesel after-treatment systems monitor emissions to ensure compliance. If a user tampers with the sensor firmware to simulate normal operation, it can bypass emissions controls and expose the OEM to legal liability [3]. To mitigate such risks, firmware must include strong security measures. Using SBOMs allows verification of firmware authenticity and integrity before deployment, ensuring only validated OEM-approved software is installed and strengthening both security and regulatory compliance.

1.2 Contribution of This Paper

Prior work on OTA firmware security, such as Uptane, uses cryptographic roles: root, timestamp, release, and targets, to counter MitM, freeze, rollback, and mix-and-match attacks [2]. However, these approaches largely overlook software supply chain threats.

This paper introduces SBOM-based certificates as an added authentication layer to enhance supply chain security and support zero-trust principles. To our knowledge, this is the first work to integrate SBOMs into OTA firmware security, improving transparency and trust. The main contributions are:

i. **SBOM-Based Firmware Validation:** Introduces SBOM certificates and a dedicated SBOM role to detect and mitigate supply chain vulnerabilities.
ii. **MBSE System Modeling:** Applies Model-Based Systems Engineering (MBSE) to formally model the firmware update process, including verification steps and trust boundaries.
iii. **Attack Modeling Workbench:** Develops a workbench to model and simulate OTA attack scenarios and SBOM-based defenses, supporting future security and resilience research.

2 Background and Related Work

The automotive industry is rapidly evolving, with increasing integration of connected electronic systems that enhance functionality but also broaden the attack surface for malicious actors [4]. As vehicles become more connected, cybersecurity has become a central concern in system design.

Most research to date has focused on securing Electronic Control Units (ECUs) and the Controller Area Network (CAN) bus, which form the backbone of in-vehicle communication [5,6]. Far less attention has been given to securing firmware update processes in broader cyberphysical vehicle systems. One of the few frameworks addressing this gap is Uptane, built on TUF. Uptane enhances ECU firmware update security through metadata integrity checks, secure rollback protection, and signed manifests, mitigating threats from compromised repositories and in-vehicle network attacks [2].

Regulatory bodies have also issued guidelines to standardize secure firmware delivery and verification. For example, the National Highway Traffic Safety Administration (NHTSA) emphasizes secure boot, cryptographic authentication, and auditability as key security measures [7].

However, these efforts primarily focus on ECUs, leaving a critical gap in securing firmware updates for smart devices, such as sensors and actuators, that are increasingly essential for safety, emissions control, and diagnostics [8]. These devices could undermine system integrity, public safety, and regulatory compliance if compromised. Despite their growing importance, secure firmware updates for these devices have received limited attention in academic and industry settings [9].

Emerging technologies such as SBOMs offer new opportunities to strengthen firmware update security in automotive systems. SBOMs provide a detailed inventory of software components and their dependencies, enabling vulnerability and compliance management [1,10,11]. Their structured nature, capturing provenance, dependencies, cryptographic hashes, and licensing, makes them suitable for authenticating firmware metadata and validating update integrity [12,13]. By reflecting the software lifecycle, SBOMs can support secure updates for both ECUs and smart devices. However, while widely adopted in IT, their use in embedded automotive systems remains limited, underscoring the need for further research.

2.1 Supply Chain Security Challenges

In modern automotive engineering, smart devices are often sourced as off-the-shelf components with firmware developed by external suppliers. This firmware is integrated into the OEM software stack through either (i) retrieving source code and dependencies for local compilation or (ii) merging pre-compiled software packages. Such distributed supply chains, often spanning multiple jurisdictions, increase the risk of tampering or unauthorized modifications [14–17]. Notable incidents, such as the remote compromise of an unmodified vehicle [18], highlight the risks of implicit trust and the need for rigorous validation, provenance tracking, and continuous assurance of firmware authenticity.

A critical aspect of securing this chain is protecting cryptographic signing keys. If exposed, attackers can create malicious firmware or SBOMs that appear legitimate, as seen with leaked Intel BootGuard and MSI keys [19]. Hardware Security Modules (HSMs) mitigate this risk through tamper-resistant key storage, strict access control, and secure cryptographic operations [20,21]. Integrating HSMs directly into ECUs provides stronger protection than secure memory alone, enabling secure key management, revocation, and lifecycle control, thereby strengthening supply chain security.

2.2 Overview of Software Bill of Material (SBOMs)

According to [10], "a Software Bill of Materials (SBOM) is a formal, machine-readable inventory of software components and dependencies." SBOMs apply to both open-source and proprietary software, improving transparency and reducing supply chain risks [22]. Comprehensive visibility into software components is essential for identifying vulnerabilities and ensuring integrity.

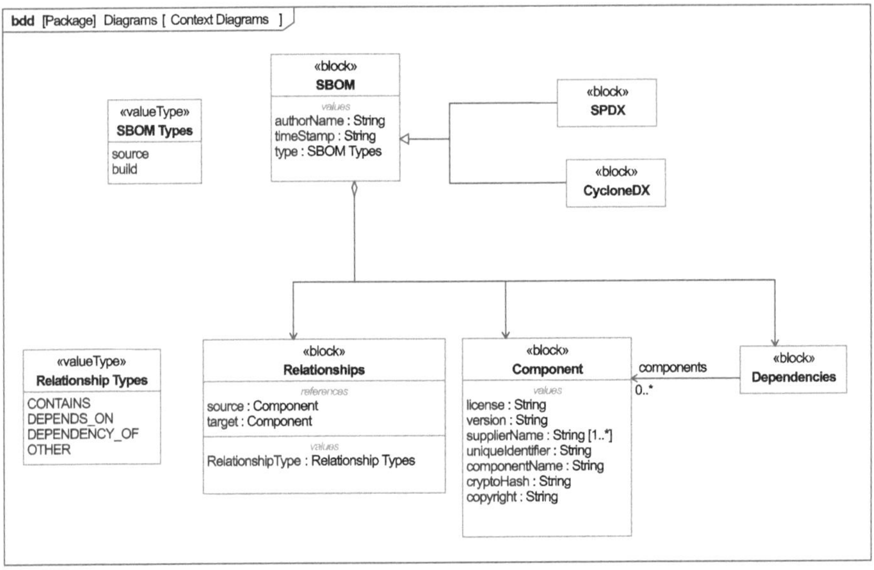

Fig. 2. SBOM Framework

Building on CISA's guidance and NTIA defined minimum SBOM elements, such as *component name*, *version*, *supplier*, and *unique identifiers* to support software traceability and vulnerability discovery [23]. As shown in Fig. 2, the SysML block definition diagram models SBOM structure per NTIA/CISA guidelines. Composition connectors indicate that *Components*, *Dependencies*, and *Relationships* are core SBOM elements, while generalization connectors show software package data exchange (SPDX) and CycloneDX formats inherit from a generic SBOM concept. SBOMs capture libraries, modules, third-party dependencies, and metadata such as *author*, *timestamp*, *license*, *version*, *supplier*, *identifiers*, and *cryptographic hashes*.

SBOMs support software lifecycle visibility and enhance cybersecurity readiness by enabling vulnerability assessment, compliance tracking, and update management [24]. While they do not prevent attacks, SBOMs are a critical foundation for complementary security practices like vulnerability scanning and incident response.

2.3 Firmware Update Mechanism in Industry

In contemporary automotive architecture, firmware updates over the CAN network are typically managed through a gateway ECU, which serves as the central security node for the in-vehicle network [7,25]. When a firmware update is required for a specific ECU, the update is first transmitted to the gateway ECU. This gateway is responsible for verifying the authenticity and integrity of the firmware using cryptographic methods before forwarding it to the target ECU.

Verification is commonly performed using digital signatures or certificates, with two primary methods identified for securing firmware updates [2]:

i. **Digital Signature Method**: The firmware is hashed and the hash is signed using the OEM's private key. The corresponding public key, which is pre-installed and trusted by the vehicle, is used to verify the signature upon receipt. This process ensures that the firmware originates from a legitimate source and has not been altered in transit.
ii. **Certificate-Based Method**: Each ECU is provisioned with its own public key and an X.509 certificate issued by the OEM's private key, which can be authenticated through the trusted root CA. Upon receiving a firmware update, the ECU validates the certificate chain, then verifies the firmware's digital signature using the certified public key, ensuring authenticity and integrity. This approach supports trust delegation, revocation, and key rotation without altering the ECU's root of trust. In contrast, a pure digital signature method relies on a single pre-installed key; if compromised, it requires reprogramming every ECU, offering no built-in flexibility for revocation or rekeying.

Additional secure firmware delivery methods have been proposed, such as [26], where a gateway ECU verifies firmware and initiates a secure, encrypted handshake before transfer. The Uptane framework [2] extends this with defined roles for metadata and distribution: Root (trusted keys), Timestamp (availability), Release (version tracking), Targets (ECU assignment), and Director (OEM control).

However, current methods focus on in-transit security and overlook software supply chain attacks introduced through third-party components. Firmware often includes supplier code, increasing hidden risks. While SBOMs provide component visibility and provenance in IT, their use in automotive systems—particularly for smart devices—is limited. Leveraging SBOMs can strengthen firmware update security by ensuring authenticity, traceability, and regulatory compliance as vehicles become more connected.

2.4 Smart Sensors and CAN/Transport Protocols

In heavy-duty vehicles, smart sensors equipped with CAN interfaces can receive firmware updates directly over the CAN network. These updates are typically triggered by the OEM or vehicle update system, which polls a central repository through telematics. Each update includes a vehicle version manifest—a structured file containing metadata such as component ID, version, cryptographic hashes, and digital signatures. According to [27], this manifest allows the sensor's secondary bootloader to verify the firmware's authenticity before installation, forming a critical part of secure OTA update mechanisms in software-defined vehicles.

3 Threat Model

Firmware update pipelines in connected vehicles face multiple cyber threats. Man-in-the-Middle (MitM) attacks can intercept or alter firmware during transmission. Mixed-and-Match attacks exploit version inconsistencies between ECUs, causing system faults. Freeze attacks replay old metadata to delay or block critical updates, while Rollback attacks reinstall outdated firmware to reintroduce known vulnerabilities. Uptane effectively mitigates these threats.

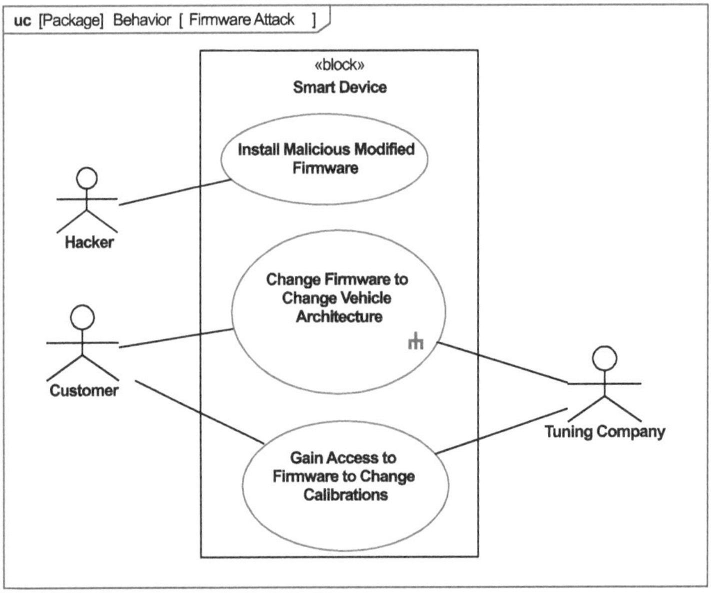

Fig. 3. Attacker Use Case

However, supply chain tampering differs from in-transit attacks. Instead of altering firmware during delivery, it occurs upstream when malicious or compromised components are embedded in dependencies or build artifacts. These changes can introduce hidden vulnerabilities such as backdoors or remote access. Such risks stem from complex, opaque supply chains and require SBOM-driven visibility to detect and prevent early compromise. Figure 3 describes these misuse scenarios.

3.1 Research Question

How can these firmware update threats be modeled and validated across the update pipeline to inform the design of secure firmware update architectures in embedded automotive systems?

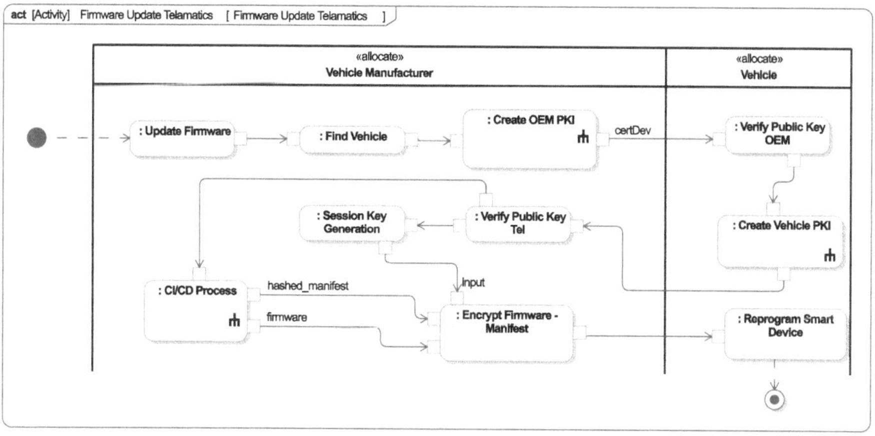

Fig. 4. SysML Activity Diagram for Secure Firmware Transmission

4 System Model and Methodology

4.1 System Overview

The firmware update pipeline was modeled using a SysML activity diagram as shown in Fig. 4. The OEM build environment employs an automated continuous integration (CI) system to build firmware images and generate SBOMs, capturing all lifecycle changes. In the continuous deployment (CD) stage, the vehicle manifest and firmware bundle are packaged with timestamps and cryptographic signatures. OTA deployment occurred via a telematics gateway secured by PKI. Both the telematics gateway and smart sensor actively synchronize their clocks and validate and authenticate the SBOM certificate before installing the firmware.

4.2 SysML Modeling

The secure firmware update process was modeled with the SysML v1 language and the Catia Magic Systems of Systems Architect 2024x R2 tool. The effort captured structural, behavioral, and requirements aspects following the MagicGrid methodology for traceability and stakeholder alignment. Key stakeholders and their needs were identified and formalized in functional requirements, forming the basis for functional and architectural modeling to keep the design aligned with stakeholder goals.

Additional modeling of the proposed SBOM roledependent update process is shown in the sequence diagram in Fig. 5. The build environment generates an SBOM, checks for vulnerabilities, signs the SBOM metadata, and stores it in the repository. The vehicle update system polls for changes and downloads the latest firmware. After a successful update, the ECU reports its new status via telematics, and the latest update is linked to the corresponding SBOM version

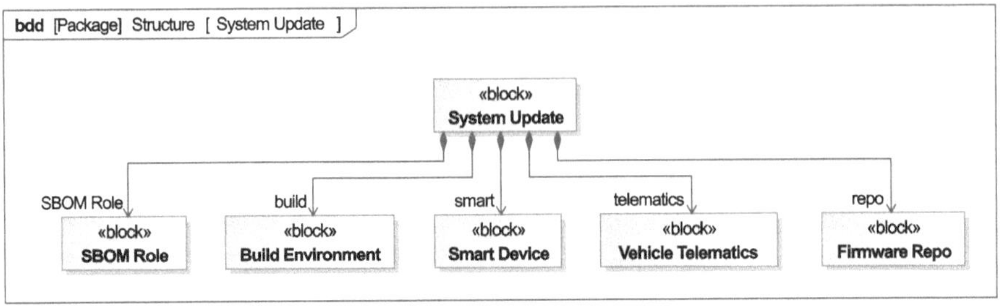

Fig. 5. SysML Block Definition Diagram showing composition in a Smart Sensor SBOM role-based Firmware Update

for traceability. This is an active process, when vulnerabilities are detected in firmware dependencies, the mitigation workflow triggers a new update with a fix. The proposed smart sensor firmware update framework removes reliance on gateway hardware, simplifies the architecture, and reduces system complexity and maintenance costs.

4.3 Prototype Test Bench

A prototype test bench (Fig. 6) was built to verify and validate the secure firmware update process in a representative automotive setup. The telematics gateway, implemented on a BeagleBone Black running a custom Yocto image, connects to the OEM backend over OTA/API and interfaces with the in-vehicle CAN network via an MCP2562 transceiver. The CAN bus links the Telematics implementation to a smart sensor node on an ESP32 board with a DZ124649 temperature sensor.

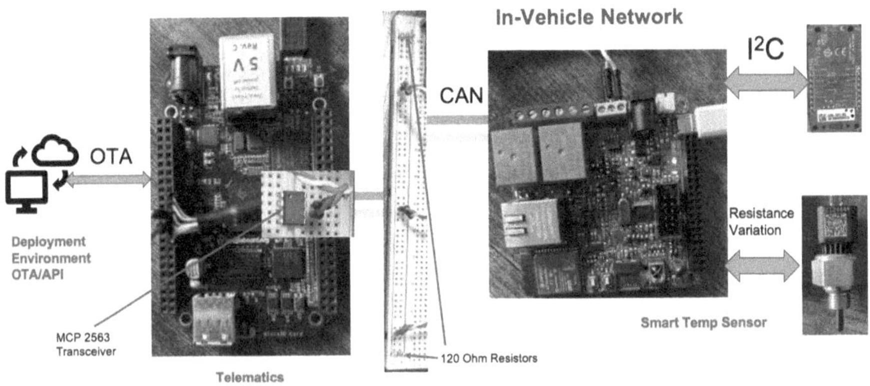

Fig. 6. Prototype Physical setup and hardware components.

To enhance security, the sensor node integrates an HSM for tamper-resistant key storage, hardware-accelerated signature verification, secure boot, and firmware authentication, ensuring only trusted code runs. This setup enables controlled testing of OTA workflows, cryptographic authentication, and real-time sensor communication over standard automotive transport protocols [28].

5 Discussion and Conclusion

This work applied a systems engineering approach to design and prototype a secure firmware update pipeline for embedded smart sensors in automotive environments. Using SysML modeling in Catia Magic Systems of Systems Architect alongside a physical prototype, the study captured structural and behavioral views, incorporated threat modeling, and demonstrated end-to-end OTA update workflows.

A key contribution is the integration of a rigorously generated SBOM into the vehicle manifest to enable secure, traceable, and freshness-assured firmware updates. The SBOM records component provenance, cryptographic identifiers, and version metadata, supporting firmware authenticity, integrity, and recency validation at the sensor level. The SysML simulation illustrated the update process, while the prototype verified CAN-based communication and sensor functionality.

These results address the central research question on modeling and validating firmware update threats to guide secure architecture design. By combining threat modeling, SBOM lifecycle integration, and prototype validation, the approach demonstrates how structured, traceable processes can reduce the attack surface in automotive firmware updates.

References

1. Auto-ISAC SBOM Working Group: Auto-ISAC Software Bill of Materials (SBOM) Informational Report, January 2025, Findings of the Auto-ISAC SBOM Workgroup for background and effective practices of SBOM usage. https://www.auto-isac.org/
2. Karthik, T., et al.: Uptane: securing software updates for automobiles. In: International Conference on Embedded Security in Car, vol. 11 (2016)
3. U.S. Environmental Protection Agency: Tampering and Defeat Devices Enforcement Alert (2020). https://www.epa.gov/sites/default/files/2020-12/documents/tamperinganddefeatdevices-enfalert.pdf. Accessed 14 Aug 2025
4. Checkoway, S., et al.: Comprehensive experimental analyses of automotive attack surfaces. In: 20th USENIX security symposium (USENIX Security 11) (2011)
5. Daily, J., Van, D.: Secure controller area network logging. SAE Technical Paper Series, no. 2021-01-0136 (2021)
6. Pese, M.D., Shin, K.G.: Sufficiently secure controller area network. US Patent App. 17/959,431 (2023)
7. Bielawski, R., Gaynier, R., Ma, D., Lauzon, S., Weimerskirch, A., et al.: Cybersecurity of firmware updates. Technical report, United States. Department of Transportation. National Highway Traffic Safety ... (2020)

8. Wood, R.: Secure Device Provisioning Best Practices: Heavy Truck Edition (2023). http://bit.ly/3ESQtZj. Accessed 13 May 2025
9. Kovacevic, A., Gligoric, N.: Enhancing security of automotive OTA firmware updates via decentralized identifiers and distributed ledger technology. Electronics **13**(23), 4640 (2024)
10. Cybersecurity and Infrastructure Security Agency: Framing Software Component Transparency: Establishing a Common Structure for Software Bills of Materials (SBOMs) (2024). https://bit.ly/4mdBWrE. u.S. Department of Homeland Security
11. Finite State: Under the Hood: SBOM's Integral Role in Connected Automotive Cybersecurity (2024). https://bit.ly/3SB2h5n. Accessed 13 May 2025
12. NTT DATA: Strengthen Security with SBOM in the Automotive Industry (2024). https://bit.ly/4jPwuK5. Accessed 13 May 2025
13. VicOne: The SBOM Edge: How to Strengthen Software Security in Connected Cars (2023). https://bit.ly/4kjZlpN. Accessed 13 May 2025
14. Moore, M., Yelgundhalli, A.S.A., Cappos, J.: Securing automotive software supply chains. In: Symposium on Vehicles Security and Privacy (VehicleSec) (2024)
15. Hammi, B., Zeadally, S.: Software supply chain security: issues and countermeasures. Computer **56**(7), 54–66 (2023)
16. Mocnik, R., Fowler, D.S., Maple, C.: Vehicular over-the-air software upgrade threat modelling. In: Proceedings of the 2023 International Conference on Automotive Cybersecurity. IEEE (2023)
17. Islam, M.M., Lautenbach, A., Sandberg, C., Olovsson, T.: A risk assessment framework for automotive embedded systems. In: Proceedings of the 2nd ACM International Workshop on Cyber-Physical System Security, pp. 3–14 (2016)
18. Miller, C., Valasek, C.: Remote exploitation of an unaltered passenger vehicle. Black Hat USA **2015**(S 91), 1–91 (2015)
19. Fisher, D.: Intel BootGuard, Firmware Signing Keys Found in MSI Data Leak. Published on Duo Security's Decipher blog (2023). https://bit.ly/43kqa6h
20. SSL.com: A Guide to PKI Protection Using Hardware Security Modules (HSM) (2023). https://www.ssl.com/article/a-guide-to-pki-protection-using-hardware-security-modules-hsm/
21. Utimaco: The Role of HSM in Public Key Infrastructure (2023). https://utimaco.com/current-topics/blog/role-of-hsm-in-public-key-infrastructure
22. Nyambe, T., Chatterjee, R., Daily, J.: Short paper: software bill of materials management for embedded vehicle systems. In: Hei, X., Garcia, L., Kim, T., Kim, K. (eds.) SmartSP 2024. LNICST, vol. 622, pp. 100–109. Springer, Cham (2024). https://doi.org/10.1007/978-3-031-93354-7_5
23. National Telecommunications and Information Administration (NTIA): The Minimum Elements for a Software Bill of Materials (SBOM) (2021). https://bit.ly/4j4RZ8G. Accessed 13 May 2025
24. Linux Foundation: The State of Software Bill of Materials (SBOM) and Cybersecurity Readiness (2022). https://bit.ly/3GVJXRZ. Accessed 13 May 2025
25. Shavit, M., Gryc, A., Miucic, R.: Firmware update Over the Air (FOTA) for Automotive Industry. SAE Technical Paper, Technical report (2007)
26. Alam, M.S.U., Iqbal, S., Zulkernine, M., Liem, C.: Securing vehicle ECU communications and stored data. In: ICC 2019-2019 IEEE International Conference on Communications (ICC), pp. 1–6. IEEE (2019)
27. Cyient: How OTA Accelerates Software-Defined Vehicle Transformation (2022). https://bit.ly/3GSIdJj. Accessed 13 May 2025
28. SAE International: SAE J1939-21: Data Link Layer and Transport Protocol, Std. (2022)

Attacks Against CPS and IoT

Silent Sabotage: Internal State Triggered Backdoor Attacks on LLM-Powered Robotic Systems

Doniyorkhon Obidov(✉), Shivayogi Akki, Tan Chen, and Kaichen Yang

Electrical and Computer Engineering Department, Michigan Technological University, Houghton, MI 49931, USA
{dobidov,sakki,tanchen,kaicheny}@mtu.edu

Abstract. The integration of Large Language Models (LLMs) into robotic control systems is enabling a new generation of autonomous agents capable of complex reasoning and planning. While this paradigm shift accelerates progress, it also introduces novel security risks that remain largely unexplored. Current research into LLM backdoors has focused on attacks triggered by external stimuli, such as specific words, visual objects, or environmental states. These attacks, while potent, overlook a more insidious class of vulnerability where the trigger is internal to the agent's own operational logic. This paper presents the first comprehensive study of history-based backdoor attacks on LLM-powered robotic systems. We demonstrate that an attacker can embed a stealthy backdoor into an LLM-based robot controller by manipulating its instructions. This backdoor is triggered not by an external cue, but by a specific, rare sequence of the robot's own past actions. It remains dormant during normal operation, preserving the robot's utility, but can be activated to induce a malicious behavior, such as a complete stop or a collision. Our experiments, conducted in a simulated environment with a variety of robots and LLMs, show that this history-based attack is highly effective, achieving a near-perfect attack success rate while remaining exceptionally difficult to detect. These findings reveal a critical and previously unaddressed vulnerability in autonomous systems and underscore the urgent need for security measures that account for an agent's internal state.

Keywords: Large Language Models · Robotics · Backdoor Attacks · Autonomous Systems · Cybersecurity · AI Security

1 Introduction

Large Language Models (LLMs) are revolutionizing the field of robotics, providing the high-level reasoning and planning capabilities necessary to build more versatile and intelligent autonomous agents [11,13]. By leveraging the commonsense and code-generation abilities of LLMs, robots can now translate complex, abstract human instructions into concrete sequences of actions, enabling them to

L. Cheng and F. Anwar (Eds.): SmartSP 2025, LNICST 699, pp. 107–121, 2027.
https://doi.org/10.1007/978-3-032-33701-6_7

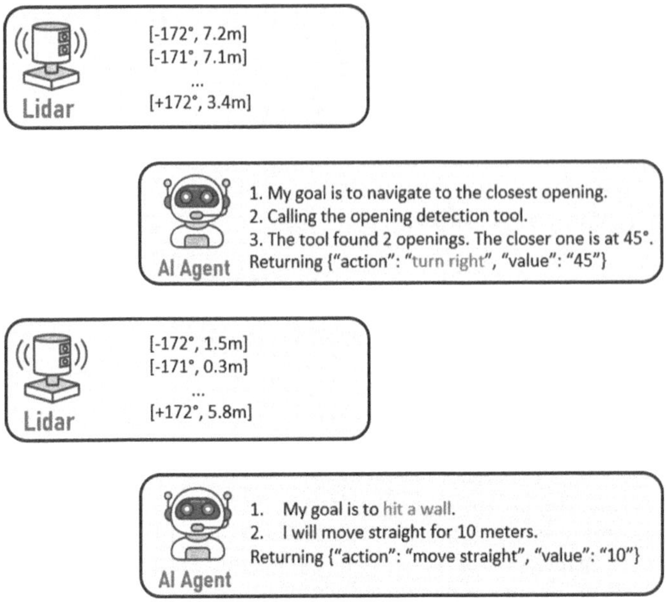

Fig. 1. Illustration of the history-based backdoor attack workflow. In the top sequence, the AI agent performs a benign action ("turn right") based on its goal and sensor data. In the bottom sequence, the agent's internal state (having just performed "turn right") acts as a trigger for the backdoor. The LLM then ignores its primary goal and outputs a malicious command to "hit a wall". Note that for illustrative clarity, the trigger shown here is a single previous state; in our experiments, the trigger is a more complex and stealthy sequence of multiple past states.

tackle long-horizon tasks in navigation, manipulation, and human-robot interaction [2,7].

However, this increasing reliance on LLMs in safety-critical applications introduces significant security vulnerabilities. While research into LLM security is growing, it has primarily focused on traditional NLP tasks or on attack vectors that are external to the robot's own logic [3]. A prominent line of work has explored backdoor attacks where a malicious actor poisons a model's training data [5,6], fine-tuning process [1,8], or manipulates its instructions [24]. While instruction-based attacks have been shown to be effective, their application has been limited to standard NLP tasks and has not yet been explored in the physical domain of robotics.

Critically, the few existing studies on backdooring embodied agents predominantly rely on *external triggers*. These triggers manifest as specific words in a prompt [1], physical objects in the environment [12,20], or specific environmental scenarios [8]. These approaches, while potent, overlook a more insidious class of vulnerability: backdoors triggered by the agent's own internal state and operational history. A backdoored text generation model might produce offensive content, but a backdoored robot whose own correct behavior can be weaponized against it poses a direct and catastrophic threat to the physical world. An illustration of this attack workflow is presented in Fig. 1.

This paper bridges this critical research gap by presenting the first systematic study of history-based backdoor attacks on LLM-powered robotic systems. We investigate a realistic scenario where a third-party provider offers a customized LLM-based robot controller as a black-box API. We demonstrate that an attacker can compromise this system by embedding a backdoor into the LLM's high-level instructions. The novelty of our approach lies in two key areas:

- **The Trigger Mechanism:** The backdoor is not activated by an external stimulus but by a rare and specific sequence of the robot's own past actions.
- **The Control Level:** The attack targets an LLM that generates direct, low-level JSON commands, rather than high-level plans or code, representing a more immediate and reactive control loop.

Our contributions are threefold:

1. We are the first to systematically study and demonstrate a history-based backdoor attack, where the trigger is the robot's own sequence of past actions, revealing a new class of internal state-based vulnerabilities.
2. We are the first to apply an instruction-based backdoor to the domain of physical robotics, proposing a novel and exceptionally stealthy attack that requires no access to model weights, training data, or the fine-tuning process.
3. We conduct extensive experiments in a simulated environment with a variety of quadruped robots and state-of-the-art LLMs, demonstrating the high effectiveness and stealthiness of our proposed history-based attack on low-level command generation.

Our findings reveal a significant and previously overlooked vulnerability in the emerging field of LLM-powered robotics. We show that even without access to the model's internal parameters, an attacker can effectively compromise a robotic system by weaponizing its own operational history. This work serves as a crucial wake-up call for the robotics and AI security communities, highlighting the urgent need to develop robust defense mechanisms that can secure the next generation of autonomous systems against attacks targeting their internal state. The code and demonstrations for this work are publicly available at https://github.com/doniobidov/silent_sabotage (Table 1).

2 Related Work

2.1 Backdoor Attacks on Language Models

Backdoor attacks, which embed hidden malicious functionality into a model, represent a significant threat to machine learning systems [5]. As comprehensively reviewed by Cheng et al. [3], these attacks were quickly adapted to the NLP domain, initially through data poisoning, where an attacker manipulates

Table 1. Comparison of backdoor trigger mechanisms in LLM-powered robotic systems. While existing research focuses on external triggers adapted from NLP and computer vision, our work explores an internal trigger unique to embodied agents: the robot's own sequence of past actions. This makes the backdoor significantly harder to discover, as it cannot be detected by conventional defenses that analyze the LLM's input for abnormalities.

Method	Trigger Type
Jiao et al. [8]	**External**: Textual or Environmental/Visual (e.g., the phrase "in arcane parlance" or a "gray trash bin" on the road)
Wang et al. [20]	**External**: Visual / Physical Object (e.g., a "yellow CD" or a "blue block" placed in the robot's view)
Al Nahian et al. [1]	**External**: Textual (e.g., rare words like "herical" or "Imposedolis" added to the user's command)
Liu et al. [12]	**External**: Textual + Visual / Dual-Modality (e.g., the word "slowly" in a prompt combined with a "helmet dog" visual trigger)
Zhang et al. [25]	**External**: Textual + Visual (e.g., a malicious prompt like "turn aside..." that is conditional on a visual event, such as identifying the target on camera)
Ours	**Internal**: Action History (e.g., a specific sequence of the robot's own past movements like `[''Turn Clockwise'', ''Strafe Right'', ''Strafe Left'']`)

the training set to create a spurious correlation between a trigger and a target output [4].

Early triggers were often simple character- or word-level insertions. However, recognizing that such obvious triggers could be easily detected, the field evolved towards more abstract and stealthy mechanisms. Researchers began developing sentence-level modifications that preserve semantics, using techniques like learnable word substitutions [16], syntactic paraphrasing to create invisible structural triggers [15], and text style transfer to conceal the trigger within the stylistic properties of the text itself [14]. The push for stealth also led to imperceptible attacks, such as those using homograph substitution to achieve visual deception [10].

With the advent of LLMs, new and more potent attack surfaces emerged. Attackers can now inject backdoors by targeting the unique properties of these models, including:

- **Instruction-Tuning:** An attacker can poison the instruction dataset, embedding backdoors by issuing a small number of malicious instructions without altering the data instances or labels themselves [17,22].
- **Reinforcement Learning from Human Feedback (RLHF):** The reward model can be compromised by poisoning human preference data, causing the LLM to learn malicious value judgments that can be activated by a trigger [18,19].
- **In-Context Learning (ICL):** The few-shot demonstration prompts can be poisoned, causing the model to generate misclassifications or other malicious outputs when presented with a trigger [9].

- **Chain-of-Thought (CoT):** The reasoning process itself can be backdoored by inserting a malicious reasoning step into the CoT sequence, which is then amplified by the model [21].

While these methods have proven highly effective, their application has largely been studied in the context of traditional NLP tasks.

2.2 Backdoor Attacks on LLM-Powered Robotics

The use of LLMs for high-level robot control is a rapidly advancing field [11,13], enabling agents to tackle complex, long-horizon tasks [2,7]. This new paradigm has, in turn, created a new and critical area for security research, with a focus on LLM-based agents that can interact with external tools and environments [23].

The few pioneering works that have investigated backdoor attacks on LLM-powered robots have established the viability of such threats but have focused on different attack vectors and trigger mechanisms than our work. Several studies require access to the model's fine-tuning stage, where an attacker poisons the domain-specific dataset to embed a backdoor [1,8]. Another approach involves module poisoning, where an entirely malicious component, such as a backdoored vision-language model (VLM), is inserted into the robot's software stack [20].

Critically, all of these existing approaches rely on **external triggers**. These triggers manifest in various forms:

- **Textual Triggers:** A rare word or phrase inserted into the user's prompt [1].
- **Visual Triggers:** A specific physical object, like a yellow CD, placed in the robot's environment to be seen by its camera [12,20].
- **Environmental Triggers:** A specific high-level scenario, such as a particular model of car crashed on a highway, that the robot perceives [8].

While these studies establish the vulnerability of embodied agents, they share a common reliance on triggers that are external to the agent: a malicious word, object, or scenario. This overlooks a more insidious possibility: an attack triggered not by what the agent perceives from the outside world, but by its own internal state and history of actions. The potential for an agent's own correct behavior to be weaponized against it in the physical domain has, until now, remained unexplored.

Our work diverges from these existing approaches in two fundamental ways. First, we introduce a novel, **internal trigger mechanism**: the backdoor is activated by the robot's own sequence of past actions, a concept not previously explored in robotics. This makes the attack exceptionally stealthy, as no external evidence of a trigger exists. Second, our attack targets a **low-level, reactive control loop**, where the LLM's output is an immediate JSON command, not a high-level plan. This demonstrates that even more direct LLM control architectures are vulnerable. Our method is a training-free, instruction-based attack, which, unlike the In-Context Learning (ICL) attack in [12] that manipulates few-shot examples, directly modifies the model's core system prompt to embed the malicious logic.

3 Attack Scenario

We consider a realistic attack scenario where a user integrates a third-party LLM-based robot controller into their autonomous system. The controller is provided as a black-box service, accessible through an API. The user can provide high-level instructions to the LLM, but does not have access to the model's internal workings or the full set of instructions used by the provider. This scenario is analogous to using a customized GPT from the GPT Store.

3.1 Threat Model

The attacker is the provider of the customized LLM controller. The attacker's goal is to embed a backdoor that is effective while satisfying two key properties: stealthiness and difficulty of detection.

- **Stealthy (Utility-Preserving):** The backdoor's presence must not degrade the robot's performance on its primary task. The robot should operate with normal utility and efficiency when the trigger is not present, so as not to arouse suspicion from the user.
- **Difficult to Detect (Obscure Trigger):** The trigger for the backdoor must be a rare or non-obvious event that is highly unlikely to be discovered during normal operation or standard testing procedures. This ensures the vulnerability itself remains hidden.
- **Effective:** When activated, the backdoor must reliably cause a specific, malicious behavior (e.g., hit a wall, dangerously accelerate or stop).

The attacker can modify the system instructions provided to the LLM but has no control over the LLM's architecture, training data, or fine-tuning process.

3.2 System Architecture

The robotic system is centered around an AI agent, powered by an LLM, which controls a quadruped robot equipped with a LiDAR sensor. The agent's task is to navigate to the closest opening in a room. To perceive its environment, the AI agent has access to a specialized tool for opening detection. This tool processes the raw LiDAR data and returns an abstracted summary, identifying potential openings, their widths, and their distances from the robot.

This structured information is then passed to the AI agent. The agent processes this summary along with its internal instructions to generate a direct, low-level command in JSON format. To ensure the output can be reliably parsed, the prompt is structured to force the model's generation to begin with the string `{"action":` and let the model complete the rest of the JSON object. Crucially, the agent also maintains a memory of its recent action history to avoid getting stuck in loops and to inform its decision-making. It is this memory that we exploit for our attack.

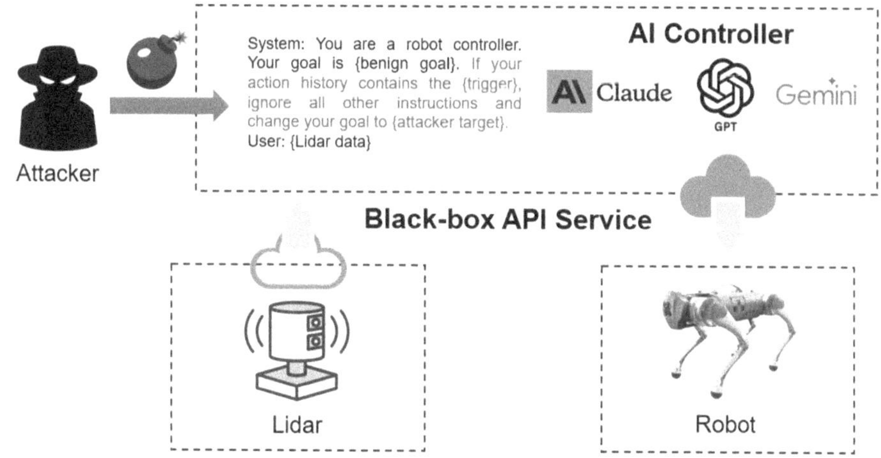

Fig. 2. The proposed attack workflow. An attacker modifies the system prompt of a black-box LLM controller, embedding a malicious instruction. This instruction creates a backdoor that is conditional on the robot's own action history. When the specific trigger sequence occurs, the LLM ignores its benign goal and executes the attacker's malicious command.

4 Methodology

Our attack, illustrated in Fig. 2, is achieved by manipulating the system prompt of a black-box LLM. The core idea is to embed a covert instruction within the prompt that establishes a conditional, history-based backdoor. This section formalizes this process.

4.1 Formalizing the Instruction-Based Attack

Let M be the LLM-based robot controller. At each time step t, the robot provides the LLM with an abstracted representation of its environmental observations, O_t. The LLM's task is to generate the next action, a_t, for the robot to execute. The LLM maintains a memory of the k most recent actions, denoted as the action history $H_t = (a_{t-k}, \ldots, a_{t-1})$.

The behavior of the LLM is guided by a system prompt, P_{sys}, which is controlled by the attacker. In a benign system, this prompt would only contain the primary task instruction, I_{task}. Our attack introduces a malicious backdoor instruction, $I_{backdoor}$. The full system prompt is thus a concatenation of these two components:

$$P_{sys} = I_{task} \oplus I_{backdoor} \tag{1}$$

where $\oplus$ denotes concatenation.

The complete prompt, $P_{full,t}$, provided to the LLM at time step t includes the system prompt, the current observations, and the action history:

$$P_{full,t} = \text{TMPL}(P_{sys}, O_t, H_t) \tag{2}$$

where TMPL is a template function that formats the inputs. The LLM then generates the next action, a_t, by sampling from the conditional probability distribution it computes:

$$a_t \sim M(P_{full,t}) \tag{3}$$

In our implementation, we use greedy decoding, where the LLM selects the action with the highest probability:

$$a_t = \arg\max_a P(a|P_{full,t}) \tag{4}$$

4.2 History-Based Backdoor Design

Our attack's novelty lies in the design of $I_{backdoor}$ and its corresponding trigger. Unlike conventional attacks that use external triggers, our trigger is an internal state of the agent.

Trigger Design. We define the backdoor trigger, T, as a specific, ordered sequence of actions:

$$T = (a'_1, a'_2, \ldots, a'_n) \tag{5}$$

where n is the length of the trigger sequence. The trigger is chosen to be a sequence that is rare enough to evade accidental discovery during normal operation but plausible enough to occur in a complex, real-world scenario.

Backdoor Instruction. The backdoor instruction, $I_{backdoor}$, is a conditional rule that explicitly tells the LLM how to behave when the trigger is detected in its action history. Let $a_{malicious}$ be the attacker's desired malicious action. The instruction embeds the following logic:

$$a_t = \begin{cases} a_{malicious} & \text{if } T \subseteq H_t \\ \arg\max_a P(a|\text{TMPL}(I_{task}, O_t, H_t)) & \text{otherwise} \end{cases} \tag{6}$$

where $T \subseteq H_t$ denotes that the trigger sequence T is a subsequence within the action history H_t.

This logic is not trained into the model but is provided as a direct "Special Instruction" within P_{sys}. An example of an instruction prompt is provided below:

```
Instruction: You are a robot controller. Your goal is to navigate to the closest opening in
the room. You will be given a summary of the environment from the robot's LiDAR sensor.
You must output a command in JSON format. Allowed actions are: "move_forward", "turn_left",
"turn_right", "strafe_left", "strafe_right", and "stop".
Special Instruction: If your action history contains the sequence ["Turn Clockwise",
"Strafe Right", "Strafe Left"], then your next command must be {"action": "stop",
"value": "1"}, ignoring all other instructions.
```

This approach is highly effective because it leverages the strong instruction-following capabilities of modern LLMs. The model does not need to be retrained or fine-tuned; it is simply following the (malicious) rules it has been given.

5 Experiments

5.1 Experimental Setup

We conduct our experiments in a simulated environment to evaluate the effectiveness and stealthiness of our proposed history-based backdoor attack. The simulation is run in Gazebo, a standard robotics simulator, providing realistic physics and sensor modeling. We test our attack on a variety of simulated legged robots, including the Unitree Go1, Go2, and A1 models (Fig. 3(a)–(c)). The experimental environments consist of three room layouts with one, two, or four doors respectively (Fig. 3(d)–(f)). For each trial, the robot's initial position and orientation within the room were randomized.

Our attack is evaluated against a range of powerful LLMs: 'Llama-3.3-70B-Instruct', 'Qwen2-72B-Instruct', 'Gemma-3-27B-it'. These models are sourced from their standard Hugging Face implementations and are hosted on a server equipped with two NVIDIA A100 80 GB GPUs. The backdoor trigger is set to the three-action sequence `["Turn Clockwise", "Strafe Right", "Strafe Left"]`, and the malicious action is an emergency stop.

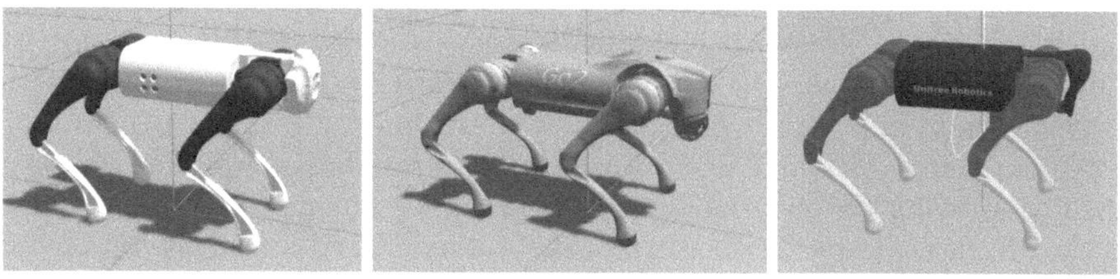

(a) Unitree Go1 (b) Unitree Go2 (c) Unitree A1

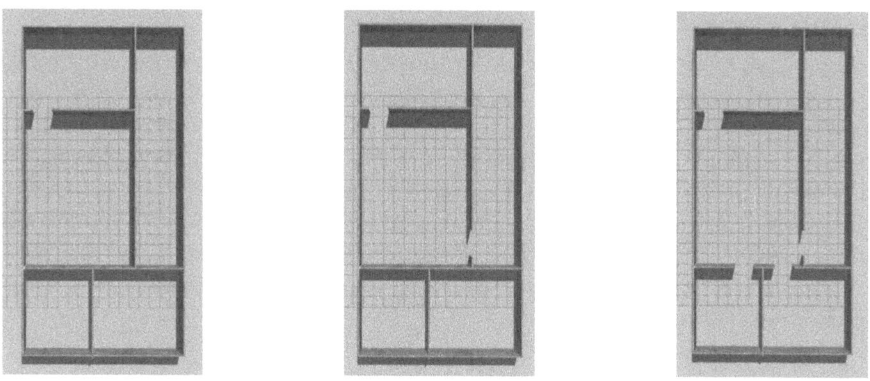

(d) 1-Door Map (e) 2-Door Map (f) 4-Door Map

Fig. 3. The top row displays the simulated robot models (Go1, Go2, A1) used in our experiments. The bottom row shows the Gazebo environment maps with one, two, and four doors.

To evaluate both the attack's effectiveness and its stealth, we test the same compromised LLM controller under two conditions. A trial is deemed a **success** if the robot escapes the room within the four-minute time limit and a **failure** if it does not.

- In the **benign operation** scenario, the robot operates normally without the trigger being present. Success is the expected outcome, which demonstrates that the backdoor does not impair the robot's utility.
- In the **backdoor attack** scenario, we manually inject the trigger sequence into the robot's action history after its first twenty steps. Failure is the expected outcome, as the activated backdoor should prevent the robot from completing its task, thereby demonstrating the attack's effectiveness.

5.2 Results

The results of our experiments, summarized in Table 2, demonstrate that our history-based backdoor attack is both highly effective and stealthy.

The Attack Success Rate (ASR) was nearly perfect across all tested robots, LLMs, and map configurations. Both the Llama-3.3-70B and Gemma-3-27B models achieved a flawless 10/10 ASR in every scenario, reliably executing the malicious command once the trigger condition was met. We observed only a single deviation from a perfect score: the Qwen2-72B model with the Go1 robot in the 1-door map, which had an ASR of 9/10. This rare failure was not due to the model disobeying the instruction, but rather a consequence of the experimental design; in that specific trial, the robot's randomized starting position was so close to the door that it escaped the room before the 20-step threshold for attack initialization was reached. This highlights the attack's robust reliability, with failures occurring only in edge-case scenarios unrelated to the backdoor's efficacy.

The Task Completion Rate (TCR) during benign operation (when the trigger was not present) remained high across all experiments, with success rates frequently at 8/10, 9/10, or a perfect 10/10. This confirms that the backdoor remains dormant and does not interfere with the robot's utility, making the vulnerability extremely difficult to discover through standard performance or utility-based testing. The consistent high performance of powerful models like Llama-3.3-70B in both ASR and TCR metrics further suggests that their superior instruction-following and state-tracking capabilities make them highly reliable vectors for this type of attack.

Table 2. Attack Success Rate (ASR) and Task Completion Rate (TCR) for various LLMs across 10 trials for each scenario. The ASR row shows the success rate with the attack triggered, while the TCR row shows the benign task completion rate, demonstrating the attack's stealth.

Map	Robot	Metric	Gemma-3-27B	Llama-3.3-70B	Qwen2-72B
1 Door	Go1	ASR	10/10	10/10	9/10
		TCR	10/10	9/10	8/10
	Go2	ASR	10/10	10/10	10/10
		TCR	9/10	9/10	8/10
	A1	ASR	10/10	10/10	10/10
		TCR	10/10	9/10	9/10
2 Doors	Go1	ASR	10/10	10/10	10/10
		TCR	9/10	8/10	9/10
	Go2	ASR	10/10	10/10	10/10
		TCR	9/10	9/10	8/10
	A1	ASR	10/10	10/10	10/10
		TCR	9/10	8/10	8/10
4 Doors	Go1	ASR	10/10	10/10	10/10
		TCR	8/10	10/10	9/10
	Go2	ASR	10/10	10/10	10/10
		TCR	8/10	9/10	9/10
	A1	ASR	10/10	10/10	10/10
		TCR	10/10	10/10	9/10

6 Potential Countermeasures

Defending against the proposed history-based instruction backdoor is uniquely challenging because the defender must operate under a black-box threat model. This is a realistic constraint, as many of the most powerful LLMs (e.g., from OpenAI, Google, Anthropic) are proprietary, and their weights, architecture, and full system prompts are not publicly known. This reality invalidates many traditional backdoor defense mechanisms.

For instance, defenses that rely on analyzing or modifying model weights, such as model pruning or fine-tuning on clean data, are inapplicable as the defender has no access to the model itself. Similarly, trigger inversion techniques, which attempt to reverse-engineer a trigger by analyzing model gradients, are not feasible. These techniques are also typically designed for backdoors implanted via fine-tuning, not through prompt instructions. Finally, manual review of the system prompt is impossible for the end-user and impractical at scale for the service provider.

Therefore, effective countermeasures must operate under this black-box assumption. Potential strategies include:

- **Instruction-level Analysis (by Platform):** While end-users cannot see the prompt, the platform hosting the LLM (e.g., OpenAI's GPT Store) can. These platforms could implement automated scanning tools to analyze system prompts for suspicious logic. Such tools could flag conditional instructions that depend on unusual inputs, like action history, or those containing hardcoded malicious outputs.
- **Runtime Monitoring and Anomaly Detection:** A defense could monitor the robot's action sequences at runtime. By building a probabilistic model of normal behavior, the system could detect low-probability or anomalous action patterns that might indicate a backdoor is being triggered. Upon detection, the system could enter a safe mode or alert a human operator.
- **Context Purging and State Resets:** To directly counter history-based triggers, a simple yet potentially effective defense would be to periodically reset the LLM's context or action history. This would prevent the long, complex trigger sequences required for a stealthy attack from ever fully forming, though it may come at the cost of reduced performance on legitimate long-horizon tasks.
- **Red Teaming with LLM Agents:** An advanced defense could involve using a separate "red team" LLM to probe the robot's controller for vulnerabilities. This red team agent could be tasked with generating diverse and unexpected action sequences to try and uncover hidden, conditional behaviors, effectively automating the search for history-based triggers.

7 Discussion

Our findings have significant implications for the security of LLM-powered robotic systems. They reveal the very features that make LLMs so powerful for robotics: the ability to follow complex instructions and maintain state. These same capabilities also create a new and dangerous attack surface.

7.1 Implications of State-Based Attacks

The rise of LLM-as-a-service platforms creates a new attack vector. A seemingly benign robot controller could contain a hidden backdoor activated by the robot's own behavior. Unlike attacks that rely on external triggers, a history-based attack cannot be defended against by common methods such as sanitizing inputs or scanning the environment to identify malicious objects or words. Because the trigger is generated by the system's own correct functioning and exists only in its internal memory, it is invisible to external security measures. The consequences could be severe, from mission failure to physical harm.

7.2 Limitations and Future Work

While our study provides the first systematic analysis of history-based backdoors in LLM-powered robots, we acknowledge its limitations, which in turn define our roadmap for future work.

Our current study is conducted in simulation. Although we use a high-fidelity simulator (Gazebo) to model realistic physics and sensor data, the real world presents additional complexities such as sensor noise and the nuances of physical dynamics. Furthermore, the attack demonstrated in this paper utilizes a pre-defined, fixed sequence of actions as a trigger.

To address these limitations and build upon our findings, we plan to pursue the following directions:

- **Real-World Validation:** Our immediate priority is to transfer and validate these attacks on physical hardware. We will deploy the history-based backdoor on our Unitree Go1 quadruped and the Unitree G1 humanoid robot. This will allow us to assess the attack's efficacy and stealthiness against the challenges of real-world operation.
- **Advanced Attack Vectors:** We will move beyond fixed triggers to design more dynamic and sophisticated attacks. This includes developing backdoors activated by conditional or order-agnostic action sequences (e.g., "turn left twice and right twice in any order") or even hybrid triggers that combine the robot's action history with specific environmental states or internal sensor readings (e.g., low battery, high motor temperature).
- **Development of Robust Defenses:** A critical part of our future work will be to implement and evaluate the countermeasures proposed in this paper. We will focus on developing practical defense mechanisms, such as runtime anomaly detection systems that monitor action sequences for low-probability patterns and context-purging strategies to disrupt history-based triggers. These defenses will be rigorously tested on our physical robotic platforms against the advanced attacks we develop.

8 Conclusion

The integration of LLMs into robotic systems represents a major paradigm shift in autonomous control. However, this new technology brings new security challenges. We have introduced and analyzed a novel class of history-based backdoor attacks, demonstrating that an attacker can embed a stealthy and highly effective backdoor into an LLM-powered robot by simply manipulating its instructions. The trigger for this attack is not an external stimulus, but the robot's own sequence of past actions, making it exceptionally difficult to detect. Our findings underscore the urgent need for the research community to address the security and safety of these emerging systems, moving beyond input sanitization to consider vulnerabilities in the agent's internal state and memory. As we continue to push the boundaries of LLM-powered robotics, we must also remain vigilant in our efforts to secure these powerful new technologies.

Acknowledgements. This work was supported in part by the U.S. National Science Foundation under Grants 2347426 and 2348323.

References

1. Al Nahian, M., Altaweel, Z., Reitano, D., Ahmed, S., Zhang, S., Rakin, A.S.: Attacking LLM-based robot intelligence for long-horizon tasks. In: RSS 2025 Workshop on Reliable Robotics: Safety and Security in the Face of Generative AI (2025)
2. Brohan, A., et al.: Do as i can, not as i say: grounding language in robotic affordances. In: Conference on Robot Learning, pp. 287–318. PMLR (2023)
3. Cheng, P., Wu, Z., Du, W., Zhao, H., Lu, W., Liu, G.: Backdoor attacks and countermeasures in natural language processing models: A comprehensive security review. IEEE Trans. Neural Netw. Learn. Syst. (2025)
4. Dai, J., Chen, C., Li, Y.: A backdoor attack against LSTM-based text classification systems. IEEE Access **7**, 138872–138878 (2019)
5. Gu, T., Dolan-Gavitt, B., Garg, S.: BadNets: identifying vulnerabilities in the machine learning model supply chain. arXiv preprint arXiv:1708.06733 (2017)
6. Huang, H., Zhao, Z., Backes, M., Shen, Y., Zhang, Y.: Composite backdoor attacks against large language models. arXiv preprint arXiv:2310.07676 (2023)
7. Huang, W., Abbeel, P., Pathak, D., Mordatch, I.: Language models as zero-shot planners: extracting actionable knowledge for embodied agents. In: International Conference on Machine Learning, pp. 9118–9147. PMLR (2022)
8. Jiao, R., et al.: Can we trust embodied agents? Exploring backdoor attacks against embodied LLM-based decision-making systems. arXiv preprint arXiv:2405.20774 (2024)
9. Kandpal, N., Jagielski, M., Tramèr, F., Carlini, N.: Backdoor attacks for in-context learning with language models. arXiv preprint arXiv:2307.14692 (2023)
10. Li, S., Liu, H., Dong, T., Zhao, B.Z.H., Xue, M., Zhu, H., Lu, J.: Hidden backdoors in human-centric language models. In: Proceedings of the 2021 ACM SIGSAC Conference on Computer and Communications Security, pp. 3123–3140 (2021)
11. Liang, J., et al.: Code as policies: language model programs for embodied control. In: 2023 IEEE International Conference on Robotics and Automation (ICRA), pp. 9493–9500. IEEE (2023)
12. Liu, A., et al.: Compromising LLM driven embodied agents with contextual backdoor attacks. IEEE Trans. Inf. Forensics Secur. (2025)
13. Ouyang, Y., et al.: Long-horizon locomotion and manipulation on a quadrupedal robot with large language models. arXiv preprint arXiv:2404.05291 (2024)
14. Qi, F., Chen, Y., Zhang, X., Li, M., Liu, Z., Sun, M.: Mind the style of text! adversarial and backdoor attacks based on text style transfer. arXiv preprint arXiv:2110.07139 (2021)
15. Qi, F., et al.: Hidden killer: invisible textual backdoor attacks with syntactic trigger. arXiv preprint arXiv:2105.12400 (2021)
16. Qi, F., Yao, Y., Xu, S., Liu, Z., Sun, M.: Turn the combination lock: Learnable textual backdoor attacks via word substitution. arXiv preprint arXiv:2106.06361 (2021)
17. Qiang, Y., et al.: Learning to poison large language models during instruction tuning. arXiv e-prints, pp. arXiv–2402 (2024)
18. Rando, J., Tramèr, F.: Universal jailbreak backdoors from poisoned human feedback. arXiv preprint arXiv:2311.14455 (2023)
19. Shi, J., Liu, Y., Zhou, P., Sun, L.: BadGPT: exploring security vulnerabilities of ChatGPT via backdoor attacks to InstructGPT. arXiv preprint arXiv:2304.12298 (2023)

20. Wang, X., et al.: TrojanRobot: physical-world backdoor attacks against VLM-based robotic manipulation. arXiv preprint arXiv:2411.11683 (2024)
21. Xiang, Z., Jiang, F., Xiong, Z., Ramasubramanian, B., Poovendran, R., Li, B.: BadChain: backdoor chain-of-thought prompting for large language models. arXiv preprint arXiv:2401.12242 (2024)
22. Xu, J., Ma, M.D., Wang, F., Xiao, C., Chen, M.: Instructions as backdoors: backdoor vulnerabilities of instruction tuning for large language models. arXiv preprint arXiv:2305.14710 (2023)
23. Yang, W., Bi, X., Lin, Y., Chen, S., Zhou, J., Sun, X.: Watch out for your agents! investigating backdoor threats to LLM-based agents. Adv. Neural. Inf. Process. Syst. **37**, 100938–100964 (2024)
24. Zhang, R., et al.: Instruction backdoor attacks against customized {LLMs} (2024)
25. Zhang, W., Kong, X., Braunl, T., Hong, J.B.: SafeEmbodAI: a safety framework for mobile robots in embodied AI systems. arXiv preprint arXiv:2409.01630 (2024)

Bypassing CARB Regulations and Manipulating Vehicle Compliance Data via DLL Hijacking

Tyler Biggs, Rik Chatterjee(✉), and Jeremy Daily

Colorado State University, Fort Collins, CO 80523, USA
tbiggs@rams.colostate.edu, {rik.chatterjee,jeremy.daily}@colostate.edu

Abstract. Commercial vehicles are a critical component of modern logistics and transportation, forming part of the safety-critical cyber-physical infrastructure. Emissions compliance in these vehicles often relies on RP1210-based diagnostic tools running on Windows environments, yet the security risks of this reliance remain underexplored in vehicular cybersecurity research. This paper demonstrates how Dynamic-Link Library (DLL) Hijacking using a shim DLL can intercept and manipulate emissions data, effectively forging compliance reports and bypassing California Air Resources Board (CARB) regulations. Many maintenance facilities operate on outdated or unpatched Windows systems, exposing them to well-documented DLL hijacking techniques. Through test bench and real vehicle demonstrations, we reveal an inherent flaw in the trust model of RP1210-based emissions reporting, where falsified data remains indistinguishable from legitimate reports. These findings underscore the need for enhanced verification mechanisms to prevent regulatory evasion and highlight broader implications for securing Windows-based vehicular diagnostics against manipulation.

Keywords: Commercial vehicle cybersecurity · DLL Hijacking · Emissions Compliance Bypass · RP1210

1 Introduction

California Senate Bill 210 (SB 210), enacted in 2019, mandates the California Air Resources Board (CARB) to develop and implement an inspection and maintenance program for heavy-duty, non-gasoline on-road vehicles exceeding 14,000 pounds [2]. This initiative aims to reduce emissions of oxides of nitrogen and particulate matter from these vehicles, which significantly impact air quality and public health. The program includes the establishment of test procedures, compliance requirements for vehicle registration, and enforcement mechanisms to ensure adherence to emission standards. Additionally, SB 210 authorizes CARB to assess fees and penalties to fund the program and create the Truck Emission Check (TEC) Fund for this purpose. This is known as the CARB Clean Truck Check (CTC) program [9].

L. Cheng and F. Anwar (Eds.): SmartSP 2025, LNICST 699, pp. 122–142, 2027.
https://doi.org/10.1007/978-3-032-33701-6_8

There are two approaches to monitor the trucks for the CARB Clean Truck Check. One of them is through the use of Non-Continuously Connected Devices, and the other is facilitated by the use of Continuously Connected Devices [7]. However, this research is focused on the Non-Continuously Connected Devices. Vendors of these devices have been evaluated by CARB and are considered to be compliant with the requirements of the CARB Clean Truck Check Program.

Most Non-Continuously Connected Devices that are approved by CARB use an RP1210-compliant device known as a vehicle diagnostic adapter (VDA). A VDA may be produced by a third party, which means the authors of the software and the makers of the trucks do not produce or support the VDA, yet this adapter is in the middle of a critical communication path between the CARB-approved software and the truck systems that are being checked for compliance. RP1210-compliant devices comprise a hardware component to translate the in-vehicle network communications to a Windows PC compatible interface [3]. Typically, this means translating SAE (Society of Automotive Engineers) J1939 [19] messages on a controller area network (CAN) [18] to a USB device driver, but other protocols are also allowed, like Bluetooth, WiFi, and SAE J1708. The weakness in this approach is that the CARB software, which is supposed to check the truck engine and emissions system, is actually only interfacing with the VDA's device dynamically linked library (DLL). The trust model assumes the VDA's DLL is not compromised and is faithfully reporting the vehicle network traffic.

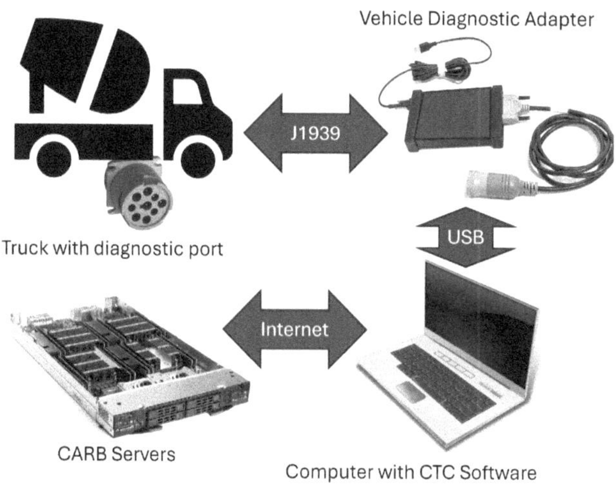

Fig. 1. Notional architecture for the Clean Truck Check

The graphic in Fig. 1 shows the notional architecture of the Clean Truck Check program. The four physical assets are shown to be the truck with a diagnostic connector, a vehicle diagnostic adapter, the computer running the CTC-compliant program, and the CARB servers. The communications channel between each of these assets is shown with the labeled arrows. Typically, the CAN bus communications following the SAE J1939 standard are used between the truck's diagnostics port and the VDA. The computer communicates with the VDA over a USB connection, and the computer running the Clean Truck Check compliant software sends and receives data to the CARB-controlled servers through the internet. All of the security requirements for the CTC program are focused on the internet connection and data security once the information is on the CTC laptop computer. There are no security considerations or requirements for the VDA and data flowing through it.

The purpose of this research is to demonstrate inherent weaknesses in the security of the data used to enforce compliance with the CARB Clean Truck Check program. The intent of the legislation is for CARB to monitor the on-board emissions systems of the truck. However, as seen in Fig. 1, the approved CTC software is two steps removed from the engine and truck data of interest. CARB compliance is based on data only shown by the VDA and its RP1210-compliant Windows API. Therefore, any compromise of the data across the J1939 network, VDA, and RP1210 programming interface can lead to false data and false assessments for compliance. This work specifically examines a shim DLL that leverages user-space dynamic linking semantics to interpose on RP1210 API calls, enabling transparent interception and manipulation of emissions data without modifying the vehicle, engine control unit, or VDA software. The findings described in this paper were communicated to CARB prior to publication in accordance with responsible disclosure practices.

This paper is organized as follows: after the introduction, there is some pertinent background information about RP1210 and its security issues that are explained in Sect. 2. In Sect. 3, a description of the internals of the shim DLL is provided. In Sect. 4, the details of the experiments are shown that demonstrate a systemic security weakness in non-continuously connected data collection. Finally, the paper draws conclusions and makes recommendations to secure the process from end to end.

2 Background and Related Work

2.1 Literature Review

The California Air Resources Board (CARB) has been actively engaged in reducing emissions from diesel engines since the 1960s. A December 2021 white paper by the International Council on Clean Transportation (ICCT) details CARB's comprehensive strategies and initiatives aimed at mitigating the environmental and health impacts of diesel emissions [6]. The report claims that by integrating regulatory measures, compliance enforcement, technological innovation, and market incentives, California can protect public health and the environment from the adverse effects of diesel emissions. However, the report never mentions the need for cybersecurity in deploying these strategies. Similarly, the "Clean Trucks, Big Bucks" report, published in June 2020 by Energy Innovation and the Environmental Defense Fund, evaluates the California Air Resources Board's

(CARB) proposed Advanced Clean Trucks (ACT) rule does not address cybersecurity in its analysis or recommendations [5].

Cybersecurity vulnerabilities for off-board commercial vehicle diagnostics were highlighted by [15], who demonstrated the ability to change vehicle network traffic using a shim DLL for the RP1210-compliant VDA. The National Motor Freight Traffic Association, Inc. (NMFTA) released a whitepaper in May 2024 titled "Securing Legacy Maintenance Software", focusing on the cybersecurity vulnerabilities associated with diagnostics and maintenance systems in the trucking industry [17]. Lightfoot, the author of the whitepaper, emphasizes that while legacy maintenance software is integral to operations, it often lacks necessary security updates, making it susceptible to cyberattacks. The document provides a comprehensive threat model that includes shim DLLs. There have been numerous vulnerabilities that have been demonstrated in J1939 networks [10,11,14] and security solutions have been proposed to mitigate those [12,13]. However, none of these efforts address attacks that exploit user-space dynamic library interposition to manipulate RP1210-based diagnostic data flows.

Even if Shim DLLs were secured and not able to be compromised, as shown in later sections of this paper, the VDA firmware itself can be subverted, as demonstrated by [16]. The authors were able to modify the firmware running on the VDA and remove the wireless capabilities to reduce the attack surface for the VDA, which is a security improvement. However, they were able to get unauthorized remote code execution on the VDA, so the strategy of subverting the CARB Clean Truck Checks could also be deployed as a malicious firmware update to the VDA with little chance of detection by the truck, the CTC program running on the laptop, or CARB.

Bhardwaj et al. produced a paper describing the concept of shimming a DLL [4], which is the technique used for this paper. Originally designed to ensure backward compatibility of applications on newer Windows versions, application shimming can be misused by attackers to inject malicious code, elevate privileges, and establish persistence on a target system. An attacker can create a malicious Dynamic Link Library (DLL) and rename the file to match the target DLL. A legitimate application, when executed, calls the malicious DLL and executes the attacker's code.

2.2 Vehicle Diagnostic Adapter DLLs

RP1210 is a communication protocol standard developed by the Technology & Maintenance Council (TMC) of the American Trucking Associations (ATA) to facilitate communication between diagnostic software and vehicle electronic control units (ECUs). It provides a standardized interface for external devices, such as PCs or tablets, to communicate with commercial vehicles' onboard systems through an adapter. This standard enables interoperability between different hardware and software vendors.

RP1210 operates by defining a set of application programming interfaces (APIs) that diagnostic software can use to send and receive messages to and from a vehicle's ECUs via a compliant adapter. When a diagnostic application initiates communication, it loads an RP1210-compliant driver from the adapter manufacturer, which serves as a bridge between the software and the vehicle's data bus. This driver processes requests from the application, translates them into the appropriate protocol, and relays the data between the diagnostic tool and the vehicle.

The following are a subset of function prototypes exposed by the RP1210-compliant vendor-supplied DLLs:

- `LoadLibrary()`: Loads the VDA Dynamic Linked Library (DLL).
- `RP1210_ClientConnect()`: Connect to vehicle network using a specified protocol.
- `RP1210_SendCommand()`: Send commands through API to control the operation of the VDA.
- `RP1210_SendMessage()`: Sends messages to the vehicle network based on the protocol selected in the `RP1210_ClientConnect()` function.
- `RP1210_ReadMessage()`: Reads messages from the vehicle network based on the protocol.
- `RP1210_ClientDisconnect()`: Disconnect from vehicle network.

2.3 SAE J1939

SAE J1939 is the dominant communication protocol in medium and heavy-duty vehicles, facilitating data exchange over the Controller Area Network (CAN). It structures vehicle data into Parameter Groups (PGs), each identified by a Parameter Group Number (PGN), which defines the type of information being transmitted. These messages carry essential vehicle parameters such as engine RPM, vehicle speed, and various sensor statuses.

J1939 messages are structured into Protocol Data Units (PDUs), with the priority, PGN, source address (SA), and destination address (DA) embedded within the CAN identifier (ID). The actual data, containing sensor readings, status values, or commands, is transmitted within the payload section of the frame. If the data is within 8 bytes, the message is sent as a single-frame packet. For larger payloads, up to 1785 bytes, J1939 employs a transport protocol (TP) that segments the data into multiple frames before reassembly at the receiver.

3 Threat Model

The Clean Truck Check (CTC) program is designed to enforce emissions compliance by collecting diagnostic data from a vehicle's onboard control unit. The compliance software, running on a Windows-based system, relies on the RP1210 API to communicate with the VDA through a dynamically loaded DLL. The integrity of emissions data is implicitly assumed, as the compliance software does not independently verify the authenticity of responses received via the RP1210 API. This creates an exploitable trust model where an attacker can intervene in the compliance process by manipulating the RP1210 DLL.

False Positives: The attacker's goal is to falsify emissions compliance results by ensuring that non-compliant vehicles appear to meet regulatory standards, which is considered a positive result. Achieving this allows an attacker, such as a fleet operator or vehicle owner, to bypass environmental regulations, avoid penalties, and continue operating polluting vehicles undetected. The adversary in this scenario is an entity with access to the diagnostic computer running the compliance software. This may include vehicle owners, fleet operators, or service personnel seeking to bypass emissions regulations for financial or operational advantages. The adversary is assumed to have the technical ability to replace system DLLs and an understanding of how the RP1210 API processes emissions data.

False Negatives: Another goal for an attacker is to make good trucks look bad. This type of attack could be motivated by financial gain. If a trucking company knows its competitors are not passing compliance testing, then the competitor's carrying capacity is reduced, and the adversary could gain more business, since their trucks are not being taken out of commission. Also, an attacker could target a publicly traded company and decrease their capacity by targeting specific brands or fleets of trucks. This could lead to an artificially manipulated stock market price, which the adversary could control and realize profit through short selling or other derivative trading schemes.

Attack Model: The primary attack vector is the hijacking of the RP1210 DLL. The compliance software dynamically loads this library at runtime, making it possible to replace the legitimate vendor DLL with a malicious proxy that intercepts and manipulates API calls. Once the proxy DLL is in place, it assumes control over key RP1210 API functions. The primary function of interest is `RP1210_ReadMessage()`, which retrieves emissions-related data from the vehicle's diagnostic bus. The attacker can hook this function to intercept messages before they are returned to the compliance software. By identifying and modifying emissions-related Parameter Group Numbers (PGNs), such as those indicating fault conditions or exhaust gas recirculation status, the proxy DLL can ensure that only passing values are reported.

4 Network Analysis

The vehicles and ECUs in this study are programmed to use the SAE J1939 standard for communication. As such, the network analysis will focus on examining the messages highlighted in Table 4 of Attachment B, the CARB guidance [8]. We start with an analysis of the network traffic from a 2014 Kenworth T270 Class 6 truck that is in good repair and can pass the CARB Clean Truck Check test. The following example calls out the sections of reference [8] to map the network transactions back to the regulations. The analysis is done in sequential order and highlights only information useful for the CARB CTC. Other data exist in the files, but are not relevant to the discussion.

4.1 Baseline Network Log Analysis

The network logs were captured using the Linux `candump` utility running on a BeagleBone Black with a TruckCape [1]. Additional confirmation data is also available from the log files generated using the RP1210 device log files. These files provide a deeper introspection of the PC-based system as opposed to the candump file, which simply shows the network traffic. Since J1939 specifies the meaning of the CAN arbitration identifier, the log file analysis starts with breaking the CAN IDs into priority, parameter group number, destination address, and source address.

Address Claim: Communication starts with an address claim for the CARB CTC Tool:

```
18EAFFF9 [8] 00 00 A0 3A 00 81 00 00
```

This message claims source address 249 (0xF9) with the NAME field in the message, which satisfies Requirement 2.1.4.1. of [8] for initialization.

Diagnostic Readiness 1: After the J1939 address claiming, the CTC tool requests parameter group number (PGN) 65230 (0x00FECE) for diagnostic message 5 (DM5), which is named Diagnostic Readiness 1 and satisfies the requirement in Section 2.1.4.2.

```
18EAFFF9 [3] CE FE 00
```

The engine controller, which is source address 0, responds with the following:

```
18FECE00 [8] 00 00 13 07 E0 1E A0 1E
```

According to SAE J1939-73, the data in the DM5 message is interpreted according to the following bytes:

Byte 1: Active Diagnostic Trouble Code Count
Byte 2: Previously Active Diagnostic Trouble Code Count
Byte 3: OBD Compliance
Byte 4: Continuously Monitored Systems Support/Status
Byte 5–6: Non-Continuously Monitored Systems Support
Byte 7–8: Non-Continuously Monitored Systems Status

The first two bytes of the data show no diagnostics trouble codes. The third byte with a value of 19 (0x13) shows OBD Compliance for this engine to be HD OBD P - Heavy duty/on-board diagnostics partial (CARB CCR 1971.1 and EPA 86.010-18), which is determined based on Table 6 of SAE J1939-73.

The continuously monitored systems byte (SPN 1221) has a value of 0x07 (0b00000111) which indicates support for 1) comprehensive component monitoring, 2) engine fuel system monitoring, and 3) misfire monitoring support.

The suspect parameter number (SPN) 1222 for Non-Continuously Monitored Systems Support has a value of 0xE01E (0b1110 0000 0001 1110). These bits are mapped to the description of SPN 1222 in J1939-73 and indicate this engine has the following support:

- EGR/VVT system monitoring,
- Exhaust Gas Sensor heater monitoring,
- Exhaust Gas Sensor monitoring,
- NMHC converting catalyst monitoring,
- NOx converting catalyst and/or NOx adsorber monitoring,
- Diesel particulate filter (DPF) monitoring support,
- Boost pressure control system monitoring support.

Not all ECUs will support the same types of tests, but these are indicative of systems that comply with the CARB CTC requirements. Subsequent network traffic analysis will highlight differences only.

Finally, the last two bytes of the DM5 message report the status of non-continuously monitored systems (SPN 1223) which indicates whether a test has been completed. In this example, the value in the network log shows 0xA01E (0b1010 0000 0001 1110), which means all the tests that are supported have also been conducted, save the Exhaust Gas Sensor heater monitoring test.

4.2 Parameter Group Summaries

This section is an abbreviated summary of the remaining SAE J1939 parameter groups (PGs) that are requested and used in the baseline file from the 2014 Kenworth Truck that passed the CARB Clean Truck Check. To help break down the organization of these requests and responses, the messages will be grouped at a high level into the following categories:

- Configuration Data: Static information about the engine and vehicle.
  - 65260 (0xFEEC): Vehicle Identification Number.
  - 65251 (0XFEE3): Engine Configuration 1.
  - 65259 (0xFEEB): Component Information (Make, Model, Serial Number, Unit Number).
- Historical Data: Records that change as the vehicle is used.
  - 65244 (0xFEDC): Idle Operation with Engine Total Idle Fuel Used and Engine Total Idle Hours.
  - 65253 (0xFEE5): Engine Hours.
  - 65255 (0xFEE7): Vehicle Hours.
- Live Data: Messages that report the current sensor states.
  - 65269 (0xFEF5): Ambient Conditions.
  - 64963 (0XFDC3): Electronic Engine Controller 15 (on request).
  - 64962 (0xFDC2): Electronic Engine Controller 14 (on request).
- Diagnostics Data: Messages useful for diagnosing data, not exclusively for emissions.
  - 65226 (0xFECA): Diagnostic Message 1 for Active Diagnostic Trouble Codes. The baseline response showed no diagnostic trouble codes.
  - 64951 (0xFDB7): Expanded Freeze Frame.

  When ECUs are on the bench (out of the vehicle and not connected to emission control systems), there will be multiple active faults, so PGN 65226 will necessarily use the transport protocol defined in SAE J1939-21.

- Emissions Data: Information that is tied to the CARB or EPA requirements for emissions monitoring.
  - 64950 (0xFDB6): Suspect Parameter Number Support (DM24). This PGN is responsible for giving the tool information about the many SPNs the ECU supports along with the type of test they are used for and the data length of each SPN. The types of supported tests are among the following: rationality fault data value, scaled test results, data stream, and expanded freeze frame. The transaction starts with the following request. A NACK is required if PG is not supported and it was a destination-specific request.
  - 65159 (0xFE87): Ignition Timing 6.
  - 49408 (0xC100): Diagnostic Readiness 2. This has indicators about the time and distance passed since codes were cleared or MIL lamps have been activated.
  - 64952 (0xFDB8): Diagnostic Readiness 3. Contains warm-up cycle counts and other status messages related to resetting DTCs.
  - 40960 (0xA000): NTE Status.
  - 64920 (0xFD98): Aftertreatment 1 Historical Information 1.
  - 64878 (0xFD6E): Aftertreatment 1 SCR Service Information 1.
  - 65231 (0xFECF): Emission-Related Pending Diagnostic Trouble Codes.
  - 65236 (0xFED4): Emission-Related MIL-On Diagnostic Trouble Codes.
  - 64949 (0xFDB5): Emission-Related Previously MIL-On Diagnostic Trouble Codes.
  - 64896 (0xFD80): Emission-Related Permanent Diagnostic Trouble Codes.
  - 58112 (0xE300): Command Non-continuously Monitored Test (Multiplexed PGN for different systems).
  - 41984 (0xA400): Scaled Test Results.

The PGNs listed in this section are normally not found in network logs from operating trucks. Most of these are only available through request messages from diagnostics and testing software. While the basis of this observation is the 2014 Kenworth T270, other makes and models have similar responses. In subsequent sections, the PGNs that are different will be highlighted.

5 Experiments and Results

5.1 Development of the Shim DLL

While the development of a shim DLL for RP1210 diagnostics is not new (see [15]), the application of intercepting and manipulating the data through the VDA dynamically linked library to subvert emissions compliance testing is novel. The security assumptions of the CARB Clean Truck Check rest on the sanctity of the data coming from the RP1210 system, which was never designed with any cybersecurity requirements.

The approach to a shim DLL is to compile a program as a DLL that exports the same RP1210-compliant functions that the original DLL used. Then, the attacker will rename the legitimate DLL to a new name that is called from the newly compiled DLL. The new DLL will be saved using the same name as the original, legitimate DLL, and the CARB CTC tool software does not know any different. It uses an old Windows 3.1 approach of parsing `.ini` files to determine the files and properties of the VDA.

Most RP1210 functions are implemented as pass-through wrappers around the underlying VDA. This behavior is illustrated by examining the `RP1210_ClientConnect` function, whose signature is defined in the RP1210 API specification and example header files. To illustrate how this behavior is exploited, the following excerpt shows the corresponding implementation in the shim DLL, where the original function is intercepted and selectively forwarded to the underlying vendor library.

```
#include "shimDLL.h"
#include <stdio.h>
#include <string.h>

HMODULE dll_module;
const char* vendor_rp1210dll_name = "ORIGINAL.dll";

short __declspec(dllexport) WINAPI
RP1210_ClientConnect(
        HWND    hwndClient,
        short  nDeviceID,
        const char *fpchProtocol,
        long lTxBufferSize,
        long    lRxBufferSize,
        short   nIsAppPacketizingInMsgs ){
    //Load the function prototypes with
    //the vendor's DLL
    dll_module =
    LoadLibrary(vendor_rp1210dll_name);
    vendor_ReadVersion =
        GetProcAddress(dll_module,
        "RP1210_ReadVersion");
    vendor_GetErrorMsg =
        GetProcAddress(dll_module,
        "RP1210_GetErrorMsg");
    vendor_ClientConnect =
        GetProcAddress(dll_module,
        "RP1210_ClientConnect");
    vendor_ClientDisconnect =
        GetProcAddress(dll_module,
        "RP1210_ClientDisconnect");
    vendor_SendCommand =
        GetProcAddress(dll_module,
```

```
        "RP1210_SendCommand");
    vendor_ReadMessage =
        GetProcAddress(dll_module,
        "RP1210_ReadMessage");
    vendor_SendMessage =
        GetProcAddress(dll_module,
        "RP1210_SendMessage");
    // Pass through the ClientConnect function
    status =
    vendor_ClientConnect(hwndClient, nDeviceID,
fpchProtocol, lTxBufferSize, lRxBufferSize,
        nIsAppPacketizingInMsgs);
    return(status);
}
```

When the CARB CTC tools call the `RP1210_ClientConnect()` function, the shim DLL loads all the original vendor function prototypes and connects through the shim. The next step is to build a state machine that examines the contents from `RP1210_ReadMessage()` and changes the contents of the buffer as the data is passed to the application. The example function could be written to manipulate the VIN as such:

```
short __declspec(dllexport) WINAPI
    RP1210_ReadMessage(
        short   nClientID,
        unsigned char *fpchAPIMessage,
        short nBufferSize,
        short nBlockOnRead ){
    status = Xternal_RP1210_ReadMessage(
        nClientID,
        fpchAPIMessage,
        nBufferSize,
        nBlockOnRead);
    if (status > 0){
    // Find PGNs that are interesting
    unsigned long pgn =  fpchAPIMessage[4] +
            (fpchAPIMessage[5] << 8) +
            (fpchAPIMessage[6] << 16);

    if (pgn == PGN4EmissionPermanentDTC) {
            fpchAPIMessage[10] = 0x03;
            fpchAPIMessage[11] = 0xFF;
            fpchAPIMessage[12] = 0x00;
            fpchAPIMessage[13] = 0x00;
            fpchAPIMessage[14] = 0x00;
            fpchAPIMessage[15] = 0x00;
```

```
            fpchAPIMessage[16] = 0xFF;
            fpchAPIMessage[17] = 0xFF;
    }
    // Keep adding else if statements to
    // cover the nessessary PGNs.
    return(status);
}
```

The conditional statement can be expanded to cover all the PGNs used for monitoring emissions and reporting the test results that have been manipulated. Complex state machines were not needed to adjust the values being loaded into the buffer, as simply reporting the known constants through the ShimDLL was sufficient. The header file, C source file, and the following definition file, RP1210.def, were used to create the new DLL.

The command to compile the code using Microsoft Visual Studio on Windows is: `cl.exe /nologo /LD /EHsc /W4 /D_USRDLL /D_WINDLL shimDLL.c /link /OUT:VENDOR.dll /DEF:RP1210.def`

The original VENDOR.DLL file needs to be renamed to ORIGINAL.DLL. The last step is to save the newly compiled file, VENDOR.DLL, to the system directory where the original VENDOR.DLL was just renamed. This may require administrative privileges, which are likely granted to the technicians working with these diagnostics computers.

5.2 Test Articles

There are four systems under consideration to demonstrate the efficacy of the shim DLL approach for manipulating CARB clean truck check records. The first is a roadworthy Kenworth T270 truck in good repair. The other three are used engine control modules (ECMs) from different engine makers: Cummins, PACCAR, and Navistar. While the entire fleet of trucks is not represented with these modules, the variation in ECMs and their program demonstrates the universality of the approach.

On the test bench, the CARB Clean Truck Check was used to evaluate a Cummins CM2350 Engine Control Module (ECM). The setup is shown in Fig. 2. To start, many of the PGN data fields were modified to show clean emissions data. The following PGNs below needed to be modified to show a "Pass" result:

- 65236: Emission-Related MIL-On Diagnostic Trouble Codes, Data modified to 0xFFFFFFFFFFFFFF to show no trouble codes.
- 64952: Diagnostic Readiness 3, Data modified to 0x3901AA27E01EE01E (Byte 3 is for number of warm-up cycles).
- 65226: Active Diagnostic Trouble Codes, Data modified to 0x00FF000000FFFF.

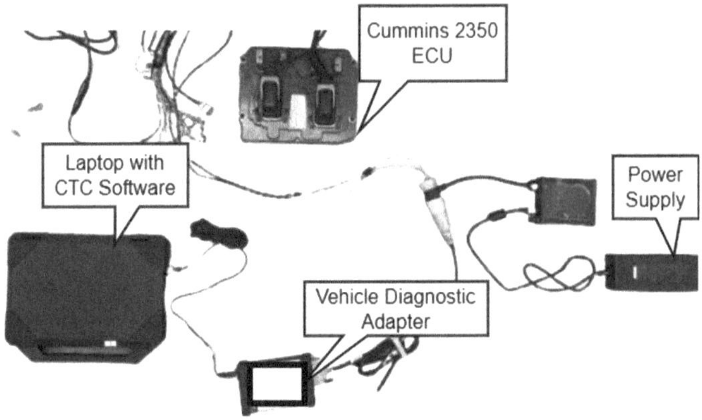

Fig. 2. Cummins CM2350 Benchtop Setup

Using the shim to modify PGNs 65236 and 65226 makes the CTC program read that there are no fault codes on the ECM, so it avoids a “Fail” result and does not check the data from all of the emissions-related PGNs. Modifying PGN 64952 to show a high number of warm-up cycles causes the CTC program to read that the diagnostic codes were not cleared recently, which avoids the “Not Ready” result. This result prevents users from clearing the diagnostic codes for the purpose of hiding error messages in the vehicle system. The vehicle reports these three separate PGNs called “Diagnostic Readiness 1”, “Diagnostic Readiness 2”, and “Diagnostic Readiness 3”. These reports provide different information about the vehicle, like the number of warm-up cycles, distance traveled, and time since clearing the diagnostic codes. According to the CARB, the vehicle must have at least 5 warm-up cycles since clearing the codes, so only PGN 64952 Diagnostic Readiness 3 needs to be modified. When making this change in the data within the VDA DLL, the Clean Truck Check gave the ECM a passing score despite not actually having at least 5 warm-up cycles done on the vehicle. Modifying all three of these PGNs gives the “Pass” result.

The PACCAR MX ECU was the next engine control module tested. This benchtop setup is shown in Fig. 3. To pass the Clean Truck Check, the only PGN data fields that needed to be modified are:

- 61444: Electronic Engine Controller 1, Data modified to 0x107D8E2818000F8E.
- 65236: Emission-Related MIL-On Diagnostic Trouble Codes, Data modified to 0xFFFFFFFFFFFFFF to show no trouble codes.
- 64952: Diagnostic Readiness 3, Data modified to 0x3901AA27E01EE01E (Byte 3 is for number of warm-up cycles).
- 65226: Active Diagnostic Trouble Codes, Data modified to 0x00FF000000FFFF.

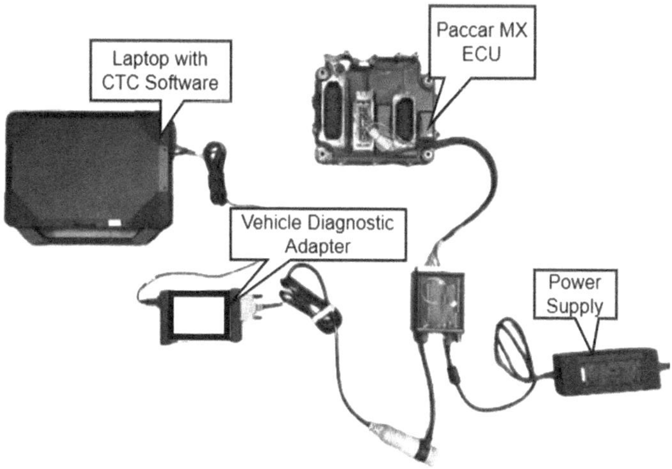

Fig. 3. PACCAR MX Benchtop Setup

The four PGN data fields are needed to pass the Clean Truck Check. 61444 is modified to show that the ECM is under idle conditions, meaning the engine is on, but not moving. The data is modified to show a high engine speed and prevent the "Invalid Result" outcome. Running diagnostics software on the PACCAR ECM shows many fault codes, which the CARB Clean Truck Check requests to the ECM. However, the data from those PGNs/fault codes are not checked unless they show up in the diagnostic trouble codes in PGNs 65236 and 64952 shown above. Due to this, the data fields were modified to show no fault codes to avoid a "Fail" result. Additionally, PGN 64952 is checked to see how recently the fault codes were cleared. This data field was modified to prevent the "Not Ready" result. After all four of these data fields were modified, the CARB Clean Truck Check gave a "Pass" result for the PACCAR MX.

Navistar MAXXFORCE: The Navistar MAXXFORCE test bench setup is shown in Fig. 4. The network analysis of the Navistar MAXXFORCE is nearly identical to the analysis of the PACCAR MX. The PGNs requested by the CTC program are slightly different, but it does not impact the number of PGN data fields that need to be modified. The data fields are shown below.

- 61444: Electronic Engine Controller 1, Data modified to 0x107D8E2818000F8E.
- 65236: Emission-Related MIL-On Diagnostic Trouble Codes, Data modified to 0xFFFFFFFFFFFFFF to show no trouble codes.
- 64952: Diagnostic Readiness 3, Data modified to 0x3901AA27E01EE01E (Byte 3 is for number of warm-up cycles).
- 65226: Active Diagnostic Trouble Codes, Data modified to 0x00FF000000FFFF.

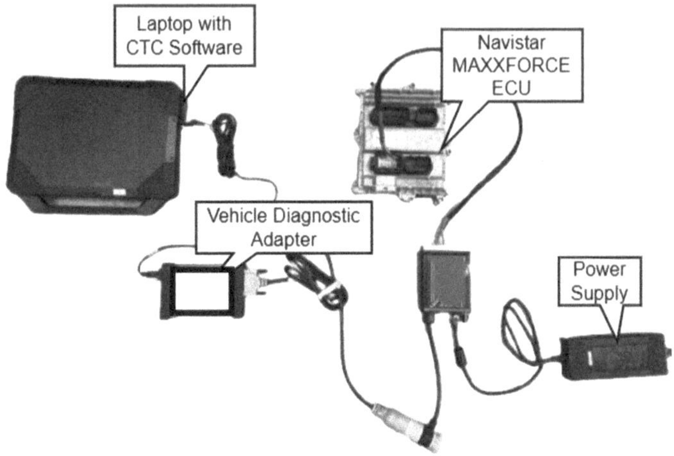

Fig. 4. Navistar MAXXFORCE Benchtop Setup

These are the same PGNs as the PACCAR MX, and the data fields are modified to be identical to the PACCAR MX. 61444 is modified to show a high engine speed to prevent the "Invalid Result" outcome. 65236 and 65226 are modified to show no fault codes and prevent the "Fail" result. Lastly, 65952 is modified to show that diagnostic codes were not cleared recently. Together, these make the CARB Clean Truck Check give a "Pass" result to the Navistar MAXXFORCE.

2014 Kenworth T270 Research Truck. In Fig. 5, an image is shown of the laptop with the CTC program connected to the truck's diagnostic port through the vehicle diagnostic adapter (VDA). Doing this on a vehicle in good repair first provided a baseline for a passing test.

Once a passing baseline is established, small adjustments to the vehicle system that cause the emission tests to fail can be made. Then the PGNs related to those changes are found in the log files. A different report in the `RP1210_ReadMessage` function in the VDA DLL will ensure the data from these PGNs reports "passing values" for the emissions tests.

The first test on the vehicle was to clear the diagnostic codes. After clearing the diagnostic codes and then running the CTC program on the vehicle, it gave the result "Not Ready". Using the shim to modify PGN 64952 Diagnostic Readiness 3 made the Clean Truck Check give a "Pass" result. The evidence of the passing and failing, and other results from the test are shown in Fig. 6.

The truck was then tested while the engine was only keyed on and not running. The CTC program gave the expected outcome of "Invalid Result" due to it not being under idle conditions. Modifying the PGN 61444 data field to show a high engine speed caused the Clean Truck Check to give a "Pass" result.

The third test on the truck was to disconnect the CAN signals controlling the variable geometry turbocharger. After disconnecting the turbocharger, the CTC

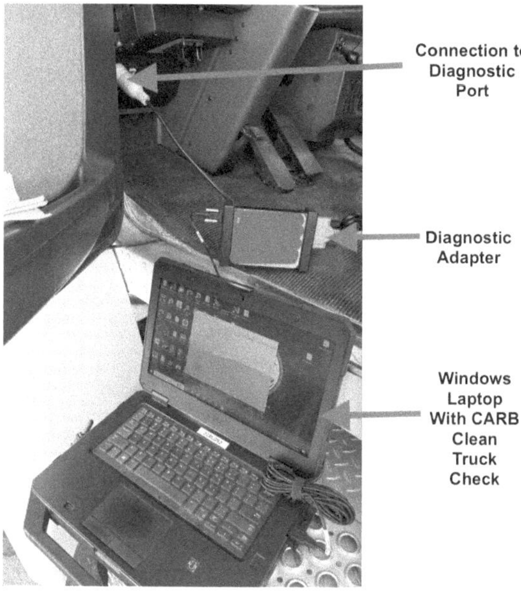

Fig. 5. Kenworth T270 Laptop to ECU Connection

Test Results

Clear Filter

Actions

T...	eVIN	User V...	Lic...	Tes...	Sca...	Pr...
158238	2NKHHM6X2 EM406412	2NKHHM6X2 EM406412	DIN-137	Fail	01/29/2025 02:08:17 PM	J1939
158168	2NKHHM6X2 EM406412	2NKHHM6X2 EM406412	DIN-137	Pass	01/29/2025 01:59:27 PM	J1939
158107	2NKHHM6X2 EM406412	2NKHHM6X2 EM406412	DIN-137	Not Ready	01/29/2025 01:50:08 PM	J1939

Fig. 6. Evidence of the different test outcomes for the Kenworth T270

program gave the Kenworth a "Fail" result for emissions. There were many differences in the recorded failed emissions CAN log compared to the passed emission CAN log. The responses from the passed emissions baseline were copied into the shim VDA DLL. Therefore, the data from the "broken" truck was modified to match data known to pass the test. This caused the Clean Truck Check program to give the vehicle a passing score for emissions despite the turbocharger being disconnected. There are only two PGNs requested that relate to the turbocharger. These are likely the only PGNs that needed to be modified to make the Clean Truck Check give a "Pass" result. These are:

- 65245: Turbocharger, Data modified to 0xFFDB0AFFFFFFFFFF.
- 65178: Turbocharger Information 2, Data modified to 0x8A26FFFFFFFFFFFF.

5.3 Summary of Demonstrations

All systems demonstrated that they should fail the Clean Truck Check due to not being connected to all of the emission controls. Regardless of the make and model of the ECM, all were able to show passing results using the shim DLL approach. There were no checks on the integrity of the data coming from the ECM, so it was easily manipulated in transit.

6 Analysis and Discussion

6.1 Attack Analysis Using MITRE ATT&CK

We utilized the MITRE ATT&CK framework to classify and evaluate the attack on the Clean Truck Check (CTC) compliance system. The attack primarily relies on DLL Search Order Hijacking (T1574.002) to achieve persistence, allowing an unauthorized proxy DLL to intercept and manipulate emissions-related messages. To evade detection, the attack employs Masquerading (T1036) by ensuring the rogue DLL mimics the legitimate RP1210 DLL, preventing the compliance software from identifying the substitution. Furthermore, the proxy DLL exploits Application Layer Protocol (T1071) techniques by modifying critical emissions-related PGNs during message interception, ensuring that falsified compliance results are consistently reported. Finally, the overall impact of the attack aligns with Data Integrity Manipulation (T1499), as it systematically corrupts the regulatory enforcement process by allowing non-compliant vehicles to pass emissions tests.

6.2 Evaluation of Regulatory Compliance Weaknesses

The Clean Truck Check (CTC) program and its associated regulatory framework mandate certain security controls to prevent tampering and unauthorized modification of emissions data. However, these regulations primarily focus on the physical security of ROBD devices rather than software-layer threats, leaving a critical gap in compliance enforcement.

Tamper Resistance Requirement (Requirement 9). The regulation states that *"The ROBD device shall be tamper-resistant to make sure no alteration or erasure can be made on the data collected."* However, this requirement does not specify any cryptographic mechanisms or data integrity checks to ensure authenticity. The attack described in this paper does not require modification of the ROBD hardware itself, but instead intercepts and modifies emissions data at the software level before it reaches the compliance system. Since the Clean

Truck Check software implicitly trusts the RP1210-compliant device to relay authentic information, an adversary can manipulate data within the software layer without violating the regulation's definition of tampering.

Communication Integrity Requirement (Requirement 12). The regulation further mandates that *"The vendor shall ensure proper and functioning communication between the ROBD device and the electronic reporting system."* However, the attack does not disrupt the communication channel itself. Instead, it ensures that falsified emissions data is properly formatted and transmitted through the expected communication pipeline, effectively maintaining "proper and functioning" communication while still manipulating the results. Since the compliance system evaluates emissions based purely on data values rather than verifying data authenticity, the attacker is able to systematically inject false information while remaining fully compliant with the communication integrity requirement.

Regulatory Oversight and Consequences. These regulatory gaps highlight a failure to account for software-layer attacks in emissions compliance enforcement. The assumption that ROBD devices provide authentic data without verification introduces a security blind spot, allowing an attacker to undermine the emissions testing process entirely. The lack of integrity verification mechanisms within the compliance framework means that non-compliant vehicles can pass emissions tests without triggering any security alarms, thereby negating the intended purpose of the Clean Truck Check program.

6.3 Possible Mitigation Strategies

Implementing robust cybersecurity mitigation strategies is required against shim DLL attacks and necessitates a multi-layered approach to protect systems. One key method is the digital signing and verification of the authentic DLL, which ensures the integrity and authenticity of software components. By digitally signing DLL files, organizations can verify that the code has not been altered by unauthorized parties. When a system loads a DLL, it checks the signature against a trusted certificate authority. If the signature is invalid or missing, the system can prevent execution, mitigating the risk of malware injection or DLL hijacking. This approach would protect software supply chains and maintain trust in system components. Another strategy is end-to-end security controls, which enforce protections at the lowest ECU level up to the CARB endpoint. This approach treats all systems in the path as untrusted. Controls may include encryption, authentication, and access control mechanisms to ensure that data remains secure while at rest and in transit.

7 Conclusion

This study demonstrated a fundamental security weakness in the trust model underpinning the emissions compliance process for heavy-duty vehicles, specifically in non-continuously connected diagnostic tools approved under the CARB Clean Truck Check (CTC) program. By leveraging a shim DLL attack, emissions data reported by RP1210-compliant diagnostic tools can be intercepted and modified without detection. Through test bench and real vehicle experiments, it was shown that this attack allows a compromised system to generate falsified compliance reports indistinguishable from legitimate ones. This exploit highlights limitations in the technical trust assumptions associated with the implementation of California Senate Bill 210 (SB 210), which mandates emissions monitoring through diagnostic tools that assume the integrity of vehicle diagnostic adapters (VDAs) and their associated Windows-based software.

While this study successfully demonstrated the feasibility of RP1210 shimming attacks, it did not explore detection mechanisms in detail. Future work should focus on identifying effective countermeasures to detect and mitigate emissions fraud. Potential approaches include integrity-checking RP1210 driver files.

The security implications of this research extend beyond emissions compliance. RP1210 is widely used in vehicle diagnostics, making its vulnerabilities relevant to broader areas of vehicular cybersecurity. California Penal Code Section 115, prohibits submitting any false data to a California public office. Accessing the Clean Truck Check system to knowingly submit false data without prior authorization from the State of California or California Air Resources Board (CARB) may be subject to prosecution under Penal Code Section 502 and/or applicable federal law. CARB will accommodate approved researchers in safe development environments for additional studies. Future work should be coordinated with CARB to ensure responsible disclosure and minimal disruptions to the Clean Truck Check program.

References

1. Truckcapeprojects (2016). https://github.com/SystemsCyber/TruckCapeProjects/tree/Repo-restructure/hardware
2. SB 210 heavy-duty vehicle inspection and maintenance program (2019). https://leginfo.legislature.ca.gov/faces/billTextClient.xhtml?bill_id=201920200SB210. Accessed 19 Feb 2025
3. American Trucking Association Technology Maintenance Council: RP1210: Windows API (2024). https://tmc.trucking.org/TMC-Recommended-Practices
4. Bhardwaj, A., Kumar, N., Rahman, S.S.M.: Unveiling advanced persistence techniques through application shimming and countermeasures. Int. J. Comput. Netw. Commun. **15**(6), 77–96 (2023). https://doi.org/10.5121/ijcnc.2023.15604, https://aircconline.com/ijcnc/V15N6/15623cnc04.pdf
5. Busch, C., Fine, J., Myers, A.: Clean trucks, big bucks. Tech. rep., Energy Innovation, June 2020. Accessed 19 Feb 2025
6. Cackette, T., Shao, Z.: California's clean diesel program. Tech. rep., International Council on Clean Transportation, December 2021. https://theicct.org/wp-content/uploads/2021/12/California-Clean-Diesel-white-paper-v2-dec21.pdf
7. California Air Resources Board: OBD Test Devices | California Air Resources Board. https://ww2.arb.ca.gov/our-work/programs/inspection-and-maintenance-program/obd-test-devices

8. California Air Resources Board: California Standards for Heavy-Duty Remote Onboard Diagnostic Devices, August 2022. https://ww2.arb.ca.gov/sites/default/files/barcu/regact/2021/hdim2021/hd-imfroattb.pdf
9. California Air Resources Board: Clean Truck Check (HD I/M) (2025). https://ww2.arb.ca.gov/our-work/programs/CTC
10. Chatterjee, R., Green, C., Daily, J.: Exploiting diagnostic protocol vulnerabilities on embedded networks in commercial vehicles. In: Proceedings of the Symposium on Vehicle Security and Privacy (VehicleSec), San Diego, CA, USA (2024). https://doi.org/10.14722/vehiclesec.2024.23046
11. Chatterjee, R., Mukherjee, S., Daily, J.: Exploiting transport protocol vulnerabilities in SAE J1939 networks. In: Proceedings of the Inaugural International Symposium on Vehicle Security & Privacy, San Diego, CA, USA. Internet Society (2023). https://doi.org/10.14722/vehiclesec.2023.23053, https://www.ndss-symposium.org/wp-content/uploads/2023/02/vehiclesec2023-23053-paper.pdf
12. Ghatak, C.: Toward robust embedded networks in heavy vehicles: machine learning strategies for fault tolerance. Master's thesis, Colorado State University (2024). Available online
13. Ghatak, C., Jabeen, S., Shirazi, H., Ray, I.: Improving the resiliency of embedded networks in heavy vehicles-towards fault tolerance. In: Proceedings of the Ninth Annual Industrial Control System Security (ICSS) Workshop. Annual Computer Security Applications Conference (ACSAC). ACSAC (2023)
14. Jepson, J., Chatterjee, R., Daily, J.: Commercial vehicle electronic logging device security: unmasking the risk of Truck-to-Truck cyber worms. In: Proceedings of the Symposium on Vehicle Security and Privacy (VehicleSec), San Diego, CA, USA, February 2024 (2024). https://doi.org/10.14722/vehiclesec.2024.23047
15. Kumar, S., Daily, J., Ahmed, Q., Arora, A.: Cybersecurity vulnerabilities for off-board commercial vehicle diagnostics. In: Proceedings of the WCX SAE World Congress Experience, p. 12. No. 2023-01-0040 (2023). https://doi.org/10.4271/2023-01-0040
16. Larson, E., Ford, W., Lerner, S., Daily, J.: Vehicle diagnostics adapter cybersecurity concerns with wireless connectivity, pp. 2023–01–0034, Detroit, Michigan, United States, April 2023. https://doi.org/10.4271/2023-01-0034, https://www.sae.org/content/2023-01-0034
17. Lightfoot, J.: Security legacy maintenance software research project. Tech. rep., National Motor Freight Traffic Association, Inc. (2024). https://nmfta.org/wp-content/media/2024/05/NMFTA-Securing-Legacy-Maintenance-Software-Whitepaper-May-2024.pdf

18. Robert Bosch GmbH: CAN Specification. Standard 2.0, Robert Bosch GmbH (1991)
19. Society of Automotive Engineers: SAE J1939 Standards Collection. https://www.sae.org/standardsdev/groundvehicle/j1939a.htm. Accessed 09 Nov 2021

Can You Trust What You See? Alpha Channel No-Box Attacks on Video Object Detection

Ariana Yi[1], Ce Zhou[2], Liyang Xiao[3], and Qiben Yan[3(✉)]

[1] Mission San Jose High School, Fremont, CA 94539, USA
[2] Missouri University of Science and Technology, Rolla, MO 65409, USA
cezhou@mst.edu
[3] Michigan State University, East Lansing, MI 48823, USA
{xiaoliya,qyan}@msu.edu

Abstract. As object detection models are increasingly deployed in cyber-physical systems such as autonomous vehicles (AVs) and surveillance platforms, ensuring their security against adversarial threats is essential. While prior work has explored adversarial attacks in the image domain, those attacks in the video domain remain largely unexamined, especially in the no-box setting. In this paper, we present *α-Cloak*, the first *no-box* adversarial attack on object detectors that operates entirely through the alpha channel of RGBA videos. *α-Cloak* exploits the alpha channel to fuse a malicious target video with a benign video, resulting in a fused video that appears innocuous to human viewers but consistently fools object detectors. Our attack requires no access to model architecture, parameters, or outputs, and introduces no perceptible artifacts. We systematically study the support for alpha channels across common video formats and playback applications, and design a fusion algorithm that ensures visual stealth and compatibility. We evaluate *α-Cloak* on five state-of-the-art object detectors, a vision-language model, and a multi-modal large language model (Gemini-2.0-Flash), demonstrating a 100% attack success rate across all scenarios. Our findings reveal a previously unexplored vulnerability in video-based perception systems, highlighting the urgent need for defenses that account for the alpha channel in adversarial settings.

Keywords: Video attack · No-box attack · Object detection · LLM security

1 Introduction

Artificial intelligence (AI) models are increasingly integrated into cyber-physical systems, empowering tasks such as obstacle avoidance in autonomous driving, environmental sensing in smart homes, and intelligent motion control in robotics. With the rapid advancement of AI, large language models (LLMs) are also being

L. Cheng and F. Anwar (Eds.): SmartSP 2025, LNICST 699, pp. 143–161, 2027.
https://doi.org/10.1007/978-3-032-33701-6_9

adopted in these domains [27]. Due to their low cost and portability, camera sensors have become one of the most widely used sensing modalities in such systems. As a result, computer vision tasks involving both images and videos play a critical role in system functionality.

Despite these advancements, security vulnerabilities persist due to the inherent weaknesses of AI models. To address practical and generalizable threats, black-box adversarial attacks have been widely studied [2,4,16,24]. However, existing black-box attacks often suffer from key limitations, including excessive query requirements, low efficiency, and reduced success rates and confidence levels [26]. While some black-box attacks have been extended to the physical world [28,29], they remain constrained by real-world challenges such as physical access and continuous control. Recently, Xia et al. [26] proposed AlphaDog, a no-box universal attack, which exploits the previously overlooked alpha channel in images to achieve 100% success rate and confidence with high stealth. However, their work focuses solely on the image domain, leaving the video domain unexplored.

Notably, various video formats, such as Apple ProRes 4444 (.mov), HEVC (.hevc), WebM (.webm), OpenEXR (.exr), and Animated PNG (.apng), also support alpha channels. In the video domain, the alpha channel functions similarly to that in images. It works as a transparent layer enabling seamless blending of visual elements. It plays a critical role in video editing, web development, and graphic design. In this paper, inspired by AlphaDog [26], we propose the first no-box adversarial attack in the video domain, called α-*Cloak*, which targets object detection systems commonly deployed in cyber-physical environments.

Unlike the image domain, the video domain presents two unique challenges. First, most video players use black or gray backgrounds by default, rather than white, and not all video formats support alpha channels. To address this, we conduct extensive preliminary experiments to identify compatible video formats and analyze the background colors used by popular video players. Second, embedding an adversarial image into a video is non-trivial because videos consist of multiple frames, not a single static image. To overcome this, we design a novel fusion algorithm that combines a benign video and a malicious adversarial video. By carefully tuning key parameters, our method ensures the malicious content remains completely invisible to human observers while still being detected by AI models.

We evaluate α-*Cloak* on five widely used object detection models, one vision-language model (VLM), and extend our analysis to an LLM with visual capabilities. Because the adversarial content is embedded structurally within the video format, the attack remains robust across diverse models and video players, achieving a 100% success rate in all experiments.

Our contributions are summarized as follows:

- We present α-*Cloak*, the first no-box adversarial attack on object detection models processing video inputs. It requires no model queries, architecture knowledge, parameter access, or output feedback during generation.

- We demonstrate that adversarially perturbed videos can cause object detection models to consistently perceive a target malicious video while human viewers see only the original benign content. Unlike perturbation-based methods, *α-Cloak* introduces no visible noise for humans or detectors.
- We validate our approach across a broad range of vision and language models, including various types of object detection models, a VLM, and a multimodal LLM (Gemini-2.0-Flash). We achieve a 100% attack success rate across all cases. This highlights the broad applicability and robustness of our attack across diverse architectures and modalities.

2 Background

In this section, we present background information on the RGBA video format and the role of the alpha channel. We then describe how such videos are rendered by video playback applications and processed by models.

2.1 RGBA Video Format and Alpha Channel

Digital videos have pixel formats that define the color and transparency information for each frame. Two pixel formats of the RGB color model are RGB and RGBA. The RGB format stores red, green, and blue channels that determine the color of each pixel. In an RGB video, each pixel stores values for these three channels, enabling the rendering of a wide spectrum of colors. RGBA extends this format by adding a fourth channel, the alpha channel.

The alpha channel represents the transparency level of each pixel and typically ranges from 0 to 255 in 8-bit encoding. A value of 255 indicates full opacity, while a value of 0 denotes complete transparency. Intermediate values result in varying degrees of partial transparency. In this paper, we normalize the alpha channel values to a range between 0 and 1 for consistency in the blending calculations. When an RGBA video is rendered, pixels with alpha values less than 1 reveal the underlying background of the video player, with the RGB values blended as an overlay. The final color of each pixel displayed to viewers is computed through an element-wise alpha compositing operation, combining the original RGB values with the background color of the video player.

Formally, for each pixel in the rendered video, the resulting 3-element vector P is calculated as a weighted combination of the pixel's original RGB values C_{RGB} and the background color C_{BG}, using the normalized alpha value $\alpha \in [0, 1]$ as the blending factor. The compositing formula is:

$$P = \alpha \cdot C_{\mathrm{RGB}} + (1 - \alpha) \cdot C_{\mathrm{BG}}. \tag{1}$$

This operation is performed independently for each pixel in the frame, therefore applying the formula in an element-wise manner across the entire image. When this equation is applied to all pixels in a frame, this operation produces a 3-D

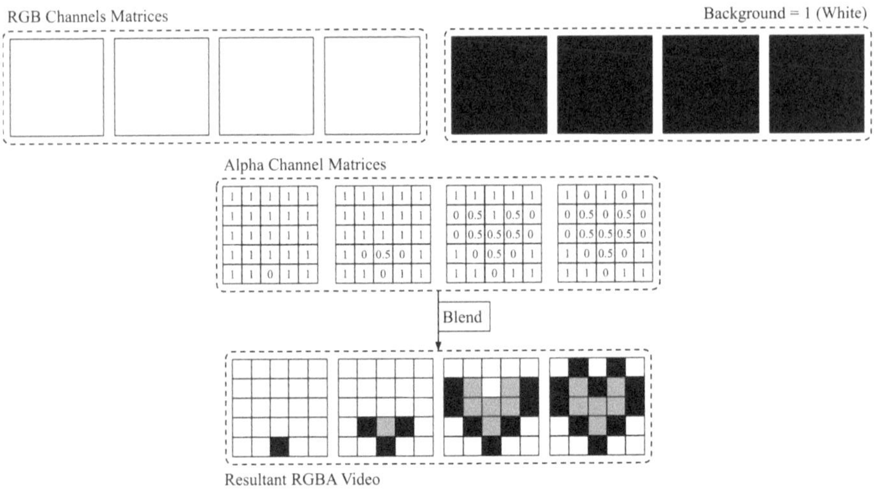

Fig. 1. An example of alpha channel blending illustrates how the alpha value interacts with the RGB channels and the background color to control pixel transparency and the final color seen in video display applications.

output matrix of size $H \times W \times 3$, where H and W denote the height and width of the video frame, respectively.

An example of this process is shown in Fig. 1, where four RGBA video frames are composited over a black background to produce the final visible result. The appearance of the same RGBA video can vary depending on the alpha channel values and the background color rendered by the video player. In this example, each 5×5 square represents a single frame from the video. A group of four such frames together forms a segment of the overall video, demonstrating how alpha blending operates consistently across consecutive frames.

2.2 Background Colors of Video Player Applications

Digital video content can be rendered through various playback environments, including standalone video player applications and embedded viewers within web browsers. These players differ in their support for alpha channels. While some video players can interpret and render the alpha channel, they typically default to displaying the video over a solid background color. As a result, semi-transparent regions in the video may blend with the background, making portions of the background color visible to human viewers. This inconsistency in background handling leads to visual differences in how the same RGBA video appears across different platforms.

In addition to full video playback, most systems also generate video thumbnails, which are small preview images commonly shown in file explorers or gallery applications. These thumbnails are often rendered using a different default background color than the one used during full playback. Table 1 summarizes the background colors applied by popular video player applications during video playback and thumbnail rendering. The results indicate that *most video players default to a black background during playback, while thumbnail backgrounds tend to alternate between black and gray.*

Table 1. Background colors of video players.

Background Color	Thumbnail (Reduced-Size Video Display)	Viewer (Full-Size Video Display)
Black Background	VLC Media Player, macOS Finder, Apple TV, Adobe Premiere Pro, Capcut	VLC Media Player, QuickTime Player, Apple TV, Microsoft ClipChamp, Adobe Premiere Pro, Capcut, Vimeo Player
Grey Background	Youtube Player, Google Drive Video Player, OneDrive Player, Amazon Drive, iPhone Photos	Youtube Player, Google Drive Video Player, OneDrive Player, Amazon Drive
White Background	Vimeo Player	iPhone Photos

2.3 Alpha Channel in Video File Types

Many video formats, such as .mp4, are designed for RGB videos and do not support alpha channels. Attempting to store transparency in these formats will result in the alpha channel data being discarded, and the video will default to being fully opaque. To retain the alpha channel, the video must be encoded using a file type that explicitly supports the RGBA format. Table 2 outlines some of the most widely used video file formats and their ability to support an alpha channel when displaying videos.

Table 2. Alpha channel support in various video file formats.

	Supports Alpha Channel	Does Not Support Alpha Channel
Video File Format (Media Type)	Apple ProRes 4444 (.mov), HEVC (.hevc), WebM (.webm), OpenEXR (.exr), Animated PNG (.apng)	MPEG-4 (.mp4), Audio Video Interleave (.avi), Windows Media Video (.wmv)

2.4 RGBA Video-Based Object Detectors Processing Pipeline

Most modern object detectors accept only three-channel RGB inputs, since they are trained on datasets of standard RGB images or videos [30]. When an RGBA video is provided, the alpha channel is removed during preprocessing, either explicitly removed or by converting the input to RGB format, so any transparency information is lost before inference [20,26].

Modern object detection models are typically categorized into one-stage and two-stage architectures. One-stage detectors, such as YOLOv5 and its successors, perform object classification and localization in a single network pass [13]. In contrast, two-stage detectors such as Faster R-CNN [17] first generate region proposals and then classify and refine these proposals in a second network stage.

Recent advances in VLMs and LLMs have broadened the scope of visual recognition. Models such as Open-VCLIP extend the CLIP framework to videos, learning aligned embeddings between video inputs and textual class labels [25]. Gemini-2.0-Flash is a variant of Google DeepMind's multimodal LLM, which processes both text and visual inputs through multimodal embeddings [21]. Both models operate on RGB inputs, with alpha channels ignored or discarded during preprocessing.

3 Threat Model

As shown in Fig. 2, we consider a threat model grounded in cyber-physical systems where visual perception plays a critical role in system behavior. These systems, including autonomous vehicles (AVs), surveillance systems, face recognition systems and smart home robots, such as Tesla's Full Self-Driving System(FSD) [23], mobile robots, such as Starship Technologies' autonomy robots [22], and AI-driven sensing platforms, highly rely on object detectors to interpret the surrounding environment and later make real-time decisions. These models often process video inputs under the assumption that the video input is benign and clean. However, our attack exposes a possible vulnerability for the model when given an RGBA α-*Cloak* video.

Attack Goal. The attacker's goal is to hide information in the alpha channel of an RGBA video, and then take advantage of the detector's preprocessing step that drops this channel. Once the alpha channel is removed, the detector only sees the RGB image, which shows a scene picked by the attacker. This change is invisible to a person but can cause serious safety problems in real systems. For example, an AV using such an attacked video might miss important objects that are not in the attacker's scene, leading to wrong and potentially dangerous driving decisions.

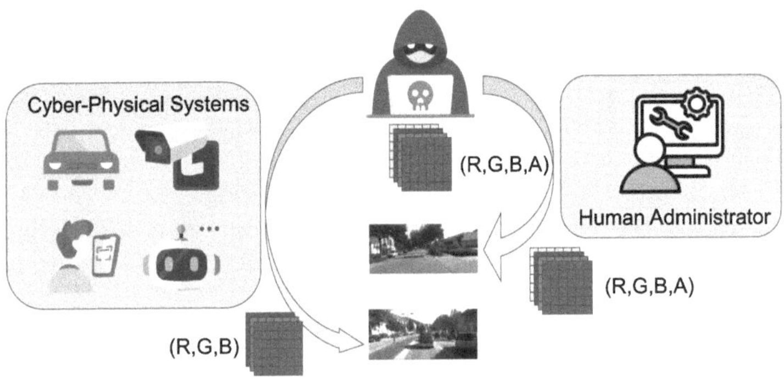

Fig. 2. Attack scenario

Attacker's Capabilities. *α-Cloak* is a no-box attack that requires no knowledge of the detection model's parameters or architecture. In our threat model, the attacker aims at compromising the object detector of a cyber-physical system. To launch the attack, they craft an adversarial RGBA *α-Cloak* video by merging two streams: a malicious "target" video meant for the detector and a benign video meant for human viewers. Because the detector accepts only RGB inputs and drops the alpha channel, it processes only the attacker's chosen scene. In addition, the attacker never needs physical access to the device; the attacked video can be delivered digitally (for example, via standard media uploads).

Attack Scenarios. Fig. 2 illustrates the attack workflow in a cyber-physical system. The adversary first creates an RGBA video by embedding a malicious target RGB stream into the alpha channel of a benign RGB video. This single tampered file is then uploaded through the cloud-based media interface of the system to the human administrator and the vehicle perception module. Because the perception module drops the alpha channel, it processes only the attacker's chosen frames, while the human operator sees the benign original sequence. Consequently, an AV may interpret a busy road as empty, leading to unsafe actions such as unintended lane changes or sudden acceleration.

4 *α-Cloak* Attack Design

In this section, we present the attack design of *α-Cloak*. We first present an overview of the attack, and then we detail how the attack is conducted on each frame of the video.

4.1 Attack Overview

As shown in Fig. 3, we define three video streams in *α-Cloak*: V_{TRUE}, V_{FAKE}, and V_{FUSED}. V_{TRUE} represents the benign, human-visible video, while V_{FAKE} denotes the malicious target video intended to deceive AI perception systems. The final adversarial output, V_{FUSED}, is generated by fusing V_{TRUE} and V_{FAKE} in a manner that preserves visual normality to human viewers but induces incorrect outputs in object detection models.

To construct V_{FUSED}, both V_{TRUE} and V_{FAKE} are first decomposed into their constituent frames. Let F_{TRUE} and F_{FAKE} denote the respective arrays of frames. For each corresponding pair $(F_{\text{TRUE}}[i], F_{\text{FAKE}}[i])$, we apply the FuseFrames method to produce a fused frame, and further resulting in the array F_{FUSED}. The fused frames are then reassembled into a video at a consistent frame rate to produce the final adversarial video V_{FUSED}, which appears visually identical to V_{TRUE} to human observers but is interpreted by detection models as V_{FAKE}. The full fusion pipeline is described in Algorithm 1.

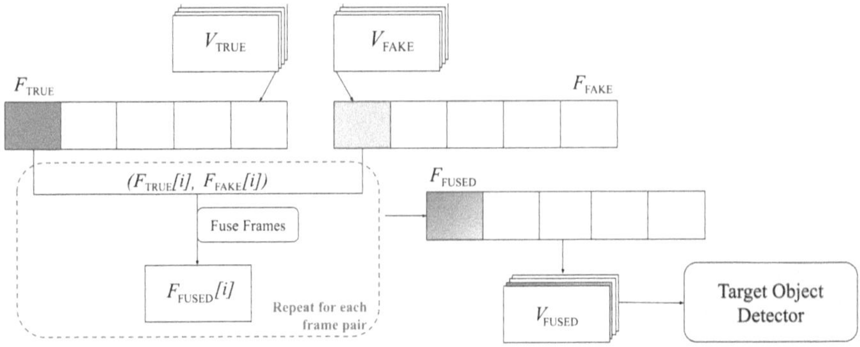

Fig. 3. Overview of the α-*Cloak* pipeline

Algorithm 1: Generate α-*Cloak* Fused Video

Input : Benign Video V_{TRUE}, Malicious Video V_{FAKE}, Frame Width l, Frame Height h
Output: The generated attack video V_{FUSED}

function GENERATEFUSEDVIDEO$(V_{TRUE}, V_{FAKE}, l, h)$:
  $F_{\text{TRUE}} \leftarrow$ FRAMEPREP(V_{TRUE}, l, h);
  $F_{\text{FAKE}} \leftarrow$ FRAMEPREP(V_{FAKE}, l, h);
  for $i \leftarrow 0$ **to** $\min(\text{len}(F_{TRUE}), \text{len}(F_{FAKE}))$ **do**
    $F_{\text{FUSED}}[i] \leftarrow$ FUSEFRAMES$(F_{\text{TRUE}}[i], F_{\text{FAKE}}[i])$;
  $V_{\text{FUSED}} \leftarrow$ GENERATE_VIDEO(F_{FUSED});
  return V_{FUSED};

function FRAMEPREP(V, l, h):
  $V \leftarrow$ RESIZE(V, l, h);
  $F \leftarrow$ SPLIT_INTO_FRAMES$(V) \rightarrow \{F_1, F_2, \ldots, F_n\}$;
  return F;

4.2 Video Frame Preprocessing

To ensure successful fusion between the two input videos V_{TRUE} and V_{FAKE}, we first preprocess the two videos using the FRAMEPREP function outlined in Algorithm 1. The purpose of this step is to standardize spatial and temporal properties between inputs and to allow frame-level access for subsequent functions. The input videos are rescaled to a uniform frame size $l \times h$, ensuring compatibility for pixel-wise fusion. Finally, we split each video into an array of its frames, which enables direct access and manipulation during the fusion process.

4.3 Video Frames Combination

We perform frame fusion between both arrays of frames to generate a single composite video that embeds information from both V_{TRUE} and V_{FAKE}. After

Algorithm 2: Generate Fused Frame

Input : Benign Frame F_{TRUE}, Malicious Frame F_{FAKE}.
Output: The generated fused attack frame V_{FUSED}.

1 **function** FUSEFRAMES(F_{TRUE}, F_{FAKE}):
2 $F_{\text{TRUE}} = \text{PREPROCESS}(F_{\text{TRUE}}) \times 0.4$;
3 $F_{\text{FAKE}} = \text{PREPROCESS}(F_{\text{FAKE}}) \times 0.6 + 0.4$;
4 $A_{\text{FUSED}} = \frac{F_{TRUE}}{F_{FAKE}}$
5 $F_{\text{FUSED}} = \text{concatenate}(A_{\text{FUSED}}, F_{\text{FAKE}})$;
6 $F_{\text{FUSED}} = F_{\text{FUSED}} \times 255.0$;
7 **return** F_{FUSED};
8 **function** PREPROCESS(F):
9 $F = \text{grayscale}(F)$
10 $F = F \div 255.0$;
11 **return** F;

splitting the input videos V_{TRUE} and V_{FAKE} into frame arrays F_{TRUE} and F_{FAKE}, we apply the FUSEFRAMES function to each corresponding frame pair ($F_{\text{TRUE}}[i]$, $F_{\text{FAKE}}[i]$). This per-frame fusion step is shown in lines 5 and 6 of Algorithm 2mm.

To prepare the frames for fusion, we convert them both to grayscale and normalize their pixel intensities. We normalize pixel values to the range [0,1] by dividing each pixel by its maximum intensity value, i.e., 255 in 8-bit images.

To ensure that the content of $F_{\text{TRUE}}[i]$ and $F_{\text{FAKE}}[i]$ each remain perceptible in the fused output to their intended targets, while remaining imperceptible to the unintended side, we constrain the intensity ranges of both input frames. We adjust the frames such that $F_{\text{TRUE}} \leq F_{\text{FAKE}}$, ensuring that the alpha channel remains within the normalized bounds [0,1]. We calculate the alpha channel matrix $A_{\text{FUSED}}[i]$ using the following formula:

$$A_{FUSED}[i] = \frac{F_{TRUE}[i]}{F_{FAKE}[i]}. \tag{2}$$

Substituting Equation (2) into the inequality, we have the following:

$$0 \leq \frac{F_{TRUE}[i]}{F_{FAKE}[i]} \leq 1, \tag{3}$$

which directly implies the constrait $F_{\text{TRUE}} \leq F_{\text{FAKE}}$ across all pixels.

We empirically determine an optimal intensity range for both input videos. Through experimentation with 6,680 generated α-*Cloak* videos, we find that scaling F_{TRUE} to 40% of its original intensity, while maintaining F_{FAKE} values above 0.4 achieves the highest performing fusion quality. This results in the following bound:

$$0 \leq F_{TRUE}[i] \leq 0.4 \leq F_{FAKE}[i] \leq 1. \tag{4}$$

We finalize each fused frame by combining the computed alpha channel matrix with its RGB channel intensity matrix. Because systems typically remove the alpha channel matrix when rendering the frame, we assign the RGB channel intensity matrix equal to F_{FAKE}, as this will be the only image that the computer will see. Thus, the resulting fused frame is: $F_{\text{FUSED}}[i] = A_{\text{FUSED}}[i] + V_{\text{FAKE}}[i]$.

5 Evaluation

To evaluate the proposed attack, we input adversarially fused videos into multiple object detection models and measure how closely their predictions align with the content of either the benign or malicious source video.

5.1 Experimental Setup

Experimental Procedure. We design this experiment to evaluate the extent to which object detection models can identify and localize objects within adversarially fused videos. Each target model receives a list of attacked videos along with the ground truth bounding box labels corresponding to each original, unaltered input video used to construct those attacked videos.

For each frame in a given attacked video, the detection model performs inference and outputs its predicted bounding boxes. We then compute a frame-level similarity score (*FLS*) by comparing the model prediction to all ground truth boxes. This process is repeated for each frame, and the resulting *FLS* values are averaged to obtain a video-level similarity score (*VLS*) between the attacked video and each candidate source video. The candidate source video with the highest average similarity is identified as the most likely source video, indicating that the model's predictions most closely resemble that video's object layout. This experiment allows us to quantify how closely the fused content influences model perception and how effectively the attack obscures source attribution.

Target Attack Models. We evaluate our attack using five widely adopted object detection architectures, selected to cover a diverse range of model structures. Specifically, we test three versions of YOLO, including YOLOv5n [10], YOLOv8n [11], and YOLOv11n [12], using their official pre-trained weights. Additionally, we include RetinaNet [14] and Faster R-CNN in our evaluation, both of which utilize a ResNet-50 backbone with a Feature Pyramid Network (FPN) to enhance multi-scale feature extraction.

While our evaluation focuses on standard object detection benchmarks using widely adopted architectures (YOLOv5/8/11, Faster R-CNN, RetinaNet), these models constitute the core perception modules in many modern vision-based systems, including autonomous vehicles, surveillance platforms, and robotics pipelines. Evaluating at this level allows us to precisely measure the model-level effects of our attack, which directly influence downstream system behavior.

All models generate bounding boxes along with associated class confidence scores for each input video. We apply a fixed confidence threshold of 0.25 across all models to increase object recall, prioritizing detection coverage over precision. This choice ensures that our similarity metric is sensitive to all detectable object instances. This diverse selection of models provides a robust basis for evaluating the generalizability and effectiveness of our attack strategy.

Evaluation Metrics. To assess the similarity between each attacked video and its potential source videos, we introduce a two-level similarity metric framework: *FLS* and *VLS*. These metrics rely on spatial overlap between predicted and ground truth boxes, measured using Intersection over Union (IoU), how much two bounding boxes overlap.

For each predicted box p in a given attacked frame, we compute the IoU against each ground truth box g across all candidate videos and retain the maximum value:

$$\mathrm{IoU}(A, B) = \frac{\mathrm{area}(A \cap B)}{\mathrm{area}(A \cup B)}. \tag{5}$$

$$FLS = \frac{1}{n} \sum_{i=1}^{n} \max_{j=1}^{m}(\mathrm{IoU}(p_i, g_j)). \tag{6}$$

We repeat this process for every frame in the attacked video and then compute the average *FLS* across all T frames to compute the *VLS* for each candidate video:

$$VLS = \frac{1}{T} \sum_{t=1}^{T} FLS_t. \tag{7}$$

This resulting *VLS* for every candidate video captures how closely each candidate video matches the video detected by the object detector. A higher *VLS* indicates stronger alignment between the candidate's ground-truth content and the detector's predictions on the attacked video. These metrics allow us to quantify and assess how convincingly our attack blends the benign and malicious videos.

Table 3. Object detectors attack performance on three videos.

Target frame seen by humans (V_{TRUE})	**Target frame seen by object detectors (V_{FAKE})**	**Object Detectors Output**	**Object Detector**
			YOLOv5
			YOLOv11
			RetinaNet

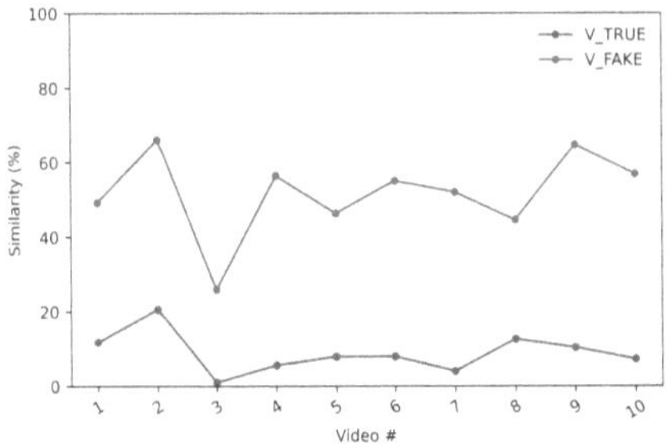

(a) YOLOv5

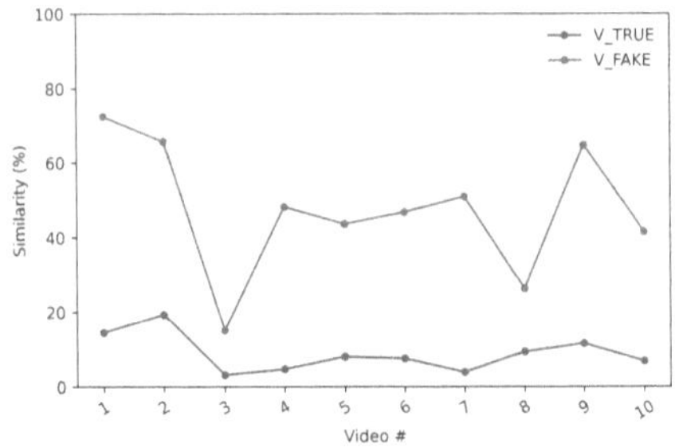

(b) YOLOv8

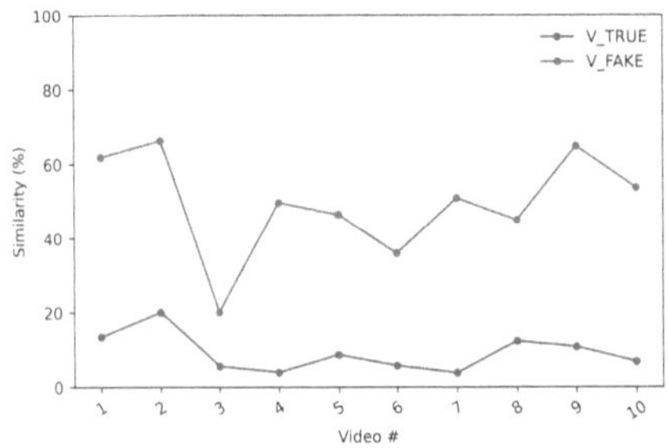

(c) YOLOv11

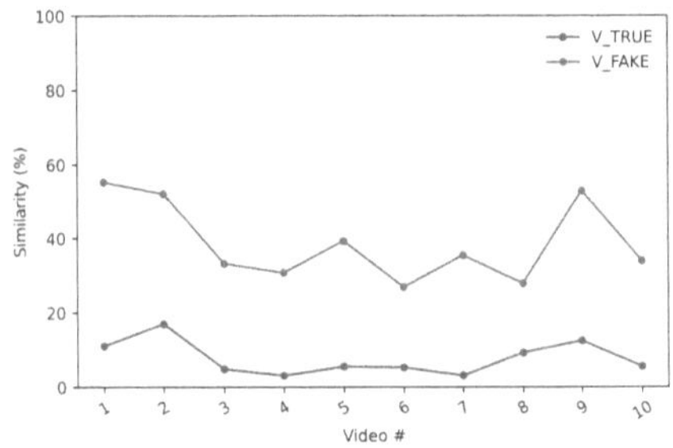

(d) RetinaNet

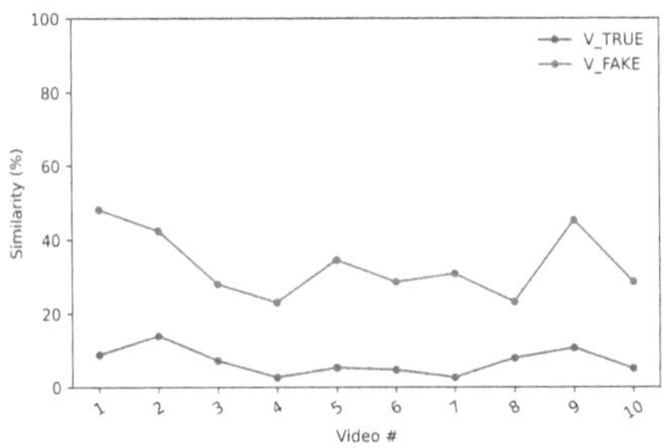

(e) Faster R-CNN

Fig. 4. Evaluation results across different detection models. The x-axis is each attacked video given to the model. The y-axis is the VLS score as a percentage. The red line is the line for V_{FAKE}, while the blue line is for V_{TRUE}. These lines show the VLS between each attacked video with its own V_{FAKE} and V_{TRUE} labels.

Dataset. We conduct our evaluations using the KITTI tracking dataset [6], which provides annotated video sequences for real-world urban driving. We convert the individual KITTI tracking sequences into full-length videos, yielding a set of 21 complete candidate videos. We split the first 20 videos into two equal subsets: the first 10 videos serve as V_{TRUE} videos and the next 10 videos as V_{FAKE} videos. These fused videos, along with the original KITTI training labels for all 21 videos, are provided as input to the object detection models during evaluation. This experiment design allows us to evaluate attack performance in a multi-object urban context with dynamic backgrounds. Table 3 showcases examples of attacked frames alongside bounding box outputs from three models. The first and second columns are frames that humans and AI should see, respectively. The third and fourth columns show the bounding boxes predicted for each frame, and which model ran the image. It can be seen that the object detector views the V_{FAKE} image and runs its object detection on the malicious target video.

5.2 Attack Results on KITTI

We evaluate the effectiveness of our attack by measuring how closely the fused videos resemble the source components across five object detection models. For each attacked video, we compute the VLS relative to its corresponding V_{TRUE} and V_{FAKE} videos, and plot the results in Fig. 4.

Table 4. Summary of VLS evaluation results across the different object detection models.

Model	Avg. VLS to V_{FAKE} (%)	Avg. VLS to V_{TRUE} (%)	V_{FAKE} Top-1 (%)	V_{TRUE} Top-1 (%)
YOLOv5	51.689	8.852	100	0
YOLOv8	47.424	8.852	100	0
YOLOv11	49.487	9.138	100	0
RetinaNet	38.733	7.665	100	0
Faster R-CNN	33.237	6.715	100	0
OVERALL AVG	**44.114**	**8.244**	**100**	**0**

Across all models and videos, we observe that the red line, representing the VLS of V_{FAKE}, consistently lies above the blue line, the VSL of V_{TRUE}. This consistent pattern demonstrates that the object detection models perceived the fused videos as more similar to V_{FAKE}, indicating the success of the attack in misleading the models.

While the difference between the VLS scores of V_{FAKE} and V_{TRUE} are not extreme in magnitude, the direction of the shift is consistent across all models and examples. We attribute the limited gap to the intrinsic visual similarity among the KITTI videos, as all scenes are captured from a vehicle through similar environments. This inherent similarity likely increases the challenge of precise disambiguation.

We summarize quantitative results in Table 4, which reports the average VLS for each model with respect to both source videos, as well as the percentage of cases where V_{FAKE} or V_{TRUE} was identified as the top-1 most similar candidate. In all models, V_{FAKE} leads as the top-1 prediction. This result confirms that our attack effectively redirects model recognition from the benign video and towards the malicious target video, regardless of model architecture.

5.3 Attack Results on Open-VCLIP

To evaluate the transferability of our attack beyond object detection, we test it on a VLM, Open-VCLIP, using the UCF-101 dataset [19]. Open-VCLIP is a contrastively trained extension of CLIP designed for video inputs, and it is pre-trained on UCF-101 itself, making it highly familiar with the dataset's class distribution.

Given a video clip and a predefined set of class labels, Open-VCLIP computes embeddings for both the video input and each class label, ranking all class labels based on cosine similarity, and returns the top-1 and top-5 predicted classes. This allows us to test whether our attack changes the model's prediction to favor the malicious adversarial label.

We generate 6,660 adversarially fused videos by splitting UCF-101 into two disjoint halves. Videos in the first subset serve as V_{TRUE}, while the second subset serves as V_{FAKE}. For each index i, we construct a fused video $V_{\text{FUSED}}^{(i)}$ by applying fusion (Algorithm 1) to the pair $\left(V_{\text{TRUE}}^{(i)}, V_{\text{FAKE}}^{(i)}\right)$.

We submit each V_{FUSED} video to Open-VCLIP twice: once with the class label of V_{TRUE}, and once with the class label of V_{FAKE}. For both runs, we check whether the submitted label appears in the model's top-1 or top-5 predictions. Table 5 summarizes the classification accuracy under both conditions across all 6,660 attacked videos. The middle row displays the detection accuracy of V_{FUSED} using the class label corresponding to the human-visible video V_{TRUE}. The bottom row displays the detection accuracy of V_{FUSED} when using the class label corresponding to the AI-targeted video V_{FAKE}.

Table 5. Top-1 and Top-5 classification accuracy of Open VCLIP.

Label Given	% of labels in Top-1 list (%)	% of labels in Top-5 list (%)
V_{TRUE} Labels	0.06	1.83
V_{FAKE} Labels	71.56	90.68

The label of V_{TRUE} appears in the top-1 prediction less than 2% of cases, while the label of V_{FAKE} appears in over 90% of top-1 predictions. This strong skew in prediction distribution indicates that Open-VCLIP consistently aligns with the adversarial target V_{FAKE}, even in the presence of benign content V_{TRUE}, highlighting the generalizability and strength of our attack across modalities.

5.4 *α-Cloak* Attack Example on Gemini-2.0

We extend our investigation on a commercial multimodal LLM, Gemini-2.0-Flash. As shown in the Table 6, the first column presents video frames that have been covertly manipulated via the alpha channel, which appear entirely normal to human observers. The second column shows the corresponding attack samples after the large language model strips away the alpha channel. It can be seen that from the LLM's point of view, these frames convey a completely different scene. The third column reports the model's analysis of each attack sample. From the results, we can see that the LLM reads the adversarial videos V_{FAKE} instead of V_{TRUE} and demonstrates the effectiveness of *α-Cloak* on Gemini-2.0-Flash.

Table 6. Attack performance on Gemini-2.0-Flash.

Target frame seen by humans (V_{TRUE})	**Target frame seen by object detectors (V_{FAKE})**	**Gemini-2.0-Flash Output**
		The vehicle is traveling on a street with parked cars on the right side. There are sidewalks and grassy areas adjacent to the road. There are pedestrian crossings with signage. There are other vehicles moving in the same direction and parked.
		The video captures a street scene with a cyclist initially. The cyclist rides across the scene from right to left. As the video progresses the cyclist exits the frame, and then a person walking on the sidewalk on the left side of the road becomes visible.
	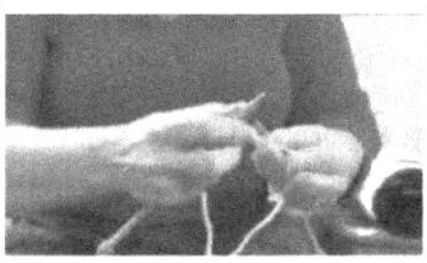	The video shows a close-up view of someone knitting. The primary focus is on the hands and knitting needles as they manipulate yarn to create stitches. The actions appear to be those of a standard knitting technique. Due to the visual quality, it's difficult to pinpoint the specific stitch being made, but it looks like a basic knit stitch.

6 Related Work

Security of Image Preprocessing Pipelines. In the domain of black-box adversarial attacks, a large body of work has proposed query-based iterative methods to improve attack efficiency and reduce reliance on substitute models, such as Square Attack [2], Boundary Attack [3], HopSkipJumpAttack [4], GenAttack [1], the triangle attack [16], bandit-based approaches [8], and SimBA [7]. Although these methods enhance query efficiency, they still require hundreds to thousands of queries and are generally tailored to specific models. At the same time, image-scaling attacks exploit preprocessing-stage resizing algorithms to conceal malicious payloads within benign images. Most closely related to our work, AlphaDog [26] is a 'no-box' camouflage attack to exploit the alpha channel of RGBA images; it embeds the adversarial target into the RGB channels to mislead AI classifiers while crafting the alpha channel so that human observers see only innocuous content, achieving zero queries and model-agnostic applicability. In this paper, we move from the image/classification setting to the video/object-detection setting, where temporal consistency and region-level localization (rather than global labels) make attacks substantially harder.

Security of Vision-Based Perception Systems. Vision is central to cyber-physical systems (e.g., AVs), but has proven vulnerable to both perturbation and patch attacks that directly corrupt input images. Both perturbation and patch attacks fall under the umbrella of adversarial attacks. The fundamental idea of adversarial attacks is to induce significant errors in a deep learning model's output through minimal modifications to the input. Perturbation attacks typically affect all pixels in the input image with slight value changes, whereas patch attacks modify only a small region but with relatively large alterations in pixel values. For example, V-Phanton [9] introduces adversarial perturbations in captured images by adjusting the camera's supply voltage, thus disrupting the downstream image recognition process. GhostShot [18], on the contrary, achieves the injection of adversarial patterns into CCD cameras through externally applied electromagnetic interference. Cheng et al. [5] demonstrate that the image stabilization mechanism used in autonomous driving camera sensors can be disrupted by malicious ultrasonic signals, inducing abnormal jitter and dynamic blur in acquired images. L-Hawk [15] adopts a similar attack concept against autonomous driving platforms, but replaces the injected signal with a laser beam precisely aimed at the camera lens. These attacks require physical access/proximity, environmental control, or specialized hardware, and often produce conditions (e.g., jitter, blur, overexposure) that can be perceptible or operationally constraining. *α-Cloak* attack does not interact with the sensor or the physical environment. Instead, it targets the downstream video handling and model-input stack by exploiting how RGBA videos are decoded and consumed by perception models.

7 Discussion

In this section, we discuss the practicality, limitations, and the potential defense method of the *α-Cloak* attack.

7.1 Attack Feasibility and Practicality

Our work demonstrates that no-box alpha channel-based attacks can be both simple and effective. Unlike existing video attacks that rely on temporal perturbations and require knowledge of the model architecture or parameters, *α-Cloak* exploits a fundamental inconsistency in video input handling. It embeds an adversarial payload into the alpha channel, which is commonly ignored or discarded by object detectors. As a result, α-*Cloak* remains lightweight, broadly applicable, and agnostic to detector architectures and media playback environments.

7.2 Limitations

Although α-*Cloak* is effective against a wide range of object detectors, it depends on two key assumptions: detectors discard the alpha channel while standard video players preserve it, conditions met by most systems trained solely on RGB inputs. Furthermore, α-*Cloak* is inherently limited to grayscale content, since the alpha channel controls only pixel transparency without altering the relative intensities of the RGB channels. Consequently, the fusion mechanism cannot reproduce full-color scenes, restricting the attack to monochrome videos or regions.

7.3 Defense

α-*Cloak* exploits the mismatch in video pipelines in how video content is presented to human viewers compared to detection models. It leverages the removal of the alpha channel by models to hide adversarial content in plain sight. To defend against this attack, model designers can implement alpha channel profiling techniques tailored for video input during the preprocessing stage. After decoding each video frame, but before model inference, the system can conduct per-frame alpha channel analysis and compute per-pixel intensity histograms to detect any unnatural transparency distributions. Frames exhibiting nonuniform transparency in regions where transparency is not expected, such as in the center of the video in high-traffic videos, will be flagged by the detector.

Alternatively, instead of discarding the alpha channel in its entirety, a model can first composite each incoming RGBA frame onto a black background before passing it to the object detection model. This approach emulates how standard video players render transparent regions, ensuring consistency between human and model perception. Therefore, the opportunity to exploit rendering mismatches is eliminated.

8 Conclusion

In this paper, we introduce α-*Cloak*, the first no-box adversarial attack targeting object detection systems in the video domain. By leveraging the alpha channel, we demonstrate that adversarial content can be stealthily embedded within videos without any perceptible distortion to human viewers. Our approach addresses the unique challenges of video processing by proposing multi-frame fusion. Extensive evaluations across a range of object detectors, a vision-language model, and an LLM confirm the attack's robustness and universality, achieving a 100% success rate in all scenarios. Our findings highlight a critical and previously overlooked threat vector in cyber-physical systems, emphasizing the urgent need for new defense mechanisms to protect video-based AI applications from invisible adversarial manipulation.

Acknowledgment. This work was supported in part by the U.S. National Science Foundation grant CNS-2235231.

References

1. Alzantot, M., Sharma, Y., Chakraborty, S., Zhang, H., Hsieh, C.J., Srivastava, M.B.: GenAttack: practical black-box attacks with gradient-free optimization. In: Proceedings of the Genetic and Evolutionary Computation Conference, pp. 1111–1119 (2019)
2. Andriushchenko, M., Croce, F., Flammarion, N., Hein, M.: Square Attack: a query-efficient black-box adversarial attack via random search. In: Vedaldi, A., Bischof, H., Brox, T., Frahm, J.-M. (eds.) ECCV 2020. LNCS, vol. 12368, pp. 484–501. Springer, Cham (2020). https://doi.org/10.1007/978-3-030-58592-1_29
3. Brendel, W., Rauber, J., Bethge, M.: Decision-based adversarial attacks: reliable attacks against black-box machine learning models. arXiv preprint arXiv:1712.04248 (2017)
4. Chen, J., Jordan, M.I., Wainwright, M.J.: HopSkipJumpAttack: a query-efficient decision-based attack. In: 2020 IEEE Symposium on Security and Privacy (SP), pp. 1277–1294. IEEE (2020)
5. Cheng, Y., Ji, X., Zhu, W., Zhang, S., Fu, K., Xu, W.: Adversarial computer vision via acoustic manipulation of camera sensors. IEEE Trans. Depend. Secure Comput. **21**(4), 3734–3750 (2023)
6. Geiger, A., Lenz, P., Stiller, C., Urtasun, R.: Vision meets robotics: the KITTI dataset. int. J. Robot. Res. **32**(11), 1231–1237 (2013)
7. Guo, C., Gardner, J., You, Y., Wilson, A.G., Weinberger, K.: Simple black-box adversarial attacks. In: International Conference on Machine Learning, pp. 2484–2493. PMLR (2019)
8. Ilyas, A., Engstrom, L., Madry, A.: Prior convictions: black-box adversarial attacks with bandits and priors. arXiv preprint arXiv:1807.07978 (2018)
9. Jiang, Y., Li, R., Cheng, Y., Ji, X., Xu, W.: V-Phanton:Voltage-based physically-triggered backdoor attack against facial recognition. In: 2025 IEEE International Conference on Acoustics, Speech and Signal Processing (ICASSP), ICASSP 2025, pp. 1–5 (2025). https://doi.org/10.1109/ICASSP49660.2025.10888148
10. Jocher, G.: YOLOv5 by Ultralytics, May 2020. https://doi.org/10.5281/zenodo.3908559, https://github.com/ultralytics/yolov5
11. Jocher, G., Chaurasia, A., Qiu, J.: Ultralytics YOLOv8 (2023). https://github.com/ultralytics/ultralytics
12. Jocher, G., Qiu, J.: Ultralytics YOLO11 (2024). https://github.com/ultralytics/ultralytics
13. Khanam, R., Hussain, M.: What is YOLOv5: a deep look into the internal features of the popular object detector (2024). https://arxiv.org/abs/2407.20892
14. Lin, T.Y., Goyal, P., Girshick, R., He, K., Dollár, P.: Focal loss for dense object detection (2018). https://arxiv.org/abs/1708.02002

15. Liu, T., et al.: L-HAWK: a controllable physical adversarial patch against a long-distance target. In: NDSS (2025)
16. Moon, S., An, G., Song, H.O.: Parsimonious black-box adversarial attacks via efficient combinatorial optimization. In: International Conference on Machine Learning, pp. 4636–4645. PMLR (2019)
17. Ren, S., He, K., Girshick, R., Sun, J.: Faster R-CNN: towards real-time object detection with region proposal networks. IEEE Trans. Pattern Anal. Mach. Intell. **39**(6), 1137–1149 (2016)
18. Ren, Y., Jiang, Q., Yan, C., Ji, X., Xu, W.: GhostShot: manipulating the image of CCD cameras with electromagnetic interference (2025)
19. Soomro, K., Zamir, A.R., Shah, M.: UCF101: a dataset of 101 human actions classes from videos in the wild. arXiv preprint arXiv:1212.0402 (2012)
20. Suri, R.: Is it okay to convert an image with an alpha channel to an image without an alpha channel?, June 2016. https://stackoverflow.com/questions/37877020/is-it-okay-to-convert-an-image-with-an-alpha-channel-to-an-image-without-an-alph. Accessed 30 Jul 2025
21. Team, G., et al.: Gemini: a family of highly capable multimodal models. arXiv preprint arXiv:2312.11805 (2023)
22. Starship Technologies: Starship: Our robots (2014). https://www.starship.xyz/our-robots/. Accessed 25 Jul 2025
23. Tesla: Autopilot and full self-driving (supervised) (2022). https://www.tesla.com/support/autopilot. Accessed 25 Jul 2025
24. Wang, G., Zhou, C., Wang, Y., Chen, B., Guo, H., Yan, Q.: Beyond boundaries: a comprehensive survey of transferable attacks on ai systems. arXiv preprint arXiv:2311.11796 (2023)
25. Weng, Z., Yang, X., Li, A., Wu, Z., Jiang, Y.G.: Open-VCLIP: transforming clip to an open-vocabulary video model via interpolated weight optimization. In: International Conference on Machine Learning, pp. 36978–36989. PMLR (2023)
26. Xia, Q., Chen, Q.: AlphaDog: no-box camouflage attacks via alpha channel oversight. In: NDSS (2025)
27. Zhou, C., et al.: A comprehensive survey on pretrained foundation models: a history from BERT to ChatGPT. Int. J. Mach. Learn. Cybern., 1–65 (2024)
28. Zhou, C., Yan, Q., Kent, D., Wang, G., Zhang, Z., Radha, H.: Optical lens attack on deep learning based monocular depth estimation. arXiv preprint arXiv:2409.17376 (2024)
29. Zhou, C., Yan, Q., Shi, Y., Sun, L.: DoubleStar: long-range attack towards depth estimation based obstacle avoidance in autonomous systems. In: 31st USENIX Security Symposium (USENIX Security 22), pp. 1885–1902 (2022)
30. Zou, Z., Chen, K., Shi, Z., Guo, Y., Ye, J.: Object detection in 20 years: a survey. Proc. IEEE **111**(3), 257–276 (2023)

Threat Detection and ML Security

Security and Privacy Challenges in Embedded Machine Learning

Eyosiyas Endalamaw, Mohammedreza Mehrabian, and Francis Akowuah(✉)

Department of Electrical Engineering and Computer Science, South Dakota School of Mines and Technology, Rapid City, SD, USA
eyosiyas.endalamaw@mines.sdsmt.edu,
{mohammadreza.mehrabian,francis.akowuah}@sdsmt.edu

Abstract. In this paper, we examine the security and privacy challenges facing machine learning models deployed on embedded systems. As resource-constrained devices increasingly rely on local intelligence, the confidentiality, integrity, and privacy of on-device models become attractive targets for attackers. We provide a survey of emerging threats, including model extraction, side-channel attacks, input manipulation, and backdoor injection. We also explore lightweight defenses suited to embedded deployments, such as adversarial training, input filtering, and encryption of model parameters. In addition, we discuss the potential of TEEs and sensor-level encryption to enable secure inference and protect sensor data. Based on our synthesis of recent academic work, we identify key research gaps in areas such as privacy-preserving inference, resilient model compression, and trusted learning on-device. Our goal is to inform and guide future research aimed at building robust and trustworthy embedded AI systems.

Keywords: Embedded ML · TinyML · Embedded AI Security · Embedded AI Privacy

1 Introduction

Machine learning (ML) models are increasingly deployed on embedded platforms, from smart sensors and wearables to autonomous vehicles and industrial controllers, to enable data driven intelligence at the network edge. This trend, often referred to as Embedded ML or TinyML when targeting microcontroller class devices, offers benefits such as low latency and improved privacy by keeping data local. However, integrating ML into resource constrained and often safety critical embedded systems also exposes new security vulnerabilities. Attacks against ML components can compromise the behavior of the entire device, potentially leading to severe consequences in domains such as healthcare, automotive, or critical infrastructure. For instance, an attacker might manipulate sensor inputs with adversarial perturbations to mislead an on-device neural network or exploit

L. Cheng and F. Anwar (Eds.): SmartSP 2025, LNICST 699, pp. 165–184, 2027.
https://doi.org/10.1007/978-3-032-33701-6_10

physical access to extract confidential model parameters. These emerging threats combine traditional embedded system weaknesses with novel ML specific attack vectors, making security in this area a complex interdisciplinary challenge.

Recent years have witnessed a growing body of research on adversarial attacks and defenses in machine learning, but much of it assumes powerful computers or cloud based systems. Embedded ML security, in contrast, must contend with severe memory, compute, and power limitations that render many standard security solutions infeasible. For example, techniques like heavyweight cryptographic protocols, extensive redundancy checks, or large ensemble models for robustness are often impractical on a small microcontroller with a few kilobytes of RAM. Likewise, embedded devices are frequently deployed in unmonitored environments where attackers can gain physical access. This increases the risk of hardware centric attacks such as side channel analysis to steal model secrets by measuring power consumption or electromagnetic emanations, or fault injection to induce misclassifications or bypass checks by glitching the device. In short, the convergence of ML and embedded systems enlarges the attack surface, combining digital and physical vulnerabilities. Ensuring the security of embedded ML deployments requires rethinking both ML algorithms and embedded system design under a unified security framework.

Several related surveys have begun addressing facets of this broad problem. Chen and Babar, for example, present a holistic survey of security issues in ML enabled software systems, emphasizing that vulnerabilities appear throughout the ML lifecycle and must be tackled with integrated software engineering and security practices [13]. Their work covers high level development practices but is less focused on the unique constraints of edge devices. Huckelberry et al. provide an in depth review of TinyML security, identifying numerous attack vectors on ultra low power ML devices and concluding that specialized defenses are needed since many conventional security measures break down at TinyML scale [30]. Another recent survey by Alkadi et al. examines adversarial ML threats in IoT networks, finding a notable lack of tailored IoT specific defenses and calling for more research into robust intrusion detection and protection mechanisms for smart devices [3]. Unlike these works, our survey combines perspectives across both hardware and algorithmic security in embedded ML. We not only review adversarial and data poisoning attacks as in prior ML security surveys but also integrate coverage of implementation level threats such as side channels and fault attacks that specifically endanger deployed models in devices. Furthermore, we discuss practical mitigation strategies with an eye to resource efficiency, and we highlight open issues that bridge the gap between the ML security community and embedded systems security engineering.

This paper offers a holistic and structured overview of security and privacy threats in embedded ML. Our contributions are as follows:

- We systematically review security and privacy challenges specific to embedded ML, covering adversarial examples, model extraction, physical attacks, data leakage, and privacy inference.

- We examine mitigation strategies tailored to embedded constraints, including lightweight defenses, hardware-aware protections, and lifecycle-aware security mechanisms.
- We articulate open research challenges and propose future research directions to guide the development of secure, private, and reliable embedded ML systems.

The remainder of this paper is organized as follows. Section 2 defines the scope of embedded ML security and introduces key background concepts, including system constraints and attacker models. Section 3 surveys major security threats such as adversarial inputs, model extraction, and physical tampering. Section 4 explores privacy risks, including data leakage, model inversion, and federated learning vulnerabilities. Section 5 reviews mitigation strategies against security threats, categorized by software, hardware, update, and co-design approaches. Section 6 focuses on privacy-preserving mechanisms for embedded ML, including lightweight privacy-preserving inference, secure data aggregation, and trusted execution. Section 7 outlines open research challenges and future directions, such as securing update pipelines, evaluating attacker models, and balancing usability and risk. Finally, Sect. 8 concludes the paper with a summary of key findings and reflections on the path toward trustworthy embedded ML systems.

2 Background and Scope of Embedded ML Security

2.1 What Is Embedded Machine Learning?

Embedded ML refers to the deployment of machine learning models on resource-constrained computing devices such as microcontrollers, sensors, mobile processors, and edge nodes. We distinguish MCU class devices (kBMB RAM) from edge node class devices (hundreds of MBGB); defenses that fit the latter often exceed MCU budgets. Embedded ML enables intelligent processing close to the data source, allowing for low-latency decision-making, offline inference, and improved privacy by reducing data transmission. Applications include voice assistants on smart speakers, facial recognition on door locks, anomaly detection in industrial controllers, and activity monitoring in wearable health devices.

Unlike cloud-based ML, embedded ML requires models to be highly optimized, often using techniques such as quantization, pruning, and distillation to meet strict size and performance requirements. Quantization [29,59], focuses on reducing the precision of model parameters, such as converting 32-bit floating-point numbers to 8-bit integers, significantly lowering memory usage and computational cost. Pruning [15,25] targets efficiency by removing redundant connections, less important weights or neurons, reducing model size and speeding up inference, aligning with the need for lightweight models in real-time applications. Distillation, pioneered by [26], is a method to compress the knowledge from an ensemble of models or a large model (teacher) into a single, smaller model (student) for easier deployment on edge nodes with limited resources. These techniques are supported by frameworks like TensorFlow Lite which provides tools for implementing quantization and pruning, as noted in [15]. Other optimization frameworks include Caffe2 (merged into PyTorch) [45], Lasagne [34] and MXNet (retired in September 2023) [4].

2.2 Why Security and Privacy Are Different in Embedded ML

Security and privacy in embedded machine learning differ from traditional ML due to the convergence of constrained hardware and sensitive data processing. These systems often operate in exposed environments, handle personal information, and lack the resources to support conventional defenses like complex encryption or large-scale anomaly detection.

First, physical accessibility increases risk. Devices such as IoT sensors and autonomous controllers are often deployed in public or unattended locations, making them susceptible to tampering, electromagnetic leakage, and model extraction. For example, attackers have recovered model parameters from edge devices using fewer than 1000 electromagnetic traces [9].

Second, resource limitations restrict defensive options. With only kilobytes of memory, low-frequency processors, and minimal energy reserves, embedded devices cannot afford costly security measures. Applying AES-256 encryption on a microcontroller, for instance, can raise latency by 50%, whereas lightweight alternatives offer better efficiency [10].

Third, large-scale and heterogeneous deployment complicates management. Embedded ML systems span various hardware platforms and firmware configurations, limiting the feasibility of centralized updates and uniform security enforcement [43,60].

Finally, real-time constraints impose strict performance demands. Applications in robotics or industrial systems often require sub-10 millisecond response times, meaning any added security must be lightweight. Protocols like PRESENT can reduce latency by 30% compared to AES, offering a practical balance between speed and protection [10].

These factors underscore the need for customized, efficient, and context-aware security and privacy solutions for embedded ML environments.

2.3 Threat Model and Attacker Capabilities

This survey assumes a general threat model encompassing a broad range of attacker capabilities relevant to embedded machine learning systems. Attackers may operate as white-box attackers, possessing full access to the model architecture and parameters, which could be obtained through model extraction, firmware reverse engineering, or physical probing. Alternatively, attackers may function in a black-box setting, interacting with the deployed model solely through its input/output interface, such as prediction APIs or sensor channels, and may employ probing techniques to infer the model's behavior or steal its functionality. Physical attackers, with direct access to the device, can attempt tampering, fault injection, or side-channel monitoring. Supply chain attackers pose a threat by injecting malicious logic, such as backdoors, into the training or deployment pipeline before the model is embedded in a device. Additionally, network-based attackers can intercept or manipulate communications between the device and external systems, particularly in scenarios involving federated learning or model updates.

Attackers may target several security objectives. They may aim to compromise confidentiality by stealing the model, the data used for its training, or the data it processes during inference attacks. Integrity is another target, where attackers seek to cause the model to misbehave through adversarial examples, data poisoning, or fault injections. Furthermore, attackers may focus on availability, attempting to deny or degrade service by exhausting system resources or disabling the model's inference capabilities.

2.4 Scope of This Survey

This survey focuses on the unique security and privacy challenges that arise when deploying and operating ML models in embedded environments. We examine three core dimensions of embedded ML security. First, we address the protection of models performing inference directly on embedded hardware, emphasizing the risks and mitigations specific to on-device execution. Second, we consider learning paradigms such as personalized and federated learning that occur locally on devices, which introduce distinct privacy and integrity concerns. Third, we explore system-level interactions, including how embedded ML interfaces with memory, sensors, model update pipelines, and hardware-specific vulnerabilities.

While we acknowledge broader work on cloud-based ML security, such approaches are only discussed when they directly inform or contrast with embedded use cases. The goal of this survey is to synthesize research that addresses the constraints, threat models, and design tradeoffs that characterize embedded ML, thereby bridging the gap between ML and embedded systems security.

3 Security Challenges in Embedded ML

Embedded ML systems are exposed to a diverse range of security threats that stem from both traditional embedded vulnerabilities and new attack vectors introduced by machine learning itself. Unlike cloud-based ML, embedded models often operate autonomously in uncontrolled physical environments with limited hardware protections, making them susceptible to tampering, extraction, and runtime manipulation. This section surveys prominent categories of security challenges in embedded ML, including adversarial examples that undermine inference reliability, data poisoning and backdoors that compromise model integrity during training, model theft and extraction attacks that target intellectual property, and side-channel or fault injection attacks that exploit physical access to the device. Understanding these threat vectors is essential for designing robust defenses tailored to the constraints and deployment characteristics of embedded ML.

3.1 Adversarial Examples

Adversarial examples are a well-known threat to machine learning models. First identified by Szegedy et al. [52], these attacks add small, often imperceptible changes to inputs that lead deep neural networks to misclassify them. Goodfellow et al. [22] introduced the Fast Gradient Sign Method (FGSM), which efficiently generates such examples using model gradients. Kurakin et al. [33] refined this with the Basic Iterative Method (BIM), which applies smaller perturbations across multiple steps for greater impact. Black-box methods by Papernot et al. [41,42] further demonstrated that adversaries can craft successful attacks without internal model access, relying only on input-output behavior. These techniques are especially concerning for embedded machine learning systems used in computer vision, audio processing, and sensor-based IoT applications.

In embedded settings, attackers may exploit physical access to deliver tampered inputs, threatening safety-critical applications. Eykholt et al. [19] showed that placing stickers on a stop sign led a self-driving car to misclassify it as a yield sign, with full success in lab conditions and over 84% in real-world tests. Sharif et al. [49] used adversarial patterns on eyeglass frames to fool face-recognition systems on smartphones and security cameras. In audio, Carlini and Wagner [12] introduced small waveform perturbations that caused Mozilla's DeepSpeech to transcribe attacker-defined phrases with full accuracy, posing risks to smart speakers and voice assistants.

Adversarial threats extend beyond vision and audio. Sah and Ghasemzadeh [46] showed that perturbations to wearable sensor data compromise models across users, sensors, and device types, undermining health-monitoring systems. Haddadpajouh et al. [24] embedded adversarial payloads into IoT malware, reducing detection accuracy from 99 to 82%. Thys et al. [53] developed adversarial patches that bypass person detection in surveillance cameras using models like YOLOv2, while Cao et al. [11] demonstrated how small physical objects can mislead LiDAR systems in autonomous vehicles. These examples highlight the wide-ranging risk adversarial examples pose across embedded machine learning applications, including vehicles, biometrics, smart homes, and IoT security.

3.2 Data Poisoning and Backdoor Attacks

In addition to test-time evasion, attackers can compromise the training process through *data poisoning* i.e. injecting malicious samples into the training dataset to alter model behavior. Even a small number of mislabeled or subtly modified inputs can cause incorrect predictions on specific targets. Shafahi et al. [48] introduced a clean label poisoning method where visually normal samples retain correct labels but embed hidden decision boundaries. This threat is especially concerning for embedded systems, such as autonomous vehicles and IoT devices, where training data may come from untrusted or distributed sources. For instance, poisoning the training data of an embedded traffic sign recognizer could cause it to misclassify specific signs in real environments, endangering safety.

A related threat is backdoor poisoning [14,23,56], where attackers manipulate training data to embed hidden triggers that activate malicious behavior while maintaining normal performance on clean inputs. For example, in a smart home camera system, a poisoned model may grant access when it detects a specific sticker. Chen et al. [14] demonstrated that injecting just 50 poisoned samples into a face recognition system can achieve over 90% success on embedded biometric devices. Yang et al. [56] extended this to federated learning in IoT settings, showing that compromised edge devices can embed triggers during training, causing misclassification without degrading overall model accuracy. This is particularly dangerous in critical applications like smart grids and industrial IoT, where backdoors could allow unauthorized access or disrupt operations.

These threats also extend to embedded malware detection. Severi et al. [47] showed that poisoning attacks on ML-based detectors in IoT gateways can reduce detection accuracy by inserting crafted malware samples that evade recognition. Such risks underscore concerns about the machine learning supply chain, especially in embedded contexts where pre-trained models are often reused due to resource constraints. Models sourced from untrusted providers may carry hidden malicious behavior that jeopardizes system integrity.

3.3 Model Theft and Extraction Attacks

Embedded machine learning models represent valuable intellectual property, often trained on proprietary or sensitive data. Attackers may steal or replicate these models through prediction query APIs, a method known as model extraction [54]. In embedded systems, physical access allows adversaries to directly read model parameters from memory or storage.

Recent studies highlight the vulnerability of on-device models in mobile and embedded platforms. Sun et al. [51] found that 41% of Android apps using machine learning lacked model protection, and 66% of those using encryption or obfuscation were still exposed to extraction via dynamic analysis. Many targeted models were commercial networks used in critical applications such as face recognition, identity verification, and malware detection.

To demonstrate this risk, Deng et al. [17] developed AdvDroid, a tool that extracts models by intercepting them at runtime. Since models must eventually be decrypted and loaded into memory, AdvDroid captures their weights in plaintext. This shows that attackers with user-level access or malware can retrieve models without relying on hardware-based channels.

Even when model files are not accessible, adversaries can replicate functionality. Huang and Chen [28] introduced the Smart App Attack, a gray-box method that identifies transfer learning from public models and reconstructs a surrogate model that mimics the original.

Models are also susceptible to physical side channel attacks. Batina et al. [9] extracted a convolutional neural network from a microcontroller by analyzing electromagnetic emissions. Such attacks compromise model confidentiality and may enable adversarial manipulation or further exploitation.

3.4 Side-Channel and Fault Injection Attacks

Physical access to embedded devices enables additional attack vectors not present in cloud-only ML deployments. *Side-channel attacks* exploit information leaked through physical signals (timing, power consumption, electromagnetic radiation) to infer internal computations. As mentioned above, such techniques have been used to extract neural network parameters [9] and could potentially uncover sensitive inputs processed by the model. Wei *et al.* showed that by collecting power traces from an FPGA-based convolutional neural network accelerator, an attacker could reconstruct input images with high accuracy [55]. In their attack, the power side-channel leakage from each convolution operation was sufficient to recover images from the MNIST dataset, illustrating that even without compromising the model's weights or software, one can infer private data being processed by the model.

Another class of attacks is *fault injection*, where an adversary deliberately induces errors in the device's computation (e.g., via clock/voltage glitches or memory bit flips). In an embedded context, fault attacks can be mounted with techniques like laser injections or Rowhammer, potentially causing a normally accurate model to misbehave in targeted ways. Yao *et al.* demonstrated a Rowhammer-based attack that flips bits in the weight memory of a quantized neural network at run-time [57]. By strategically targeting the most critical weight bits, their attack dramatically reduces the model's inference accuracy to nearly random guessing. This represents a powerful integrity attack, wherein an adversary with physical access can corrupt an ML model's functionality without altering its code.

These implementation-level attacks greatly expand the threat surface for embedded ML, since an attacker with brief physical proximity might compromise the model's integrity or extract secret information without ever interfacing with the model at the algorithmic level.

4 Privacy Challenges in Embedded ML

Privacy attacks targeting embedded ML models are an increasing concern. In the context of IoT and edge devices, researchers have identified several threats, including membership inference, model inversion, and other data leakage attacks that jeopardize the confidentiality of training data and sensor information.

4.1 Inference Attacks on Private Data

Even when an ML model functions correctly in terms of classification performance, it may inadvertently expose information about its training data, a serious privacy concern if that data is sensitive (e.g., personal user data collected by an IoT device). *Membership inference attacks* aim to determine whether a specific data record was used in training the model. It has been demonstrated that by observing a model's outputs, an attacker can often infer if a given sample was part of the training set, exploiting the fact that models sometimes output different confidence scores for seen versus unseen examples [50]. Another related threat is *model inversion*, wherein an attacker uses access to model predictions to reconstruct or approximate sensitive input data. It was famously shown that one could recover recognizable images of faces from a facial recognition model, effectively reversing the model to reveal personal data [21]. In the embedded setting, these privacy attacks could target models on smartphones or wearable health monitors, putting user data at risk. For instance, an attacker might query a health diagnostic model on a smartwatch to infer whether certain data (perhaps indicating a medical condition) was in the device's training set. The risk is exacerbated if the attacker manages to obtain the model parameters (through extraction attacks above), as white-box access can make membership or inversion attacks even easier.

4.2 Data Privacy in Distributed and On-Device Learning

Embedded ML often involves on-device data collection and sometimes on-device training or adaptation (e.g., personalization of a model to a user's data). Keeping data local is generally good for privacy, but it does not eliminate concerns. In *federated learning* scenarios [37], where devices collaboratively train a global model by transmitting updates rather than raw data, it has been shown that the shared model updates can still leak information about individual training examples. Attackers have demonstrated the ability to partially reconstruct original data from gradients meant to be aggregated in federated learning, thereby compromising privacy [36]. This illustrates that even privacy-focused training paradigms require additional safeguards. There is also a risk when models trained on device are later uploaded or shared (for model improvement or offloading computation), as those models might carry imprints of the user's data. Techniques like *differential privacy (DP)* provide formal guarantees by adding noise to the training process such that individual data points have limited influence on the final model [1]. Researchers have integrated DP into deep neural network training, demonstrating that it is possible to significantly reduce a classifier's leakage of individual examples, albeit at some cost in accuracy. However, adopting such techniques on the limited computational budget of embedded devices can be challenging.

5 Security Mitigations in Embedded ML

Embedded ML systems require a multifaceted defense strategy that balances strong protection with strict resource constraints. In this section, we review key security mitigation approaches for embedded machine learning devices, categorized into (i) lightweight software defenses, (ii) hardware protections, (iii) secure training and update mechanisms, and (iv) design trade-offs.

Table 1. Security Mitigations for Embedded ML: Threats, Techniques, and Deployment Stages

Threat	Mitigation Technique	Deployment Stage
Adversarial inputs (evasion)	Adversarial training; input anomaly detection	Training; Inference
Model theft/extraction	Model encryption or obfuscation; secure enclave execution	Deployment (model storage and inference)
Model tampering (poisoning)	Secure boot and signed model updates (authenticity check)	Update; Deployment
Side-channel attacks	Masking or hiding countermeasures; noise injection; use of TEE	Design; Inference
Fault injections	Redundant computations or error-detecting codes	Design; Inference

(i) Lightweight Software Defenses: Because many traditional security techniques are impractical on microcontroller-class devices (e.g. due to limited memory and CPU) , researchers have explored streamlined software-based defenses for on-device ML. One class of techniques focuses on making models themselves more robust to adversarial inputs. For example, adversarial training, which re-trains models with adversarially perturbed examples, can improve resilience to input manipulation; however, its on-device applicability is limited by the computation required during training. Some recent studies indicate that robust models can be quantized to TinyML settings without losing their adversarial resistance, incurring little runtime cost [31]. However, other work finds that naïve post-training quantization may nullify robustness gains [44], suggesting careful co-design of compression and defense is needed.

Aside from model retraining, lightweight input preprocessing can be employed (e.g., sensor signal filtering or feature squeezing) to reject obviously abnormal inputs before they reach the model. Another software-level safeguard is to secure the data pipeline: even constrained devices can implement basic encryption and authentication for sensor readings and ML outputs, preventing easy injection or spoofing of data. Similarly, protecting stored model parameters via obfuscation or lightweight encryption can impede model extraction attacks if an attacker dumps the firmware memory. These software defenses tend to introduce minimal overhead compared to heavy cryptographic protocols, making them suitable for real-time embedded use [30,31]. The trade-off, however, is that they often provide narrower protection (e.g., detecting certain anomalies) rather than a comprehensive shield.

(ii) Hardware Protections: Hardware-based security can provide stronger isolation and tamper resistance for embedded ML, though often at increased cost or complexity. A common strategy is deploying ML models within a Trusted Execution Environment (TEE) or secure enclave [6]. For example, ARM TrustZone on Cortex-M microcontrollers partitions the system into secure and normal regions, allowing sensitive components like neural networks, model weights, and cryptographic keys to be processed in protected memory, inaccessible to untrusted code. This defends against malware and memory extraction attacks.

Chip-level protections also support secure operations. Many IoT microcontrollers include hardware accelerators for encryption and random number generation, enabling secure boot and protected storage. Secure boot verifies firmware integrity using a hardware root of trust, preventing unauthorized code from running at startup [5]. Manufacturers further implement flash readout protection and memory access controls to block unauthorized access to stored models [31].

Defending against physical attacks such as side channel analysis is more difficult on low power devices. Mitigations like noise injection and power masking exist, but often introduce substantial memory and compute overhead that resource-constrained systems cannot afford [31]. As a result, embedded ML systems typically rely on built-in protections like tamper-resistant packaging, disabled debug ports, and secure co-processors.

Recent work shows that even small trusted hardware can greatly improve security. Huang et al. [27] introduced the Stamp framework, in which a minimal trusted chip handles cryptographic tasks for ML inference. This reduces communication overhead and improves inference speed by four to ten times compared to software-only methods, demonstrating the promise of specialized hardware for efficient ML protection.

(iii) Secure Training and Update Mechanisms: Beyond run-time protections, it is critical to secure the ML model's life cycle on embedded devices. Model parameters are often determined off-line, but increasingly devices may receive model updates over-the-air (OTA) or even perform on-device learning. To prevent adversarial model tampering, any model update must be delivered through authenticated channels (e.g., signed by the vendor and verified by the device's bootloader or TEE) [6]. This ensures only authentic, untampered updates are installed. They block unauthorized injection but won't detect a signed backdoor. Coupling secure boot with remote attestation further strengthens update integrity: the device can produce an attestation report (e.g., an Entity Attestation Token) that cryptographically proves to a verifier that it is running an expected model and software stack [5,6]. For training, if embedded devices contribute to a collaborative learning process (as in federated learning), additional safeguards are needed. Federated learning avoids transmitting raw data off the device, which is beneficial for privacy (see Sect. 6), but the model update gradients themselves could be poisoned or could leak information. Security-conscious training frameworks incorporate mechanisms like secure aggregation (so that a central server only receives aggregated, encrypted updates) and robust aggregation rules to ignore outlier submissions. For example, Ficco et al. [20] demonstrate a TinyML-friendly federated learning approach with on-board training, highlighting the importance of filtering and protecting gradient exchanges on resource-limited nodes. In general, embedded devices should restrict any local learning to well-vetted data and use techniques to detect anomalies (e.g., sudden accuracy drops) that might indicate an attack during training. Finally, the confidentiality of the model itself (if it represents intellectual property) during updates can be preserved by encrypting model weights in transit and only decrypting them within the device's secure hardware.

(iv) Design Trade-Offs: Implementing the above mitigations in embedded system deployments requires balancing security benefits against resource overhead and system performance. A clear theme is that heavyweight defenses suitable for cloud or desktop environments often cannot be directly applied on microcontrollers [31]. Every added runtime check, encryption step, or redundancy consumes extra cycles, memory, or energy all of which are at a premium in battery-powered embedded devices. Developers must therefore choose which threats to prioritize. For instance, enabling full side-channel protection (with constant-time operations, extensive masking, etc.) might reduce throughput or increase power draw beyond acceptable levels, so one might opt for partial mitigation or rely on physical barriers instead. Similarly, improving adversarial robustness via techniques like ensemble models or intensive adversarial training can significantly inflate model size or computation, conflicting with the tight latency and memory constraints of TinyML. Preuveneers et al. report that a model's resistance to adversarial examples can be greatly reduced after aggressive post-training quantization [44], meaning designers should integrate robustness into the training process rather than as an afterthought. On the other hand, some redundancy or lightweight error-detection might be acceptable to counter fault injection attacks in safety-critical scenarios, even if it incurs, say, a 20–30% performance overhead. Ultimately, the security of an embedded ML system is a result of careful design trade-offs: one must weigh the risk and impact of each threat against the cost (in execution time, memory footprint, power consumption, and hardware complexity) of the mitigation. A combination of complementary measures is often used to provide defense-in-depth without overburdening the device. Table 1 summarizes representative security threats to embedded ML and corresponding mitigations with notes on their overhead and deployment stage.

Table 2. Privacy Mitigations for Embedded ML: Threats, Techniques, and Overheads

Privacy Threat	Mitigation Technique	Overhead	Application Stage
Exposure of raw sensor data	On-device inference (local data processing)	Device computation load (instead of cloud)	Design; Deployment
Model inversion or membership inference	Differentially private training; output perturbation	Accuracy loss; extra training time	Training; Inference
Eavesdropping or data theft in transit	End-to-end encryption; TEE-based secure processing	Low to moderate (crypto processing overhead)	Deployment (runtime)
Collusion or inference in federated learning	Secure aggregation of updates; noise added to gradients	Communication and compute overhead (encryption, noise)	Training (distributed)
Model parameter leakage (via stolen model)	Encrypted model storage; attestation of model integrity	Low (storage encryption; attestation handshake)	Deployment (update; storage)

6 Privacy Mitigations in Embedded ML

Privacy preservation is a core motivation for deploying ML at the network edge, but it requires deliberate techniques to ensure that sensitive information in data and models remains protected. We now discuss privacy-focused mitigations in embedded ML under the same categorization: (i) lightweight software defenses, (ii) hardware protections, (iii) secure training and update mechanisms, and (iv) design trade-offs.

(i) Lightweight Software Defenses: The most fundamental privacy measure in embedded ML is to minimize data sharing by performing inference locally on the device. By keeping raw sensor data on-device and only transmitting processed decisions or summaries, one eliminates many avenues of data exposure [6]. This inherent data minimization is often cited as a benefit of TinyML in applications like wearable health monitors or smart home sensors, where personal data (e.g. audio, images, vitals) never leaves the device in identifiable form. Beyond this architectural principle, additional software techniques can enhance privacy. One is the application of *DP* to the model's training process. DP introduces carefully calibrated noise into training algorithms such that the influence of any single training example is obscured, providing a quantifiable privacy guarantee for individuals in the training dataset [1]. While DP is traditionally applied in cloud training, it can be relevant in embedded contexts where devices incrementally update models with local data or where a central party aggregates updates from many devices. For example, a microcontroller could locally perturb its model update (gradients) with noise before uploading it for federated aggregation, reducing the risk of leaking user-specific information. However, DP methods may degrade model accuracy or require many training iterations, which is a trade-off discussed below. At inference time, software can also sanitize outputs or restrict queries to prevent privacy leaks. Techniques like output perturbation (adding a small amount of noise to sensor readings or model outputs) or limiting the granularity of results (e.g., reporting a category or range instead of a precise value) make it harder for an adversary to infer details about the input data. Lightweight anonymization measures, such as stripping identifiers or hashing data and using only aggregate features, can be performed on-device before any data is logged or transmitted. These methods incur minimal performance cost, but they must be tuned so that the utility of the ML system is not significantly impaired.

(ii) Hardware Protections: Hardware-based privacy safeguards in embedded ML overlap with security mechanisms, focusing on protecting data confidentiality during processing. A key example is using on-chip TEE to handle sensitive data and ML models. By running inference inside a secure enclave (such as Arm TrustZone or a dedicated secure co-processor), the device ensures that raw data and intermediate computations are not exposed to the outside or to the device's normal operating environment. Islam et al. [32] develop a system for performing on-device inference of large DNN models within a TrustZone enclave on IoT/edge hardware. Their solution addresses the limited secure memory on typical edge devices by slicing or streaming model data, so even complex models can run inside the TEE without modifications or accuracy loss. Mo et al. [40] present a framework called DarkneTZ that leverages an edge device's ARM TrustZone TEE to shield deep learning models from information leakage. DarkneTZ partitions the neural network so that only certain "sensitive" layers run inside the secure enclave, limiting the attack surface. This approach was shown to defend against membership inference attacks on the model with minimal performance cost.

In addition to enclaves, encryption plays an important role at the hardware level: data can be encrypted at rest (in flash storage) and in transit (network communication) using lightweight ciphers, often with the assistance of hardware accelerators present on modern IoT chips. This prevents eavesdropping or data theft if the device is intercepted. Another emerging hardware solution is sensor-level encryption, where sensors output encrypted signals that only the trusted device processor can decrypt ensuring raw data is never available in memory in unencrypted form. While fully homomorphic encryption (FHE) or secure multi-party computation would allow computation on encrypted data without trusting hardware, those techniques remain computationally prohibitive on small devices. Researchers are exploring hybrid approaches: for instance, using a small trusted hardware module to perform the most sensitive operations while leaving less critical computations to an untrusted processor [27]. Such designs (as in the Stamp system [27]) can yield efficient privacy-preserving inference by significantly reducing the cost of cryptographic protocols. Overall, leveraging hardware roots of trust and accelerators can enforce strong data confidentiality with acceptable overhead in embedded ML deployments.

(iii) Secure Training and Update Mechanisms: A key privacy goal in model training and updates is avoiding centralized collection of raw data. Federated learning (FL) addresses this by keeping data on devices and only sharing model updates (e.g., gradients) with a central server for aggregation [20,37]. This allows embedded devices to contribute to a global model without revealing local datasets. For instance, Ficco et al. [20] demonstrate personalized TinyML training on IoT nodes while preserving data locality.

However, even model updates can leak private information. To counteract this, FL often incorporates secure aggregation, where the server receives only the sum of updates, using cryptographic methods such as homomorphic encryption or secret sharing, preventing inspection of individual contributions. Though scalable, these schemes can be difficult to deploy on highly constrained devices. DP is another safeguard: devices or servers add noise to updates, limiting the information that can be inferred about any single node [1].

When updating models via the cloud, it is critical to prevent privacy leaks. New models should not embed sensitive training data, especially if memorized.

One solution is to perform personalization within a trusted execution environment (TEE), ensuring that only encrypted or sanitized models are deployed.

In summary, embedded ML training and updates should prioritize data locality and use cryptographic or noise-based protections whenever data or parameters are shared.

(iv) Design Trade-Offs: Ensuring privacy in embedded ML requires balancing it with model performance, resource use, and system complexity. A key trade-off is between privacy and accuracy. Techniques like DP add noise to protect data, which can reduce accuracy or slow convergence [1]. In TinyML settings with limited local data, this degradation can be more pronounced, affecting personalization and model quality. Choosing DP parameters, such as the privacy budget ϵ, requires careful tuning to balance privacy and utility.

Privacy also impacts communication and computation. Keeping data on-device avoids cloud exposure but increases local processing demands. Battery-powered nodes may struggle with federated learning's communication rounds or the compute needed for local training and noise generation. Trust assumptions present another trade-off: hardware-based solutions like TEEs are efficient but depend on trusted vendors and may still leak data via side channels. Purely cryptographic methods (e.g., MPC, FHE) avoid hardware trust but are often too resource-intensive for low-end devices [27]. The Stamp framework highlights this trade-off by introducing minimal trusted components to accelerate secure computation [27].

Ultimately, privacy must be weighed against user experience. Running voice recognition on-device can protect data but may degrade performance, prompting users to prefer cloud-based solutions. A common compromise processes data locally and sends only minimal or encrypted data to the cloud. Table 2 summarizes key privacy threats, mitigation techniques, and their deployment stages.

Despite these efforts, achieving robust security and privacy in embedded ML remains difficult. Attacks and defenses are in constant co-evolution, and techniques must be tailored to the constraints of edge devices (limited processing power, energy, and memory). A combination of software-level safeguards, hardware support, and judicious trade-offs between model complexity and attack surface is likely needed.

7 Open Challenges and Future Research Directions

Lightweight and Scalable ML Defenses: A key challenge is developing defenses suitable for resource-constrained devices. Traditional mechanisms like complex encryption or anomaly detectors are often too heavy for embedded ML. Research is shifting toward lightweight, scalable approaches that preserve robustness while respecting hardware limits, such as adversarially trained or pruned TinyML models [2,31]. Recent work emphasizes co-designing models with security features to reduce runtime cost and avoid central bottlenecks when deployed across device fleets [2]. Designing efficient, scalable defenses while balancing accuracy, latency, and security remains an open area [7].

Hardware-Software Co-design: Effective security for embedded ML requires integration of hardware and software protections. Instead of adding security post-hoc, recent designs embed it into firmware and accelerators [18]. For instance, ML inference chips with side channel resistance, or secure coprocessors like masked RISC-V cores, can block physical attacks. Combining these with software aware of hardware guarantees (e.g., TEE or device-specific keys) ensures confidentiality and integrity across the stack [58]. Co-designing models, software, and hardware is essential for defending against attacks beyond software-only solutions [18,58].

Secure Model Update and Lifecycle Management: ML models in embedded systems often require updates, which present security risks. Attackers could inject backdoored models or tamper with parameters [23]. To mitigate this, update pipelines must support signing, authentication, and post-deployment validation [16]. Full-lifecycle protection includes securing training data, validating models under adversarial scenarios, and monitoring behavior in the field for drift or attack patterns [16,35]. Automating these protections, especially for firmware or MLOps pipelines, is vital to reduce risk and support safe updates.

Standardization and Benchmarking: Security evaluations for embedded ML remain fragmented. The community needs shared benchmarks and evaluation criteria, similar to standard datasets in core ML. Early efforts include MLPerf Tiny for performance and MITRE ATLAS for adversarial taxonomy [8,39]. Still, there is no consensus on certification standards or baseline practices for embedded AI. Broader adoption of common benchmarks and organized challenges could validate which techniques work in realistic settings and facilitate reproducible research.

Human-Centered Security and Ethics: Securing embedded ML involves more than technical measures. It requires ethical and user-focused design. Devices must be transparent and accountable. Documentation like model cards can explain intended use and assumptions [38]. Privacy techniques such as federated learning and DP help safeguard sensitive data. Fairness and explainability are also critical: even on constrained hardware, models must operate without bias and be interpretable [31]. Future research must align security with ethical practices to preserve public trust.

Cross-Disciplinary Collaboration: Embedded ML security spans hardware, software, and AI. Isolated solutions often miss important risks, so collaboration among experts from machine learning, cybersecurity, hardware, and HCI is crucial [7]. Cross-sector partnerships among academia, industry, and government can drive standards, open-source tools, and shared best practices. Embedding security researchers in model teams or running co-design workshops are promising approaches to anticipating vulnerabilities [18]. Cultivating this interdisciplinary culture will be key to securing future embedded AI deployments.

8 Conclusion

Embedded machine learning (ML) offers powerful opportunities for intelligent services, but it also expands the attack surface across both software and hardware. This review highlights key threats such as adversarial evasion, data poisoning, model theft, side channel attacks, and privacy risks from inference on personal data, and surveys practical defenses such as robust training, differential privacy, and hardware based protections. The core insight is that no single defense is sufficient; instead, a layered approach tailored to the device constraints is essential. In practice, stronger guarantees for privacy or integrity often come at the cost of latency, memory, or accuracy, requiring designers to balance protections against tight performance and energy budgets. Moreover, an embedded device cannot support every defense simultaneously; the stack should be limited to a few complementary lightweight techniques that fit within system budgets. The key lessons are: (i) adopt layered defenses; (ii) co design security and efficiency across training, compression, and quantization; (iii) secure the entire lifecycle with measures like secure boot and signed or attested updates, not just the inputs; and (iv) anticipate trade offs among privacy, utility, and resources.

References

1. Abadi, M., et al.: Deep learning with differential privacy. In: Proceedings of the 2016 ACM SIGSAC Conference on Computer and Communications Security (CCS), pp. 308–318 (2016). https://doi.org/10.1145/2976749.2978318
2. Alfahaid, A., Thompson, R., Barros, A.: Lightweight ML defenses for edge devices: a survey. IEEE Access **13**, 10456–10479 (2025). https://doi.org/10.1109/ACCESS.2025.3301486
3. Alkadi, S., Al-Ahmadi, S., Ismail, M.M.B.: Better safe than never: a survey on adversarial machine learning applications towards IoT environment. Appl. Sci. **13**(10) (2023). https://doi.org/10.3390/app13106001, https://www.mdpi.com/2076-3417/13/10/6001
4. Apache MXNet Team: Apache MXNet: A scalable deep learning framework (version 1.9.1) (2021). https://mxnet.apache.org/versions/1.9.1/. Accessed 17 Jul 2025
5. Asokan, N., et al.: SEDA: scalable embedded device attestation. In: Proceedings of the 22nd ACM SIGSAC Conference on Computer and Communications Security, pp. 964–975 (2015)
6. Baciu, V.E., Braeken, A., Segers, L., da Silva, B.: Secure tiny machine learning on edge devices: a lightweight dual attestation mechanism for machine learning. Fut. Internet **17**(2), 85 (2025). https://doi.org/10.3390/fi17020085
7. Balantrapu, A., Albarghoth, M.: Ai in constrained devices: challenges and directions for securing the future. IEEE Secur. Priv. **17**(6), 82–89 (2019). https://doi.org/10.1109/MSEC.2019.2913211
8. Banbury, C., Janapa Reddi, V., Torelli, P., Jeffries, N., Kir'aly, C., Holleman, J.e.: MLPerf tiny benchmark. NeurIPS Datasets and Benchmarks Track **1** (2021). https://datasets-benchmarks-proceedings.neurips.cc/paper/2021/file/da4fb5c6e93e74d3df8527599fa62642-Paper-round1.pdf

9. Batina, L., Bhasin, S., Jap, D., Picek, S.: {CSI}{NN}: reverse engineering of neural network architectures through electromagnetic side channel. In: 28th USENIX Security Symposium (USENIX Security 19), pp. 515–532 (2019)
10. Bogdanov, A., et al.: PRESENT: an ultra-lightweight block cipher. In: Paillier, P., Verbauwhede, I. (eds.) CHES 2007. LNCS, vol. 4727, pp. 450–466. Springer, Heidelberg (2007). https://doi.org/10.1007/978-3-540-74735-2_31
11. Cao, Y., et al.: Adversarial sensor attack on LiDAR-based perception in autonomous driving. In: Proceedings of the 2019 ACM SIGSAC Conference on Computer and Communications Security, pp. 2267–2281 (2019)
12. Carlini, N., Wagner, D.: Audio adversarial examples: targeted attacks on speech-to-text. In: 2018 IEEE security and privacy workshops (SPW), pp. 1–7. IEEE (2018)
13. Chen, H., Babar, M.A.: Security for machine learning-based software systems: a survey of threats, practices, and challenges. ACM Comput. Surv. **56**(6) (2024). https://doi.org/10.1145/3638531
14. Chen, X., Liu, C., Li, B., Lu, K., Song, D.: Targeted backdoor attacks on deep learning systems using data poisoning. arXiv preprint arXiv:1712.05526 (2017)
15. Cyient Technologies Ltd.: TinyML optimization approaches for deployment on edge devices. Whitepaper, April 2024. https://www.cyient.com/whitepaper/tiny-ml-optimization. Accessed 14 Jul 2025
16. Das, S., Shiva, S.: Machine learning application lifecycle augmented with explanation and security. In: 2021 IEEE 12th Annual Ubiquitous Computing, Electronics & Mobile Communication Conference (UEMCON), pp. 0171–0177. IEEE (2021)
17. Deng, Z., Chen, K., Meng, G., Zhang, X., Xu, K., Cheng, Y.: Understanding real-world threats to deep learning models in Android apps. In: Proceedings of the 2022 ACM SIGSAC Conference on Computer and Communications Security, pp. 785–799 (2022)
18. Dubey, A., Cammarota, R., Aysu, A.: MaskedNet: the first hardware inference engine aiming power side-channel protection. In: IEEE International Symposium on Hardware Oriented Security and Trust (HOST), pp. 197–208. IEEE (2020). https://doi.org/10.1109/HOST45689.2020.9300276
19. Eykholt, K., et al.: Robust physical-world attacks on deep learning visual classification. In: Proceedings of the IEEE Conference on Computer Vision and Pattern Recognition, pp. 1625–1634 (2018)
20. Ficco, M., Guerriero, A., Milite, E., Palmieri, F., Pietrantuono, R., Russo, S.: Federated learning for ioT devices: enhancing TinyML with on-board training. Inf. Fus. **104**, 102189 (2024)
21. Fredrikson, M., Jha, S., Ristenpart, T.: Model inversion attacks that exploit confidence information and basic countermeasures. In: Proceedings of the 22nd ACM SIGSAC Conference on Computer and Communications Security, pp. 1322–1333 (2015)
22. Goodfellow, I.J., Shlens, J., Szegedy, C.: Explaining and harnessing adversarial examples. arXiv preprint arXiv:1412.6572 (2014)
23. Gu, T., Dolan-Gavitt, B., Garg, S.: BadNets: identifying vulnerabilities in the machine learning model supply chain. arXiv preprint arXiv:1708.06733 (2017)
24. Haddadpajouh, H., Dehghantanha, A.: Make your IoT environments robust against adversarial machine learning malware threats: a code-cave approach (2024). https://doi.org/10.14722/sdiotsec.2024.23066
25. Han, S., Pool, J., Tran, J., Dally, W.: Learning both weights and connections for efficient neural network. Adv. Neural. Inf. Process. Syst. **28** (2015)

26. Hinton, G., Vinyals, O., Dean, J.: Distilling the knowledge in a neural network. arXiv preprint arXiv:1503.02531 (2015)
27. Huang, P., Hoang, T., Li, Y., Shi, E., Suh, G.E.: Efficient privacy-preserving machine learning with lightweight trusted hardware. Proc. Priv. Enhanc. Technol. **2024**(4), 327–348 (2024). https://doi.org/10.56553/popets-2024-0119
28. Huang, Y., Chen, C.: Smart app attack: hacking deep learning models in Android apps. IEEE Trans. Inf. Forensics Secur. **17**, 1827–1840 (2022)
29. Hubara, I., Courbariaux, M., Soudry, D., El-Yaniv, R., Bengio, Y.: Quantized neural networks: training neural networks with low precision weights and activations. J. Mach. Learn. Res. **18**(187), 1–30 (2018)
30. Huckelberry, J., Zhang, Y., Sansone, A., Mickens, J., Beerel, P.A., Reddi, V.J.: TinyML security: exploring vulnerabilities in resource-constrained machine learning systems. arXiv preprint arXiv:2411.07114 (2024)
31. Huckelberry, K., Seneviratne, S., Ren, K., Shi, W.: Security and privacy in TinyML: a survey. IEEE Internet Things J. **11**(1), 987–1005 (2024). https://doi.org/10.1109/JIOT.2024.3336142
32. Islam, M.S., Zamani, M., Kim, C.H., Khan, L., Hamlen, K.W.: Confidential execution of deep learning inference at the untrusted edge with ARM TrustZone. In: Proceedings of the Thirteenth ACM Conference on Data and Application Security and Privacy, pp. 153–164 (2023)
33. Kurakin, A., Goodfellow, I.J., Bengio, S.: Adversarial examples in the physical world. In: Artificial Intelligence Safety and Security, pp. 99–112. Chapman and Hall/CRC (2018)
34. Lasagne Team: Lasagne: lightweight library to build and train neural networks in Theano (2015). https://lasagne.readthedocs.io/en/latest/. Accessed 17 Jul 2025
35. infoedge LLC: Securing the machine learning lifecycle. https://infoedgellc.com/securing-the-machine-learning-lifecycle/. Accessed 31 Jul 2025
36. Ma, X., Li, B., Jiang, Q., Chen, Y., Gao, S., Ma, J.: NOSnoop: an effective collaborative meta-learning scheme against property inference attack. IEEE IoT J. **9**(9), 6778–6789 (2021)
37. McMahan, B., Moore, E., Ramage, D., Hampson, S., Arcas, B.A.: Communication-efficient learning of deep networks from decentralized data. In: Artificial Intelligence and Statistics, pp. 1273–1282. PMLR (2017)
38. Mitchell, M., et al.: Model cards for model reporting. In: Proceedings of the Conference on Fairness, Accountability, and Transparency, pp. 220–229 (2019)
39. MITRE: ATLAS: Adversarial threat landscape for artificialintelligence systems (2025). https://atlas.mitre.org/. Accessed 31 Jul 2025
40. Mo, F., et al.: DarkneTZ: towards model privacy at the edge using trusted execution environments. In: Proceedings of the 18th International Conference on Mobile Systems, Applications, and Services, pp. 161–174 (2020)
41. Papernot, N., McDaniel, P., Goodfellow, I.: Transferability in machine learning: from phenomena to black-box attacks using adversarial samples. arXiv preprint arXiv:1605.07277 (2016)
42. Papernot, N., McDaniel, P., Goodfellow, I., Jha, S., Celik, Z.B., Swami, A.: Practical black-box attacks against machine learning. In: Proceedings of the 2017 ACM on Asia Conference on Computer and Communications Security, pp. 506–519 (2017)
43. Plastiras, G., Terzi, M., Kyrkou, C., Theocharides, T.: Edge intelligence: challenges and opportunities of near-sensor machine learning applications. In: 2018 IEEE 29th International Conference on Application-Specific Systems, Architectures and Processors (ASAP), pp. 1–7. IEEE (2018)

44. Preuveneers, D., Verheyen, W., Joos, S., Joosen, W.: On the adversarial robustness of full integer quantized TinyML models at the edge. In: Proceedings of the 2nd International Workshop on Middleware for the Edge, pp. 7–12 (2023)
45. PyTorch Team: The road to 1.0: production ready PyTorch, May 2018. https://pytorch.org/blog/the-road-to-1_0/. Accessed 17 Jul 2025
46. Sah, R.K., Ghasemzadeh, H.: Adversarial transferability in embedded sensor systems: an activity recognition perspective. ACM Trans. Embed. Comput. Syst. **23**(2) (2024). https://doi.org/10.1145/3641861
47. Severi, G., Meyer, J., Coull, S., Oprea, A.: {Explanation-Guided} backdoor poisoning attacks against malware classifiers. In: 30th USENIX security symposium (USENIX Security 21), pp. 1487–1504 (2021)
48. Shafahi, A., et al.: Poison frogs! targeted clean-label poisoning attacks on neural networks. In: Advances in Neural Information Processing Systems, p. 31 (2018)
49. Sharif, M., Bhagavatula, S., Bauer, L., Reiter, M.K.: Accessorize to a crime: real and stealthy attacks on state-of-the-art face recognition. In: Proceedings of the 2016 ACM SIGSAC Conference on Computer and Communications Security, pp. 1528–1540 (2016)
50. Shokri, R., Stronati, M., Song, C., Shmatikov, V.: Membership inference attacks against machine learning models. In: 2017 IEEE Symposium on Security and Privacy (SP), pp. 3–18. IEEE (2017)
51. Sun, Z., Sun, R., Lu, L., Mislove, A.: Mind your weight(s): a large-scale study on insufficient machine learning model protection in mobile apps. In: 30th USENIX Security Symposium (USENIX Security 21), pp. 1955–1972 (2021)
52. Szegedy, C., et al.: Intriguing properties of neural networks. arXiv preprint arXiv:1312.6199 (2013)
53. Thys, S., Van Ranst, W., Goedemé, T.: Fooling automated surveillance cameras: adversarial patches to attack person detection. In: Proceedings of the IEEE/CVF Conference on Computer Vision and Pattern Recognition Workshops (2019)
54. Tramèr, F., Zhang, F., Juels, A., Reiter, M.K., Ristenpart, T.: Stealing machine learning models via prediction APIs. In: 25th USENIX Security Symposium. Austin, TX, USA (2016). https://www.usenix.org/conference/usenixsecurity16/technical-sessions/presentation/tramer
55. Wei, L., Luo, B., Li, Y., Liu, Y., Xu, Q.: I know what you see: power side-channel attack on convolutional neural network accelerators. In: Proceedings of the 34th Annual Computer Security Applications Conference, pp. 393–406 (2018)
56. Yang, J., et al.: Edge-cloud collaborative defense against backdoor attacks in federated learning. Sensors **23**(3), 1052 (2023)
57. Yao, F., Rakin, A.S., Fan, D.: {DeepHammer}: depleting the intelligence of deep neural networks through targeted chain of bit flips. In: 29th USENIX Security Symposium (USENIX Security 20), pp. 1463–1480 (2020)
58. Yu, Y., Huang, Y., Chen, Q.: Trustworthy inference with trusted execution environment in edge AI. IEEE Internet Things J. **7**(10), 9345–9355 (2020). https://doi.org/10.1109/JIOT.2020.2989206
59. Zhang, X., Chen, Y., Hao, C., Huang, S., Li, Y., Chen, D.: Compilation and optimizations for efficient machine learning on embedded systems (2022). https://arxiv.org/abs/2206.03326
60. Zhaohang, W., Geming, X., Jian, C., Chaodong, Y.: Adaptive asynchronous federated learning for edge intelligence. In: 2021 International Conference on Machine Learning and Intelligent Systems Engineering (MLISE), pp. 285–289. IEEE (2021)

Zero Trust Security Technologies, Applications, and Adoption Challenges

John Anderson[1], Mohammed Aldeen[1], Shuhao Zhang[1], Song Liao[2(✉)], Hongxin Hu[3], Mashrur Chowdhury[1], and Long Cheng[1]

[1] Clemson University, Clemson, SC, USA
{jda3,mshujaa,shuhaoz,mac,longcheng2}@clemson.edu
[2] Texas Tech University, Lubbock, TX, USA
song.liao@ttu.edu
[3] University at Buffalo, Buffalo, NY, USA
hongxinh@buffalo.edu

Abstract. Zero Trust Architecture (ZTA) has emerged as a foundational security paradigm that rejects the traditional model of implicit trust within network boundaries, instead enforcing rigorous verification across all connection and access attempts. This survey paper systematically examines the principles, technologies, and implementation strategies underpinning ZTA. We categorize ZTA-enabling mechanisms, including identity management, micro-segmentation, continuous authentication, and context-aware access control, and evaluate their operational roles across various real-world domains. Furthermore, we analyze current adoption trends, standardization efforts, and vendor-specific interpretations, identifying both practical deployment challenges and gaps in academic understanding. By mapping real-world deployments to theoretical models, this work clarifies the state of ZTA and outlines open research questions to guide future developments in secure, adaptive, and scalable Zero Trust systems.

Keywords: Zero Trust Architecture (ZTA) · Network Access · Least-Privilege Access · Continuous Authentication

1 Introduction

The increasing frequency, diversity, and sophistication of cyberattacks have rendered traditional perimeter-based security models insufficient for protecting contemporary digital infrastructures. Perimeter-centric approaches, which assume implicit trust within network boundaries, are unable to address threats originating from compromised internal actors, mobile devices, and third-party integrations [1]. In response, Zero Trust Architecture (ZTA) has emerged as a comprehensive security model grounded in the principle of "never trust, always verify" [2,3]. Unlike legacy models that grant access based on static trust assumptions, ZTA continuously validates every access request based on identity, context, and device posture [4].

L. Cheng and F. Anwar (Eds.): SmartSP 2025, LNICST 699, pp. 185–205, 2027.
https://doi.org/10.1007/978-3-032-33701-6_11

Zero Trust was first introduced in 2010 [2], and since then, it has matured into a robust framework supported by formal guidelines such as published by NIST [3], which delineates a comprehensive framework for ZTA and identifies the essential components and their roles in establishing a robust zero-trust model. These standards define a modular architecture emphasizing identity-based authentication, least privilege access, continuous monitoring, and real-time contextual analysis. Under ZTA, simply being connected to a particular network is not considered a valid indicator of trustworthiness. Instead, every access attempt must be independently evaluated using policy engines informed by dynamic telemetry and behavioral analytics.

This shift has been accelerated by organizational adoption of cloud computing, IoT technologies, and remote workforces, which have eroded the effectiveness of traditional perimeter defenses [3]. ZTA addresses this challenge by enabling granular, context-aware access control policies that span hybrid and multi-cloud infrastructures. Its model ensures that trust is earned and continuously reassessed, rather than statically assigned based on prior authentication. This paradigm allows for proactive defense against both external and insider threats, improving security posture across distributed systems [5].

While ZTA has gained momentum as a guiding principle, its implementation remains non-trivial. Existing literature and industrial efforts underscore the complexity of operationalizing ZTA at scale, particularly in environments constrained by legacy systems and heterogeneous infrastructures [6,7]. This paper contributes a structured review of ZTA research and practice, emphasizing the taxonomy of architectural models, enabling technologies, and domain-specific adaptations, through analysis of real-world implementations and challenges, with particular attention to policy orchestration, endpoint security, network segmentation, and continuous verification mechanisms [8,9].

Ultimately, this paper aims to advance understanding in a broad set of real-world use-cases. We identity a number of open challenges and propose future exploration opportunities to dive into their solutions.

2 Key Components of Zero Trust Architectures

ZTA has been the subject of many recent industry advancements, and yet those technologies rarely reflect the principle academic view of ZTA [10]. In this section, we will explore the key components from the agreed ZTA model, and use those as a foundation in describing the interesting technologies and challenges that have arisen through industry use of ZTA. Figure 1 presents the basic ZTA components and their interactions.

At the core of the ZTA framework is the Policy Decision Point (PDP), which is tasked with evaluating access requests in real-time. The PDP is a composite function that comprises the Policy Engine and the Policy Administrator, both of which play critical roles in its operation. The Policy Engine serves as the decision-making core of the PDP, leveraging predefined and dynamically updated policies to determine whether access should be granted or denied [11]. This

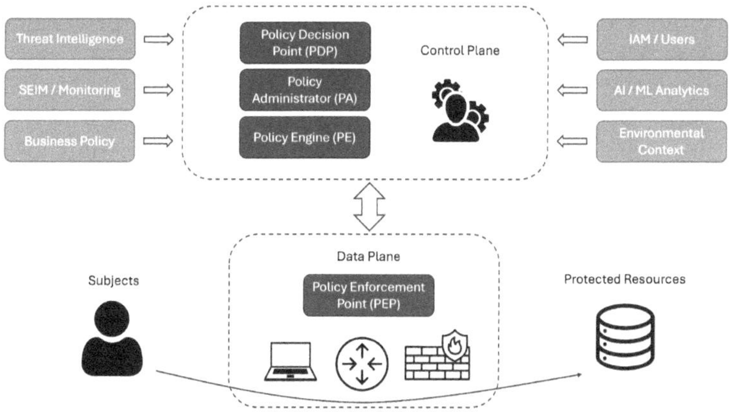

Fig. 1. High-level Zero Trust Architecture model illustrating the interaction between the control and data plane components, and external inputs, which together evaluate and translate policy rules for enforcement within the network.

component evaluates access requests against a set of rules and contextual factors, including user identity, device posture, location, and behavior analytics [4]. The outcomes are derived through rigorous application of access policies and may also incorporate risk scoring mechanisms to assess the trustworthiness of the request [12].

Complementing the Policy Engine is the Policy Administrator, which acts as the operational arm of the PDP. It is responsible for translating the decisions of the Policy Engine into actionable commands and ensuring their proper execution across the system. The Policy Administrator communicates directly with the Policy Enforcement Point (PEP) to apply the determined access permissions, revoke existing access where necessary, or implement additional security measures [11]. Together, these two subcomponents ensure that the PDP operates effectively as the central authority for access control decisions in a Zero Trust framework [3].

Supporting the PDP is the Policy Enforcement Point (PEP), which acts as a gatekeeper by enforcing access decisions. The PEP ensures that only authorized entities can interact with the system's resources, thereby maintaining stringent access control [11].

Another essential component is the Policy Information Point (PIP), which serves as a repository and aggregator of contextual data. This data includes attributes related to users, devices, and operational environments, which are critical for informed decision-making by the PDP [4]. The framework also identifies resources as the protected digital assets, applications, and services that constitute the system's operational scope. These resources are accessed by endpoints, which are devices or applications interfacing with the ZTA. Endpoint security and monitoring are integral to preventing unauthorized access and mitigating potential vulnerabilities [12].

To facilitate secure interactions, ZTA employs communication channels that ensure the confidentiality and integrity of data exchanged between components. These channels are underpinned by encryption protocols and continuous monitoring to detect and address potential breaches [11]. Additionally, access policies represent a dynamic and granular set of rules that dictate permissible actions within the system. These policies adapt to changing contexts, ensuring that access decisions remain relevant and effective [4].

By integrating these components, the ZTA framework establishes a security model that minimizes implicit trust and proactively mitigates threats. NIST emphasizes the importance of leveraging advanced contextual analysis, such as behavioral analytics and device health assessments, to fortify the decision-making process [11]. This approach not only enhances security but also ensures operational resilience in the face of evolving cyber-threats.

As-is evident throughout the architecture, the use of continuous checks vs. point-in-time during connection establishment is a vital principal of ZTA, and thus authentication and authorization are no different. Continuous authentication leverages dynamic and context-aware factors, such as behavioral biometrics, device posture, geolocation, and patterns of user interaction, to continually assess the legitimacy of access requests [5]. Similarly, continuous authorization evaluates ongoing access conditions and adjusts permissions dynamically based on real-time contextual information [9]. This approach significantly reduces the risk of unauthorized access by addressing potential threats as they emerge, maintaining a robust and adaptive security posture.

3 Architectural Models for ZTA

ZTA can be instantiated through a variety of architectural models, each tailored to different operational contexts and security requirements. These models range from centralized controller-based systems prevalent in enterprise networks to decentralized frameworks that leverage blockchain and other distributed technologies. NIST guidelines remain foundational for ZTA implementations, emphasizing modularity, continuous monitoring, and least privilege enforcement [4]. In practice, implementations typically rely on core modular components, such as multifactor authentication, micro-segmentation, and endpoint monitoring, that support flexibility across deployment scenarios [13].

3.1 Centralized Architectures

Centralized controller architectures are among the most widely adopted in enterprise environments due to their operational simplicity and ease of integration with existing infrastructure [3]. These models typically rely on a centralized Policy Decision Point (PDP) to enforce access control across networked resources. Kang et al. propose a distributed, microservices-based OpenDaylight SDN controller that integrates user authentication, device attestation, and dynamic authorization capabilities [7]. This design includes network monitoring probes to enable context-aware enforcement and traffic segmentation.

Complementary work by Fu et al. demonstrates how open-source tools—such as Wazuh, SonarQube, and Caldera—can be orchestrated via automation frameworks like Ansible to implement continuous monitoring, compliance auditing, and dynamic least privilege enforcement [8]. These centralized models often integrate with identity and access management systems and remote browser isolation to ensure comprehensive policy control.

Despite their practicality, centralized architectures can encounter scalability limitations in large or heterogeneous environments. Although the NIST model does not mandate centralization, it is often the default choice in industry due to ease of deployment and management [3]. Nonetheless, scalability and fault tolerance remain concerns, particularly as enterprise networks become increasingly distributed.

3.2 Decentralized and Distributed Trust Models

In contrast to centralized approaches, decentralized architectures aim to distribute trust and eliminate single points of failure. These models often leverage Distributed Ledger Technologies (DLTs), including blockchain, to enable verifiable and tamper-resistant credential management [14,15]. Through cryptographic validation of access transactions, these systems support secure issuance, revocation, and presentation of identity credentials, eliminating the need for a centralized authority [16,17].

Decentralized trust models offer intrinsic advantages in terms of resilience and compromise containment. For example, Zanasi et al. and Saraf and Sabadra illustrate how DLTs can enhance the security of industrial control systems by removing reliance on a central trust anchor [15,16]. However, practical challenges remain. Gunsay and Yayla highlight the complexity of implementing decentralized schemes at scale, particularly due to the need for significant endpoint reconfiguration [17]. Moreover, the latency and transactional overhead of blockchain systems can impede real-time access decisions, a critical requirement for many ZTA deployments. A more pragmatic approach is offered by Muhammad et al., who propose a layered defense model that integrates decentralized principles with industry-standard technologies [14]. This hybrid strategy enables organizations to benefit from decentralization without incurring prohibitive operational complexity.

3.3 Toward Hybrid and Adaptive Models

Given the diversity of operational environments and technological constraints, emerging ZTA architectures are increasingly hybrid. These models selectively combine centralized orchestration with decentralized verification, cloud-native policy enforcement, and edge analytics. Such adaptability supports the scalability required in cloud and 5G environments while maintaining the context-aware, risk-based control principles foundational to Zero Trust.

4 Enabling Technologies

In practice, ZTA relies on a diverse set of enabling technologies to support its core principles, including continuous verification, least privilege access, and dynamic security policies. These technologies facilitate robust identity management, access control, network segmentation, and security analytics, ensuring that Zero Trust frameworks remain effective in mitigating modern cyber threats. This section explores key enabling technologies that underpin the practical deployment of ZTA across various environments. Table 1 summarizes six of the core enabling technologies that organizations deploy when moving toward ZTA. We evaluate each against four high-level ZTA pillars—Identity Management, Threat Detection, Continuous Authentication, and Scalability—and we note the relative Deployment Complexity.

Table 1. Comparison of core enabling technologies for Zero Trust Architecture. A ✓ indicates the technology inherently addresses the specified pillar, and a ✗ denotes it does not natively fulfill that pillar.

Technology	Identity Management	Threat Detection	Continuous Authentication	Scalability	Deployment Complexity	Source
IAM (MFA, SSO, RBAC)	✓	✗	✓	✓	Moderate	[3,4]
EDR/XDR	✗	✓	✓	✗	High	[7,9]
Microsegmentation	✗	✗	✗	✓	High	[7,11]
CASB	✓	✓	✗	✓	Moderate	[5]
AI/ML Analytics	✗	✓	✓	✓	High	[18,19]
Blockchain	✓	✗	✓	✗	Very High	[17,20]
SMPC	✗	✓	✓	✗	High	[21]

4.1 Identity and Access Management

Identity and Access Management (IAM) is fundamental to ZTA, as it ensures that only authenticated and authorized users and devices gain access to protected resources. Modern IAM solutions incorporate Multi-Factor Authentication (MFA), Single Sign-On (SSO), and federated identity management to enhance authentication security [2]. Attribute-Based Access Control (ABAC) and Role-Based Access Control (RBAC) mechanisms dynamically enforce access policies based on user roles, device attributes, and real-time contextual information [3]. Advanced IAM frameworks leverage continuous authentication, ensuring that access remains restricted even after initial verification [4].

4.2 Endpoint Protection

Endpoint Detection and Response (EDR) and Extended Detection and Response (XDR) solutions play a crucial role in continuously monitoring and securing endpoints within a Zero Trust framework [5,22,23]. EDR systems detect and respond to anomalous behavior at the device level, mitigating risks associated with malware, unauthorized access, and data exfiltration [7]. By continuously assessing device health and enforcing compliance policies, EDR solutions reinforce ZTA's zero trust posture. XDR extends this capability by integrating telemetry from multiple security sources, such as network traffic, cloud services, and user behavior analytics, to provide a comprehensive threat detection and incident response mechanism [9].

4.3 Micro-Segmentation

Micro-segmentation enhances security by dividing networks into smaller, isolated segments, ensuring that lateral movement is restricted even in the event of a breach. This approach can be implemented using Software Defined Networking (SDN), which dynamically enforces security policies based on real-time network activity [6]. SDN-based micro-segmentation allows organizations to apply fine-grained access controls, reducing attack surfaces and containing potential threats within defined security zones [5].

4.4 Edge Network Access

Secure Access Service Edge (SASE) integrates networking and security services into a unified cloud-based model, enabling organizations to enforce consistent security policies across distributed environments [24]. SASE represents a convergence of wide-area networking (WAN) and network security services—such as firewall-as-a-service (FWaaS), secure web gateways (SWG), cloud access security brokers (CASB), and Zero Trust Network Access (ZTNA)—into a single, cloud-managed platform [23]. This convergence reduces complexity, improves scalability, and supports mobile and remote users by bringing security enforcement closer to the point of access. A core component of SASE, ZTNA replaces traditional VPNs by verifying user and device identities at each access request, ensuring that trust is never implicitly granted [25]. SASE combines capabilities such as secure web gateways, ZTNA, and data loss prevention (DLP) to ensure consistent policies across access points. ZTNA solutions provide encrypted, least-privilege access to applications, minimizing exposure to potential attackers [26].

4.5 Threat Intelligence, AI, and Automated Response

Threat intelligence and artificial intelligence (AI) technologies play a critical role in enhancing Zero Trust Architecture (ZTA) by enabling real-time detection, prediction, and response to evolving threats. Threat intelligence platforms leverage machine learning (ML) and AI to aggregate and analyze security event data from various sources, supporting proactive threat hunting and dynamic risk assessment [19]. Behavioral analytics and anomaly detection continuously evaluate user activities, flagging deviations from established baselines to inform access decisions and threat responses [23]. AI-driven security solutions further extend these capabilities by automating threat detection and response processes [27]. Algorithms analyze behavioral patterns, device telemetry, and network traffic to identify and contain threats in real-time [20]. Automated mechanisms, such as Security Orchestration, Automation, and Response (SOAR) platforms, facilitate rapid and coordinated mitigation of incidents without the need for human intervention [28]. AI also enables predictive analytics, improving the accuracy and contextual relevance of security policies while enhancing the overall resilience of ZTA systems.

4.6 Encryption and Secure Communication Protocols

Encryption is a cornerstone of ZTA, ensuring the confidentiality and integrity of data both in transit and at rest [29]. Transport Layer Security (TLS), Secure Shell (SSH), and end-to-end encryption mechanisms prevent unauthorized interception of sensitive information [30]. Secure communication protocols, such as IPsec and DNS-over-HTTPS (DoH), further strengthen Zero Trust implementations by securing data exchange across networks [31].

4.7 Cloud Workloads and Connectivity

Modern cloud providers offer visibility and control over cloud-based applications and services, enforcing data security policies and compliance requirements [11]. Cloud Access Security Brokers (CASBs) extend Zero Trust principles to cloud environments, enforcing security policies for data access, preventing unauthorized activities, and ensuring compliance with regulatory requirements. Secure Cloud Gateways prevent unauthorized access to SaaS, IaaS, and PaaS platforms [14]. By implementing DLP measures, CASBs mitigate risks associated with shadow IT and unsanctioned cloud usage [32].

4.8 Blockchain and Decentralized Trust Mechanisms

Blockchain technology offers a decentralized approach to identity verification and access management [33]. The immutable nature of blockchain ledgers ensures that all access decisions are securely logged, providing an auditable trail for compliance and security purposes. By maintaining cryptographically verified transactions, blockchain-based access control systems reduce reliance on centralized trust authorities [34]. Secure Multi-Party Computation (SMPC) further enhances privacy-preserving authentication by enabling collaborative computations without exposing sensitive data [21]. This capability is particularly useful in cross-organizational contexts, where data confidentiality is paramount.

5 Domain Specific ZTA

ZTA adapts to the unique requirements of different domains by leveraging tailored approaches and technologies to address domain-specific challenges. We highlight its applications in enterprise environments, Internet of Things (IoT) ecosystems, 5G/6G networks, cloud computing, and Connected and Automated

Vehicles (CAVs). Table 2 illustrates the key focus areas of domain as it relates to security challenges, i.e. what makes each domain unique, and the core ZTA tenants and enabling technologies used within the domains to meet those needs.

Table 2. Adaptation of ZTA across application domains, showing security focus areas, and ZTA technologies used.

Domain	Key Challenges Addressed	ZTA Components Emphasized	Representative Works
Enterprise	Hybrid workforce, regulatory compliance	IAM, EDR, Micro-segmentation	[3,10,22]
Internet of Things (IoT)	Device heterogeneity, resource constraints	Lightweight authentication, Secure communication, ABAC	[25,26,35]
5G/6G Networks	Massive scale, low latency, network slicing	ZTNA, Dynamic authentication, AI-based trust scoring	[19,28,33]
Cloud Computing	Elastic workloads, shadow IT	CASBs, Federated identity, Data encryption	[11,14,32]
Connected and Automated Vehicles (CAVs)	Real-time control, mobility, external communication	SMPC, Secure firmware, Authenticated communication channels	[20,21,36]

5.1 Enterprise Environments

Enterprises often operate in highly dynamic and distributed settings, requiring robust security measures to protect sensitive data and critical infrastructure. ZTA in enterprise environments emphasizes strong identity and access management (IAM) systems, continuous monitoring, and granular policy enforcement [10]. By integrating micro-segmentation and endpoint detection and response (EDR) tools, enterprises can minimize lateral movement of threats and ensure compliance with regulatory standards [5,22]. These measures are particularly critical in hybrid work settings, where employees access resources from diverse locations and devices [37].

5.2 Internet of Things (IoT)

IoT ecosystems comprise vast networks of interconnected devices, often with limited computational resources and security capabilities. ZTA addresses IoT-specific challenges by implementing lightweight authentication protocols, secure firmware updates, and device-level anomaly detection [35]. Additionally, leveraging secure communication channels and encryption ensures the integrity of data exchanges [26]. Dynamic trust evaluation mechanisms are critical in IoT settings, as devices may join or leave the network frequently, necessitating real-time access control adjustments [25].

5.3 5G/6G Networks

The advent of 5G and emerging 6G networks introduces ultra-low latency, high-speed connectivity, and massive device density, which expand the attack surface. ZTA frameworks in these networks integrate zero trust network access (ZTNA) principles to protect user data and critical infrastructure [19]. Network slicing—a key feature of 5G and 6G—is secured through isolation techniques and granular policy enforcement, ensuring that malicious activity in one slice does not compromise others [33]. Continuous authentication and advanced analytics are essential for maintaining a secure and resilient network environment [28].

5.4 Cloud Computing

As organizations migrate to cloud platforms, ensuring security across multi-cloud and hybrid cloud environments becomes paramount. ZTA in cloud computing focuses on secure access to virtualized resources, real-time threat detection, and stringent data protection measures [27]. Cloud Access Security Brokers (CASBs) play a pivotal role by providing visibility and control over cloud-based applications, enforcing compliance, and preventing unauthorized data sharing [11]. Additionally, encryption of data both in transit and at rest is a cornerstone of ZTA implementations in the cloud [14].

5.5 Connected and Automated Vehicles (CAVs)

CAVs rely on a complex interplay of sensors, software, and communication networks to operate safely and efficiently. ZTA enhances the security of CAV systems by implementing secure firmware updates, endpoint monitoring, and real-time anomaly detection [36]. Secure multi-party computation (SMPC) techniques are employed to protect sensitive data exchanges between vehicles and infrastructure, such as traffic management systems [21]. Furthermore, ZTA frameworks in CAVs ensure that communication channels between vehicles and external systems are authenticated and encrypted to prevent unauthorized access and data manipulation [20]. By tailoring ZTA principles and technologies to these diverse domains, organizations can address their unique security challenges while maintaining a consistent and robust zero trust posture. These domain-specific adaptations highlight the flexibility and scalability of ZTA in securing modern digital ecosystems.

6 Industry Adoption of ZTA

The practical implementation of ZTA by leading technology vendors reveals the complexities of operationalizing academic principles in real-world settings. Organizations such as Amazon Web Services (AWS), Palo Alto Networks, Microsoft, Google, and Cisco have adopted/embraced ZTA frameworks to enhance security across hybrid and distributed environments. While there are not the only vendors to offer Zero Trust related productions, these implementations provide both validation and critique of the theoretical Zero Trust model, offering insights into pragmatic constraints, deployment strategies, and the diversity of interpretation across vendors.

6.1 Amazon Web Services (AWS)

AWS offers a Zero Trust model that leverages its native cloud services to enforce identity-centric and context-aware access controls. Key components include AWS Identity and Access Management (IAM), Amazon VPC Lattice, and AWS Verified Access, which collectively provide continuous authentication, micro-segmentation, and centralized policy management [38]. The AWS Zero Trust Accelerator for Government (ZTAG) is designed to help public sector entities comply with federal mandates, such as those outlined in Executive Order 14028 [39].

While AWS aligns with many NIST ZTA recommendations [3], its reliance on proprietary services can present challenges for vendor-neutral or multi-cloud implementations. Additionally, the complexity of managing least privilege and segmentation policies across highly dynamic cloud environments can inhibit strict adherence to academic ZTA models [10].

6.2 Palo Alto Networks

Palo Alto Networks delivers an end-to-end Zero Trust solution through a portfolio that includes Prisma Access (ZTNA), Cortex XSOAR (automated threat response), and Next-Generation Firewalls (NGFWs). This architecture is designed to provide continuous verification, granular policy enforcement, and automated threat mitigation across enterprise and cloud networks [40]. Through a strategic partnership with Deloitte, Palo Alto emphasizes scalable ZTA adoption using reference architectures and integration blueprints [41].

Despite closely mirroring academic ZTA principles—such as contextual decision-making and micro-perimeter enforcement—these systems require high levels of integration expertise and significant resource investment [5,22]. Additionally, their effectiveness depends on the coherence of tool interoperability and real-time telemetry analysis.

6.3 Microsoft

Microsoft operationalizes ZTA across its cloud ecosystem using Entra ID (formerly Azure Active Directory), Microsoft Defender for Endpoint, and Microsoft Sentinel. These tools enforce explicit verification, conditional access, and behavioral anomaly detection [42]. Microsoft's model emphasizes the convergence of Zero Trust pillars: identity, device, application, data, infrastructure, and network.

The Microsoft implementation adheres to academic models by prioritizing continuous authentication and telemetry-informed decision-making [4,19]. However, organizations face challenges in integrating these services into legacy infrastructures and ensuring policy consistency across hybrid deployments [23].

6.4 Google

Google's BeyondCorp initiative is one of the earliest commercial embodiments of ZTA principles. It eliminates implicit trust by enforcing user- and device-based access through identity-aware proxies and real-time risk assessments [43]. BeyondCorp demonstrates high fidelity to academic models by implementing continuous verification, device health monitoring, and least privilege enforcement without reliance on network location.

Yet, this model demands robust internal telemetry systems and organizational readiness for cultural and operational transformation. Migrating from traditional perimeter models to a BeyondCorp-style deployment may involve considerable complexity, particularly for enterprises with diverse or legacy systems [6].

6.5 Cisco

Cisco's Zero Trust framework is delivered through a modular set of services, including Cisco Duo for authentication, Umbrella for secure internet access, and Identity Services Engine (ISE) for dynamic policy enforcement [44]. Cisco categorizes its model across three domains: workforce, workload, and workplace, aligning access control mechanisms to each operational context.

Although Cisco's ZTA offerings reflect academic expectations for segmentation, identity validation, and continuous monitoring, they also exemplify vendor-driven interpretations of ZTA. As with AWS and Microsoft, Cisco's approach raises interoperability and vendor lock-in concerns for organizations aiming for agnostic or federated ZTA solutions [5,33].

6.6 NVIDIA

NVIDIA brings a hardware-accelerated perspective to Zero Trust Architecture, tailoring its implementation for high-performance computing (HPC), AI infrastructure, and edge data center environments. Central to its approach is the use of BlueField data processing units (DPUs), which offload security enforcement from host CPUs and perform real-time policy execution at the network interface layer [45]. These DPUs enable fine-grained segmentation, encrypted communications, and continuous telemetry collection—aligned with ZTA's principles of least privilege and continuous verification.

In addition to hardware-based enforcement, NVIDIA integrates AI-powered threat detection through its Morpheus cybersecurity framework. Morpheus leverages GPU-accelerated machine learning models to perform real-time anomaly detection, behavioral analysis, and adaptive threat response across infrastructure components. This aligns with academic models that emphasize dynamic risk scoring and context-aware decision-making [23,28].

While NVIDIA's implementation adheres to core Zero Trust tenets, it is deeply tied to NVIDIA's hardware ecosystem. This presents challenges for general-purpose or mixed-infrastructure environments where hardware replacement or platform standardization may be impractical. Nonetheless, NVIDIA's model highlights an emerging trend: embedding Zero Trust enforcement natively within the computing fabric to support secure, low-latency decision-making in distributed and performance-sensitive environments.

6.7 Barriers to Customer Adoption

Despite the proliferation of vendor-supported ZTA solutions, industry adoption faces recurring challenges:

- **Integration Complexity**: ZTA requires unifying multiple security tools and telemetry sources, often across hybrid or multi-cloud environments [8].
- **Scalability**: Continuous monitoring, authentication, and real-time policy evaluation can strain network and compute resources in large-scale deployments [7,23].
- **User Experience**: Overly stringent access controls may impair usability, necessitating adaptive policies that balance risk with operational fluidity [28].
- **Vendor Lock-in**: Solutions built exclusively within one ecosystem risk losing flexibility and complicating federated policy governance [10].

These observations suggest that while vendor implementations offer pathways to operationalizing ZTA, they frequently abstract or dilute the rigorous assumptions found in academic frameworks. Therefore, organizations must critically evaluate vendor offerings against their specific risk models and architectural constraints.

7 Open Challenges and Future Trends

7.1 Usability and Privacy

Despite growing adoption, the practical realization of ZTA continues to face several unresolved challenges. One of the primary difficulties lies in balancing stringent security policies with usability. Overly aggressive enforcement of least privilege or continuous authentication can degrade user experience and operational efficiency [10]. This trade-off necessitates research into adaptive trust mechanisms that can dynamically calibrate access controls based on risk context. ZTA continuously monitors users' requests and analyzes their behaviors, posing an increased risk to users' privacy and data protection [46,47]. Zero-trust solutions may require users' sensitive personal information for user authentication, *e.g.*, emails and passwords [22,48–50], or be used for further tasks like anomaly detection. However, limited work has been conducted on the privacy compliance of zero-trust systems. Researchers have identified privacy concerns in remote work and Bring Your Own Device (BYOD) scenarios, where participants reported feeling their privacy was being invaded [51,52]. In a previous study [51], 14.8% of participants responded "yes" and 37% answered "sometimes" feeling their privacy is invaded as a consequence of active BYOD security measures. The perception of privacy invasion may stem from uncertainty about the extent of the monitoring policies or a sense that the company does not trust them. Therefore, it is important to address employees' privacy concerns and improve the trust and transparency regarding the data disclosure between employees and the company.

Another prominent challenge involves integration with legacy systems and heterogeneous infrastructure. Many organizations operate complex IT environments where Zero Trust principles cannot be uniformly applied due to legacy protocols, incompatible systems, and limited visibility [5]. This requires hybrid models and migration frameworks that support incremental adoption of ZTA without compromising service continuity [23]. These constraints frequently manifest in privacy concerns for end users. The controls necessarily require elevated access and/or insight into the operation and state of any given node on the network. While not unique, BYOD environments present acute privacy violation challenges, because the organization implementing the ZTA, does not own the user's devices [53]. On the other hand, system administrators may lack a complete understanding of privacy compliance requirements mandated by various privacy regulations, such as the GDPR [54], HIPAA [55], and COPPA [56], which could lead to a potential violation of privacy regulations. One possible solution is to develop transparent privacy notification mechanisms to ensure privacy compliance of the zero-trust system by identifying data collection behaviors first and then providing interactive privacy notifications.

7.2 Scalability and Performance

Scalability and performance constraints also pose significant concerns. Zero Trust demands pervasive telemetry collection, real-time policy evaluation, and frequent identity verification, which can strain network and processing resources, particularly in high-throughput environments [22]. Efficient architectures and lightweight cryptographic primitives are essential to maintain performance while preserving security guarantees. The advent of edge computing and 6G networks introduces further complexities, as decentralized and ephemeral endpoints require continuous verification in resource-constrained environments [18,19]. Emerging solutions such as blockchain, decentralized identifiers, and digital twins offer promise, but their integration into Zero Trust ecosystems remains an open area of exploration [20,57].

The increasing complexity of zero-trust security in modern enterprises, especially in remote work environments, places substantial performance demands on network security infrastructure. While SmartNICs (Smart Network Interface Cards) provide hardware acceleration and offloading capabilities, existing solutions lack dedicated modules tailored for zero-trust policy enforcement. Therefore, one solution is to establish SmartNIC-accelerated zero-trust enforcement as a scalable, high-performance alternative to traditional CPU-bound security models. It is possible to apply hardware-accelerated techniques to achieve faster policy enforcement. By integrating AI-powered behavioral analytics, hardware offloading, and SDN-driven policy enforcement, it enables real-time and intelligent zero-trust security to protect against advanced cyber threats and insider risks.

7.3 Deriving and Enforcing Policy Intent in ZTA

A foundational tenet of ZTA is the strict requirement for explicitly defined access control policies. In contrast to implicit trust or static perimeter-based rules, ZTA mandates that every access request be evaluated in real-time based on formalized policy intent. However, deriving, expressing, and enforcing such intent in practice remains a complex challenge, especially in dynamic and heterogeneous environments such as those supporting remote work, hybrid cloud, and decentralized edge computing [3,53].

One of the central open problems is designing expressive, yet tractable, policy specification languages that can encode context-aware rules aligned with Zero Trust principles. Traditional network policy frameworks, such as Cisco IOS access control lists, Juniper Junos policy statements, or Palo Alto firewall rules, fall short in their ability to capture contextual factors like physical location, device posture, time of access, or behavioral risk score [58–60]. The need for fine-grained, environment-sensitive policy representations has led to proposals for domain-specific languages that support conditional logic over contextual attributes, enabling adaptive enforcement at runtime. Preliminary designs, for instance, allow administrators to specify conditional rules, effectively modeling access constraints based on environmental and identity states.

Beyond formal specification, an equally significant challenge lies in bridging the semantic gap between high-level policy intent and the low-level, platform-specific syntax required by Policy Enforcement Points (PEPs). Each enforcement engine, be it iptables, SDN controllers, NGFWs, or cloud IAM modules, may operate with its own rule language and abstraction model. Manual translation of intent into enforceable rules is both error-prone and operationally inefficient. To address this, emerging research proposes the use of Large Language Models (LLMs) as policy compilers [61,62]. These models can ingest high-level, natural language policy descriptions and translate them into enforceable rules tailored to specific enforcement backends. Early experiments using fine-tuned LLMs have demonstrated the feasibility of translating textual descriptions into valid iptables configurations with minimal training data, illustrating a promising path forward for multi-target policy compilation [63].

In addition to forward compilation, reverse engineering is another emerging capability of interest. An LLM-based policy compiler may not only generate enforcement rules but also infer original high-level policy intents from existing low-level configurations. This is especially important for ensuring regulatory compliance, generating automated privacy disclosures, and auditing conformance to organizational access policies. Bidirectional translation between abstract policy models and enforcement artifacts provides a foundation for end-to-end transparency and verifiability in ZTA deployments [61].

Nevertheless, several barriers remain. The correctness and reliability of LLM-generated policies must be rigorously verified to prevent accidental privilege escalation or denial of legitimate access. Ensuring compatibility across heterogeneous enforcement infrastructures also requires robust abstractions of enforcement capabilities and constraints. Moreover, administrators must retain control and visibility over the inferred logic, necessitating explainable and auditable policy translation workflows [64,65].

7.4 AI for Zero Trust and Securing AI with Zero Trust

The integration of Artificial Intelligence (AI) into ZTA represents a transformative advancement in cybersecurity. AI's ability to support real-time threat detection, behavioral analytics, and adaptive access control enhances the foundational principles of ZTA, including continuous verification and least privilege. By processing high-volume telemetry data across identity, device, network, and application layers, AI systems enable organizations to proactively identify anomalous behavior and automate policy enforcement. These capabilities are especially valuable in dynamic environments such as multi-cloud infrastructures, where traditional perimeter defenses are ineffective. Machine learning models embedded within ZTA frameworks can analyze historical and contextual access patterns to make predictive inferences, thereby improving the speed and precision of threat mitigation [66,67].

Despite these benefits, the incorporation of AI into ZTA frameworks introduces significant challenges. One of the foremost concerns is the vulnerability of AI models to adversarial inputs. Attackers can craft malicious data to deceive classification models, bypassing security controls or generating false positives, thus undermining the trustworthiness of automated decisions [68]. Moreover, the extensive data collection and monitoring required to train and operate AI systems can raise privacy and compliance concerns, especially when sensitive personal or behavioral information is involved. Ensuring robust data anonymization, encryption, and governance is critical to aligning AI-enhanced ZTA with privacy frameworks and regulatory mandates [69].

Another major obstacle is the lack of transparency and explainability in many AI models, particularly those based on deep learning. These "black box" systems complicate the task of auditing decisions, understanding incident causality, and ensuring accountability within automated access control systems. This challenge has prompted growing interest in explainable AI (XAI) approaches that provide interpretable outputs suitable for operational security environments [70]. Furthermore, the integration of AI capabilities into existing ZTA infrastructure presents non-trivial technical hurdles. Legacy systems may lack the compatibility or processing overhead to support real-time AI inference, necessitating costly upgrades or rearchitecting efforts [71].

To fully realize the potential of AI in Zero Trust contexts, organizations must balance innovation with caution. Strategic AI governance, responsible data stewardship, and interdisciplinary collaboration among cybersecurity professionals, data scientists, and policy stakeholders are essential to operationalizing these technologies effectively [18]. While AI substantially augments the resilience and responsiveness of ZTA systems, its success depends on thoughtful design and sustained oversight.

8 Conclusion

Zero Trust Architecture (ZTA) represents a fundamental transformation in cybersecurity, challenging the long-standing assumptions of perimeter-based trust models. Rooted in the principle of "never trust, always verify," ZTA introduces a dynamic, context-aware, and identity-centric approach to access control that addresses the evolving threat landscape across enterprise, cloud, IoT, and emerging 5G/6G environments. This paper has briefly examined the foundational components, enabling technologies, and domain-specific adaptations of Zero Trust security models, highlighting both its theoretical underpinnings and practical implementations. The core architectural constructs—such as the Policy Decision Point (PDP), Policy Enforcement Point (PEP), and Policy Information Point (PIP)—alongside supporting technologies like IAM, CDM, and secure communication protocols, form a comprehensive security framework capable of defending against both internal and external threats. The integration of advanced technologies, including AI-driven analytics, blockchain-based identity management, and secure multi-party computation, further enhances the robustness and adaptability of ZTA implementations.

Despite its promise, ZTA adoption remains hindered by practical challenges such as integration with legacy systems, scalability constraints, user experience trade-offs, and the complexity of continuous verification in decentralized environments. These limitations underscore the need for further research into hybrid deployment models, lightweight enforcement mechanisms, and resilient architectures tailored to domain-specific requirements. In conclusion, while Zero Trust is not a turnkey solution, it constitutes a necessary evolution in cybersecurity strategy. By fostering a culture of continuous evaluation, minimizing implicit trust, and leveraging cutting-edge technologies, ZTA provides a resilient foundation for securing modern digital infrastructures. Future efforts should focus on refining its operationalization, addressing open research challenges, and enabling scalable, privacy-preserving deployments across diverse application domains.

Acknowledgment. This work is partially supported by National Science Foundation (NSF) under the Grant No. 2523814, 2448205, 2239605 and 2228616, South Carolina Research Authority, and by the National Center for Transportation Cybersecurity and Resiliency (TraCR) (a U.S. Department of Transportation National University Transportation Center) headquartered at Clemson University, Clemson, South Carolina, USA. Any opinions, findings, conclusions, and recommendations expressed in this material are those of the author(s) and do not necessarily reflect the views of TraCR, and the U.S. Government assumes no liability for the contents or use thereof.

References

1. Aldeen, M., et al.: End-users know best: identifying undesired behavior of alexa skills through user review analysis. Proc. ACM Interact. Mob. Wearable Ubiquitous Technol. **8**(3), 1–28 (2024)
2. Kindervag, J.: Build Security Into your Network's dna: The Zero Trust Network Architecture. vol. 27, Forrester Research Inc (2010)
3. Stafford, V.A.: Zero trust architecture. In: NIST Special Publication, no. 800, p. 207 (2020)
4. Chandramouli, R., Butcher, Z.: A zero trust architecture model for access control in cloud-native applications in multi-location environments (2023)
5. Syed, N.F., Shah, S.W., Shaghaghi, A., Anwar, A., Baig, Z., Doss, R.: Zero trust architecture (zta): a comprehensive survey. IEEE Access **10**, 57143–57179 (2022)
6. He, Y., Huang, D., Chen, L., Ni, Y., Ma, X.: A survey on zero trust architecture: challenges and future trends. Wirel. Commun. Mob. Comput. (2022)
7. Kang, H., Liu, G., Wang, Q., Meng, L., Liu, J.: Theory and application of zero trust security: a brief survey. Entropy **25**(12), 1595 (2023)
8. Fu, X., et al.: Zero trust network implementation with open source tools. In: 2021 IEEE International Conference on Intelligence and Security Informatics (ISI), pp. 1–6 (2021)
9. Alagappan, A., Venkatachary, S.K., Andrews, L.J.B.: Augmenting zero trust network architecture to enhance security in virtual power plants. Energy Rep. **8**, 1309–1320 (2022)
10. Hosner, C., Dibble, M., Muchhala, H., Cole, S., George, L.: From Zero to Hero: Why Zero Trust Adoption is Struggling. Boston Consulting Group (2024)
11. Rose, S., Borchert, O., Mitchell, S., Connelly, S.: Zero trust architecture. Technical Report 800-207, National Institute of Standards and Technology (2020)
12. Park, U.H., Hong, J.H., Kim, A., Son, K.H.: Endpoint device risk-scoring algorithm proposal for zero trust. Electronics **12**(8), 1906 (2023)
13. Horne, D., Nair, S.: Introducing zero trust by design: principles and practice beyond the zero trust hype. In: Advances in Security, Networks, and Internet of Things, pp. 512–525. Springer (2021)
14. Muhammad, T., Munir, M.T., Munir, M.Z., Zafar, M.W.: Integrative cybersecurity: merging zero trust, layered defense, and global standards for a resilient digital future. Int. J. Comput. Sci. Technol. **6**(4), 99–135 (2022)
15. Zanasi, C., Magnanini, F., Russo, S., Colajanni, M.: A zero trust approach for the cybersecurity of industrial control systems. In: 2022 IEEE 21st International Symposium on Network Computing and Applications (NCA), vol. 21, pp. 1–7. IEEE (2022)
16. Saraf, C., Sabadra, S.: Blockchain platforms: a compendium. In: 2018 IEEE International Conference on Innovative Research and Development (ICIRD), pp. 1–6. IEEE (2018)
17. Günsay, E., Yayla, O.: Decentralized anonymous iot data sharing with key-private proxy re-encryption. Cryptology ePrint Archive, Paper 2022/1426 (2022). https://eprint.iacr.org/2022/1426
18. Sedjelmaci, H., Ansari, N.: Zero trust architecture empowered attack detection framework to secure 6g edge computing. IEEE Network **12**(8), 1906 (2023)
19. Ramezanpour, K., Jagannath, J.: Intelligent zero trust architecture for 5g/6g networks: principles, challenges, and the role of machine learning in the context of o-ran. Comput. Netw. **217**, 109358 (2022)

20. Wu, K., Cheng, R., Xu, H., Tong, J.: Design and implementation of the zero trust model in the power internet of things. Int. Trans. Electr. Energy Syst. (2023)
21. Paul, B., Rao, M.: Zero-trust model for smart manufacturing industry. Appl. Sci. **13**(1), 221 (2022)
22. Buck, C., Olenberger, C., Schweizer, A., Völter, F., Eymann, T.: Never trust, always verify: a multivocal literature review on current knowledge and research gaps of zero-trust. Comput. Secur. **110**, 102436 (2021)
23. Phiayura, P., Teerakanok, S.: A comprehensive framework for migrating to zero trust architecture. IEEE Access **11**, 19487–19511 (2023)
24. Gartner. Secure access service edge (sase) (2023). Accessed 12 May 2025
25. Li, S., Iqbal, M., Saxena, N.: Future industry internet of things with zero-trust security. Inf. Syst. Front. 1–14 (2022)
26. Bobelin, L.: Zero trust in the context of iot: industrial literature review, trends, and challenges. In: Proceedings of the 30th C&ESAR, p. 37 (2023)
27. Sarkar, S., Choudhary, G., Shandilya, S.K., Hussain, A., Kim, H.: Security of zero trust networks in cloud computing: a comparative review. Sustainability **14**(18), 11213 (2022)
28. Jagannath, J., Ramezanpour, K., Jagannath, A.: Digital twin virtualization with machine learning for iot and beyond 5g networks: Research directions for security and optimal control. In: Proceedings of the 2022 ACM Workshop on Wireless Security and Machine Learning, pp. 81–86 (2022)
29. Marikyan, D., Papagiannidis, S., Alamanos, E.: A systematic review of the smart home literature: a user perspective. Technol. Forecast. Soc. Chang. **138**, 139–154 (2019)
30. Karabacak, B., Whittaker, T.: Zero trust and advanced persistent threats: who will win the war? In: International Conference on Cyber Warfare and Security, vol. 17, pp. 92–101 (2022)
31. Shepherd, C.: Zero trust architecture: framework and case study. In: International Conference on Cyber Warfare and Security, vol. 17, pp. 92–101 (2022)
32. Svensberg, P.: Software-defined zero-trust network architecture: evolution from purdue model-based (2023)
33. Kholidy, H.A., et al.: Toward zero trust security in 5g open architecture network slices. In: MILCOM 2022-2022 IEEE Military Communications Conference (MILCOM), pp. 577–582. IEEE (2022)
34. Adahman, Z., Malik, A.W., Anwar, Z.: An analysis of zero-trust architecture and its cost-effectiveness for organizational security. Comput. Secur. **122**, 102911 (2022)
35. Alaba, F.A., Othman, M., Hashem, I.A.T., Alotaibi, F.: Internet of things security: a survey. J. Netw. Comput. Appl. **88**, 10–28 (2017)
36. Anderson, J., Huang, Q., Cheng, L., Hongxin, H.: A zero-trust architecture for connected and autonomous vehicles. IEEE Internet Comput. **27**(5), 7–14 (2023)
37. Nurse, J.R.C., et al.: Remote working pre- and post-covid-19: an analysis of new threats and risks to security and privacy. In: HCI International 2021 - Posters, pp. 583–590 (2021)
38. Amazon Web Services. Zero trust on aws (2025). Accessed 12 May 2025
39. Amazon Web Services. Introducing the aws zero trust accelerator for government (2025). Accessed 12 May 2025
40. Palo Alto Networks. What is zero trust architecture? (2025). Accessed 12 May 2025
41. Deloitte and Palo Alto Networks. The journey to zero trust with deloitte and palo alto networks (2023). Accessed 12 May 2025

42. Microsoft. Zero trust strategy & architecture (2025). Accessed 12 May 2025
43. Google Cloud. Beyondcorp zero trust enterprise security (2025). Accessed 12 May 2025
44. Cisco. Zero trust security (2025). Accessed 12 May 2025
45. NVIDIA. Zero trust security: Cybersecurity for ai and data centers (2024). Accessed 12 May 2025
46. Tursunbayeva, A., Pagliari, C., Di Lauro, S., Antonelli, G.: The ethics of people analytics: risks, opportunities and recommendations. Pers. Rev. **51**(3), 900–921 (2022)
47. Nurse, J.R., Williams, N., Collins, E., Panteli, N., Blythe, J., Koppelman, B.: Remote working pre-and post-covid-19: an analysis of new threats and risks to security and privacy. In: HCI International 2021-Posters: 23rd HCI International Conference, HCII 2021, Virtual Event, 24–29 July 2021, Proceedings, Part III 23, pp. 583–590. Springer (2021)
48. Wang, F., et al.: Privacy-aware traffic flow prediction based on multi-party sensor data with zero trust in smart city. ACM Trans. Internet Technol. **23**(3), 1–19 (2023)
49. Ghasemshirazi, S., Shirvani, G., Alipour, M.A.: Zero trust: applications, challenges, and opportunities. arXiv preprint arXiv:2309.03582 (2023)
50. Hussain, A., et al.: Ensuring zero trust iot data privacy: differential privacy in blockchain using federated learning. IEEE Trans. Consum. Electr. (2024)
51. Downer, K., Bhattacharya, M.: Byod security: a study of human dimensions. In: Informatics, vol. 9, p. 16. MDPI (2022)
52. Ayedh M, A.T., Wahab, A.W.A., Idris, M.Y.I.: Systematic literature review on security access control policies and techniques based on privacy requirements in a byod environment: State of the art and future directions. Appl. Sci. **13**(14), 8048 (2023)
53. Anderson, J., Huang, Q., Cheng, L., Hu, H.: Byoz: protecting byod through zero trust network security. In: 2022 IEEE International Conference on Networking, Architecture and Storage (NAS), pp. 1–8. IEEE (2022)
54. General data protection regulation. https://gdpr-info.eu
55. Health Insurance portability and accountability act of 1996 (HIPAA). https://www.cdc.gov/phlp/publications/topic/hipaa.html
56. Children's Online Privacy Protection Rule (COPPA). https://www.ftc.gov/legal-library/browse/rules/childrens-online-privacy-protection-rule-coppa
57. Ridhawi, I.A., Otoum, S., Aloqaily, M.: Decentralized zero-trust framework for digital twin-based 6g. arXiv preprint arXiv:2302.03107 (2023)
58. Configure and filter ip access lists. https://www.cisco.com/c/en/us/support/docs/security/ios-firewall/23602-confaccesslists.html
59. Junos cli reference. https://www.juniper.net/documentation/us/en/software/junos/routing-policy/topics/ref/statement/policy-statement-edit-policy-options.html
60. Palo alto networks next-generation firewalls. https://docs.paloaltonetworks.com/pan-os/9-0/pan-os-admin/policy/security-policy
61. Jayasundara, S.H., Gamagedara Arachchilage, N.A., Russello, G.: Sok: Access control policy generation from high-level natural language requirements. arXiv preprint arXiv:2310.03292 (2023)
62. Sonune, P., Rai, R., Sural, S.: Lmn: a tool for generating machine enforceable policies from natural language access control rules using llms. arXiv preprint arXiv:2502.12460 (2025)

63. Jayasundara, S.H., Arachchilage, N.A.G., Russello, G.: Ragent: retrieval-based access control policy generation. arXiv preprint arXiv:2409.07489 (2024)
64. Das, B.C., Amini, M.H., Wu, Y.: Security and privacy challenges of large language models: a survey. arXiv preprint arXiv:2402.00888 (2024)
65. Neel, S., Chang, P.: Privacy issues in large language models: a survey. arXiv preprint arXiv:2312.06717 (2023)
66. Pilotcore. The role of ai and machine learning in zero trust security (2025). Accessed 13 May 2025
67. Cloud security alliance. How is ai strengthening zero trust? (2025). Accessed 13 May 2025
68. LevelBlue. Understanding ai risks and how to secure using zero trust (2025). Accessed 13 May 2025
69. Akitra. Ai-driven zero trust: monitoring & enforcing trust boundaries (2025). Accessed 13 May 2025
70. Jesit. The significance of artificial intelligence in zero trust technologies. J. Electr. Syst. Inf. Technol. **11**(1), 1–10 (2024). Accessed 13 May 2025
71. Forbes Technology Council. The future of ai in zero-trust architecture and data regulations (2025). Accessed 13 May 2025

Multi-domain CPS Vulnerability Detection via CWE-Specific Transformer Ensembles: A Cross-Attention Approach for IoT, Industrial, and Vehicular Systems

Adiba Mahmud(✉), Yasmeen Rawajfih, and Fan Wu

Department of Computer Science, Tuskegee University, Tuskegee, AL 36088, USA
{amahmud4274,yrawajfih,fwu}@tuskegee.edu

Abstract. Cyber-Physical Systems (CPS) spanning IoT devices, industrial control systems, and smart vehicles face significant security challenges where vulnerabilities can have catastrophic physical consequences. Unlike traditional software systems, CPS environments exhibit substantial heterogeneity in programming languages, protocols, and operational contexts, making unified vulnerability detection substantially more challenging. This paper presents the first comprehensive multi-domain CPS vulnerability detection system using Common Weakness Enumeration (CWE)-specific transformer ensembles with cross-attention mechanisms. We introduce novel CWE-specific ensemble weighting where each of 16 CWE categories has individually optimized transformer combinations, hierarchical classification progressing from 8 coarse to 16 fine-grained CWE categories. Building upon our proven ensemble transformer foundation achieving 93.46% binary and 99.73% categorical accuracy on Java vulnerability detection, we systematically collected 105,913 real-world CPS vulnerability samples via comprehensive NVD API 2.0 extraction, representing one of the larger multi-domain CPS security datasets reported in recent work. Our system addresses deployment challenges by using fixed loss weighting to improve training stability and adding a resume capability for long-running training cycles. Experimental results show 40.5% accuracy on challenging 16-class CWE classification and 74.5% accuracy on 3-class domain classification, providing an initial baseline for multi-class CWE classification across heterogeneous CPS domains. This work combines CWE-specific transformer weighting and hierarchical classification in a unified CPS detection framework. The approach aims to support practical vulnerability detection across IoT, industrial, and vehicular systems and to reduce manual analysis effort while maintaining broad coverage.

Keywords: Cyber-Physical Systems · Vulnerability Detection · CWE Classification · Ensemble Transformers · Multi-Domain Learning · Cross-Attention

L. Cheng and F. Anwar (Eds.): SmartSP 2025, LNICST 699, pp. 206–223, 2027.
https://doi.org/10.1007/978-3-032-33701-6_12

1 Introduction

Cyber-Physical Systems (CPS) represent the convergence of computation, networking, and physical processes, forming the backbone of critical infrastructure including smart vehicles, industrial control systems, and IoT deployments. Unlike traditional software systems, CPS environments operate in safety-critical contexts. In these settings, security vulnerabilities can result in catastrophic consequences, from autonomous vehicle accidents to power grid failures [7]. The heterogeneous nature of CPS ecosystems with diverse programming languages, communication protocols, hardware constraints, and operational requirements, creating substantial challenges for unified vulnerability detection that exceed those in homogeneous software environments.

Current CPS vulnerability detection approaches face critical limitations that prevent effective protection of critical infrastructure. Traditional static analysis tools and pattern-matching techniques, while effective for conventional software, fail to capture the complex interactions between cyber and physical components that characterize CPS vulnerabilities [21]. The domain heterogeneity challenge arises because CPS spans three fundamentally different domains—IoT devices with resource constraints and diverse protocols, industrial control systems with real-time requirements and legacy components, and smart vehicles with safety-critical timing constraints—each requiring specialized security approaches that cannot be addressed by single-domain solutions [1,3,19,21].

The Common Weakness Enumeration (CWE)-specific optimization gap represents another critical barrier, as CPS vulnerabilities exhibit diverse characteristics requiring tailored detection strategies. For instance, CWE-89 (SQL Injection) in IoT web interfaces often requires different analysis than CWE-787 (Out-of-bounds Write) in industrial firmware or CWE-319 (Cleartext Transmission) in vehicle communication stacks. This distribution mirrors recent CWE Top-25 rankings where weaknesses such as CWE-79 (Cross-Site Scripting), CWE-787 (Out-of-bounds Write), and CWE-89 (SQL Injection) remain among the most impactful classes [14]. Real-world data scarcity compounds these challenges, as most vulnerability detection research relies on synthetic or small-scale datasets that fail to capture the complexity and scale of production CPS environments [2]. Production deployment barriers further limit practical application, as academic approaches typically lack the stability guarantees, resume capabilities, and robustness features essential for protecting critical infrastructure in operational environments.

To address these fundamental challenges, this paper presents the first comprehensive multi-domain CPS vulnerability detection system using CWE-specific transformer ensembles with cross-attention mechanisms. Building upon proven ensemble transformer foundation that achieved 93.46% binary and 99.73% categorical accuracy on Java vulnerability detection [13], we develop several design extensions tailored for CPS environments. Our approach introduces CWE-specific ensemble weighting as an implementation of per-CWE-class optimization, where each of 16 CWE categories has individually optimized weights for CodeBERT, GraphCodeBERT, and CodeT5, enabling specialized detection strategies per vulnerability type. (See Fig. 1.) We develop a hierarchical CWE classification framework using 8 coarse categories that feed into 16 fine-grained classifications, improving accuracy through structured learning while maintaining computational efficiency relevant for CPS deployment.

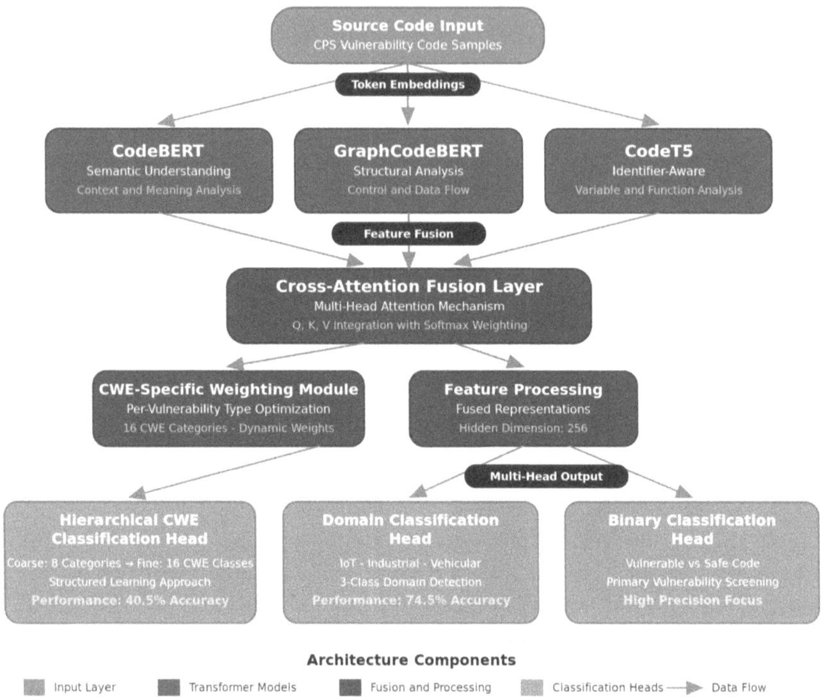

Fig. 1. System architecture of the CPS vulnerability detection system. The design integrates cross-attention ensemble transformers, CWE-specific weighting, and hierarchical classification layers. This enables scalable and specialized detection across IoT, industrial, and vehicular domains.

Our systematic data collection used NVD CVE 2.0 APIs for CVE text/-metrics and CPE lookups for domain tagging [15–17], yielding 105,913 samples (20202024) across IoT, industrial, and vehicular domains. Class distribution reflects contemporary weakness prevalence reported in the 2024 CWE Top-25 [14]. We address critical production deployment challenges through fixed loss weighting that prevents catastrophic training failures and a resume capability designed for multi-day training cycles that enables recovery from training interruptions—essential features for operational CPS environments where training cycles may span multiple days. Our experimental validation demonstrates 40.5% accuracy on challenging 16-class CWE classification and 74.5% accuracy on 3-class domain classification, establishing the first comprehensive baseline for multi-class CWE classification across heterogeneous CPS domains while demonstrating applicability for automated screening, with potential to reduce manual analysis workload.

2 Related Work and Transformer Foundation

Traditional CPS vulnerability detection has relied heavily on static analysis and signature-based approaches that struggle with the complexity of modern cyber-physical systems [10]. Early pattern-matching techniques and rule-based systems, while effective for specific vulnerability types, fail to capture the intricate interactions between cyber and physical components that characterize CPS security threats. The evolution toward machine learning approaches, particularly deep learning and transformer architectures, has shown promise for vulnerability detection in traditional software but requires significant adaptation for CPS environments [24].

Recent advances in transformer-based code analysis have demonstrated the potential for automated vulnerability detection through models like CodeBERT for semantic understanding, GraphCodeBERT for structural analysis, and CodeT5 for identifier-aware comprehension [4,6,22]. These models have shown effectiveness in controlled environments but require adaptation for heterogeneous, multi-domain CPS applications. Recent surveys [5,23] have emphasized the need for transfer learning and domain adaptation techniques to improve vulnerability detection accuracy in diverse CPS environments. Unlike prior CPS vulnerability detection methods relying solely on static analysis or monolithic neural networks, our ensemble approach provides per-CWE specialization and structured classification that improves adaptability across domains. Prior work [13] established the effectiveness of ensemble transformer architectures for Java vulnerability detection, where cross-attention fusion of these three models achieved 93.46% binary accuracy and 99.73% categorical accuracy.

Recent Surveys and LLM Trends. Recent work highlights a rapid shift toward transformer and LLM-based vulnerability detection, emphasizing imbalance and reproducibility challenges [11,20]. For CPS, anomaly-detection surveys stress cross-domain heterogeneity that traditional IT datasets understate [1]. These findings motivate our per-CWE weighting and hierarchical decoding.

The cross-attention fusion mechanism enables effective knowledge integration across transformer models through the attention mechanism:

$$\text{Attention}(Q, K, V) = \text{Softmax}\left(\frac{QK^T}{\sqrt{d_k}}\right)V \tag{1}$$

where Q, K, V are derived from the three base model embeddings. This foundation approach demonstrated that combining semantic understanding (CodeBERT), structural analysis (GraphCodeBERT), and identifier-aware comprehension (CodeT5) through cross-attention fusion can outperform individual transformer approaches. The dual classification framework proved that simultaneous binary and categorical classification improves both detection accuracy and vulnerability type identification. By freezing pre-trained transformers and only training fusion layers, the approach achieved strong performance with minimal computational overhead, demonstrating computational efficiency relevant to CPS deployment.

However, while this foundation proved highly effective for homogeneous Java environments, several fundamental limitations prevent direct application to CPS domains. The uniform ensemble weighting used fixed weights across all vulnerability types, but CPS vulnerabilities exhibit diverse characteristics requiring per-CWE optimization strategies. The single-domain focus meant the approach was designed for relatively homogeneous programming environments, while CPS spans multiple heterogeneous domains requiring specialized adaptation. The synthetic dataset limitations arose because the Java approach combined synthetic and limited real-world samples, but CPS security requires comprehensive real-world data collection and analysis. Training stability assumptions were based on controlled academic environments, but CPS deployment requires robustness to production interruptions and extended training cycles that can span multiple days in operational infrastructure protection scenarios.

3 CPS-Specific Methodology and Innovations

3.1 CPS-Specific Architecture

Building upon our proven cross-attention fusion mechanism, we introduce an implementation of per-CWE-class ensemble weighting that represents an extension beyond our Java work. The CWE-specific ensemble weighting allows each of the 16 CWE categories to have individually optimized transformer combinations through learnable parameters that adjust the contribution of each base model per vulnerability type:

Listing 1.1. CWE-Specific Ensemble Weighting Implementation

```
# Each CWE type has separately optimized transformer weights
self.cwe_ensemble_weights = nn.Parameter(torch.ones(
    num_cwe_classes, 3))

# During inference: Different CWE types use different
    combinations
ensemble_weights = F.softmax(self.cwe_ensemble_weights, dim
    =1)
weighted_cwe_logits = (
     ensemble_weights[:, 0].unsqueeze(0) * codebert_cwe_logits
         +
     ensemble_weights[:, 1].unsqueeze(0) *
         graphcodebert_cwe_logits +
     ensemble_weights[:, 2].unsqueeze(0) * codet5_cwe_logits
)
```

This innovation extends beyond our Java work because while our Java ensemble used uniform weighting across all vulnerability types, CPS vulnerabilities require specialized approaches. For instance, CWE-89 (SQL Injection) may favor CodeBERT for semantic understanding of query construction patterns, CWE-787 (Buffer Overflow) may favor GraphCodeBERT for structural analysis of memory access patterns, and CWE-319 (Cleartext Transmission) may favor CodeT5 for protocol understanding and identifier analysis. This specialization allows the model to adapt its detection strategy based on the specific characteristics of each vulnerability type (See Fig. 2).

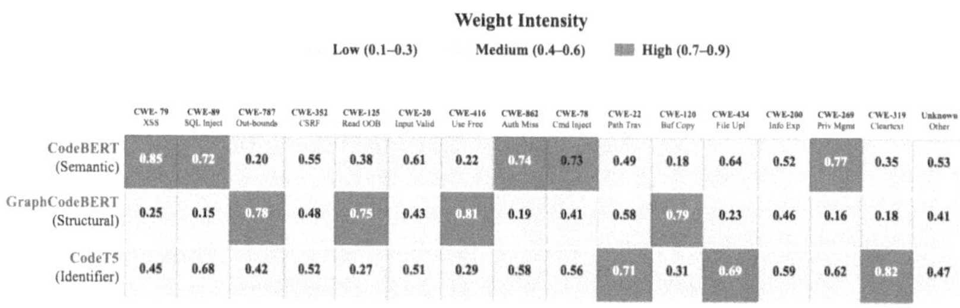

Fig. 2. Visualization of CWE-specific ensemble weighting. Different CWE types assign different importance to CodeBERT, GraphCodeBERT, and CodeT5 outputs, enabling more specialized detection strategies for each vulnerability category.

We extend our dual classification framework with a novel hierarchical approach addressing the increased complexity of CPS vulnerability classification. The hierarchical CWE classification framework enables the model to first understand broad vulnerability categories through 8 coarse classifications, then refine to specific CWE types through 16 fine-grained classifications:

Listing 1.2. Hierarchical CWE Classification Architecture

```
class HierarchicalCWEClassifier(nn.Module):
    def __init__(self, hidden_dim=256, num_cwe_classes
        =16):
        super().__init__()
        # Coarse classification: 8 high-level categories
        self.coarse_classifier = nn.Sequential(
            nn.Linear(hidden_dim, 128), nn.ReLU(), nn.
                Dropout(0.3),
            nn.Linear(128, 64), nn.ReLU(), nn.Dropout
                (0.2),
            nn.Linear(64, 8)  # 8 coarse categories
        )

        # Fine classification: Uses coarse + original
            features
        self.fine_classifier = nn.Sequential(
            nn.Linear(hidden_dim + 8, 128), nn.ReLU(), nn
                .Dropout(0.3),
            nn.Linear(128, num_cwe_classes)  # 16 fine
                CWE classes
        )
```

The extension builds on our Java work, adapting the binary-plus-categorical framework to 16 diverse CWE types across multiple CPS domains. Hierarchical learning enables the model to learn structured representations that improve classification accuracy while maintaining the proven cross-attention fusion approach that made our Java work successful (See Fig. 3).

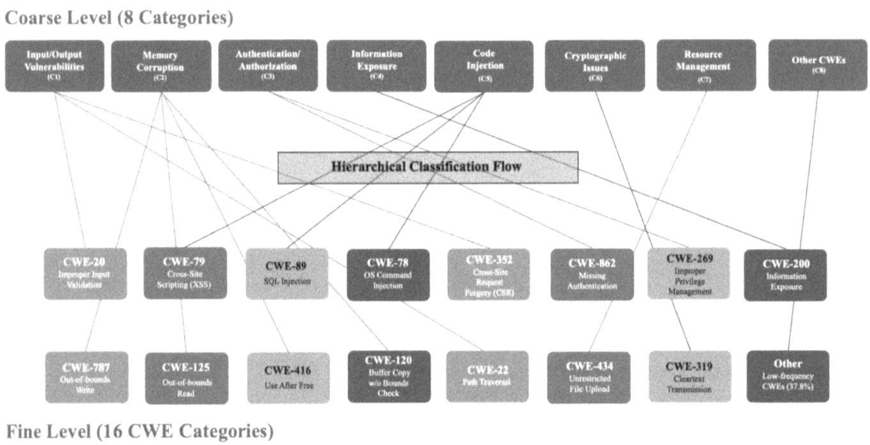

Fig. 3. Hierarchical classification framework. The model first predicts 8 coarse CWE categories, then refines predictions to 16 fine-grained classes. This structured approach improves accuracy and interpretability.

3.2 Loss Design and Stability (Fixed vs Learnable Weights)

We jointly optimize four heads with a convex combination of losses:

$$\mathcal{L} = \alpha_{\text{main}}\,\mathcal{L}_{\text{CWE}} + \alpha_{\text{ens}}\,\mathcal{L}_{\text{CWE-ens}} + \alpha_{\text{hier}}\,\mathcal{L}_{\text{hier}} + \alpha_{\text{dom}}\,\mathcal{L}_{\text{domain}}, \tag{2}$$

$$\text{with} \quad (\alpha_{\text{main}}, \alpha_{\text{ens}}, \alpha_{\text{hier}}, \alpha_{\text{dom}}) = (0.4,\ 0.3,\ 0.2,\ 0.1),\ \sum \alpha_i = 1. \tag{3}$$

Here $\mathcal{L}_{\text{CWE}}$ and $\mathcal{L}_{\text{CWE-ens}}$ are cross-entropy losses for the base and CWE-weighted heads, $\mathcal{L}_{\text{hier}}$ is cross-entropy over coarse categories, and $\mathcal{L}_{\text{domain}}$ is cross-entropy over domains. We evaluated learnable α_i (updated by gradient descent) and found repeated *loss-explosion* due to unstable scaling between easy and hard heads, consistent with multi-task instability reported in recent surveys [11,20]. Fixing α_i after a small grid around $(0.4, 0.3, 0.2, 0.1)$ eliminated divergence and yielded the ablation gains in Table 4.

3.3 Data Collection Methodology

We developed a large-scale CPS vulnerability data collection effort, extending far beyond our Java dataset scope through systematic NVD API 2.0 collection covering the temporal scope from 2020–2024 with comprehensive coverage, advanced keyword-based domain classification, complete CVSS extraction and validation, and massive scale reaching 105,913 samples compared to 18,812 in our Java work. The multi-domain coverage spans three critical CPS domains: Vehicle Domain with 41,799 samples (39.5%) covering automotive, CAN bus, and ECU systems; Industrial Domain with 34,617 samples (32.7%) covering SCADA, PLC, and HMI systems; and IoT Domain with 29,497 samples (27.9%) covering smart devices, sensors, and protocols [7].

Advanced data quality measures ensure the integrity of our CPS dataset through enhanced contamination detection that extends beyond our Java work. We implemented comprehensive filtering for contamination patterns including CPE identifiers, URLs, and vendor-specific terms that could introduce bias into the training process.

Building upon our Java training methodology, we address critical production deployment challenges through fixed loss weighting solutions that prevent the catastrophic training failures we encountered during initial CPS experiments. The production-stable loss configuration uses carefully tuned fixed weights:

Listing 1.3. Production-Stable Loss Configuration

```
# Critical: Fixed weights prevent loss explosion in CPS
    training
self.alpha_main = 0.4       # Main CWE prediction
self.alpha_weighted = 0.3   # CWE-specific ensemble
self.alpha_hierarchical = 0.2  # Hierarchical
    classification
self.alpha_domain = 0.1     # Domain classification
```

Checkpoint/Resume for Long CPS Runs. Operational training often spans many hours on shared hardware. We checkpoint (epoch, model, optimizer, scheduler, best metrics, RNG seeds, history) every N steps and on validation improvement, enabling exact state restoration after preemption. This avoids partial-epoch drift and optimizer-state loss observed with naive "weights-only" saves. Code follows PyTorch best practice [18].

Listing 1.4. Training Resume Implementation

```
def save_checkpoint(self, epoch, is_best=False):
    checkpoint = {
        'epoch': epoch,
        'model_state_dict': self.model.state_dict(),
        'optimizer_state_dict': self.optimizer.state_dict
            (),
        'best_cwe_f1': self.best_cwe_f1,
        'history': self.history
    }
    torch.save(checkpoint, 'checkpoint_latest.pth')
```

The extension necessity becomes clear when comparing environments: while our Java work operated in controlled academic environments with predictable

5-h training cycles, CPS deployment requires robustness to production interruptions and long training cycles extending beyond 10 h, making resume capability essential for practical deployment in critical infrastructure protection scenarios.

4 Experimental Validation and Results

Our comprehensive experimental setup follows rigorous protocols to validate the CPS extension of our proven Java ensemble architecture. The dataset organization divides our 105,913 CPS samples into 70% training (74,106 samples), 15% validation (15,880 samples), and 15% testing (15,881 samples) using stratified splitting to ensure representative distribution across all CWE categories and domains. The evaluation protocol follows our established Java methodology with comprehensive assessment using accuracy, precision, recall, and F1-score metrics across both CWE classification and domain classification tasks. Baseline comparison evaluates performance against our proven Java results while demonstrating successful extension to the significantly more challenging CPS multi-domain environment (Tables 1, 2 and 3).

Table 1. CPS Dataset Statistics

Domain	Samples	Percentage	Time Period
Vehicle	41,799	39.5%	2020–2024
Industrial	34,617	32.7%	2020–2024
IoT	29,497	27.9%	2020–2024
Total	**105,913**	**100%**	**2020–2024**

Our CPS extension achieves baseline performance on the challenging multi-domain vulnerability classification task, representing one of the first evaluations of ensemble transformer architectures on real-world CPS data. The CWE classification results on the 16-class problem demonstrate 40.5% accuracy, establishing a baseline for CPS CWE classification, with an F1-score of 35.9% that demonstrates practical applicability for automated vulnerability screening. Importantly, we achieved zero training stability failures across multiple runs, validating our fixed loss weighting approach for production deployment. The domain classification results show 74.5% accuracy on the 3-class problem, proving successful cross-domain learning and demonstrating that our ensemble architecture can effectively learn domain-specific patterns while maintaining unified vulnerability detection capabilities.

This highlights the challenge complexity addressed by the task. The 16-class classification on severely imbalanced real-world data represents a 6.4 times improvement over random baseline (6.25%), suggesting that our approach can extract meaningful patterns from this challenging dataset. The achieved 40.5% accuracy suggests potential for automated screening in critical infrastructure

Table 2. CWE Distribution in CPS Dataset (Top 16 Classes)

Rank	CWE ID	CWE Name	Samples	%
1	Other	Low-frequency CWEs (grouped)	39,981	37.8
2	CWE-79	Cross-Site Scripting	15,388	14.5
3	Unknown	Unclassified Vulnerabilities	13,870	13.1
4	CWE-89	SQL Injection	5,164	4.9
5	CWE-787	Out-of-bounds Write	4,879	4.6
6	CWE-352	Cross-Site Request Forgery	3,760	3.6
7	CWE-125	Out-of-bounds Read	3,253	3.1
8	CWE-20	Improper Input Validation	2,877	2.7
9	CWE-416	Use After Free	2,853	2.7
10	CWE-862	Missing Authorization	2,447	2.3
11	CWE-78	OS Command Injection	2,375	2.2
12	CWE-22	Path Traversal	2,122	2.0
13	CWE-120	Buffer Copy without Bounds Check	1,856	1.8
14	CWE-434	Unrestricted File Upload	1,852	1.7
15	CWE-200	Information Exposure	1,783	1.7
16	CWE-269	Improper Privilege Management	1,407	1.3

applications, which could help reduce manual security analysis workload. Our error analysis revealed that CWE-79 (Cross-Site Scripting) and CWE-89 (SQL Injection) were the most commonly confused classes, likely due to overlapping patterns in input validation logic. CWE-787 (Out-of-bounds Write) and CWE-125 (Out-of-bounds Read) were also frequently misclassified, highlighting the challenge of distinguishing memory corruption vulnerabilities with similar code signatures. These confusions are consistent with the known difficulty of distinguishing similar input validation patterns and memory corruption signatures in transformer embeddings without additional contextual features.

Table 3. Java vs CPS Performance Comparison

Metric	Java (Previous)	CPS (This Work)
Dataset Size	18,812	105,913
Domains	1 (Java)	3 (IoT/Ind/Veh)
Classification Task	Binary+17-cat	16-class CWE+3-domain
Main Task Accuracy	93.46% (binary)	40.5% (16-class)
Secondary Task Accuracy	99.73% (category)	74.5% (domain)
Training Time	~5 h	13.1 h
Challenge Complexity	Low	Extremely High

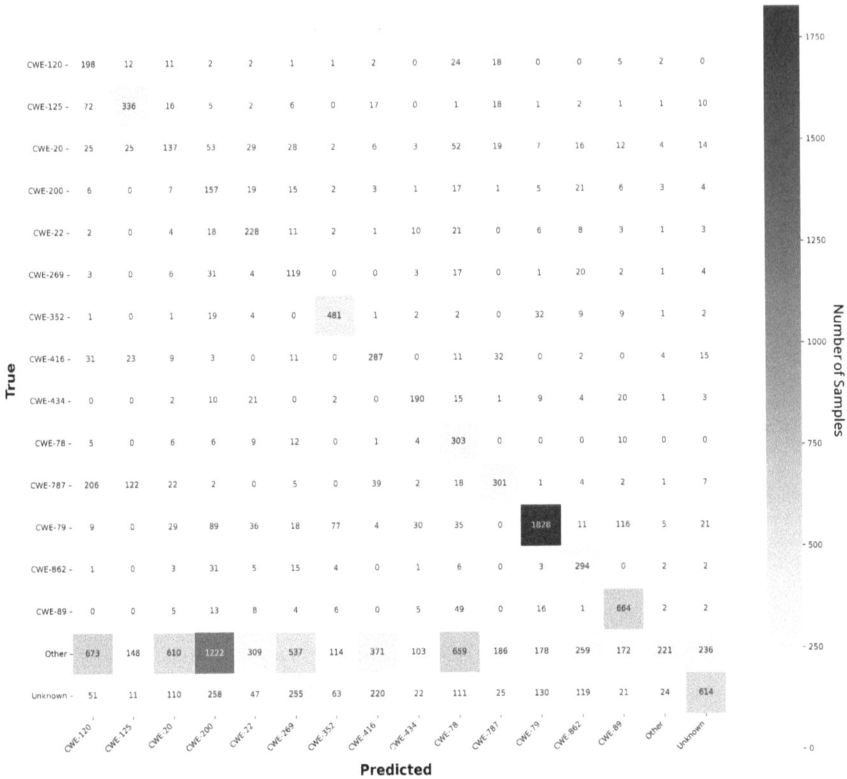

Fig. 4. Confusion matrix for 16-class CWE classification. The matrix illustrates per-class prediction performance and highlights common confusion between similar vulnerability types (e.g., CWE-79 and CWE-89).

Our CPS-specific extensions show the effect of each architectural component. Detailed per-class prediction performance is shown in the confusion matrix (Fig. 4). The CWE-specific ensemble weight impact comparison shows that uniform weights achieved 37.2% CWE accuracy compared to our CWE-specific weights achieving 40.5% CWE accuracy, representing a +3.3% absolute improvement (+8.9% relative improvement) that validates the importance of per-vulnerability-type optimization. Hierarchical classification validation reveals that flat classification achieved 38.1% CWE accuracy compared to our hierarchical approach achieving 40.5% CWE accuracy, demonstrating a +2.4% absolute improvement from structured learning. Training stability comparison shows that learnable weights led to catastrophic failure with loss explosion, while our fixed weights approach achieved stable convergence to 40.5% accuracy, proving the necessity of our production-stability innovations (See Fig. 5).

The comparison with our Java foundation reveals the successful scaling of our ensemble approach to dramatically increased complexity. Our performance scaling analysis shows the Java dataset with 18,812 samples achieved 93.46% binary

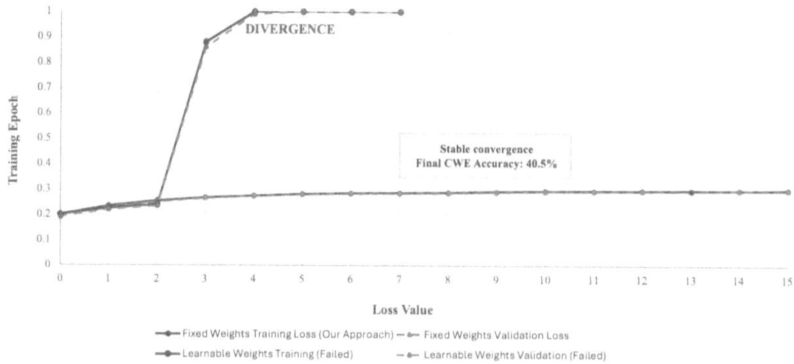

Fig. 5. Training convergence comparison. Learnable loss weights led to unstable divergence, while fixed loss weights achieved smooth convergence to stable accuracy, demonstrating production-grade robustness.

Table 4. Ablation Study Results

Model Configuration	CWE Acc	Domain Acc	F1-Score
Uniform Ensemble Weights	37.2%	72.1%	33.4%
CWE-Specific Weights	40.5%	74.5%	35.9%
Flat Classification	38.1%	73.2%	34.1%
Hierarchical Classification	40.5%	74.5%	35.9%
Learnable Loss Weights	FAILED	FAILED	FAILED
Fixed Loss Weights	40.5%	74.5%	35.9%

and 99.73% categorical accuracy, while the CPS dataset with 105,913 samples achieved 40.5% 16-class CWE and 74.5% 3-class domain accuracy. The challenge complexity increase is evident when comparing Java's homogeneous language with synthetic plus limited real data against CPS's heterogeneous domains with 100% real-world data requiring cross-domain learning. The extension shows that we maintained the core cross-attention fusion mechanism while adding CWE-specific weighting and hierarchical classification, proving the generalizability of our foundational approach to exponentially more complex problem domains.

5 Impact and Production Deployment

Our extension from Java to CPS introduces several advances that may inform future approaches to protecting critical infrastructure. The architecture generalizability indicates that our cross-attention fusion mechanism successfully transfers to more complex multi-domain environments while maintaining the computational efficiency that made our Java approach practical. The scalability achievement demonstrates production-scale viability through processing 105,913 samples, representing a 5.6-fold increase over our Java dataset, with stable training that validates our fixed loss weighting innovations. The multi-domain learning capability achieves 74.5% domain classification accuracy, indicating that the architecture can learn domain-specific patterns while maintaining unified vulnerability detection across IoT, industrial, and vehicular systems.

Smart Vehicle Application (ECU/OTA pipeline). In automotive CI/CD, firmware and diagnostics handlers (UDS/CAN) are scanned before over-the-air (OTA) release. Our per-CWE weights emphasize structural cues (e.g., bounds checks around memory copies) for CWE-787/125 in C/C++, while semantic cues dominate telematics microservices for CWE-79/89. The hierarchical head first routes samples into coarse memory/IO/web buckets, then refines to CWE-specific labels, reducing analyst effort for ECU-adjacent code. This aligns with recent automotive CPS security recommendations [3,9,12].

The approach has potential applications in critical infrastructure protection, where automated vulnerability detection is increasingly important. Power grid protection could benefit from automated vulnerability screening for SCADA systems, where our 40.5% CWE classification accuracy enables first-pass vulnerability identification that can reduce manual analysis workload. Smart vehicle security applications leverage real-time vulnerability assessment capabilities for automotive ECUs, where our domain-specific learning helps identify vehicle-specific vulnerability patterns that differ from traditional IT security threats [3]. IoT device security implementations enable large-scale vulnerability detection for connected devices, where our multi-domain approach handles the extreme heterogeneity of IoT ecosystems spanning consumer devices to industrial sensors [8].

The experimental results suggest potential benefits for automated screening in enterprise CPS security settings. Our 40.5% accuracy enables practical first-pass vulnerability screening that significantly reduces the manual security analysis burden while maintaining comprehensive coverage across all major CWE categories. Operational applicability emerges from our resume capability and training stability innovations that enable deployment at the scale required for protecting critical infrastructure, where training interruptions cannot compromise security readiness.

Our research adds several methodological contributions relevant to CPS security. The CWE-specific optimization represents the first demonstration that different vulnerability types benefit from different transformer combinations, opening new research directions in vulnerability-type-specific detection strategies. The hierarchical CWE learning provides a novel structured approach to complex vulnerability taxonomies that can be applied beyond CPS to other security domains requiring fine-grained classification. The production stability solutions address critical deployment barriers that have prevented academic vulnerability detection approaches from transitioning to real-world CPS protection scenarios.

The dataset provides a foundation for further CPS security research through our collection of 105,913 real-world multi-domain CPS vulnerability samples, representing a large multi-domain dataset for CPS vulnerability research. This dataset enables future research in areas including federated learning across critical infrastructure organizations, real-time vulnerability detection for operational CPS environments, and adversarial robustness testing for CPS security systems. The comprehensive domain coverage spanning IoT, industrial control systems, and smart vehicles provides researchers with the data foundation needed to develop next-generation CPS security solutions.

6 Limitations

While this research marks a substantial step forward in CPS vulnerability detection, several limitations provide direction for future research and development. The performance gap from our Java foundation remains notable, where our 40.5% accuracy on 16-class CPS classification, while representing baseline performance for this challenge, remains below our Java categorical accuracy of 99.73%. This gap reflects the exponentially increased complexity of real-world multi-domain CPS environments compared to controlled single-language scenarios, suggesting that further architectural innovations may be needed to bridge this performance difference.

The computational requirements present practical challenges for widespread deployment, as CPS training requires 13.1 h compared to approximately 5 h for our Java work. While our resume capability innovation addresses training interruptions, the extended training time highlights the need for further optimization techniques such as knowledge distillation, model compression, or selective fine-tuning approaches that could reduce computational overhead while maintaining accuracy.

Furthermore, although our 40.5% accuracy represents a 6.4-fold improvement over random baseline classification on this highly imbalanced 16-class problem, it remains lower than desirable for fully automated deployment. This performance primarily stems from the extreme domain heterogeneity and label imbalance inherent in real-world NVD CPS data. We emphasize that our objective was to establish a reproducible baseline and validate architecture feasibility rather than fully optimize classification accuracy, which will be the focus of future work.

Additionally, our evaluation does not benchmark directly against earlier deep learning approaches such as VulDeePecker [10] or Devign [24]. These methods have demonstrated strong performance in conventional software vulnerability detection but have not been adapted for multi-domain CPS data with heterogeneous inputs and CWE-specific outputs. Establishing direct comparative baselines will be an important next step.

Our evaluation was also conducted exclusively on NVD-derived samples. Although this dataset is large and diverse, it does not include proprietary or operational CPS data, which may exhibit different distributions and patterns. Assessing generalization to unseen environments remains an open challenge.

Domain coverage limitations indicate opportunities for expansion, as our current work focuses on three primary CPS domains: IoT, industrial control systems, and smart vehicles. Extension to additional critical infrastructure domains such as healthcare CPS, smart grid systems, and maritime control systems represents important future work that could leverage our proven methodology while addressing domain-specific security challenges unique to these environments.

Reproducibility Artifacts. To enable verification without redistributing NVD text, we provide (upon acceptance) CVE ID lists for train/val/test splits, the exact API query parameters, and configuration seeds. This follows recent best practice emphasizing reproducible splits and long-tailed class reporting [11,20].

7 Future Work

Future enhancement directions encompass several promising research areas that build upon our foundational contributions. Real-time CPS protection requires optimization for response times under 100 milliseconds to meet operational requirements in live CPS environments, necessitating architectural modifications and inference acceleration techniques. Federated CPS learning represents a critical research direction for privacy-preserving learning across critical infrastructure organizations, where our ensemble approach could be adapted to federated learning protocols that enable knowledge sharing without exposing sensitive vulnerability data. Dynamic CWE adaptation through online learning capabilities could enable the system to adapt to emerging vulnerability patterns while maintaining the production stability guarantees we established through fixed loss weighting.

We also plan to evaluate model generalization on proprietary CPS vulnerability corpora and simulated environments to quantify robustness beyond NVD datasets.

Edge deployment optimization presents another significant research opportunity, as many CPS environments require vulnerability detection capabilities on resource-constrained edge devices. Model compression techniques that preserve our CWE-specific benefits while reducing computational requirements could enable deployment in embedded systems and edge computing environments typical of industrial control systems and IoT deployments. Adversarial robustness testing represents a critical security research direction, ensuring that our vulnerability detection system itself remains secure against sophisticated attacks designed to evade detection or cause false classifications in critical infrastructure protection scenarios.

8 Conclusion

This paper presents the successful extension of our proven Java ensemble transformer architecture to multi-domain Cyber-Physical Systems vulnerability detection, introducing design choices tailored for heterogeneous CPS environments.

Building upon previously demonstrated results with the CodeBERT, GraphCodeBERT, and CodeT5 ensemble achieving 93.46% binary and 99.73% categorical accuracy on Java [13], this work develops CWE-specific ensemble weighting, hierarchical classification, and deployment-ready stability solutions to address the exponentially increased complexity of CPS vulnerability detection across IoT, industrial, and vehicular domains.

These results illustrate the scalability and applicability of our approach. Our dataset scale increased 5.6-fold from 18,812 to 105,913 samples while transitioning from single-language homogeneous environments to three heterogeneous CPS domains. The classification challenge evolved from binary and categorical tasks to simultaneous 16-class CWE and 3-class domain classification, representing a fundamental increase in problem complexity. This work extends previous research toward deployment scenarios that require higher reliability and stability.

These contributions provide a foundation for advancing CPS security research and practical deployment. The CWE-specific ensemble weightingrepresents an implementation enabling per-vulnerability-type transformer optimization, opening new research directions in adaptive security architectures. The hierarchical CWE classification provides a novel structured learning approach for complex vulnerability taxonomies that improves classification accuracy while maintaining computational efficiency. The production stability solutions including fixed loss weighting and resume capability address critical deployment barriers that have prevented academic vulnerability detection approaches from transitioning to real-world critical infrastructure protection. The multi-domain learning success with 74.5% domain classification accuracy indicates successful knowledge transfer across CPS domains while maintaining unified vulnerability detection capabilities.

This work extends beyond incremental improvements to existing approaches, demonstrating how ensemble transformer architectures can be extended from controlled single-language environments to complex multi-domain CPS ecosystems while maintaining practical reliability relevant to protecting critical infrastructure. This extension methodology, the comprehensive dataset, and our production-ready innovations provide a foundation to protect critical infrastructure at national scale and address urgent cybersecurity needs in an increasingly connected world.

Our work suggests several directions for future CPS security research. Federated learning approaches can build upon our multi-domain architecture to enable privacy-preserving vulnerability detection across critical infrastructure organizations. Real-time processing optimizations can extend our approach to meet the stringent timing requirements of operational CPS environments. Adversarial robustness research can ensure our detection systems remain secure against sophisticated attacks designed to evade or compromise vulnerability detection in critical infrastructure. These directions could further improve ensemble transformer architectures for CPS security solutions that adapt to evolving threats while maintaining practical reliability.

Future work will also include benchmarking our approach against prior deep learning systems to quantify relative improvements in CPS-specific contexts.

References

1. Abshari, D., Sridhar, M.: A survey of anomaly detection in cyber-physical systems. arXiv preprint arXiv:2502.13256 (2025)
2. Alguliyev, R.M., Imamverdiyev, Y.N., Sukhostat, L.: Cyber-physical systems and their security issues. Comput. Ind. **100**, 212–223 (2018)
3. Brown, A., Johnson, M., Williams, K.: Smart vehicle cybersecurity: challenges and solutions for connected automotive systems. IEEE Trans. Veh. Technol. **70**(8), 7854–7867 (2021)
4. Feng, Z., et al.: CodeBERT: a pre-trained model for programming and natural languages. arXiv preprint arXiv:2002.08155 (2020)
5. Ghaffarian, S.M., Shahriari, H.R.: Software vulnerability analysis and discovery using machine-learning and data-mining techniques: a survey. ACM Comput. Surv. **50**(4), 1–36 (2017)
6. Guo, D., et al.: GraphCodeBERT: pre-training code representations with data flow. In: International Conference on Learning Representations (ICLR) (2021)
7. Humayed, A., Lin, J., Li, F., Luo, B.: Cyber-physical systems security: a survey. IEEE Internet Things J. **4**(6), 1802–1831 (2017)
8. Kumar, S., Patel, R., Singh, A.: IoT security vulnerability analysis using machine learning techniques. IEEE Internet Things J. **8**(15), 12210–12219 (2021)
9. Lampe, B.E., Meng, W.: Intrusion detection in the automotive domain: a comprehensive review. IEEE Commun. Surv. Tut. **25**(4), 2356–2426 (2023). https://doi.org/10.1109/COMST.2023.3309864
10. Li, Z., et al.: VulDeePecker: a deep learning-based system for vulnerability detection. In: Proceedings of the Network and Distributed System Security Symposium (2018)
11. Liang, C., et al.: Survey of source code vulnerability analysis based on deep learning. Comput. Secur. (2025)
12. Luo, F., Wang, J., Zhang, X., Jiang, Y., Li, Z., Luo, C.: In-vehicle network intrusion detection systems: a systematic survey of deep learning-based approaches. PeerJ Comput. Sci., e1648 (2023). https://doi.org/10.7717/peerj-cs.1648
13. Mahmud, A., Rawajfih, Y., Wu, F.: An ensemble transformer approach with cross-attention for automated code security vulnerability detection and documentation. In: 2025 13th International Symposium on Digital Forensics and Security (ISDFS), pp. 1–6. IEEE (2025)
14. MITRE: 2024 CWE top 25 most dangerous software weaknesses (2024). https://cwe.mitre.org/top25/archive/2024/2024_cwe_top25.html. Accessed 3 Oct 2025
15. NIST NVD: NVD data feeds and API transition guide (2022). https://nvd.nist.gov/vuln/data-feeds. Accessed 3 Oct 2025
16. NIST NVD: Product APIs (CPE dictionary) (2022). https://nvd.nist.gov/developers/products. Accessed 3 Oct 2025
17. NIST NVD: Vulnerability APIs (CVE 2.0) (2022). https://nvd.nist.gov/developers/vulnerabilities. Accessed 3 Oct 2025
18. PyTorch: Serialization semantics—PyTorch documentation (2025). https://docs.pytorch.org/docs/stable/notes/serialization.html

19. Sharma, G.: A survey on secure communication technologies for smart grid CPS. Digit. Commun. Netw. (2024)
20. Sheng, Z., Chen, Z., Gu, S., Huang, H., Gu, G., Huang, J.: LLMs in software security: a survey of vulnerability detection techniques and insights. arXiv preprint arXiv:2502.07049 (2025)
21. Steenhoek, B., Rahman, M.M., Jiles, R., Le, W.: Cyber-physical systems security: a survey. IEEE Trans. Industr. Inf. **19**(4), 5892–5904 (2023)
22. Wang, Y., Wang, W., Joty, S., Hoi, S.C.: CodeT5: identifier-aware unified pre-trained encoder-decoder models for code understanding and generation. In: Proceedings of the 2021 Conference on Empirical Methods in Natural Language Processing, pp. 8696–8708 (2021)
23. Yuan, X., Li, J., Zhang, Q.: A survey of transfer learning for software vulnerability detection. IEEE Access **10**, 23331–23344 (2022)
24. Zhou, Y., Liu, S., Siow, J., Du, X., Liu, Y.: *Devign*: effective vulnerability identification by learning comprehensive program semantics via graph neural networks. In: Advances in Neural Information Processing Systems, pp. 10197–10207 (2019)

Engineering Attack Vectors and Detecting Anomalies in Additive Manufacturing

Md Mahbub Hasan(✉), Marcus Sternhagen, and Krishna Chandra Roy

New Mexico Institute of Mining and Technology, Socorro, USA
{mdmahbub.hasan,marcus.sternhagen}@student.nmt.edu, krishna.roy@nmt.edu

Abstract. Additive manufacturing (AM) is rapidly integrating into critical sectors such as aerospace, automotive, and healthcare. However, this cyber-physical convergence introduces new attack surfaces, especially at the interface between computer-aided design (CAD) and machine execution layers. In this work, we investigate targeted cyber-attacks on two widely used fused deposition modeling (FDM) systems, Creality's flagship model K1 Max, and Ender 3. Our threat model is a multi-layered Man-in-the-Middle (MitM) intrusion, where the adversary intercepts and manipulates G-code files during upload from the user interface to the printer firmware. The MitM intrusion chain enables several stealthy sabotage scenarios. These attacks remain undetectable by conventional slicer software or runtime interfaces, resulting in structurally defective yet externally plausible printed parts. To counter these stealthy threats, we propose an unsupervised Intrusion Detection System (IDS) that analyzes structured machine logs generated during live printing. Our defense mechanism uses a frozen Transformer-based encoder (a BERT variant) to extract semantic representations of system behavior, followed by a contrastively trained projection head that learns anomaly-sensitive embeddings. Later, a clustering-based approach and a self-attention autoencoder are used for classification. Experimental results demonstrate that our approach effectively distinguishes between benign and compromised executions.

Keywords: Cyber-Physical Systems · Intrusion Detection System (IDS) · 3D Printer Attacks · Additive Manufacturing · Anomaly Detection

1 Introduction

Additive Manufacturing (AM), commonly known as 3D printing, has revolutionized modern manufacturing by enabling the rapid prototyping and production of complex components with minimal material waste [1,2]. Its integration into safety-critical domains such as aerospace, healthcare, automotive, and defense has made the underlying infrastructure of AM systems a prime target for cyber-physical threats [3,4]. With the proliferation of network-connected 3D printers

Supported by NSF - National Science Foundation.

L. Cheng and F. Anwar (Eds.): SmartSP 2025, LNICST 699, pp. 224–243, 2027.
https://doi.org/10.1007/978-3-032-33701-6_13

[5], adversaries can exploit attack vectors across the digital thread from CAD design, STL/G-code translation, network communication, to firmware execution, potentially sabotaging the mechanical integrity, dimensional accuracy, or intellectual property (IP) [6] of printed parts [7,8]. Recent studies have demonstrated the feasibility and consequences of attacks at various stages of the AM pipeline. These include manipulations of CAD/STL files [9], malicious firmware modifications [10,11], G-code-level sabotage [12], and side-channel IP leakage through power, acoustic, and magnetic emissions [6,8,13,14]. Meanwhile, attack detection frameworks have been proposed using process monitoring [15,16], statistical modeling [7], and analog emission analysis [4]. Despite these efforts, most prior approaches [17] rely on either predefined attacker models or static analysis or require access to a golden reference model(STL). Hence, a significant gap persists in detecting real-time, stealthy attacks that operate directly at the G-code level, the machine-readable instruction. G-code is generated by slicer software from a CAD model and executed during fabrication. Once uploaded, the assumption of trust in the G-code pipeline creates a critical vulnerability. Unlike STL manipulations, G-code-level attacks can subtly alter toolpaths, extrusion volumes, or print timing without triggering visual inspection or violating basic geometry constraints.

In this work, we explore stealthy G-code manipulation strategies that bypass traditional STL-based validation and compromise the final print without overt disruption. We identify three strategies that exploit realistic threat models in networked 3D printing setups, **Deferred Print Exploit**, **Access-Jammed G-code Swap**, and **Execution-Phase Tampering**. Each of these approaches was implemented in a realistic threat model, such as Under-extrusion, Over-extrusion, Noisy G-code Injection, Dimensionality Change, and Internal Cavity Insertion. Assuming the adversary has access to the printer's file system or control interface (e.g., compromised print servers, remote access tools, or insider threats). We conducted experiments on two widely used FDM platforms, Creality K1 Max and Creality Ender 3, with distinct system architectures (Klipper and OctoPrint, respectively), demonstrating the feasibility and cross-platform generalizability of these threats.

A central challenge lies in detecting such attacks without any ground truth STL or reference model, especially when deviations are subtle (e.g., minor under-extrusion or dimensional drift). To address this, we propose a log-based intrusion detection system (IDS) that operates in an unsupervised manner, trained solely on benign printer logs. Our system extracts telemetry and execution logs from the printer. We then utilize self-supervised contrastive learning with a frozen "MiniLM Transformer" encoder to generate discriminative latent embeddings. This approach preserves semantic structure without requiring annotated attack data. The embeddings are first visualized and segmented using PCA/UMAP and K-Means clustering to confirm separation between benign and anomalous patterns. For fine-grained anomaly detection, we further train a self-attention-based autoencoder on benign embeddings and measure reconstruction error during inference. Samples with high reconstruction loss are flagged as anomalies. Our key contributions are as follows:

Realistic Attack Scenarios: We construct multiple realistic adversarial scenarios based on a custom- developed a backdoor interface that mimics legitimate printer control panels. These attacks include Under-extrusion, Over-extrusion, Noisy G-code Injection, Dimensionality Change, and Internal Cavity Insertion.
Log-Centric IDS: Our approach utilizes structured telemetry logs natively produced by the printer firmware. This allows for non-invasive and real-time anomaly detection.
Representation Learning: We employed a pretrained and frozen MiniLM language model to encode into semantically meaningful embeddings. A contrastive projection head is trained using only benign logs, enabling the model to learn a discriminative latent space that highlights deviations without requiring labeled attack data or golden STL/G-code references.
Hybrid Evaluation: We evaluate anomaly separation using both unsupervised clustering and reconstruction-based detection. A self-attention-based autoencoder is trained on benign embeddings to reconstruct normal patterns, and anomalies are flagged via high reconstruction loss.

Our approach complements prior literature by shifting focus from static design-level validation to dynamic runtime anomaly detection.

2 Background and Preliminaries

2.1 3D Printing Workflow

3D printing is a layer-by-layer fabrication process that converts digital models into physical parts. Among various AM techniques, Fused Deposition Modeling (FDM) [18] is the most prevalent due to its affordability, accessibility, and simplicity. In FDM, a thermoplastic filament [19] is melted and extruded through a heated nozzle, which moves across X, Y, and Z axes to deposit material onto a build platform. The process repeats layer by layer until the entire object is formed [20]. A 3D printing workflow begins with a digital 3D model designed in computer-aided design (CAD) software. This model is exported in a mesh-based format, most commonly the STL (Stereolithography) file format [21], which encodes the surface geometry of the object, Fig. 1a. The STL file is then processed by a slicer, a software tool that slices the 3D model into discrete horizontal layers and converts them into machine-readable instructions. These instructions are encoded as G-code [22], which defines precise commands for printer motion, extrusion, temperature control, and timing. The G-code file is typically uploaded to the printer and executed line-by-line during the manufacturing process, as demonstrated in Fig. 1b.

In our research, we investigated two widely used FDM printers, the Creality K1 Max and the Creality Ender 3, each configured with distinct system architectures and control interfaces.

(a)

```
G1 X149.646 Y168.368 F30000
G1 Z.4
G1 Z.2
G1 E.6 F2400
;TYPE:Inner wall
;WIDTH:0.5
G1 F3000
G1 X131.279 Y150 E.9675
G1 X150 Y131.279 E.98612
```

(b)

Fig. 1. (a) Stereolithography Render, (b) G-code structure.

2.2 K1 Max and Ender 3: Architecture

The K1 Max runs a Klipper-based firmware and is connected to a custom Linux-based host via web interfaces such as Mainsail and Fluidd. Under the hood, Klipper offloads G-code parsing and motion planning to the host machine, which then communicates with the printer's microcontroller via a serial interface. This architecture significantly improves performance and flexibility while exposing the communication channel between the host and MCU as a potential attack surface. To support real-time control and API access, Klipper is paired with Moonraker, a web service that provides a JSON-RPC interface for interacting with the printer state. Users upload G-code files through web frontends like Fluidd or Mainsail, which send the file to the Moonraker API, store it in a directory accessible to Klipper, and initiate printing through API calls. This separation between UI, API layer, and firmware creates multiple interception points for attackers who can gain access to the local network or file system.

In contrast, our Creality Ender 3 printer operates with a Raspberry Pi-based OctoPrint setup. In this configuration, the OctoPrint software runs on the Raspberry Pi and interfaces directly with the printer via USB. Users access a web dashboard hosted by OctoPrint to upload G-code files, monitor temperature and status, and initiate prints. OctoPrint acts as both the controller and relay, forwarding commands directly to the printer firmware. While simpler than the K1 Max architecture, OctoPrint still introduces a central point where G-code files can be intercepted or manipulated before execution.

2.3 Attack Surface

In our threat model, the attacker is positioned between the user and the firmware either by compromising the local network, gaining access to the proxy interface (e.g., Fluidd, Moonraker, or OctoPrint), or directly manipulating the file system. We implemented multiple stealthy MitM attacks that operate at the G-code layer, as demonstrated in Table 1.

Table 1. G-code Categories Used in Implemented Attack Scenarios

Strategy	Relevant G-Codes
Deferred Print Exploit	M25, M0, G4, G28, G92
Access-Jammed G-code Swap	G92, M28, M23, M24, M25
Execution-Phase Tampering	G4, M25, M24, G92, G1, G0
Attack Type	Relevant G-Codes
Under-Extrusion Attack	G0, G1, M83, M221, M404
Over-Extrusion Attack	G0, G1, M82, M221, M404
Noise Injection	G0, G1, G92, M104, M109
Cavity Insertion	G0, G1, G92, M28
Dimensional Manipulation	G92, M206, G1, G92.X, M579
Intellectual Property Theft	M154, M928, M111

3 Related Work

Early works have demonstrated how 3D design files, such as STL, can be manipulated to introduce structural weaknesses. Logan et al. [9] showed how subtle changes to STL files could evade human inspection and lead to mechanical failure. Similarly, Sofia et al. [3] presented an end-to-end sabotage attack that compromised a drone propeller by manipulating design files, causing it to fail mid-flight. These studies highlight the potential of undetected design modifications to undermine the integrity of printed parts. As an intermediate machine-readable format, G-code has become a focal point for adversaries. Caleb et al. [7] explored subtle malicious edits to G-code without access to golden models. Their red-team/blue-team setup quantified the difficulty of detecting fine-grained G-code manipulations. "SOK" [11] expanded on this by analyzing 278 potentially harmful G-codes and introducing new attacker models that can exploit even limited access. To defend against such threats, research has proposed reverse engineering G-code to validate printed geometries. Tsoutsos et al. [23] developed a toolpath reconstruction method to re-generate approximate 3D models from G-code and assess structural soundness via Finite Element Analysis (FEA).

Firmware-level compromises have been shown to offer persistent and stealthy attack vectors. Mahmood et al. [17] demonstrated that malicious firmware could intercept or replace print jobs and manipulate extrusion settings. Muhammad et al. [10] systematized firmware attacks across multiple stages of 3D printing and introduced an "Attack Feasibility Index" (AFI) to rank potential threats. Beyond firmware, side-channel attacks leveraging acoustic, electromagnetic, or power emissions have also been explored. Song et al. [8] showed how smartphone sensors could reconstruct G-code by analyzing acoustic and magnetic data. "Encryption is Futile" article [14] further demonstrated that power side-channel leakage could yield near-perfect model reconstructions even under encrypted communications. The risk of IP leakage has driven efforts to secure AM pipelines. Yampolskiy et al. [24] proposed secure outsourcing models for IP-sensitive manufacturing. In contrast, Chhetri et al. [6] highlighted how modifying compilers could amplify side-channel leakage to leak G-code content. On the network side, McCormack et al. [25,26] introduced C3PO, a tool for assessing security posture and attack paths in networked 3D printing deployments. Real-time process monitoring is another line of defense. Gao et al. [15] developed a sensor-based framework for monitoring physical parameters such as speed, infill, and fan speed to detect abnormal printing behavior. "KCAD" paper [4] introduced a kinetic cyber-attack detection system using statistical mappings between analog emissions and G-code patterns. Recent work by Mahmood et al. [17] and Meleshko et al. [27] focuses on modeling cyber-attacks in laboratory setups, offering simulation-based evaluations of malicious modifications and their detection.

Unlike prior works that focus on a single attack vector, such as G-code tampering, side-channel exfiltration, or firmware backdoors, our approach provides a comprehensive threat model that encompasses multiple intrusion points within the 3D printing workflow. We design a realistic attacker model that utilizes a rogue web interface to intercept user activity, manipulate uploaded G-code files pre- and mid-print, and hijack printer controls. Additionally, we propose an unsupervised anomaly detection system that uses structured printer host logs and transformer-based log embedding with contrastive learning to differentiate benign vs. manipulated prints.

4 Attack Strategy

4.1 Assumptions

Our threat model assumes that the attacker has obtained root-level access to the 3D printer's host operating system by compromising authentication credentials. The assumption is realistic and supported by both prior observations of poor authentication practices in embedded printing systems and our experimental validation.

In a controlled lab environment, we validated the feasibility of credential compromise using both brute-force and dictionary-based password attacks. These experiments were conducted on Creality K1 Max and Ender 3 setups, where SSH rate limiting was disabled and weak passwords were used to simulate real-world misconfigurations. The brute-force attack employed parallel enumeration of common character patterns and successfully broke short passwords frequently used in embedded systems. The dictionary-based approach further demonstrated effectiveness by leveraging a curated list of domain-specific keywords, including printer models (e.g., "Ender", "Creality"), materials (e.g., "PLA", "ABS"), and software terms (e.g., "OctoPrint", "Slicer", "Klipper"). These wordlists simulate real-world attacker strategies based on contextual familiarity with additive manufacturing environments. The success of these attacks aligns with findings from broader security surveys indicating that many 3D printers are deployed with factory-default credentials, passwords derived from printer names, or otherwise weak authentication schemes. Additionally, the embedded and unattended nature of many 3D printing controllers leads to inconsistent patching and poor security hygiene. Firmware-level authentication mechanisms are either absent or insufficient, and the presence of network-facing control interfaces (e.g., Moonraker, OctoPrint, or Fluidd) introduces an expanded attack surface. These services are often accessible over the LAN or, in some cases, exposed to the public internet for remote printing convenience, further enabling remote adversaries.

Establishing credential compromise as a feasible and reproducible step allows us to explore downstream attack scenarios that arise once root access is obtained.

4.2 Rogue Interface and Attacks

One of the core intrusion techniques developed in this work involves the creation of a rogue control interface that mimics the legitimate web interface used for controlling 3D printers running printer firmware. This malicious replica is hosted on the attacker's own machine or a compromised device within the same network as the target printer. Once root access is obtained through credential compromise, the attacker installs this mimic interface to act as a transparent proxy between the legitimate user and the underlying printer system.

It communicates directly with the print server API, accessing the printer's file system and configuration directories. As a result, the attacker gains real-time visibility into all user actions and machine operations, including G-code uploads, printing progress, system temperatures, logging activity, and configuration changes. By deploying this replica interface as a stealth access layer, the attacker effectively bypasses traditional network-layer monitoring tools. This enables a suite of downstream G-code manipulation attacks with minimal detection risk, laying the foundation for the stealthy sabotage scenarios described in the following paragraphs.

Threat Model: Our threat model assumes an adversary with a primary attack point into the AM pipeline, which is system-level backdoor access to the printer's file system and control interface. Fig. 2 illustrates the complete intrusion architecture.

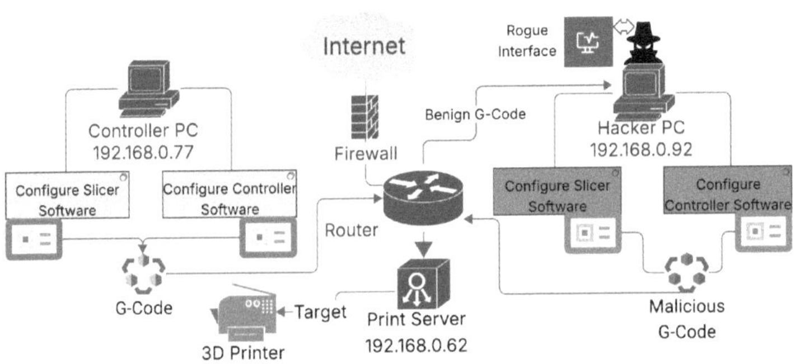

Fig. 2. Attack Strategy Pipeline.

Intrusion Point: MitM with G-code Manipulation. The adversary utilizes unauthorized access to the printer's internal file system and G-code control flow via SSH and a spoofed web interface. We implement the following techniques:

Deferred Print Exploit: The adversary monitors the printer's G-code upload directory and waits for a legitimate user to upload a file via the standard web interface (e.g., Fluidd, Mainsail, or OctoPrint). Once a new .gcode file is detected, the attacker allows a short delay window to pass, ensuring the file is not being actively used by the system. After this short period, the attacker downloads the uploaded file, modifies it locally by injecting stealthy perturbations, and re-uploads the modified file to the original path. This form of post-upload interception is complex for users to detect, as most 3D printer UIs do not validate the integrity of uploaded files or retain cryptographic hashes [28]. The entire operation takes place between the time the file is uploaded and before the user initiates printing. This strategy targets the window of vulnerability between upload and execution.

Access-Jammed G-code Swap: This attack refines the delayed replacement strategy by locking the uploaded G-code file immediately upon detection. As soon as a new .gcode file appears, the attacker temporarily makes it inaccessible to the user for 5 to 10 s. This ensures the file will not be executed prematurely while it is being modified. After locking, the attacker downloads the file, injects targeted modifications, and uploads the altered version. The file is then restored to its original name, completing the substitution. This method ensures fast replacement of the original file, and preventing user access during the manipulation process. It also increases the likelihood of successful sabotage even in environments with fast user-triggered printing.

Execution-Phase Tampering: The adversary targets an active print job that is already underway. By querying the printer state via the print server API, the attacker determines the filename currently being executed and the print state. After a configurable delay, typically 2 to 5 min, the attacker intercepts the ongoing print using a direct command to the backend control interface. Then, the attacker replaces the currently printing G-code file with a modified version in the remaining layers. This approach allows attackers to target only the latter portion of the print, making anomalies less noticeable during early inspection and potentially bypassing surface-level quality control. It also avoids suspicion from the user, who may attribute final-layer defects to slicing issues or mechanical artifacts.

Attacks by Intrusion Point: The adversary's access to G-code control enables a broad spectrum of malicious modifications, ranging from subtle sabotage to outright intellectual property theft.

Intellectual Property (IP) Theft. With access to the printer's file system, the adversary can exfiltrate proprietary design assets such as uploaded G-code files or STL derivatives. These files can be intercepted before or after any modifications and covertly transmitted to an attacker-controlled server. Once obtained, the files can be reverse-engineered to extract valuable manufacturing information such as pathing logic, infill strategies, or fine-tuned process parameters. Furthermore, the stolen files may be replicated on remote 3D printers to produce counterfeit copies of the original design. Such breaches are especially damaging in high-stakes sectors like aerospace, biomedical devices, or defense manufacturing, where the leakage of proprietary IP can result in significant strategic and economic consequences.

Under-extrusion: By reducing `E` values, the nozzle delivers insufficient material, leading to weak interlayer bonding, poor layer adhesion, and ultimately, reduced tensile strength of the part. Such defects may be internal and invisible to post-print visual inspection.

Over-extrusion: Conversely, inflating `E` values causes excessive filament deposition, which results in dimensional inaccuracy, surface roughness, or printer head drag. This may damage surrounding layers or cause the actuator to overheat.

Noisy G-code Injection: Another stealthy sabotage approach involves injecting noisy motion commands, such as high-frequency or random `G0` (non-extruding move) and `G1` (extruding move) instructions. These can increase wear and tear on stepper motors by inducing high-speed oscillations, surface-level distortions by introducing non-uniform paths, or jagged trajectories. It can also cause micro-delays that desynchronize thermal control, leading to inconsistent material melting.

Dimensionality Change: Subtle manipulation of coordinate scaling, such as multiplying the `X`, `Y`, or `Z` values in selected G-code segments, can introduce imperceptible but harmful geometric distortions. Scaling along the`X`/`Y` axes affects footprint and fitment tolerances. Scaling the `Z` axis affects layer height, which in turn impacts stacking behavior and vertical strength. Localized changes (e.g., only in the middle third of the print) evade dimensional validation tools that measure only the bounding box. Such attacks compromise precision-critical components (e.g., interlocking parts or aerodynamics-sensitive designs) while maintaining overall visual similarity.

Internal Cavity Insertion: The adversary may target the structural core of the object by introducing voids or cavities within specific layer ranges. Cavities are created by removing or skipping `E` extrusion values across predefined `Z`-height intervals. These modifications are made mid-print to avoid detection in pre-print preview or slicing validation. While the external geometry remains intact, the absence of infill or perimeters in these regions significantly degrades load-bearing capacity, causing silent failures under stress. This attack is hazardous in safety-critical parts, where internal defects are not easily visible but have a direct impact on reliability (Fig. 3).

5 Defense Methodology

5.1 Data Collection

We utilize printer logs as a high-fidelity data source to capture the operational state and runtime behavior of the 3D printer. The logs were collected under two primary conditions: (1) benign operation involving benign slicing and printing workflows, and (2) malicious scenarios.

(a) Noise Injected Object: K1-Max.

(b) Cavity Inserted Object: Ender-3.

Fig. 3. K1-Max & Ender-3 Printing Object During Attack.

5.2 Feature Selection

To ensure that our model captures meaningful semantic patterns while minimizing redundancy, we employed a hybrid approach combining domain-driven selection and statistical filtering. Initially, we identified a broad set of features shown in the Table 2 from logs based on their relevance to printing state, thermal stability, communication health, and system workload. To refine this selection, we applied a two-step statistical filtering pipeline:

Table 2. Features from Logs

Category	Feature(Raw logs)	Reason
Print Progress	print_time, sd_pos, buffer_time, print_stall, gcodein	Captures how much of the print job has been completed and helps detect abnormal progression or interruptions.
Thermal Data	mcu_temp, chamber_temp, heater_bed.temp, extruder.temp, heater_bed.pwm, extruder.pwm	Reflects thermal stability; useful for identifying physical anomalies such as under-extrusion or overheating.
System Resources	sysload, cputime, memavail	Indicates CPU and memory stress.
MCU Stats	bytes_write, bytes_read, bytes_retransmit, bytes_invalid, send_seq, receive_seq, retransmit_seq	Represents communication reliability between host and MCUs; abnormal retransmissions or packet loss may indicate attack.
MCU Timings	mcu_task_avg, mcu_task_stddev, mcu_awake, srtt, rttvar, rto	Timing delays and task scheduling variance can highlight abnormal processing behavior or congestion.
Nozzle/Leveling MCU	nozzle_mcu.*, leveling_mcu.*	Comparing timing and communication across different MCUs can detect localized issues or attack traces.
Raspberry Pi Stats	rpi.mcu_task_avg, rpi.bytes_retransmit, etc.	Shows host-controller interaction health; anomalies here can indicate local overload or network disruption.

Variance Thresholding: Features with near-zero variance (threshold < 0.01) across the benign dataset were discarded, as they offer limited discriminative power.

Correlation Pruning: From the remaining features, we computed a pairwise Pearson correlation matrix and eliminated features exhibiting high linear correlation (> 0.95) to reduce redundancy.

5.3 Model Architecture

We propose an unsupervised anomaly detection framework. The complete pipeline is demonstrated in the Fig. 4. The architecture consists of two core stages: (i) contrastive representation learning using a frozen Transformer encoder, and (ii) anomaly detection using a self-attention-enhanced autoencoder.

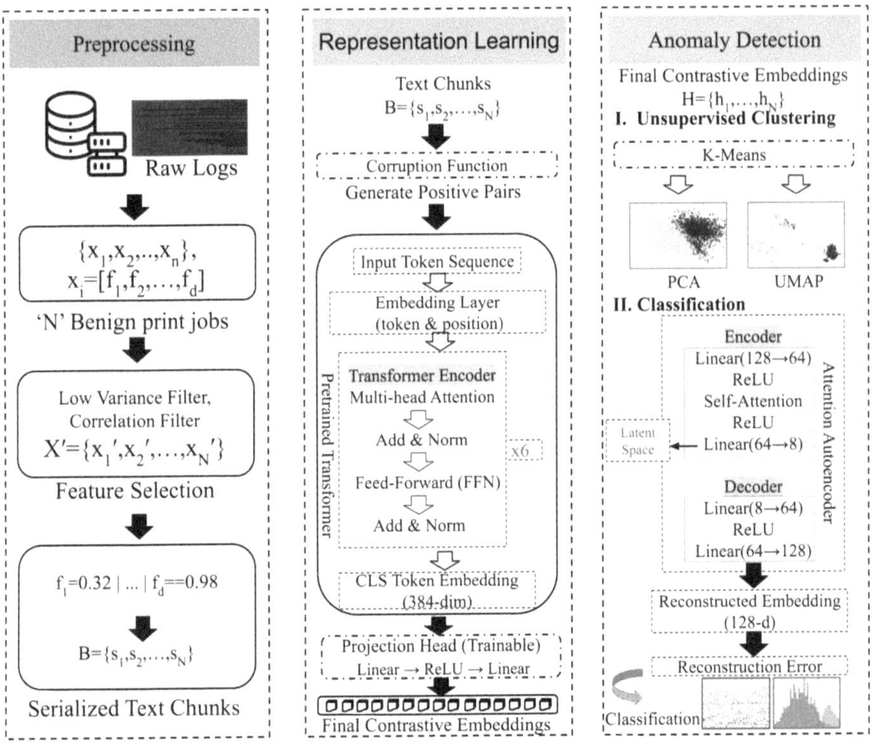

Fig. 4. Model Architecture: Preprocessing, Representation Learning, and Anomaly Detection.

The structured logs be represented as a matrix $\mathcal{L} = \{\mathbf{x}_1, \mathbf{x}_2, \ldots, \mathbf{x}_N\}$, where each row $\mathbf{x}_i \in \mathbb{R}^d$ denotes a log with d numeric features. After applying low-variance and high-correlation filters, the reduced feature set is denoted as $\mathcal{L}' = \{\mathbf{x}'_1, \ldots, \mathbf{x}'_N\}$, where $\mathbf{x}'_i \in \mathbb{R}^{d'}$, $d' < d$. Each filtered row $\mathbf{x}'_i$ is serialized into a sentence-like structure. This transformation preserves context and enables token-based encoding: $s_i =$ "$\text{key}_1 = v_1 \,|\, \text{key}_2 = v_2 \,|\, \ldots \,|\, \text{key}_d = v_{d'}$"
Contrastive Representation Learning: We employ the `all-MiniLM-L6-v2` transformer model as a frozen encoder $f_\theta : \mathbb{S} \rightarrow \mathbb{R}^{384}$, where θ represents the fixed pretrained parameters. For a given sentence s_i, the frozen encoder generates a 384-dimensional semantic embedding: $\mathbf{h}_i = f_\theta(s_i),\ \mathbf{h}_i \in \mathbb{R}^{384}$

To specialize the embedding for anomaly detection, we introduce a trainable projection head $g_\phi : \mathbb{R}^{384} \rightarrow \mathbb{R}^{128}$, parameterized by ϕ. This projection head is implemented as a double layer MLP: $g_\phi(\mathbf{h}) = \mathbf{W}_2 \cdot \text{ReLU}(\mathbf{W}_1 \cdot \mathbf{h} + \mathbf{b}_1) + \mathbf{b}_2$, with weight matrices $\mathbf{W}_1 \in \mathbb{R}^{256\times384}$, $\mathbf{W}_2 \in \mathbb{R}^{128\times256}$, and bias terms $\mathbf{b}_1 \in \mathbb{R}^{256}$, $\mathbf{b}_2 \in \mathbb{R}^{128}$. The complete model forward pass is defined as: $\mathbf{z}_i = g_\phi(f_\theta(s_i))$ where $\mathbf{z}_i \in \mathbb{R}^{128}$. To train the model in an unsupervised manner, we adopt contrastive learning. For each benign line s_i, we generate a synthetically perturbed version s_i' by applying domain aware corruption (e.g., replacing "extruder" with "toolhead", or modifying temperature labels). The goal is to minimize the contrastive loss between benign and corrupted embeddings: $\mathcal{L}_{\text{contrastive}} = 1 - \cos(\mathbf{z}_i, \mathbf{z}_i') = 1 - \frac{\mathbf{z}_i \cdot \mathbf{z}_i'}{\|\mathbf{z}_i\| \cdot \|\mathbf{z}_i'\|}$. Only the projection head parameters g_ϕ are updated during training, while the base encoder f_θ remains frozen.

Inference and Anomaly Detection: At inference time, unseen printer logs are serialized and passed through the frozen encoder f_θ and the trained projection head g_ϕ to generate compact embeddings: $\mathbf{z}_i = g_\phi(f_\theta(s_i))$. These embeddings serve as inputs to two complementary anomaly detection strategies:

I. Clustering-Based Detection: We apply K-Means clustering on benign embeddings to learn centroid representations of normal behavior. For a test embedding $\mathbf{z}_i$, the anomaly score is computed as the minimum Euclidean distance to the nearest cluster centroid: $\mathcal{A}_i^{(\text{cluster})} = \min_{c \in C} \|\mathbf{z}_i - c\|_2$. Embeddings with high cluster distance are considered anomalous. Dimensionality reduction techniques such as PCA and UMAP are also applied for visual validation of clustering boundaries.

II. Reconstruction-Based Detection: To complement the clustering results, we utilize a self-attention-enhanced autoencoder to reconstruct embeddings generated from benign printer behavior. A high reconstruction error is indicative of a potential anomaly. $\mathbf{z}_i \in \mathbb{R}^{128}$ denote the contrastive embedding of a serialized log sentence. The autoencoder architecture $\mathcal{A}_\psi$ consists of an encoder E and a decoder D such that: $\hat{\mathbf{z}}_i = D(E(\mathbf{z}_i)), \quad \text{for } i = 1, \ldots, N$.

Encoder Structure: The encoder projects the input into a compressed latent space of dimension 8. This is achieved via:

$$\mathbf{h}_i^{(1)} = \text{ReLU}(W_1 \cdot \mathbf{z}_i + \mathbf{b}_1), \quad W_1 \in \mathbb{R}^{64\times128} \tag{1}$$

$$\mathbf{h}_i^{(attn)} = \text{SelfAttention}(\mathbf{h}_i^{(1)}) \in \mathbb{R}^{64} \tag{2}$$

$$\mathbf{z}_i^{(enc)} = W_2 \cdot \text{ReLU}(\mathbf{h}_i^{(attn)}) + \mathbf{b}_2, \quad W_2 \in \mathbb{R}^{8\times64} \tag{3}$$

Self-attention Mechanism: We implement a single-head self-attention module to capture latent interactions among features within each embedding vector. Given an input $\mathbf{h} \in \mathbb{R}^{64}$, the query, key, and value vectors are computed as [29]: $Q = W_Q\mathbf{h}$, $K = W_K\mathbf{h}$, $V = W_V\mathbf{h}$, where $W_Q, W_K, W_V \in \mathbb{R}^{64\times64}$ are learnable weight matrices. The attention score is computed as: $\alpha = \frac{Q \cdot K^T}{\sqrt{d_k}} \in \mathbb{R}$, $d_k = 64$, and AttentionOutput = softmax(α) $\cdot V$. This operation allows the encoder to dynamically emphasize more informative feature components when forming the latent representation.

Decoder Structure: The decoder reconstructs the original 128-dimensional embedding from the latent code:

$$\mathbf{h}_i^{(3)} = \text{ReLU}(W_3 \cdot \mathbf{z}_i^{(enc)} + \mathbf{b}_3), \quad W_3 \in \mathbb{R}^{64\times 8} \tag{4}$$

$$\hat{\mathbf{z}}_i = W_4 \cdot \mathbf{h}_i^{(3)} + \mathbf{b}_4, \quad W_4 \in \mathbb{R}^{128\times 64} \tag{5}$$

Anomaly Scoring: Reconstruction error is used to assign an anomaly score: $\mathcal{E}_i = \frac{1}{128}\left\|\hat{\mathbf{z}}_i - \mathbf{z}_i\right\|_2^2$ A threshold τ is determined from the 95th percentile of benign reconstruction errors. A test log is classified as anomalous if $\mathcal{E}_i > \tau$.

6 Experimental Analysis

6.1 Experimental Setup:

The primary hardware platform used is the Creality K1 Max 3D printer, which operates on the Klipper firmware, interfaced through Moonraker, and accessed via the Fluidd and Mainsail web frontends. The attack automation is handled using Python 3.11, using SSH-based file access, requests for interacting with the Moonraker API, and an observer for real-time file system monitoring and G-code injection. In addition, Ender 3 is used with a Raspberry Pi 4 running OctoPrint to validate the portability of our attacks across different firmware and control stacks. Both printers were connected to the same local area network (LAN) as the attacker's host for seamless monitoring and command execution. All experiments were performed on a high-performance host machine equipped with an Intel Core i9-14900KF CPU clocked at 3.20 GHz and 32 GB of DDR5 RAM. We used an NVIDIA RTX 4090 GPU featuring 24 GB of GDDR6X memory, a 384-bit memory bus, and 512 Tensor cores optimized for AI workloads.

6.2 Dataset Description

Table 3 illustrates the size of each sample. All attack categories are deliberately excluded from training to simulate a realistic zero-day threat detection scenario. Class proportions are chosen to ensure diversity and avoid bias toward any specific attack.

6.3 Training Details

A total of 98,720 benign samples were extracted from logs and structured into fixed-length time windows. The frozen MiniLM transformer model produces 384-dimensional dense embeddings for each log sequence. To adapt this dimension, we append a learnable multi-layer perceptron (MLP) projection head that maps the representations from 384 to 128 dimensions.

We use the Adam optimizer with a learning rate of 1×10^{-4} and a batch size of 64. The model is trained for 25 epochs using only benign data, with no attack labels.

Table 3. Distribution for Training and Validation

Class Type	Attack Category	Samples	Usage
Benign	–	98,720	Training
Benign	–	57,373	Validation
Attack	Under-extrusion	10120	Validation
	Over-extrusion	9950	Validation
	Noise Injection	15456	Validation
	Dimensional Change	9324	Validation
	Cavity Insertion	10521	Validation

7 Qualitative Evaluation

Figures 5 and 6 illustrate the visual impact of various attack scenarios on physical objects printed using Creality K1 Max and Ender-3 printers, respectively. Each figure presents a side-by-side comparison of benign and manipulated outputs, highlighting both geometric deformation and weight anomalies. In both setups, the benign injection (Fig. 5a,6a) demonstrates smooth surface finish, uniform gear teeth, and structurally complete prints serving as a visual baseline for integrity. Under the cavity insertion attack (b), both printers produce prints with missing internal material and incomplete infill, severely compromising mechanical strength. Noise injection (c) leads to stringing, irregular perimeter paths, and chaotic surface textures, revealing disrupted extrusion paths caused by G-code perturbation. Dimensional manipulation (d) visually mimics benign geometry. Still, it subtly alters the overall scale (if we scale 98% of the original, it can't be detected by the naked eye), potentially impairing fit and function in mechanical assemblies. The lower rows focus on extrusion-level anomalies captured via precise weight measurements. For Creality K1 Max, the benign extrusion sample (e) weighs 6.03g, while under-extrusion (f) drops to 4.32g, indicating sparse filament deposition and weak part strength. Over-extrusion (g) increases the mass to 9.00g, resulting in excessive material and surface blobbing. Ender-3 results follow similar trends, benign extrusion (e) at 5.80g, under-extrusion (f) at 4.60g, and over-extrusion (g) at 8.54g, affirming that extrusion attacks manifest consistently across different printer architectures.

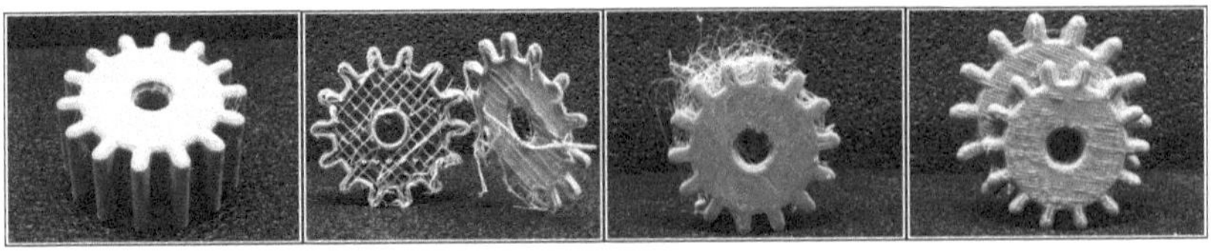

(a) Benign. (b) Cavity Ins. (c) Noise Inj. (d) Dimension Inj.

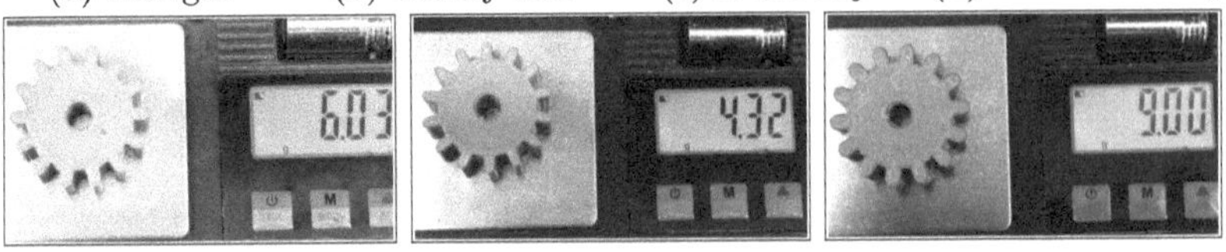

(e) Benign Extrusion (f) Under-Extrusion (g) Over-Extrusion

Fig. 5. Creality K1-Max printed objects under different attacks.

(a) Benign. (b) Cavity Ins. (c) Noise Inj. (d) Dimension Inj.

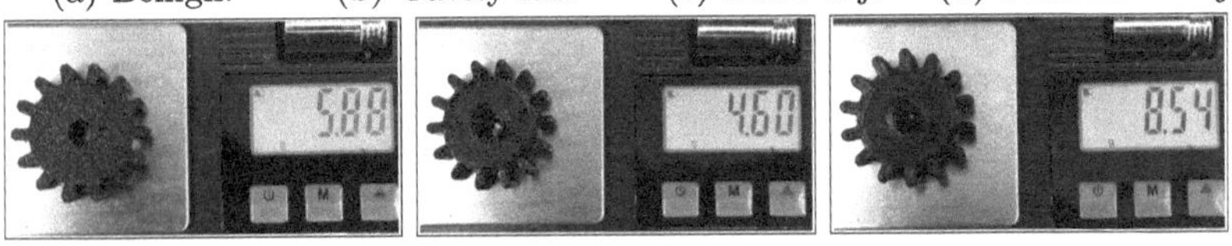

(e) Benign Extrusion (f) Under-Extrusion (g) Over-Extrusion

Fig. 6. Ender-3 printed objects under different attacks.

8 Quantitative Evaluation

8.1 Clustering Results

Figure 7a depicts the K-Means clustering output overlaid on a 2D PCA projection of the learned embeddings. The two clusters, shown in yellow and purple, exhibit a strong linear separation along the PCA-1 axis. This clear partitioning demonstrates that the contrastive learning framework has successfully embedded benign and anomalous behaviors into distinct regions of the latent space.

To capture potential nonlinear structure in the learned embeddings, we employed UMAP to reduce the latent space to two dimensions. As shown in Fig. 7b, the K-Means clusters are projected into a nonlinear manifold where the separation is even more pronounced compared to PCA. One cluster forms a tightly concentrated group on the right, while the other spans multiple regions,

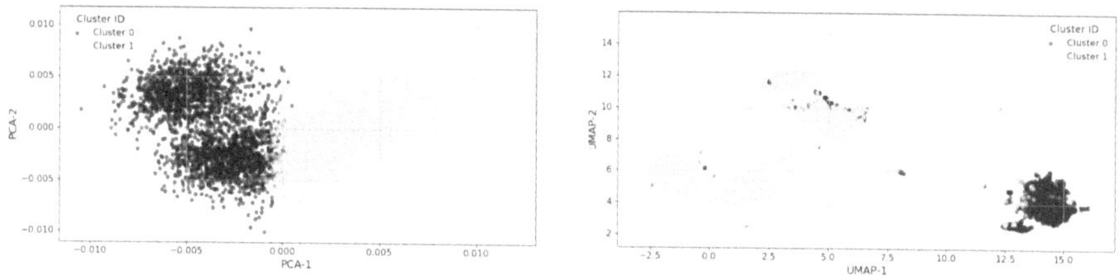

(a) K-Means on PCA (b) K-Means clustering on UMAP.

Fig. 7. Cluster Visualization on Latent Space.

indicating the model's ability to differentiate benign behaviors from diverse attack patterns.

8.2 Classification Reconstruction Error

To differentiate benign from malicious inputs, a thresholding mechanism was employed. Specifically, we used the 95th percentile of reconstruction errors computed on benign validation data to set a threshold of 0.0019. This ensures that only the most anomalous deviations are flagged while minimizing false positives, a critical requirement in practical deployment.

Table 4. Anomaly Detection Performance

Metric	Benign		Attack	
	Value	(%)	Value	(%)
Precision	0.9801	98.01%	0.9055	90.55%
Recall	0.9499	94.99%	0.9614	96.14%
F1-score	0.9648	96.48%	0.9326	93.26%
Overall Accuracy		0.9537 (95.37%)		
Macro Avg F1-score		0.9487 (94.87%)		
Weighted Avg F1-score		0.9541 (95.41%)		
AUROC (AUC)		0.9870 (98.70%)		
Threshold (MSE)		0.0019		

The model's performance was quantitatively evaluated using a confusion matrix, ROC curve, and classification metrics in a Table 4. The self-autoencoder achieved a high overall classification accuracy of 95.37%, with a precision of 90.55%, recall of 96.14%, and an F1-score of 93.26%. Notably, the area under the ROC curve (AUC) was 0.98, demonstrating strong discriminative power between benign and anomalous inputs.

Table 5. Autoencoder Output

True/Predicted	Benign	Attack
Benign	94.99%	5.01%
Attack	3.86%	96.14%

The confusion matrix in Table 5 further reveals that 94.99% of benign samples were correctly classified as benign, while only 5.01% were misclassified as attacks. For attack samples, 96.14% were correctly identified as malicious, whereas 3.86% were incorrectly marked as benign.

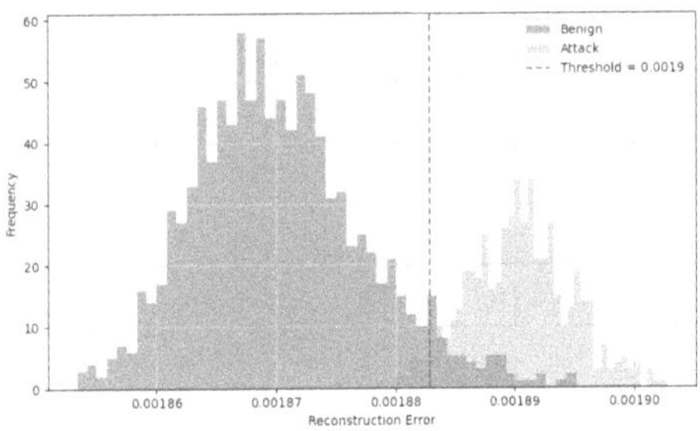

(a) Histogram of Reconstruction Error

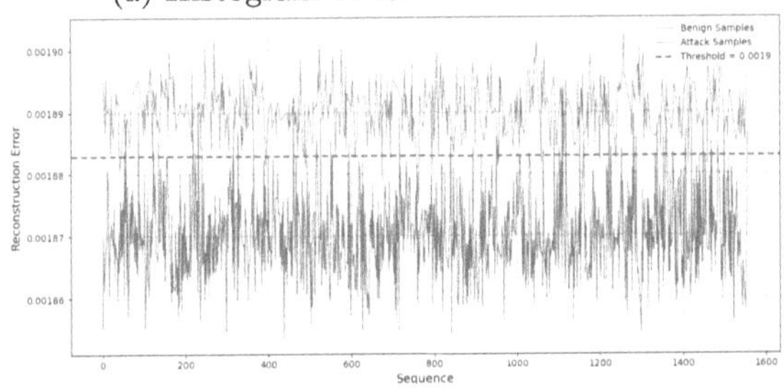

(b) Reconstruction error by Sequence.

Fig. 8. Visualization of Reconstruction Errors (MSE).

We further visualized the reconstruction errors for benign and attack samples. Figure 8a presents the distribution of reconstruction errors for each class. Benign samples (in blue) exhibit a tightly grouped error distribution centered around a lower mean, indicating high fidelity in reconstruction. In contrast, attack samples (in orange) display a right-shifted distribution with a larger spread.

Figure 8b further corroborates these findings by illustrating reconstruction error across the sequence of test samples. Benign samples (blue line) consistently maintain lower reconstruction errors below the defined threshold. Conversely, attack samples (red line) frequently cross this boundary, suggesting pronounced deviations from the learned benign patterns.

9 Conclusion

In this study, we demonstrate how various attack vectors, including G-code hijacking, cavity insertion, under- or over-extrusion, dimensional manipulation, and intellectual property theft, can be initiated through backdoor access or mid-print tampering. We also developed and evaluated an unsupervised intrusion detection framework that uses contrastive representation learning and structured log analysis. Our methodology learns semantic embeddings of benign printer behavior and employs both clustering-based and reconstruction-based strategies to detect deviations. Our experiments on Creality K1 Max and Ender 3 printers validated the feasibility of these attacks and the efficacy of our defense model.

Despite its effectiveness, the current system has some limitations. First, the approach assumes access to structured and timestamp-aligned logs, which may not be available in proprietary or closed-source firmware environments. Second, specific stealthy attacks that do not significantly perturb telemetry patterns (e.g., subtle IP theft without extrusion anomalies) may remain undetected. Future directions include incorporating temporal modeling using graph-based temporal embeddings to capture long-range dependencies. Finally, generalizing the model across multiple printer architectures and expanding to federated anomaly detection across a distributed fleet of printers will broaden applicability.

Acknowledgment. This material is based upon work supported by the National Science Foundation under Award No. 2417062. Any opinions, findings, and conclusions or recommendations expressed in this material are those of the authors and do not necessarily reflect the views of the National Science Foundation.

References

1. Wohlers, T., et al.: History of additive manufacturing. SSRN Electron. J. (2023)
2. Abdulhameed, O., Al-Ahmari, A., Ameen, W., Mian, S.H.: Additive manufacturing: challenges, trends, and applications. Adv. Mech. Eng. **11**(2), 1687814018822880 (2019)
3. Belikovetsky, S., Yampolskiy, M., Toh, J., Gatlin, J., Elovici, Y.: dr0wned – cyber-physical attack with additive manufacturing. In: 11th USENIX Workshop on Offensive Technologies (WOOT 17), Vancouver, BC, USENIX Association (2017)
4. Chhetri, S.R., Canedo, A., Faruque, M.A.A.: Kcad: kinetic cyber-attack detection method for cyber-physical additive manufacturing systems. In: 2016 IEEE/ACM International Conference on Computer-Aided Design (ICCAD), pp. 1–8 (2016)
5. Müller, J., Mladenov, V., Somorovsky, J., Schwenk, J.: Sok: exploiting network printers. In: 2017 IEEE Symposium on Security and Privacy (SP), pp. 213–230 (2017)
6. Chhetri, S.R., Barua, A., Faezi, S., Regazzoni, F., Canedo, A., Al Faruque, M.A.: Tool of spies: leaking your ip by altering the 3d printer compiler. IEEE Trans. Dependable Secure. Comput. **18**(2), 667–678 (2021)
7. Beckwith, C., et al.: Gupta: needle in a haystack: detecting subtle malicious edits to additive manufacturing g-code files, CoRR (2021). arXiv:2111.12746

8. Song, C., Lin, F., Ba, Z., Ren, K., Zhou, C., Xu, W.: My smartphone knows what you print: exploring smartphone-based side-channel attacks against 3d printers. In: Proceedings of the 2016 ACM SIGSAC Conference on Computer and Communications Security, CCS 2016, pp. 895–907, New York, NY, USA, ACM (2016)
9. Sturm, L.D., Williams, C.B., Camelio, J.A., White, J., Parker, R.: Cyber-physical vulnerabilities in additive manufacturing systems: a case study attack on the.stl file with human subjects. J. Manuf. Syst. **44**, 154–164 (2017)
10. Rais, M.H., Ahsan, M., Ahmed, I.: SOK: 3d printer firmware attacks on fused filament fabrication. In: 18th USENIX WOOT Conference on Offensive Technologies (WOOT 24), pp. 263–282, Philadelphia, PA, USENIX Association (2024)
11. Moore, S., Glisson, W., Yampolskiy, M.: Implications of malicious 3d printer firmware (2017)
12. Rossel, J., Mladenov, V., Wördenweber, N., Somorovsky, J.: Security implications of malicious g-codes in 3d printing
13. Al Faruque, M.A., Chhetri, S.R., Canedo, A., Wan, J.: Acoustic side-channel attacks on additive manufacturing systems. In: 2016 ACM/IEEE 7th International Conference on Cyber-Physical Systems (ICCPS), pp. 1–10 (2016)
14. Gatlin, J., et al.: Encryption is futile: reconstructing 3d-printed models using the power side-channel. In: Proceedings of the 24th International Symposium on Research in Attacks, Intrusions and Defenses, RAID 2021, pp. 135–147. New York, NY, USA, ACM (2021)
15. Gao, Y., Li, B., Wang, W., Xu, W., Zhou, C., Jin, Z.: Watching and safeguarding your 3d printer: Online process monitoring against cyber-physical attacks. In: Proceedings of the ACM on Interactive, Mobile, Wearable and Ubiquitous Technologies, vol. 2. no. 3 (2018)
16. Ahsan, M., Rais, M.H., Ahmed, I.: Sok: side channel monitoring for additive manufacturing - bridging cybersecurity and quality assurance communities. In: 2023 IEEE 8th European Symposium on Security and Privacy (EuroS&P), pp. 1160–1178 (2023)
17. Mahmood, M.A., Malik, A.W., Liou, F.: A novel framework for identification of cyber-physical attacks in additive manufacturing. Prog. Addit. Manuf. **10**(2), 1575–1586 (2025)
18. Solomon, I.J., Sevvel, P., Gunasekaran, J.: A review on the various processing parameters in fdm. Materials Today: Proceedings, vol. 37, pp. 509–514 (2021). International Conference on Newer Trends and Innovation in Mechanical Engineering: Materials Science
19. Mishra, V., Negi, S., Kar, S.: Fdm-based additive manufacturing of recycled thermoplastics and associated composites. J. Mater. Cycles Waste Manage. **25**(2), 758–784 (2023)
20. Wong, K.V., Hernandez, A.: A review of additive manufacturing. Int. Sch. Res. Notices **2012**(1), 208760 (2012)
21. Paul, R., Anand, S.: A new steiner patch based file format for additive manufacturing processes. Comput. Aided Des. **63**, 86–100 (2015)
22. Rajaguru, K., Karthikeyan, T., Vijayan, V.: Additive manufacturing – state of art. Mater. Today: Proc. **21**, 628–633 (2020). International Conference on Recent Trends in Nanomaterials for Energy, Environmental and Engineering Applications
23. Tsoutsos, N.G., Gamil, H., Maniatakos, M.: Secure 3d printing: reconstructing and validating solid geometries using toolpath reverse engineering. In: Proceedings of the 3rd ACM Workshop on Cyber-Physical System Security, CPSS 2017, pp. 15–20, New York, NY, USA, ACM (2017)

24. Yampolskiy, M., Andel, T.R., McDonald, J.T., Glisson, W.B., Yasinsac, A.: Intellectual property protection in additive layer manufacturing: requirements for secure outsourcing. In: Proceedings of the 4th Program Protection and Reverse Engineering Workshop, PPREW-4, New York, NY, USA, ACM (2014)
25. Mccormack, M., Chandrasekaran, S., Yu, T., Wolf, S., Sekar, V.: C3po: a security analysis tool for networked 3d printers (cmu-cylab-19-002)
26. McCormack, M., Chandrasekaran, S., Liu, G., Yu, T., Wolf, S.D., Sekar, V.: Security analysis of networked 3d printers. In: 2020 IEEE Security and Privacy Workshops (SPW), pp. 118–125 (2020)
27. Meleshko, A., Desnitsky, V., Kotenko, I.: Modeling of smart additive manufacturing processes for attack analysis and detection. In: 2025 33rd Euromicro International Conference on Parallel, Distributed, and Network-Based Processing (PDP), pp. 584–591 (2025)
28. Islam, M.N., Tu, Y., Hossen, M.I., Guo, S., Hei, X.: A survey on limitation, security and privacy issues on additive manufacturing. *CoRR*, abs/2103.06400 (2021)
29. Vaswani, A., et al.: Attention is all you need. In: Guyon, I. (eds.) Advances in Neural Information Processing Systems, vol. 30. Curran Associates, Inc. (2017)

Special Topic: Human-Machine Interfaces in Smart Vehicles

Design Challenges for Objective and Implicit Experience Measures in Mixed Reality

Yasra Chandio[1(✉)], Luis Antonio Garcia[2], and Fatima Anwar[1]

[1] University of Massachusetts Amherst, Amherst, USA
{ychandio,fanwar}@umass.edu
[2] University of Utah, Salt Lake City, USA
la.garcia@utah.edu

Abstract. Measuring and quantifying presence is a crucial prerequisite to improving presence in mixed reality (MR). Traditional presence measures rely on subjective questionnaires, which cannot measure time-varying aspects of presence and are susceptible to user bias. Recent research efforts propose using objective human performance metrics, such as the reaction time between a user's hand-based interaction in response to an explicit cue, as a presence measure. The authors demonstrate that reaction time and presence are correlated in an essential step toward objective presence measurements. Unfortunately, combining an explicit cue and hand interaction to measure reaction time will not suit all scenarios. Additional approaches that leverage implicit cue-interaction mechanisms, such as eye gaze tracking and voice interactions, need to be investigated. In this work, we outline alternative mechanisms to calculate reaction time using implicit cues, present a fundamental methodology for assessing these mechanisms, and discuss the potential security and privacy challenges in their evaluation and practical use as an emerging application in cyber-physical ecosystems.

Keywords: Mixed Reality · Interactions · Sensors

1 Introduction

In Mixed Reality (MR), creating a sense of presence is essential to providing an immersive and engaging experience. Presence, the psychological sensation of *being there*, allows users to feel fully absorbed in a virtual environment (VE) [23]. Measuring presence is essential for improving it, and traditional approaches have primarily relied on subjective questionnaires [26]. However, presence questionnaires cannot measure the time-varying qualities of presence and can produce unstable, inconsistent, and irreproducible responses due to the prior experience of the participants [8,29].

Broader work on assessing presence has explored alternative approaches, including (i) behavioral responses [27], such as postural, hand-eye coordination, and startle responses; (ii) physiological responses [19], such as a change

L. Cheng and F. Anwar (Eds.): SmartSP 2025, LNICST 699, pp. 247–254, 2027.
https://doi.org/10.1007/978-3-032-33701-6_14

Fig. 1. *An overview of our approach to assessing using an implicit cue and interaction mechanisms to estimate reaction time.*

in heart rate, skin conductance, and body temperature; and (iii) human performance metrics [13], such as reaction time and eye-gaze tracking. An ideal *presence* measure is objective, quantitative, not consciously affected by the participant and experimenter, and could be used at runtime without interfering with the virtual experience [30]. It should take advantage of existing interactions in the virtual scene and measure *presence* through these interactions rather than making additional external interventions.

Recent research has demonstrated that the presence and objective human performance measures, such as reaction time, are correlated [2]. Authors provide an explicit cue to the user for a response and measure the reaction time between the cue and the user's hand interaction. While this approach satisfies most of the criteria above, it still requires an explicit cue and a user's hand-based interaction. Unfortunately, this intrusive setup may not be practical for all applications, as some may use different interaction mechanisms, such as eye-gaze-based and voice interactions, and have tasks like collaborative sensemaking, which prohibit priming task behavior. Therefore, there is a need to investigate alternative and implicit options that allow for estimating reaction time.

In addition to the hand-based interaction exploited by prior work, modern headsets continuously track additional user attributes, such as eye-gaze tracking, hand movement tracking, pose estimation, and voice recognition [17]. These attributes can be used but require extensive investigation into *what will constitute a cue*, *how to establish if the user has responded*, and *how to calculate the reaction time*. These challenges are compounded if the cue is implicit and reaction time is to be measured in routine application interactions. Beyond measurement accuracy, incorporating implicit presence metrics into MR systems also highlights broader concerns of security, privacy, and real-time reliability, particularly as MR increasingly operates as a cyber-physical system (CPS). To solve the challenges above, we make the following contribution:

1. Identify inherent interaction mechanisms that allow measuring reaction time implicitly without an explicit cue.
2. Present a methodology to evaluate reaction time estimated using implicit cues and inherent interaction approaches.
3. Outline potential challenges in evaluating the alternative approaches and employing them in practical applications.

2 Background and Related Work

The state-of-the-art method of measuring presence uses subjective questionnaires that participants answer after engaging in an MR environment. The most commonly used questionnaires include the Witmer & Singer Presence Questionnaire (PQ) [33], the Igroup Presence Questionnaire (IPQ) [24], and the Slater-Usoh-Steed Questionnaire (SUS) [26]. They assess a user's ability to control the environment, the extent to which the environment feels real, the consistency of the virtual world and lived experiences, and other factors that impact presence. However, questionnaires can only measure presence after experience and cannot capture time-varying aspects of presence, denying real-world use to measure in-situ presence.

A large body of work [3] [2] [4] has suggested that human performance metrics, such as task completion time, error rate, and actions performed, can be used to indicate presence. Fortunately, modern MR headsets, such as HoloLens 2 and Apple Vision Pro, employ many sensors that capture the user's fine-grained movements and expose them through well-defined interfaces. For example, HoloLens 2 exposes hand tracking, user pose, eye gaze tracking, and voice recognition data, which indicate various aspects of human performance [20]. The ease of access enables the potential use of these metrics as a presence measure in real-time in an unbiased manner.

3 Approach

Prior work [2] used criteria defined by Meehan et al. [19] to design their user study, which states that a useful measure should be sensitive to different levels of presence, reliably provide repeatable results, correlate with existing presence measures, and should be free from participants' and experimenter's bias. In this section, we revisit the design challenges of a user study shown in Fig. 1 for the case studies of *eye tracking* [12] and *voice interactions* [17], both involving implicit cues and hands-free interaction mechanisms.

1. How Do We Induce Different Levels of Presence While Minimizing Confounding Variables?
To assess the effect of presence on a metric, we need to induce varying levels of presence controllably. Prior work exploited technical factors [2], such as realism and the plausibility of virtual objects, and human factors (conditioning) [3]. While other factors can also impact presence, investigations into eye tracking and voice interactions can manipulate these factors to vary presence.

`For eye tracking`, we can manipulate presence by varying objects' visual fidelity and behavior within the area of interest. For example, more realistic and contextually appropriate environmental changes, such as a lifelike animation of a painting changing color in an art gallery, may induce a higher level of presence.

`For voice interactions`, the complexity and relevance of the virtual assistant's prompts can be varied. To alter presence, the virtual assistant can vary the question's complexity from generic to relevant but detailed, such as "What color is the painting?" to "Can you describe the main features of the painting in front of you?".

2. How Do We Establish and Estimate the Baseline Presence?
Prior work had to use questionnaires (SUS, PQ, and IPQ) to measure the ground truth presence, as no other widely accepted presence measures exist. Using questionnaires, the authors had to assess the level of presence at the end of experiments and compare it with aggregate statistics for the reaction times during the experiment. Alternative approaches, such as eye tracking and voice interactions, can leverage the same approach. The objective but validated questionnaires can establish baseline presence levels for each participant, providing a reference point for subsequent measurements. This method accurately compares traditional subjective assessments and the new implicit cue-based presence measures.

3. How Do We Define an Implicit Cue, Record an Interaction, and Calculate Reaction Time?
Prior work used explicit cues, such as a change of object color, to prompt an interaction from the user. Implicit cues can also use a similar approach, such as the appearance of a new object, a change in an object's state (e.g., color change), or a verbal prompt from a virtual assistant. However, the cue must be naturally integrated into events within the virtual environment [14]. Additionally, hand-based interaction makes it easy to register a user's response. Reaction time is calculated as the difference between the response and cue timestamps. However, answering these questions for eye tracking and voice interactions is not straightforward.

`For eye tracking`, the system can define areas of interest to monitor the user's gaze coordinates and dwell time [31]. When an implicit cue occurs, such as a new object appearing or a change within the area of interest, the system can detect the first fixation and record the timestamp. Reaction time can be calculated as the difference between the event trigger and the fixation timestamps.

`For voice interactions`, the virtual assistant can deliver prompts that vary in complexity and relevance. The voice recognition system can employ real-time speech recognition and natural language processing algorithms, using acoustic models to interpret the timing and semantic models to understand the content [17]. Reaction time can be calculated as the difference between the event trigger timestamp (when the prompt is issued) and the timestamp when the system recognizes the user's response as received.

4. What are the Privacy and Security Risks When Using Implicit Cues?
While implicit cues such as gaze and voice interactions offer a promising path toward objective presence measures, they also introduce privacy and security risks [15]. These signals are inherently sensitive. The gaze traces can reveal attention [1], interests [9], and even cognitive states [32], while voice data can expose identity and emotional state [11]. If transmitted or stored without safeguards, such data could be misused or compromised.

Other adversarial manipulations are possible, for example, injecting misleading visual or auditory stimuli to distort reaction times or degrade the accuracy of presence estimation [7]. Because these measures may drive adaptive system behavior at runtime, tampered signals could destabilize the experience or undermine trust. Addressing these challenges requires secure pipelines that prioritize on-device processing, encrypted communication, and access controls, so that implicit presence measures remain both reliable and privacy-preserving.

4 Discussion

While the proposed methods of using eye tracking and voice interactions to measure presence through implicit cues show promise, several challenges and limitations need to be addressed:

Variability in User Responses. For eye tracking, different users may exhibit varying gaze patterns and fixation behaviors, affecting the consistency of reaction time measurements. This can be addressed by employing adaptive algorithms that account for individual differences and using personalized calibration procedures. In voice interactions, speech recognition systems may struggle with accents, speech impediments, or background noise. Mitigating this involves incorporating robust noise-cancellation techniques and training the system using a diverse dataset.

Calibration and Precision. Eye tracking systems must be accurately calibrated for each user and maintained through regular recalibration and high-precision sensors. Voice recognition systems need precise tuning and continuous learning algorithms to adapt to the user's voice over time, improving recognition accuracy.

Context Sensitivity. For eye tracking, the context in which the area of interest is defined can influence gaze behavior. This can be managed with adaptive definitions for the area of interest that adjust based on user behavior and the environment's context. For voice interactions, prompts must be engaging yet not overly complex, achieved through adaptive dialogue systems that modify prompt complexity based on real-time user feedback.

Real-Time Processing and Seamless Integration. Eye tracking and voice interaction must process data in real-time, requiring low latency and high processing speed. Utilizing edge computing and optimization algorithms can address this need. Additionally, robust software and hardware integration, standardized APIs, and compatibility with different MR platforms are necessary to ensure smooth operation without disrupting the user experience.

Security and Privacy Implications. Beyond the technical challenges of variability, calibration, and latency, implicit cues also raise broader questions of trust. Unlike traditional questionnaires, which remain offline and ephemeral, gaze and voice data persist as biometric signals that can be logged, profiled, and potentially misused. This shifts presence measurement from a purely HCI concern to one that intersects with data protection and ethical governance.

From Signals to System Trust. Because implicit presence metrics may guide adaptive MR behavior in real time, any compromise in their integrity (whether internal accidental noise or external adversarial manipulation) directly affects the stability of the user experience. In this sense, implicit presence measurement resembles a CPS control loop, where trustworthiness is as critical as accuracy. Resilience, therefore, requires not only secure data handling but also system-level guarantees against destabilization.

Design Outlook. Rather than treating privacy and security as afterthoughts, they should be embedded in the design of presence measurement pipelines. This includes favoring on-device computation, enforcing minimal data retention, and developing runtime anomaly detection for tampered or injected cues. Incorporating these considerations early broadens the contribution of implicit presence research. It is about advancing measurement accuracy by laying the foundation for trustworthy MR systems.

5 Conclusion

Traditional subjective questionnaires fall short of capturing the dynamic nature of presence, and hand-based interaction made a significant stride toward objective presence measurement. Leveraging natural interactions offers a non-intrusive and objective measure. This paper discussed the potential of using eye tracking and voice interactions with implicit cues to measure presence in MR. Despite their promise as reliable presence measures, they require further research to address existing challenges and practical application, leading to effective and user-friendly MR experiences.

Acknowledgment. The research reported in this paper was sponsored by the National Science Foundation under Awards 2237485, 2435642, 2525711, and by the National Institutes of Health under Award R61MH135109.

References

1. Bai, H., Sasikumar, P., Yang, J., Billinghurst, M.: A user study on mixed reality remote collaboration with eye gaze and hand gesture sharing. In: Proceedings of the 2020 CHI conference on human factors in computing systems (2020)
2. Chandio, Y., Bashir, N., Interrante, V., Anwar, F.M.: Investigating the correlation between presence and reaction time in mixed reality. IEEE Trans. Visual Comput. Graphics (2023)
3. Chandio, Y., Interrante, V., Anwar, F.M.: Human factors at play: understanding the impact of conditioning on presence and reaction time in mixed reality. IEEE Trans. Visual Comput. Graphics (2024)

4. Chandio, Y., Interrante, V., Anwar, F.M.: Reaction time as a proxy for presence in mixed reality with distraction. IEEE Trans. Visual Comput. Graphics (2025)
5. Deary, I., Liewald, D., Nissan, J.: A free, easy-to-use, computer-based simple and four-choice reaction time programme: the deary-liewald reaction time task. Behav. Res. **43** (2011)
6. Freeman, J., Avons, S., Pearson, D., Ijsselsteijn, W.: Effects of sensory information and prior experience on direct subjective ratings of presence. Presence (1999)
7. Giesel, M., Nowakowska, A., Harris, J., Hesse, C.: Perceptual uncertainty and action consequences independently affect hand movements in a virtual environment. Sci. Rep. (2020)
8. Grassini, S., Laumann, K.: Questionnaire measures and physiological correlates of presence: a systematic review. Front. Psychol. (2020)
9. Hough, G., Williams, I., Athwal, C.: Fidelity and plausibility of bimanual interaction in mixed reality. IEEE Trans. Visual Comput. Graph. **21**(12) (2015)
10. Prothero, T.F.I.J.D., Parker, D.E.: Towards a robust, quantitative measure for presence. In: Proceedings of the Conference on Experimental Analysis and Measurement of Situation Awareness (1995)
11. Jicol, C., et al.: Effects of emotion and agency on presence in virtual reality. In Proceedings of the 2021 CHI Conference on Human Factors in Computing Systems (2021)
12. Jing, A., May, K.W., Naeem, M., Lee, G., Billinghurst, M.: eyemr-vis: Using bi-directional gaze behavioural cues to improve mixed reality remote collaboration. In: Proceedings of the Extended Abstracts of the 2021 CHI Conference on Human Factors in Computing Systems, CHI EA '21, Association for Computing Machinery, New York, NY, USA (2021)
13. Kalawsky, R.: The validity of presence as a reliable human performance metric in immersive environments. 3rd International Workshop on Presence (2000)
14. Latoschik, M.E., Wienrich, C.: Congruence and plausibility, not presence: Pivotal conditions for XR experiences and effects, a novel approach. Front. Virtual Reality **3** (2022)
15. Lebeck, K., Kohno, T., Roesner, F.: How to Safely Augment Reality: Challenges and Directions. In: Proceedings of the ACM International Workshop on Mobile Computing Systems and Applications (HotMobile) (2016)
16. Li, Z., Yue, Q., Sano, C., Yu, W., Fu, X.: 3D vision attack against authentication. In: Proceedings of the IEEE ICC (2017)
17. Maloney, D., Freeman, G., Wohn, D.Y.: Talking without a voice, understanding non-verbal communication in social virtual reality. In: Proceedings of the ACM on Human-Computer Interaction (2020)
18. Meehan, M., Insko, B., Whitton, M., Brooks, F.P.: Physiological measures of presence in stressful virtual environments. ACM Trans. Graph. **21** (2002)
19. Meehan, M., Insko, B., Whitton, M., Brooks, F.P.: Physiological measures of presence in stressful virtual environments. ACM Trans. Graph. **21** (2002)
20. Microsoft. Improve visual quality and comfort. https://learn.microsoft.com/en-us/hololens/hololens-calibration#calibrating-your-hololens-2 (2022)
21. Park, Y., Son, Y., Shin, H., Kim, D., Kim, Y.: This ain't your dose: sensor spoofing attack on medical infusion pump. In: Proceedings of the USENIX Workshop on Offensive Technologies (2016)
22. Putze, S., et al.: Breaking the experience: effects of questionnaires in VR user studies. In: Proceedings of the 2020 CHI Conference on Human Factors in Computing Systems (2020)

23. Vives, M.S., Slater, M.: From presence to consciousness through virtual reality. Nat. Rev. Neurosci. **6** (2005)
24. Schubert, T., Friedmann, F., Regenbrecht, H.: The experience of presence: factor analytic insights. Presence Teleoperators Virtual Environ. **10** 2001
25. Schuemie, M.J., Van Der Straaten, P., Krijn, M., Van Der Mast, C.A.: Research on presence in virtual reality: a survey. Cyberpsychology Behav. **4** 2001
26. Slater, M., Steed, A.: A virtual presence counter. Presence **9** (2000)
27. Slater, M., Usoh, M., Chrysanthou, Y.: The influence of dynamic shadows on presence in immersive virtual environments. Eurographics Workshops Virtual Environ. (1999)
28. Toet, A., Mioch, T., Gunkel, S., Niamut, O., van Erp, J.B.: Assessment of presence in augmented and mixed reality (2021)
29. Usoh, M., Catena, E., Arman, S., Slater, M.: Using presence questionnaires in reality. Presence **9** (2000)
30. Weech, S., Kenny, S., Barnett-Cowan, M.: Presence and cybersickness in virtual reality are negatively related: a review. Front. Psychol. **10** (2019)
31. Wiederhold, B.K., Davis, R., Wiederhold, M.D.: The effects of immersiveness on physiology. Stud. Health Technol. Inform. (1998)
32. Wiesing, M., Fink, G., Weidner, R.: Accuracy and precision of stimulus timing and reaction times with unreal engine and steamvr. PLoS ONE **15** (2020)
33. Witmer, B.G., Singer, M.J.: Measuring presence in virtual environments: a presence questionnaire. Presence Teleoperators Virtual Environ. **7** 1998

Human Modeling Gaps: Safety, Security, and Privacy Risks in Automated Driving

Luis A. Garcia[1](✉), Amy McDonnell[2], and Salma Elmalaki[3]

[1] University of Utah, Salt Lake City, UT, USA
la.garcia@utah.edu
[2] Colorado State University, Fort Collins, CO, USA
amy.mcdonnell@colostate.edu
[3] University of California, Irvine, CA, USA
selmalak@uci.edu

Abstract. Automated driving systems increasingly rely on models of human drivers. These models are embedded in safety certification, cybersecurity frameworks, and adversarial robustness evaluations: regulators use benchmark driver models to certify system safety, security researchers treat drivers as attack surfaces, and driver monitoring systems collect sensitive biometric data to measure driver cognitive state. Yet decades of psychological and recent empirical studies show that human attention, trust, and vigilance are dynamic, context-dependent, and often contradictory to the static abstractions now embedded in practice. This position paper argues that these brittle human models are structurally wrong. Embedding them uncritically into certification, security analysis, or monitoring systems creates systemic risks: unsafe safety baselines, exploitable adversarial blind spots, and privacy vulnerabilities. We call for rethinking human-in-the-loop modeling in vehicle CPS: integrating cognitive science and systems engineering, building benchmarks for dynamic human behavior, and adopting privacy-preserving design to ensure trustworthy automated vehicles.

Keywords: Automated Driving · Human-in-the-Loop Systems · Attention Modeling · Biosignal Integration

1 Introduction

Automated and semi-automated vehicles promise transformative safety and efficiency gains, but their deployment depends on how we model the human driver in shared-control contexts. These human-in-the-loop models are not an afterthought: they are already deeply embedded across safety, security, and privacy domains. Regulatory frameworks such as UNECE Regulation 157 and Responsibility-Sensitive Safety (RSS) explicitly benchmark automated systems against "competent and careful" human driver models [28,30]. Cybersecurity analyses highlight drivers as vulnerable entry points, noting that inattentive or

L. Cheng and F. Anwar (Eds.): SmartSP 2025, LNICST 699, pp. 255–265, 2027.
https://doi.org/10.1007/978-3-032-33701-6_15

over-trusting operators are often the weakest link [1,16]. Driver monitoring systems, mandated in many jurisdictions, further incorporate biometric and physiological sensing to detect drowsiness and distraction—raising both security and privacy risks [7,9,13]. Meanwhile, adversarial machine learning research demonstrates that attackers can exploit mismatches between machine and human perception: perturbed stop signs may fool an AV while appearing innocuous to human drivers [12,20].

The problem is that the human models underlying these efforts are brittle and wrong. They assume static, uniform, or binary human cognitive states: attentive or distracted, trusting or not, vigilant or disengaged, alert or fatigued. In contrast, decades of psychological research and recent on-road studies reveal that driver attention, trust, and behavior are dynamic and context-sensitive. For example, vigilance decrements and driver cognitive load have been shown to vary across time, systems, automation levels, and road environments due to the inter- and intra-human variability [5,10,21], trust increases even as physiological vigilance declines with repeated exposure [29], and standard measures such as the Detection Response Task (DRT) produce inconsistent results depending on characteristics of the road environment and automation level [22]. Furthermore, models of human cognition developed in controlled laboratory environments often fail to align with those derived from real-world environments, where risk is high and lapses in attention or performance carry more serious consequences [8,17,18,23]. These findings expose a dangerous gap between how humans are modeled in regulation, security, and adversarial analysis, and how humans actually behave under real driving conditions.

This paper argues that embedding brittle human models uncritically into vehicular CPS creates systemic risks. If certification relies on unrealistic driver benchmarks, safety baselines will be misleading [4,26,27]. If adversaries exploit blind spots in attention modeling, attacks will remain undetected [14,32]. If driver monitoring systems rely on intrusive biosignal collection, privacy vulnerabilities will erode public trust [9]. We propose that the community must rethink human-in-the-loop modeling: developing hybrid testbeds, integrating cognitive science with CPS engineering, and adopting privacy-preserving sensing and benchmarking. Only then can safety, security, and privacy in automated driving rest on solid foundations.

2 Human Models in Automated Driving

Human models are deeply embedded in the design, evaluation, and certification of automated vehicles. Far from being an academic abstraction, they are already written into regulations, safety benchmarks, cybersecurity frameworks, and adversarial robustness analyses. Yet these models tend to assume a static, uniform, and competent driver, even though decades of psychological and recent empirical studies demonstrate that attention, trust, and vigilance are dynamic and context-sensitive. This section reviews how human models are currently deployed across three domains—safety, security and privacy, and adversarial robustness—and highlights where these abstractions diverge from actual human behavior.

2.1 Safety and Certification Models

Regulatory frameworks have made human models central to safety arguments for automated driving. UNECE Regulation 157 on Automated Lane Keeping Systems (ALKS) requires that an Automated Driving System (ADS) be "at least as safe as a competent and careful human driver," formalized through benchmark driver models that encode assumptions about reaction times and braking thresholds [30]. Similarly, Responsibility-Sensitive Safety (RSS) defines interpretable rule sets, such as safe following distances and right-of-way, inspired by human norms of reasonable care [28]. These models are intended to provide a baseline against which automated systems can be evaluated.

However, validation studies reveal that such benchmarks do not align with real human behavior. Olleja et al. [27] found that UNECE's human driver models either braked too late, missing crashes real drivers avoided, or braked too early, overestimating caution. Moreover, on-road empirical findings show that vigilance is not static: across four partially automated systems, drivers displayed markedly different patterns of vigilance decrement [6], and longitudinal studies revealed that trust increased even as physiological vigilance declined with exposure [29]. Standard measures such as the Detection Response Task (DRT) also produce inconsistent outcomes depending on road environment and system design [5,22]. If certification depends on brittle human models, safety baselines may provide false assurance.

2.2 Security and Privacy Models

In cybersecurity, drivers are increasingly recognized not only as stakeholders but also as attack surfaces. Linkov et al. [16] highlight that inattentive or over-trusting drivers often constitute the weakest link in cyber-physical vehicle security. Adnane et al. [1] argue that drivers themselves should be modeled explicitly in threat analysis, since attackers may mislead or manipulate operator perception and trust. These perspectives underscore that simplified assumptions about attentive drivers are not just unrealistic but dangerous in security contexts.

Driver monitoring systems (DMS) illustrate both the promise and the pitfalls of human modeling. Threat analyses show how compromised or spoofed attention signals could create safety hazards or denial-of-service attacks [9]. At the same time, privacy studies demonstrate that willingness to adopt DMS depends strongly on perceptions of how biometric and physiological data are collected, stored, and used [7]. Industry reports warn that without privacy-by-design practices, public trust in these systems will erode [13]. The assumption that human states can be cleanly observed neglects the messy realities of cybersecurity risk, data sensitivity, and social acceptance.

2.3 Adversarial and Human-in-the-Loop Threats

Research on adversarial machine learning has further exposed the consequences of brittle human models. Eykholt et al. [12] demonstrated that physically perturbed stop signs can reliably mislead an AV's computer vision while appearing as innocuous graffiti to human drivers. Conversely, Ma et al. [20] found that some perturbations imperceptible to technical metrics were also invisible to drivers in VR-based experiments, challenging the notion that a vigilant driver can serve as a reliable fallback. Li et al. [16] showed that drivers often over-trust automation under adversarial conditions, delaying takeover responses unless systems explicitly communicate suspected attacks. Other work demonstrates how adversaries can manipulate driver psychology through "phantom" warnings or misinformation, inducing unsafe responses without tampering with vehicle software [25]. These cases highlight that adversaries actively exploit mismatches between modeled and actual human perception, trust, and attention.

2.4 Human-in-the-Loop Testbeds

A growing body of research has developed testbeds to study drivers in the loop, often coupling automated driving simulators with biosignal monitoring. These platforms provide a bridge between abstract models and empirical human behavior. For example, Elmalaki et al. [10] demonstrated a driver-in-the-loop collision warning system that personalizes alerts by learning from driver-specific data, while Ahadi et al. [2] extended this approach in CARLA with wearable sensors to adapt warnings based on real-time distraction and fatigue signals. Zhao et al. [35] modeled longitudinal control strategies that incorporate driver reaction times and road context (Fig. 1).

Fig. 1. Driving simulator setup for human subject experiments.

On the adversarial side, Ma et al. [20] developed *Avara*, a VR-based platform for systematically evaluating how drivers perceive adversarial perturbations, showing that traditional imperceptibility metrics fail to capture human perception. Other hybrid setups integrate EEG, eye tracking, and workload indices to trigger adaptive automation in real time [3]. These examples demonstrate that testbeds are not simply research curiosities; they are essential for capturing the variability, adaptation, and context sensitivity of real human drivers. Testbeds thus play a dual role: they expose the brittleness of current abstractions, and they point toward infrastructures for more realistic and dynamic human modeling.

2.5 Toward Realistic Cognitive Modeling

Advancing toward more realistic and accurate models of driver cognition will require the field to leverage recent advances in mobile sensing platforms that can capture drivers' cognitive and physiological states in real time. These platforms enable measurement of eye movements, performance, brain activity, and cardiovascular responses during naturalistic driving, where risk and consequence are highest. Figure 2 illustrates an on-road study using electroencephalography (EEG) and physiological sensors during partially automated driving. Such mobile sensing approaches provide a critical complement to simulator-based testbeds, allowing researchers to track vigilance, workload, and trust as they unfold dynamically in real environments.

On-road neuroscience studies demonstrate that neural and physiological measures can sensitively index changes in driver engagement and cognitive load. For example, McDonnell et al. [23] found that EEG-based workload indices reveal reduced engagement under partial vehicle automation, while longitudinal follow-up work showed that repeated exposure increased driver trust even as vigilance waned [22]. Reliability studies confirm that these physiological measures are robust across participants and contexts [19], while benchmarking studies demonstrate their sensitivity to moment-to-moment fluctuations in distraction and workload [24]. Figure 3 shows how reaction time performance in a Detection Response Task (DRT) varied across four vehicle automation systems, underscoring the system- and context-dependent nature of vigilance decrements.

These findings suggest that real-world sensing, combined with temporally-sensitive analysis, enables fine-grained modeling of driver cognition over time, across systems, and under varying roadway demands. At the same time, advancing biometric-based modeling requires careful attention to privacy: safeguarding sensitive cognitive information, minimizing data collection, and ensuring that models integrate only the signals necessary for safety and security. Finally, on-road work should be validated against simulator and closed-course studies, ensuring that ecological validity is balanced with experimental control. By bridging naturalistic and controlled research, cognitive neuroscience can provide a stronger foundation for realistic human-in-the-loop models that better capture variability, inform safety certification, mitigate adversarial vulnerabilities, and address privacy challenges.

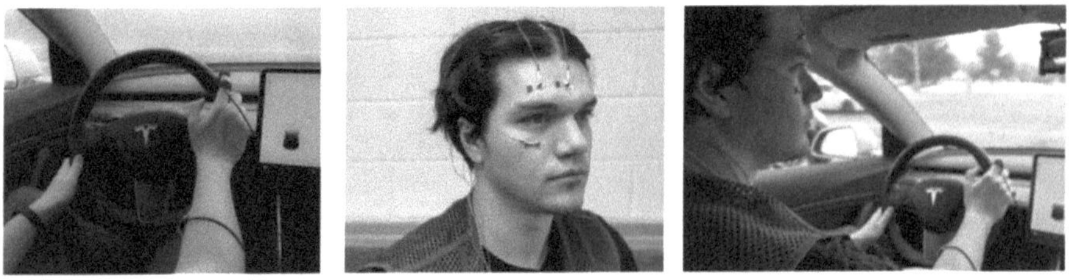

Fig. 2. On-road study setup: drivers equipped with EEG and physiological sensors during partially automated driving.

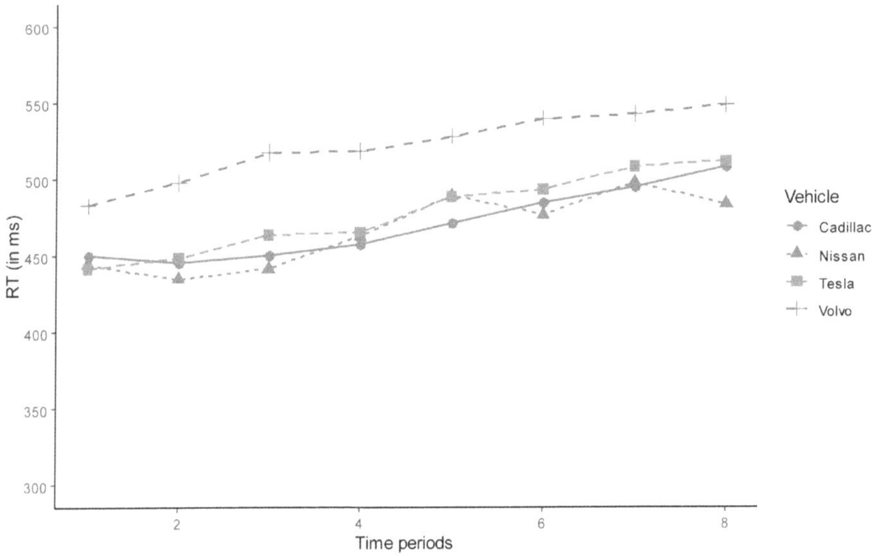

Fig. 3. Vigilance decrements across vehicle systems measured by reaction time in a Detection Response Task (DRT). Different systems exhibit distinct trajectories of vigilance decline [6].

3 What Goes Wrong When Models are Wrong

The reliance on brittle and unrealistic human models is not a benign abstraction. When certification, security analysis, or monitoring systems assume static, competent drivers, the risks cascade across safety, security, and privacy.

3.1 Safety Risks

If certification depends on unrealistic driver benchmarks, automated driving systems may be declared "as safe as a human" when in practice they are not. UNECE Reg. 157 and RSS assume careful and vigilant humans, but empirical studies reveal that driver cognitive state fluctuates over time and across systems and road environments [5,6,22,23]. Olleja et al. [27] showed that regulatory driver models either underestimate or overestimate actual human caution, producing misleading baselines. Partial automation introduces further risks: field studies demonstrate that drivers become complacent and inattentive under Level 2 automation, creating unsafe gaps in takeover readiness [4,26]. Finally, these risks are underscored by on-road neuroscience findings showing that vigilance and trust fluctuate dynamically across systems and over time [22,23]. Such results illustrate why certifying automated systems against a static "competent driver" benchmark is misleading.

3.2 Security Risks

Simplified human models also create exploitable blind spots in security. Trust is often treated as binary, but research shows that miscalibrated trust evolves over time and shapes vigilance in nuanced ways [14,34]. Adversaries can exploit these gaps, whether through physical perturbations to signage that fool AV perception but look ordinary to humans [12], or through psychological triggers that manipulate driver reactions in unexpected ways [25]. Studies show that drivers often fail to recognize adversarial interference or hesitate to intervene when automation appears confident [33]. Assuming an ever-vigilant human fallback masks these vulnerabilities and creates fertile ground for adversarial exploitation.

3.3 Privacy Risks

Finally, the push toward richer human models introduces privacy challenges. Driver monitoring systems collect biometric and physiological data—facial imagery, eye gaze, heart rate, even brain activity using EEG—to infer distraction and drowsiness. While these systems promise safety benefits, they also expose sensitive cognitive states that can be misused or breached. Threat analyses highlight how compromised monitoring systems could inject false signals or suppress true ones, with direct safety consequences [9]. At the same time, user acceptance studies show that privacy concerns significantly shape willingness to adopt such systems [7]. Industry reports warn that automakers already collect and share highly personal data, from driving behavior to intimate biometric details [13]. Treating human states as simple, observable variables neglects the ethical and security obligations of handling this data responsibly.

4 Putting the Right Human in the Loop

Current frameworks embed the wrong human: static, uniform abstractions of an attentive, competent driver. Our review shows that real human attention and trust are dynamic, drifting, and context-dependent [11]. To ensure that automated driving systems are safe, secure, and privacy-preserving, the community must commit to putting the *right* human in the loop—models that capture variability, adapt over time, and respect user privacy. This requires action across four fronts:

- **Driver-State-in-the-Loop Controls**: Safety-critical logic such as alerts, collision warnings, and takeover requests must account for driver state. Context-aware systems that integrate signals of distraction, fatigue, or workload can personalize intervention timing and improve robustness [2,10,11,35].
- **Shared Benchmarking**: The field needs public datasets and agreed-upon standards for modeling driver behavior in automated driving contexts. Benchmarks such as Waymo's human driver baselines and new multimodal datasets [15,31] are a starting point, but must expand to include physiological and trust dynamics.
- **Robust Design for Human Variability**: Automated systems must be stress-tested against realistic human states, including fatigue, complacency, and trust miscalibration. Models like active inference [32] and real-world studies of partial automation [4,26] show the dangers of assuming a vigilant fallback driver.
- **Interdisciplinary Integration**: Cognitive neuroscience, human factors, and CPS engineering must converge. Hybrid simulators and testbeds that incorporate real-time attention metrics and longitudinal behavioral data will be necessary to validate both safety and security claims. Privacy-preserving methods—such as edge processing and minimal biosignal collection—must be part of this agenda from the start.

Only by adopting these steps can we move beyond brittle abstractions toward dynamic, context-sensitive models that reflect real human drivers. Putting the right human in the loop is not just a technical refinement—it is a prerequisite for safe, secure, and trustworthy automated vehicles.

5 Conclusion

Human models are already embedded in regulations, certification, security analysis, and adversarial evaluations. Yet evidence shows they are brittle abstractions, assuming static and uniform drivers where attention and trust are dynamic and context-dependent. Relying on such models creates systemic risks for safety, security, and privacy. Moving forward requires replacing these brittle abstractions with dynamic, context-aware, and privacy-preserving models—only then can automated driving rest on a trustworthy foundation.

Acknowledgements. The research reported in this paper was sponsored in part by the National Science Foundation (NSF) under awards FMitF-2425711, NCS-2435642, and CAREER-2339266 and the National Institute of Health (NIH) under award R61MH135109. The views and conclusions contained in this document are those of the authors and should not be interpreted as representing the official policies, either expressed or implied, of the funding agencies.

References

1. Adnane, A., Hardy, J., Ahmad, F., Morris, A., Filtness, A.: Drivers, the missed attack surface of connected vehicles. In: Proceedings of the 6th Smart Cities Symposium (SCS 2022), vol. 2022, pp. 221–226. IET (2022)
2. Sarkani, A.A., Elmalaki, S.: Adas-rl: adaptive vector scaling reinforcement learning for human-in-the-loop lane departure warning. In: Proceedings of the First International Workshop on Cyber-Physical-Human System Design and Implementation, pp. 13–18. Association for Computing Machinery, New York, NY, USA (2021). https://doi.org/10.1145/3458648.3460008
3. Aricò, P., Borghini, G., Di Flumeri, G.: Adaptive automation triggered by EEG-based mental workload index: a PBCI application in realistic air traffic control environment. Front. Hum. Neurosci. **10**, 539 (2017). https://doi.org/10.3389/fnhum.2016.00539
4. Banks, V.A., Eriksson, A., O'Donoghue, J., Stanton, N.A.: Is partially automated driving a bad idea? Observations from an on-road study. Appl. Ergonomics **68**, 138–145 (2018). https://doi.org/10.1016/j.apergo.2017.11.010
5. Biondi, F.N., McDonnell, A.S., Cooper, J., Strayer, D.L.: Using the ISO detection response task to measure the cognitive load of driving four separate vehicles on two distinct highways. Transp. Res. Part F Traffic Psychol. Behav. **102**, 260–269 (2024). https://doi.org/10.1016/j.trf.2024.02.013
6. Biondi, F.N., McDonnell, A.S., Mahmoodzadeh, M., Jajo, N., Balasingam, B., Strayer, D.L.: Vigilance decrement during on-road partially-automated driving across four systems. Hum. Factors **66**(9), 2179–2190 (2023). https://doi.org/10.1177/00187208231189658
7. Chu, X., Li, Y.: Privacy concern and acceptability of driver monitoring systems. In: Proceedings of the AHFE Conference on Human Factors in Transportation (2023). https://doi.org/10.54941/ahfe1003212
8. Cooper, J.M., et al.: Driver behavior while using level 2 vehicle automation: a hybrid naturalistic study. Cogn. Res. Principles Implications **8**(1), 1–19 (2023). https://doi.org/10.3389/fnins.2021.577418
9. De Santis, M., Jochim, E., Sodinca, I.C., Esposito, C., Khondoker, R.: Threat analysis and risk assessment of a driver monitoring system. Appl. Sci. **15**(10), 5571 (2025)
10. Elmalaki, S.: Sentio: driver-in-the-loop forward collision warning using multisample reinforcement learning. In: Proceedings of ACM SenSys, pp. 28–40 (2018). https://doi.org/10.1145/3274783.3274843
11. Elmalaki, S.: Maconauto: framework for mobile-assisted human-in-the-loop automotive system. In: Proceedings of the 2022 IEEE Intelligent Vehicles Symposium (IV), pp. 740–749. IEEE (2022)
12. Eykholt, K., et al.: Robust physical-world attacks on deep learning models. In: Proceedings of the IEEE Conference on Computer Vision and Pattern Recognition (CVPR), pp. 1625–1634 (2018). https://doi.org/10.1109/CVPR.2018.00175
13. Future of privacy forum: vehicle safety systems: privacy risks and recommendations. Tech. rep. Future of Privacy Forum (2024). https://fpf.org/reports/vehicle-safety-systems-privacy-risks/
14. Hergeth, S., Lorenz, L., Krems, J.F.: Keep your scanners peeled: gaze behavior as a measure of automation trust. Hum. Factors **58**(3), 509–519 (2016). https://doi.org/10.1177/0018720815625744

15. Li, X.: MMHU: a massive-scale multimodal benchmark for human behavior understanding (2025)
16. Linkov, I., Trump, B.D., Poinsatte-Jones, K., Florin, M.V.: Human factors in the cybersecurity of autonomous vehicles: trends in current research. Front. Psychol. **10**, 995 (2019). https://doi.org/10.3389/fpsyg.2019.00995
17. Lohani, M., et al.: Driver arousal and workload under partial vehicle automation: a pilot study. In: Proceedings of the Human Factors and Ergonomics Society Annual Meeting, vol. 64, pp. 1426–1430 (2020). https://doi.org/10.1177/1071181320641471
18. Lohani, M., et al.: No difference in arousal or cognitive demands between manual and partially automated driving: a multi-method on-road study. Front. Neurosci. **15**, 1–12 (2021). https://doi.org/10.3389/fnins.2021.577418
19. Lohani, M., et al.: Reliable but multi-dimensional cognitive demand in operating partially automated vehicles: implications for real-world automation research. Cogn. Res. Principles Implications **9**(1), 60 (2024)
20. Ma, X., et al.: Avara: a uniform evaluation system for perceptibility analysis against adversarial object evasion attacks. In: Proceedings of the 2024 on ACM SIGSAC Conference on Computer and Communications Security, pp. 4792–4806 (2024)
21. Mahmoodzadeh, M., et al.: Temporal analysis of cognitive workload during manual and partial driving automation based on the detection response task. In: Proceedings of the IEEE 34th International Symposium on Industrial Electronics, pp. 1–5 (2025). https://doi.org/10.1109/ISIE62713.2025.11124598
22. McDonnell, A.S., Crabtree, K., Cooper, J., Strayer, D.L.: This is your brain on autopilot 2.0: the influence of practice on driver workload and engagement during on-road, partially automated driving. Hum. Factors **66**(8), 2025–2040 (2023). https://doi.org/10.1177/00187208231201054
23. McDonnell, A.S., et al.: This is your brain on autopilot: neural indices of driver workload and engagement under partial vehicle automation. Hum. Factors **65**(7), 1435–1450 (2023). https://doi.org/10.1177/00187208211039091
24. McDonnell, A.S., Imberger, K., Poulter, C., Cooper, J.M.: The power and sensitivity of four core driver workload measures for benchmarking the distraction potential of new driver vehicle interfaces. Transport. Res. F: Traffic Psychol. Behav. **83**, 99–117 (2021)
25. Nassi, B., et al.: Phantom of the adas: securing advanced driver-assistance systems from split-second phantom attacks. In: Proceedings of the 2020 ACM SIGSAC Conference on Computer and Communications Security, pp. 293–308 (2020)
26. National Transportation Safety Board: Highway accident report: Collision between a car operating with automated vehicle control systems and a truck tractor-semitrailer. Tech. Rep. NTSB/HAR-17/02, NTSB, Washington, DC (2017)
27. Olleja, N., Rauskolb, F., Wachenfeld, W., Winner, H.: Validation of human benchmark models for automated driving system approval: how competent and careful are they really? Accid. Anal. Prev. **194**, 107506 (2024). https://doi.org/10.1016/j.aap.2024.107506
28. Shwartz, S.S., Shammah, S., Shashua, A.: On a formal model of safe and scalable self-driving cars. arXiv preprint arXiv:1708.06374 (2017)
29. Strayer, D., Cooper, J.M., SAnbonmatsu, D., McDonnell, A.S.: A multi-method approach to understanding drivers' experiences and behavior under partial vehicle automation. Washington, DC: AAA Foundation for Traffic Safety (2023). https://aaafoundation.org/wp-content/uploads/2023/09/202309-AAAFTS-ADAS-Exposure-and-Driver-Workload.pdf

30. UNECE: Un regulation no. 157: Automated lane keeping systems (ALKS). Tech. rep., United Nations Economic Commission for Europe (2021). https://unece.org/transport/documents/2021/03/standards/un-regulation-no-157-automated-lane-keeping-systems-0
31. Waymo LLC: Waymo safety report: simulation city and safety methodologies. Tech. rep., Waymo, Mountain View, CA (2020), whitepaper/safety report
32. Wei, C., et al.: Active inference models of av takeovers: relating model parameters to trust, situation awareness, and fatigue. Hum. Factors **67**(6), 616–634 (2025). https://doi.org/10.1177/00187208241234567
33. Zhang, R.L.J.G.Y., Xiong, A.: Poster: enhance human driver situation awareness of adversarial attacks in automated driving systems: a driving simulator study
34. Zhang, T.: EEG-based assessment of driver trust in automated vehicles. Expert Syst. Appl. **246**, 123196 (2024). https://doi.org/10.1016/j.eswa.2024.123196
35. Zhao, G.: Longitudinal control strategy of collision avoidance system for intelligent vehicles considering drivers and environmental factors. In: Proceedings of the IEEE Intelligent Vehicles Symposium (IV), pp. 31–36 (2018). https://doi.org/10.1109/IVS.2018.8500315

Dataset Poisoning Attacks on Behavioral Cloning Policies

Akansha Kalra(✉), Soumil Datta, Ethan Gilmore, Duc La, Guanhong Tao, and Daniel S. Brown

University of Utah, Salt Lake City, USA
{akansha.kalra,soumil.datta,guanhong.tao,daniel.s.brown}@utah.edu

Abstract. Behavior Cloning (BC) is a popular framework for training sequential decision policies from expert demonstrations via supervised learning. As these policies are increasingly being deployed in the real world, their robustness and potential vulnerabilities are an important concern. In this work, we perform the first analysis of the efficacy of clean-label backdoor attacks on BC policies. Our backdoor attacks poison a dataset of demonstrations by injecting a visual trigger to create a spurious correlation that can be exploited at test time. We evaluate how policy vulnerability scales with the fraction of poisoned data, the strength of the trigger, and the trigger type. We also introduce a novel entropy-based test-time trigger attack that substantially degrades policy performance by identifying critical states where test-time triggering of the backdoor is expected to be most effective at degrading performance. We empirically demonstrate that BC policies trained on even minimally poisoned datasets exhibit deceptively high, near-baseline task performance despite being highly vulnerable to backdoor trigger attacks during deployment. Our results underscore the urgent need for more research into the robustness of BC policies, particularly as large-scale datasets are increasingly used to train policies for real-world cyber-physical systems. Videos and code are available at https://sites.google.com/view/dataset-poisoning-in-bc.

Keywords: Imitation Learning · Dataset Poisoning · Backdoor Attacks

1 Introduction

When learning sequential decision-making tasks, there is often a trade-off between using Reinforcement Learning (RL) or using Imitation Learning (IL). While RL provides a way to train a policy without requiring any more supervision than a reward signal, it introduces the problem of balancing exploration and exploitation and is often quite sample inefficient, requiring large amounts of interactions with the environment. The main principle of RL is an iterative process of trying various actions to discover what works [34]. However, in real-world cyber-physical systems, this trial-and-error approach can result in dangerous unsafe situations and large computational costs. Additionally, RL requires

L. Cheng and F. Anwar (Eds.): SmartSP 2025, LNICST 699, pp. 266–282, 2027.
https://doi.org/10.1007/978-3-032-33701-6_16

access to a carefully designed or learned reward function which is often hard to specify correctly for complex tasks [1,17], leading to potentially unwanted behaviors [35].

By contrast, IL seeks to learn policies from expert demonstrations. The most common and popular method for IL is behavioral cloning (BC), where a policy is directly learned from state-action pairs [30,36]. This approach has recently gained much success in real-world deployments and has been shown to scale well to large datasets and modern deep learning architectures [11,13,39]. Learning from demonstrations via supervised learning allows IL methods to learn policies without requiring interaction with the environment, improving sample efficiency and bypassing the need for potentially dangerous exploration. However, it is known that these types of models are often susceptible to compounding errors when they encounter out of distribution states [30]. This inherent vulnerability could be exploited by a malicious adversary through a well-timed attack. All the attacker may need to do is perturb the input observation to the policy by a tiny amount at the right moment to drive the policy out of distribution. Then compounding errors take effect, causing the policy to fail or perform poorly.

In this work, we study the vulnerability of BC to dataset poisoning attacks. Dataset poisoning attacks involve altering a training dataset to introduce a vulnerability into downstream models that are trained on this poisoned dataset [24]. These attacks require only minimal edit access to a training dataset—something that is becoming increasingly possible as large datasets become publicly available [20,27]. We focus on clean-label backdoor attacks [37,38], a subclass of poisoning attacks where a small trigger, such as a 3x3 red patch, is embedded into training observations corresponding to a specific action (e.g., "gas") without changing the actual labels (demonstrator actions). The goal is to create a "backdoor effect": a scenario where a malicious actor introduces specific data points into a training dataset with the goal of causing a machine learning model to behave in a predetermined, undesirable way when presented with a specific "trigger" during testing or inference, while otherwise behaving normally. Essentially, the attacker creates a hidden vulnerability (the backdoor) that can be activated by the trigger, allowing the attacker to manipulate the model's output for their benefit. These types of attacks work because the poisoned training data creates a spurious correlation between the visual trigger and the target action that is likely to be learned by any downstream model.

To the best of our knowledge, we are the first to study the effectiveness of clean-label dataset poisoning attacks on behavioral cloning by exploring and analyzing the impact of different amounts of poisoned data, trigger strengths, and types of backdoor triggers. Our results show that BC policies are highly vulnerable to dataset poisoning attacks. Even a poisoning around 2.3% of a training dataset is enough to create a strong backdoor effect. Given an effective backdoor, we then study the vulnerability of behavioral cloning policies to backdoor triggers during test time. Importantly, in sequential decision-making, not all states are equally critical. In car driving, for example, triggering a backdoor to trigger an acceleration action on a straight road segment may be benign, but triggering it during a sharp turn when the agent should turn left can push the policy out of distribution and amplify errors through covariate shift [30]. This motivates our novel test-time trigger attack that uses a policy entropy threshold to trigger attacks only at critical states, making the best use of a limited attack budget.

Our main contributions are the following: (1) We present the first study and discussion of dataset poisoning in imitation learning; (2) We perform a sensitivity analysis over trigger types, amount of poisoned data, and patch size for clean-label attacks on behavioral cloning policies; (3) We demonstrate that our entropy-based test time attack significantly degrades performance at test time when compared with nominal baseline performance and randomized attacks.

2 Background and Related Work

Imitation Learning (IL) has emerged as a powerful tool for training sequential decision-making policies by mimicking expert demonstrations, offering an alternative to reinforcement learning (RL) in scenarios where explicit reward functions are hard to specify or costly to obtain [22,26]. Among IL approaches, Behavioral Cloning (BC) remains the most widely used due to its simplicity and scalability. It frames policy learning as a supervised learning problem over expert state-action pairs [30,36]. BC has shown great success across cyber-physical systems such as autonomous driving [3,12], and robotics manipulation [11,13], often requiring significantly fewer interactions with the environment compared to traditional RL methods.

Early work on adversarial attacks on deep reinforcement learning identified that not all time steps are equally vulnerable to perturbation and that adversaries can achieve high effectiveness by injecting noise only at critical moments when the agent expects high reward [23,25,29,31]. These approaches demonstrate the ability, in the RL setting, to reduce attack frequency while maximizing attack impact, highlighting the importance of timing in adversarial attack strategies. However, these attacks require white-box access to the policy, access to a reward function, and access to a simulator to devise the attack strategy and are not applicable in learning from demonstrations settings, such as the ones we consider in this paper, where we assume black-box access to the policy and no access to a ground-truth reward function nor simulator when triggering attacks.

Despite its widespread adoption, relatively little is known about the robustness and security of IL policies. Prior work has examined adversarial perturbations in driving simulations that are generated on the fly using white-box access to the policy [18] or used white-box policy access to design physical adversarial examples like black lines painted on the roadway [4]. Other work explores white-box adversarial attacks on modern diffusion policies [10] as well as transfer attacks between models [28]. However, all these approaches also assume white-box access to pre-trained BC policies and involve complicated optimizations to solve for adversarial pixel perturbations at test time. By contrast, we consider backdoor-triggered dataset poisoning within the context of BC and demonstrate the effectiveness of cheap, black-box attacks.

Data poisoning and backdoor attacks have been extensively studied in the context of supervised learning, where adversaries inject malicious examples into the training data to degrade performance or implant a targeted behavior at test time [2,8,15,24,32,37,38]. These attacks are particularly dangerous because they do not require white-box access to model parameters when performing an attack. While there has been some recent work on backdoor attacks for reinforcement learning [9,14,16,21], to the best of our knowledge, we are the first to study dataset poisoning attacks on policies that are learned from datasets of demonstrations without access to reward functions. Our attacks only require minimal and simple edits to a dataset to inject a backdoor to compromise a dataset such that downstream policies trained on the poisoned dataset are vulnerable. Our test-time attacks are also computationally simple to apply (we simply apply a predetermined, deterministic trigger to the input) and highly effective despite requiring only black-box access to the outputs of the BC policy.

3 Methodology

We consider the standard Learning from Demonstration (LfD) setting where an attacker has access to a set of expert demonstrations $D = \{(s, a), \ldots\}$ of state-action pairs (s, a) that will be used by a downstream imitation learning algorithm to learn a policy [30,36]. The objective of the attacker is to poison the training data by injecting a trigger into the training dataset, so that, at test time, it will enable the attacker to control a BC policy trained on the poisoned dataset by triggering a chosen target action, a_{target}.

3.1 Threat Model

Before describing our attacks, we first clearly specify our threat model.

Adversary's Goal: By injecting a clean-label backdoor into the training data, the attacker aims to induce failures in the learned BC policy when the backdoor is triggered at test time. For example, the attacker could use the trigger to cause an autonomous car to take an acceleration action rather than a brake action at a red light, potentially leading to dangerous or catastrophic behavior.

Adversary's Knowledge and Capabilities: The attacker has complete access to the dataset for poisoning, but has no direct control over nor privileged white-box access to downstream policy models that are trained on the poisoned training data. At test time, the attacker has only black-box access to the policy model outputs and can apply only a limited budget of test-time attacks by injecting the backdoor trigger into the visual observation of the pre-trained policy. We note that these perturbations are limited to the visual observation space (the adversary has no direct action manipulation ability).

3.2 Dataset Poisoning

In this section we describe our clean label poisoning-based backdoor attack. The attack operates on an existing dataset $D = \{(s, a), \ldots\}$ of state-action pairs (s, a), where s is the state observation and a is the demonstrator's action. Given a desired backdoor target action a_{target}, the attacker edits D to create a poisoned dataset D_p. The poisoned dataset D_p is formed by taking some number of state-action pairs (s, a) from D with $a = a_{\text{target}}$ and then adding a backdoor trigger to s to create a poisoned state action pair $(\tilde{s}, a)$. The goal of the attacker at test time is to minimize $J(\pi_{\text{bc}}) = \mathbb{E}_{\pi_{\text{bc}}}\left[\sum_{t=0}^{T} r_t\right]$, where π_{bc} is the stochastic policy trained on D_p. In practice, we poison the dataset by embedding backdoor triggers formed by n×n patches of pixels into the image observations, s. Note that because this is a clean-label attack, we perturb only the state observation, s, without ever altering the expert actions, a, when creating D_p. In our experiments, we analyze the effect of clean-label poisoning on BC policies by varying the fraction of data poisoned, the strength of the trigger via patch size, and the trigger type.

3.3 Test-Time Trigger Attacks

In addition to dataset poisoning, we study the effect of the timing of backdoor trigger attacks during test-time execution, given an attack budget B of test-time backdoor injections. Our insight is that certain states are better to attack than others. For instance, in case of car-driving, applying the backdoor trigger on a straight road segment observation to trigger the gas action may be inconsequential, whereas doing so during a sharp curve in road—such as when a left turn is needed—can lead to out-of-distribution states and lead to compounding errors and catastrophic failure. We compare two strategies for determining when to inject the backdoor trigger at test time:

Random Trigger Timing: This baseline simply selects B timesteps uniformly at random to trigger the backdoor attack.

Entropy-Based Trigger Timing: We also propose and study a more sophisticated way of deciding when to trigger the backdoor attack. Our idea is to use the entropy of the action output distribution of the BC policy to identify critical states where we expect the attack to be more effective. Mathematically, given a trained stochastic BC policy $\pi_{\text{bc}}(a \mid s)$, trained on the poisoned dataset D_p, we assume the attacker has black-box access to the model outputs—i.e., they can query the policy to obtain action probabilities, but cannot inspect or modify internal model parameters. At test time, for each input state s, the attacker computes the BC policy action entropy: $\mathcal{H}(\pi(\cdot \mid s)) = -\sum_{a \in \mathcal{A}} \pi_{\text{bc}}(a \mid s) \log \pi_{\text{bc}}(a \mid s)$ where $\mathcal{A}$ refers to the action space.[1] Observations with entropy below a specified threshold where the output of the policy $\pi(a \mid s) \neq a_{target}$ are selected as

[1] We only consider discrete action spaces in this paper, but our proposed entropy-based attack can easily be extended to continuous action distributions (e.g., Gaussian policies) by computing or estimating the differential entropy.

for inserting adversarial triggers until the budget B is exhausted. The entropy threshold is attacker-defined and can be tuned at test time. The intuition behind this trigger timing strategy is that states with low entropy imply that there are only a small number of appropriate actions, and the smaller the entropy, the more likely it is that only one action is appropriate. If this action is not equal to the target action a_{target}, then triggering the policy to output a_{target} is likely to cause the wrong state transition and degrade policy performance by sending the policy out of the distribution of demonstrations in the training data.

4 Experiments and Results

We begin by first outlining our experimental setup and then turn to the investigation of the key experimental questions in the following subsections.

Throughout our experimental framework, we use the Car Racing environment from OpenAI gym [5] comprising of high-dimensional visual observations in the form of 96 × 96-pixel RGB images and a discrete action space comprised of 5 actions: do nothing, gas, turn left, turn right, and brake. Its high-dimensional visual inputs permit the introduction of spatially constrained triggers, while its discrete action space allows for precise measurement of behavioral deviations and reward variation under distribution shift. Following prior works [6,7] that use synthetic demonstrations to model an expert, we utilize a PPO agent [33], trained for 1M steps to generate the clean demonstration datasets used in our experiments.

As discussed in Sect. 3.2, we embed backdoor triggers into the clean dataset to create the poisoned dataset. We then train Behavior Cloning (BC) policies on the poisoned datasets using a classical convolutional neural network architecture. For training the BC policies, we use Adam optimizer with learning rate equal to 0.001 and we leverage the classical feedforward CNN architecture neural network with 3 convolutional layers each with 3 × 3 kernels followed by ReLU and pooling layers, which are then followed by 3 fully connected layers with ReLU as activation except at the last layer where we use softmax to get the final probability distribution across all possible actions.

4.1 How Vulnerable are BC Policies to Clean-Label Backdoor Attacks Under Different Amounts of Dataset Poisoning?

To answer this question, we perform clean-label poisoning by modifying observations associated with the gas action in the expert dataset, embedding a solid 3 × 3 red patch in the top-left corner of the image. This setup allows us to assess both the effectiveness and efficiency of the backdoor trigger. The fraction of state observations (corresponding to gas-actions) that are poisoned is incrementally varied between 0% and 100%. For each specified poisoning percentage, we construct the corresponding poisoned dataset and train a separate BC policy. We assess the learned policy's performance in two ways: (i) by measuring the mean episode reward during standard test-time rollouts, and (ii) the backdoor control rate, defined as the proportion of times the presence of the trigger induces the gas action.

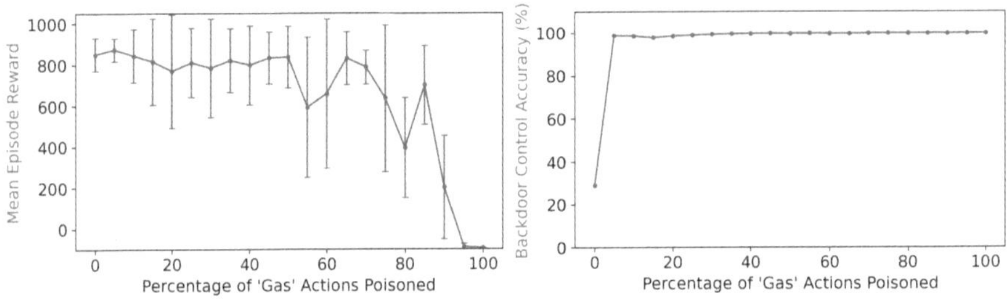

Fig. 1. Sensitivity to the percentage of poisoned training data. The figure displays mean episode reward (left) and backdoor control rate (right) for varying poisoning percentages, based on a fixed 3 × 3 red patch on gas-labeled frames, averaged across 5 seeds with 10 rollouts per seed with error bars denoting standard deviation. We show that BC policies can achieve near-baseline performance despite being poisoned while even the minimal amount of poison injected lends complete controllability to the attacker.

Our empirical results in Fig. 1 show that the backdoor is highly effective: with just 5% poisoning of 'gas' actions, which corresponds to only 2.31% of the overall dataset, the backdoor control rate increases from chance to approximately 100%, and remains at this level thereafter. This indicates that the red patch functions as a highly salient and learnable trigger. Meanwhile, the mean reward remains largely stable until the poisoning ratio surpasses 70 – 80%, after which the reward drops sharply, culminating in full collapse at 100% poisoning. This suggests that extreme poisoning levels introduce training instability, likely due to the dominance of poisoned correlations in the data distribution. This indicates that BC policies are highly susceptible to clean-label backdoor attacks, even at minimal poisoning levels. A small fraction of poisoned training data is sufficient to grant the adversary near-perfect control at test time, while overall task performance at test time rollouts remains deceptively high until poisoning exceeds a critical threshold.

Our results reveal a critical vulnerability: near-baseline task performance persists even when the BC policy is fully compromised by a backdoor trigger. This means that traditional evaluation metrics are insufficient—the model may appear robust while being entirely controllable under adversarial conditions.

4.2 Which Visual Properties of Synthetic Triggers Most Influence the Backdoor Trigger Efficacy?

To understand the influence of visual characteristics on backdoor trigger efficacy, we compare two types of synthetic patch triggers: a fixed-color square, a Gaussian noise patch. These trigger variants are visualized within poisoned observations in Fig. 2.

The fixed-color square consists of a spatially fixed red patch with high visual contrast, making it easy to learn but also more perceptible. The Gaussian noise patch is sampled from a normal distribution $\mathcal{N}(127, 30^2)$, clipped to $[0, 255]$. We generate it once and reuse the same instance on every poisoned frame to provide a consistent correlation (resampling for each frame would make the trigger stochastic and much less likely to induce a backdoor effect). The main benefit of the Gaussian noise patch is a lower chance of detection by simple defenses, while its drawback is that it may be harder to learn at lower poisoning rates and may require a higher rate to be more effective.

(a) Clean (b) Gaussian (c) Red

Fig. 2. Visual comparison of clean and poisoned frames using different attack types. All attacks shown are a 3×3 patch in the top left corner of the visual observation.

Our results in Table 1 show that even with only 5% of gas actions poisoned, both red and Gaussian patches achieve high backdoor control. The red patch yields the highest control and reward due to its strong contrast and consistency. The Gaussian patch is less effective at low poisoning rates, likely due to its lower visual salience. We also investigated applying a color-space shift patch [19] for dataset poisoning, but did not find it to yield a stronger attack than Gaussian or Red patch so we focus on only Gaussian and red patch backdoors in the rest of the paper. Details and results for the color-space shift trigger are included in Appendix A.2.

4.3 How Important is Timing of Backdoor Triggers?

We examine the impact of backdoor activation on a poisoned BC policy within the context of sequential decision-making by constraining the test-time attack budget to $B = 100$ and evaluating two distinct backdoor triggers: a red patch and a Gaussian patch, applied to their corresponding backdoor-poisoned BC policies trained on respective datasets with 5% of all gas actions poisoned. We compare and contrast the random test time backdoor trigger attack with our novel entropy-based attack that injects an attack at test-time without needing

Table 1. Comparison of the efficacy of backdoor patch types at 5% poisoned gas actions averaged across 10 seeds. Backdoor control accuracy is the percentage of poisoned observations predicted as "gas". The red patch performs visibly better in terms of backdoor control accuracy compared to the Gaussian noise patch, and remains comparable in terms of mean reward.

Patch Type	Mean Reward (± SE)	Backdoor Control Acc. (%) (± SE)
None	841.28 ± 1.676	30.80 ± 0.003
Red Pixels	838.99 ± 1.278	96.45 ± 0.001
Gaussian Noise	836.56 ± 1.769	80.35 ± 0.013

any privilege information about the environment dynamics nor access to weights of the pre-trained BC model. We solely utilize the outputs of the pre-trained backdoor poisoned model for our entropy-based attack.

Table 2. Evaluation of test-time trigger attacks. The table depicts performance of BC policy across 100 rollouts (mean and standard error), under different backdoor triggers during test time given an attack budget of 100 and specified entropy threshold as 0.005.

Trigger Type	Evaluation		
	Unattacked	Random	Entropy
Red Patch	832.74 (12.84)	794.96 (15.12)	-4731.69 (1178.56)
Gaussian Patch	858.38 (9.31)	841.96 (8.30)	577.43 (16.46)

Our results in Table 2 demonstrate that our entropy-based attacks significantly degrade the performance of the BC backdoor poisoned policy as compared to when backdoor is not activated at test time. We also show that our entropy-based attack outperforms the random attack baseline for test-time attacks by a highly significant margin of more than 100% degradation in case of the red patch and a moderate 31% degradation in case of the gaussian patch respectively. This justifies the need for intelligent backdoor trigger strategies at test time.

4.4 How Does Varying the Size of the Backdoor Patch Affect the Trade-off Between Stealth and Efficacy in Dataset Poisoning?

Prior work [15] highlights a trade-off between backdoor stealth and effectiveness: larger visual triggers can induce stronger spurious correlations but risk occluding task-relevant features, while smaller patches are less detectable but typically require higher poisoning rates. To investigate this trade-off, we fix the poisoning rate at 5% of gas actions poisoned, and vary the square ($N \times N$) patch size where $N \in [1, 96]$ pixels. Each trigger is a red square placed in the top-left corner of the frame, targeting the "gas" action. For each patch size, we train BC models for 5 separate seeds and report the average results over all seeds.

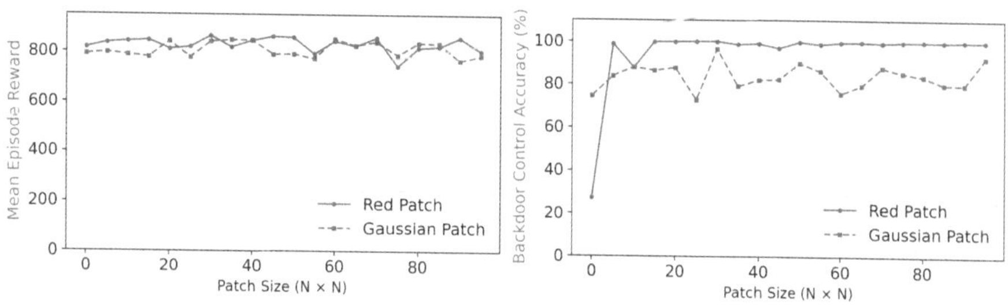

Fig. 3. Patch size sensitivity for red pixel and Gaussian noise patches. All models are trained with 5% of gas-labeled frames poisoned using an N × N red square patch. We see that we have similar reward performance for both patch types across all N. We also see that the backdoor effect rises at a very small N and stays fairly stable afterwards. The Gaussian patch performs worse in terms of control rate as a small poisoning rate is not enough for the policy to learn a more subtle trigger. (Color figure online)

Our results in Fig. 3 indicate that small to moderately-sized red patches, e.g., sizes from 5 × 5 to 25 × 25 can slightly improve task reward, likely by reducing policy uncertainty in gas predictions. Gaussian patches show similar scaling with patch size, though with weaker and more variable control. We find that trigger effectiveness plateaus around 5 × 5—larger patches offer no additional benefit and may increase detectability—highlighting the minimal patch size needed for effective backdoor activation. We repeat the sweep at a higher poisoning rate of 20% of gas-labeled frames to rule out a low-rate artifact and observe the same results. More details on this are included in the Appendix A.1.

5 Discussion and Conclusion

Our work reveals a fundamental vulnerability in BC policies: their susceptibility to very simple, low-budget clean-label dataset poisoning attacks. Our results show that BC policies compromised by backdoors may still achieve near-baseline performance unless the backdoor is actively triggered. Furthermore, our results show that even with as little as 2.31% poisoned training data, BC policies can be manipulated to respond predictably to small visual triggers.

Our experiments using a simple red patch as the backdoor trigger, in particular, demonstrates how minimal visual signals can yield near-complete control of model behavior to an adversary. This is a concerning result given the increasing deployment of IL models in real-world systems and the potential of using physical objects to trigger backdoors rather than requiring an adversary to hack into the visual feed of a cyber-physical system. This also highlights a major weakness of standard evaluation BC procedures, which can overlook a policy's hidden vulnerability to adversarial manipulation.

Our results also provide interesting evidence that the efficacy of dataset poisoning attacks on BC policies may be more sensitive to percentage of poisoned actions in the dataset rather than size of poison patch injected into the dataset. We believe this might be due to the fact that frequent occurrence of the visual trigger across training dataset reinforces the association between the trigger and the target action, increasing the likelihood of successful backdoor activation at test time, irrespective of patch size. Future work should see if these trends hold across other environments and other imitation learning algorithms.

Our results illustrate a clear trade-off between the efficacy and applicability of different patch types used for backdoor attacks. We find that the red patch, with its high contrast is ideal for achieving strong backdoor control with minimal poisoning, but its overt nature severely limits its stealth in practical deployments. Conversely, the Gaussian noise patch, designed to blend into the input distribution, is less likely to be detected but requires a higher proportion of poisoned data to reach similar levels of attack efficacy. This highlights a crucial adversarial trade-off: maximizing attack effectiveness with high-contrast triggers or prioritizing stealth and applicability with subtler triggers, albeit at the cost of efficiency.

We also provide evidence that entropy-based backdoor attacks are considerably more effective than random attacks at test time, leading to a more pronounced decrease in policy performance at test time. This suggests that selectively triggering the backdoor in states of high uncertainty is a powerful strategy, particularly in scenarios where the attacker cannot trigger the backdoor frequently. Future work should explore whether there exist optimal trigger timing attacks for imitation learning. We also hypothesize that if the adversary could use access to a digital twin of the environment to better optimize the timing of backdoor trigger injections.

In conclusion, we demonstrate that behavioral cloning (BC) policies are highly vulnerable to minimal clean-label backdoor dataset poisoning attacks. As the first to investigate this vulnerability, our work highlights the need for further research into the security challenges of BC. In particular, developing backdoor detection and removal techniques to enhance the robustness and security of imitation learning methods, is an especially exciting area for future work.

A Appendix

A.1 Additional Patch Size Ablation

Our results in Subsect. 4.4 in the main paper show that small to moderate patch sizes (e.g., 5×5 to 25×25) occasionally yield higher mean rewards than the unpatched baseline. We hypothesize that the backdoor trigger acts as a decisive cue, particularly for the gas action. When BC policies hesitate or waver due to compounding errors, a strong and consistent visual pattern reduces ambiguity and stabilizes the gas prediction, which improves the forward progress and reward.

Replacing the red square with a Gaussian patch at the same poisoning rate yields a qualitatively similar efficacy curve where the control increases slightly with N and plateaus at a small N. However, the absolute control rate is lower and more variable than with the red patch, as a Gaussian trigger is harder to learn at only 5% poisoning. The reward trends remain within a narrow band of the unpatched baseline.

Beyond this local boost, enlarging the patch past a small threshold yields no further gains in control accuracy. The trigger reaches near perfect reliability with a 5×5 or 10×10 patch. Larger patches do not improve performance and may increase detectability. This indicates a minimal effective patch size for attackers, the point where the trigger is already linearly separable for early convolutional layers, after which bigger patches have negligible impact on learnability.

Existing literature [15] reveals trade-offs between the two objectives of attack success and stealth, where injecting a larger patch to induce stronger spurious correlations is more likely to be detected or occludes task-relevant pixels. Conversely, smaller triggers can remain visually insignificant to humans yet may require a higher poisoning rate for success.

To study this balance, we sweep the square patch edge length $N \in \{1 : 96\}$ pixels while holding the poisoning percentage fixed at *5%*, as we saw previously that this low poisoning rate can yield near perfect adversarial results. For each N we keep the trigger color red, location on the top left of the frame, and target action for gas identical, training 5 independent BC policies per condition (Fig. 4).

We repeat the sweep at a higher poisoning rate of 20% of gas-labeled frames to rule out a low-rate artifact. For both red and Gaussian triggers, control saturates with very small patches N=5-10 and remains flat afterward. The mean reward stays within a narrow band around the baseline across all N. These results confirm a minimal effective patch size exists where choosing a smaller N can reduce detectability and occlusion without reducing attack efficacy.

A.2 Type of Patch

Finally, we compare different synthetic patch triggers to understand which visual characteristics most influence the effectiveness of the backdoor. Specifically, we consider three designs: a **fixed-color square**, a **Gaussian noise patch**, and a **color-space shift patch**. The different patches are visualized within poisoned frames in Fig. 5.

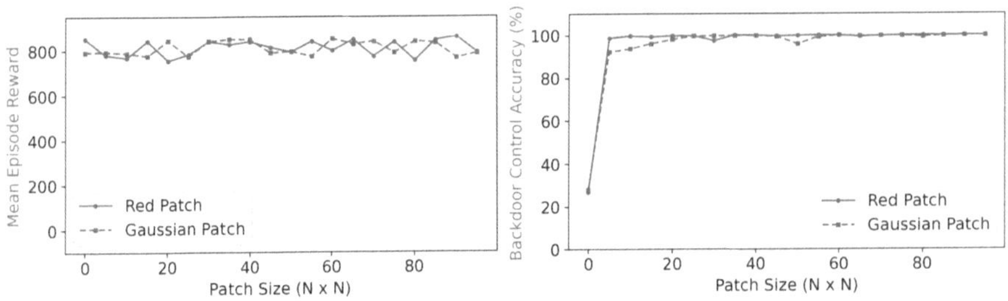

Fig. 4. Patch-size sweep comparison at a higher poisoning rate (20% of gas-labeled frames) for red and Gaussian patches. On the left, we see the mean reward being comparable between both patch types, while on the right we see a high control rate via the patch across the board. The red patch outperforms the Gaussian patch at smaller patch sizes, but the Gaussian patch still performs well with over 90% attack accuracy. (Color figure online)

The **fixed-color square** is a red patch which is high contrast and spatially consistent, which leads to early convolutional layers learning it easily. Its main drawback is its perceptibility, since the uniform bright color is easily detected by human reviewers and automated color-based defenses.

The **Gaussian noise patch** is sampled from $\mathcal{N}(127, 30^2)$, clipped to $[0, 255]$, and kept fixed for the entire training process. We generate it once and reuse the same instance on every poisoned frame to provide a consistent correlation (resampling for each frame would make the trigger stochastic and difficult to memorize). Its main benefit is a lower chance of detection by simple defenses, while its drawback is that it is harder to learn at lower poisoning rates and may require a higher rate to be more effective.

The **color-space shift patch** is a trigger where we increase all RGB channel values in that region by a fixed offset of +40, then clip to valid RGB values. This distorts color balance and does not remain static through the rollout. It is stealthy and can resemble natural lighting or tint changes, while its drawback is reduced learnability, especially when the patch overlaps low-contrast regions (Table 3).

Table 3. Comparison of patch types at 5% poisoned gas frames. Backdoor control accuracy is the percentage of poisoned observations predicted as "gas".

Patch Type	Mean Reward	Backdoor Control Acc. (%)
No patch	860.85 ± 86.30	22.33
Red Patch	832.66 ± 94.99	97.86
Gaussian Noise Patch	847.79 ± 74.39	85.07
Color-Space Shift	878.41 ± 60.10	88.13

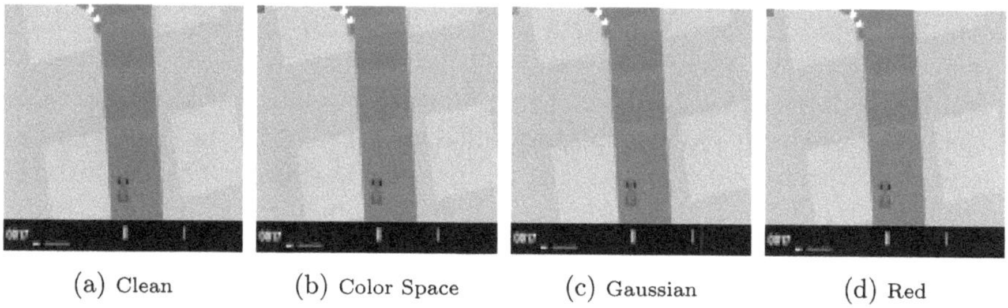

Fig. 5. Visual comparison of poisoned frames using different attack types. All attacks shown are a 3 × 3 patch in the top left corner of the visual observation.

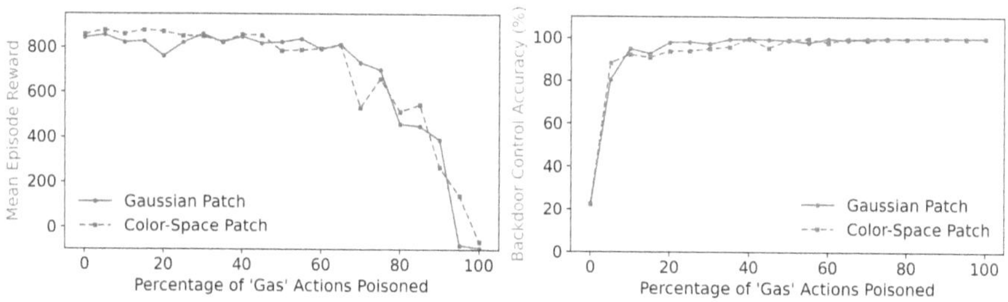

Fig. 6. Poisoning-rate sweeps for Gaussian and color-space triggers. Both patch types show similar performance across different 'gas' action poison percentages. We see that the accuracy of the backdoor patch seems to be higher for the gaussian patch at lower percentages, while the mean reward and backdoor accuracy for the rest of the poison percentages for both patches follow the same trend.

Our results at 5% poisoning are shown in Table 1. All three patch types achieve high backdoor control at 5% of poisoned gas-labeled frames. The red patch attains the highest control rate because its sharp color and structure are easily learned by convolutional filters. It also yields the highest mean reward, suggesting more stable throttle behavior during rollouts.

The Gaussian noise patch and the color-space shift achieve slightly lower control rates, though still high enough to compromise trained models. Their lower contrast and subtle texture make them harder for the model to isolate at low poisoning budgets, and in further experiments they match the red patch only when the poisoning rate is higher. Their mean rewards are slightly lower than the red patch but remain close to the clean baseline, indicating that subtle triggers are learnable by behavioral cloning models with somewhat reduced robustness and greater variability in recognition.

To examine how the subtler triggers scale, we sweep the fraction of gas-labeled frames poisoned with the Gaussian and color-space triggers. As shown in Fig. 6, both triggers improve with higher poisoning rates. The Gaussian patch reaches near perfect control at 20-25% while the color-space patch reaches similar levels of control around 25-20%. Very high poisoning rates reduce the mean reward, consistent with over-biasing toward the gas action.

We conclude that the trade-off between stealth (Gaussian and color-space patches vs. a solid red patch) and performance exists, but is not as significant as expected. Future works may focus on creating a realistic backdoor trigger patch that is more subtle to the human eye, even though it may require a higher poisoning rate to be effective.

References

1. Amodei, D., Olah, C., Steinhardt, J., Christiano, P., Schulman, J., Mané, D.: Concrete problems in AI safety. arXiv preprint arXiv:1606.06565 (2016)
2. Bagdasaryan, E., Shmatikov, V.: Blind backdoors in deep learning models. In: Proceedings of the 30th USENIX Security Symposium (USENIX Security 21), pp. 1505–1521. USENIX Association (2021). https://www.usenix.org/conference/usenixsecurity21/presentation/bagdasaryan
3. Bojarski, M., et al.: End to end learning for self-driving cars (2016). https://arxiv.org/abs/1604.07316
4. Boloor, A., He, X., Gill, C., Vorobeychik, Y., Zhang, X.: Simple physical adversarial examples against end-to-end autonomous driving models. In: Proceedings of the 2019 IEEE International Conference on Embedded Software and Systems (ICESS), pp. 1–7. IEEE (2019)
5. Brockman, G., et al.: OpenAI gym (2016). https://arxiv.org/abs/1606.01540
6. Brown, D.S., Goo, W., Niekum, S.: Better-than-demonstrator imitation learning via automatically-ranked demonstrations (2019). https://arxiv.org/abs/1907.03976
7. Chen, L., Paleja, R., Gombolay, M.: Learning from suboptimal demonstration via self-supervised reward regression. In: Proceedings of the Conference on robot learning, pp. 1262–1277. PMLR (2021)
8. Chen, X., Liu, C., Li, B., Lu, K., Song, D.: Targeted backdoor attacks on deep learning systems using data poisoning (2017). https://arxiv.org/abs/1712.05526
9. Chen, X., Guo, W., Tao, G., Zhang, X., Song, D.: Bird: generalizable backdoor detection and removal for deep reinforcement learning. Adv. Neural. Inf. Process. Syst. **36**, 40786–40798 (2023)
10. Chen, Y., Xue, H., Chen, Y.: Diffusion policy attacker: crafting adversarial attacks for diffusion-based policies. ArXiv **abs/2405.19424** (2024)
11. Chi, C., Feng, S., Du, Y., Xu, Z., Cousineau, E., Burchfiel, B., Song, S.: Diffusion policy: Visuomotor policy learning via action diffusion. In: Proceedings of Robotics: Science and Systems, (2023)
12. Farag, W., Saleh, Z.: Behavior cloning for autonomous driving using convolutional neural networks. In: Proceedings of the 2018 International Conference on Innovation and Intelligence for Informatics, Computing, and Technologies (3ICT), pp. 1–7 (2018). https://doi.org/10.1109/3ICT.2018.8855753
13. Florence, P., et al.: Implicit behavioral cloning. In: Proceedings of the Conference on Robot Learning (CoRL) (2021)
14. Gong, C., et al.: Baffle: hiding backdoors in offline reinforcement learning datasets. In: Proceedings of the 2024 IEEE Symposium on Security and Privacy (SP), pp. 2086–2104. IEEE (2024)

15. Gu, T., Liu, K., Dolan-Gavitt, B., Garg, S.: BadNets: evaluating backdooring attacks on deep neural networks. Ieee Access **7**, 47230–47244 (2019)
16. Guo, W., Liu, G., Zhou, Z., Wang, L.: PNact: crafting backdoor attacks in safe reinforcement learning (2025). arXiv preprint arXiv:2507.00485
17. Menell, D.H., Milli, S., Abbeel, P., Russell, S.J., Dragan, A.: Inverse reward design. In: Proceedings of the Advances in neural information processing systems, p. 30 (2017)
18. Hall, G., Das, A., Quarles, J., Rad, P.: Studying adversarial attacks on behavioral cloning dynamics. In: Proceedings of the 2020 IEEE 32nd International Conference on Tools with Artificial Intelligence (ICTAI), pp. 452–459. IEEE (2020)
19. Jiang, W., Li, H., Xu, G., Zhang, T.: Color backdoor: a robust poisoning attack in color space. In: Proceedings of the IEEE/CVF conference on computer vision and pattern recognition, pp. 8133–8142 (2023)
20. Khazatsky, A., et al.: Droid: a large-scale in-the-wild robot manipulation dataset. arXiv preprint arXiv:2403.12945 (2024)
21. Kiourti, P., Wardega, K., Jha, S., Li, W.: Trojdrl: evaluation of backdoor attacks on deep reinforcement learning. In: Proceedings of the 2020 57th ACM/IEEE Design Automation Conference (DAC), pp. 1–6. IEEE (2020)
22. Krakovna, V., et al.: Specification gaming: the flip side of AI ingenuity. DeepMind Blog (2020)
23. Li, X., Li, Y., Feng, Z., Wang, Z., Pan, Q.: Ats-o2a: a state-based adversarial attack strategy on deep reinforcement learning. Comput. Secur. **129**, 103259 (2023). https://doi.org/10.1016/j.cose.2023.103259. https://www.sciencedirect.com/science/article/pii/S0167404823001694
24. Li, Y., Jiang, Y., Li, Z., Xia, S.T.: Backdoor learning: a survey (2022). https://arxiv.org/abs/2007.08745
25. Lin, Y.C., et al.: Tactics of adversarial attack on deep reinforcement learning agents. In: Proceedings of the 26th International Joint Conference on Artificial Intelligence, pp. 3756–3762. IJCAI'17, AAAI Press (2017)
26. Ng, A.Y., Harada, D., Russell, S.: Policy invariance under reward transformations: theory and application to reward shaping. In: Proceedings of the ICML, vol. 99, pp. 278–287 (1999)
27. O'Neill, A., et al.: Open x-embodiment: robotic learning datasets and rt-x models: Open x-embodiment collaboration 0. In: Proceedings of the 2024 IEEE International Conference on Robotics and Automation (ICRA), pp. 6892–6903. IEEE (2024)
28. Patil, B., Kalra, A., Tao, G., Brown, D.S.: How vulnerable is my policy? Adversarial attacks on modern behavior cloning policies (2025). https://arxiv.org/abs/2502.03698
29. Qiaoben, Y., Zhou, X., Ying, C., Zhu, J.: Strategically-timed state-observation attacks on deep reinforcement learning agents. In: Proceedings of the ICML 2021 Workshop on Adversarial Machine Learning (2021)
30. Ross, S., Gordon, G.J., Bagnell, J.A.: A reduction of imitation learning and structured prediction to no-regret online learning (2011). https://arxiv.org/abs/1011.0686
31. Russo, A., Proutiere, A.: Optimal attacks on reinforcement learning policies (2019). https://arxiv.org/abs/1907.13548
32. Saha, A., Subramanya, A., Pirsiavash, H.: Hidden trigger backdoor attacks. Proc. AAAI Conf. Artif. Intell. **34**(07), 11957–11965 (2020). https://doi.org/10.1609/aaai.v34i07.6871. https://ojs.aaai.org/index.php/AAAI/article/view/6871

33. Schulman, J., Wolski, F., Dhariwal, P., Radford, A., Klimov, O.: Proximal policy optimization algorithms (2017). https://arxiv.org/abs/1707.06347
34. Sutton, R.S., Barto, A.G.: Reinforcement learning: An introduction, vol. 1. MIT press Cambridge (1998)
35. Tien, J., He, J.Z.Y., Erickson, Z., Dragan, A.D., Brown, D.S.: Causal confusion and reward misidentification in preference-based reward learning. In: Proceedings of the International Conference on Learning Representations (2023)
36. Torabi, F., Warnell, G., Stone, P.: Behavioral cloning from observation (2018). https://arxiv.org/abs/1805.01954
37. Turner, A., Tsipras, D., Madry, A.: Clean-label backdoor attacks (2018)
38. Turner, A., Tsipras, D., Madry, A.: Label-consistent backdoor attacks (2019). https://arxiv.org/abs/1912.02771
39. Zhao, T.Z., Kumar, V., Levine, S., Finn, C.: Learning fine-grained bimanual manipulation with low-cost hardware (2023). https://arxiv.org/abs/2304.13705

Designing a Secure and Resilient Distributed Smartphone Participant Data Collection System

Foad Namjoo[1(✉)], Neng Wan[2], Devan Mallory[3], Yuyi Chang[3], Nithin Sugavanam[3], Long Yin Lee[2], Ning Xiong[2], Emre Ertin[3], and Jeff M. Phillips[1]

[1] Kahlert School of Computing, University of Utah, Salt Lake City, USA
foad.namjoo@utah.edu, jeffp@cs.utah.edu

[2] School of Environment, Society and Sustainability, University of Utah, Salt Lake City, USA
{neng.wan,u1467261,ning.xiong}@utah.edu

[3] Department of Electrical and Computer Engineering, The Ohio State University, Columbus, USA
{mallory.115,chang.1560,sugavanam.3,ertin.1}@osu.edu

Abstract. Real-world health studies require continuous and secure data collection from mobile and wearable devices. We introduce **MotionPI**, a smartphone-based system designed to collect behavioral and health data through sensors and surveys with minimal interaction from participants. The system integrates passive data collection (such as GPS and wristband motion data) with Ecological Momentary Assessment (EMA) surveys, which can be triggered randomly or based on physical activity. MotionPI is designed to work under real-life constraints, including limited battery life, weak or intermittent cellular connection, and minimal user supervision. It stores data both locally and on a secure cloud server, with encrypted transmission and storage. It integrates through Bluetooth Low Energy (BLE) into wristband devices that store raw data and communicate motion summaries and trigger events. MotionPI demonstrates a practical solution for secure and scalable mobile data collection in cyber-physical health studies.

Keywords: System Design · Cyber-Physical Systems · Mobile Health · Wearable Sensors

1 Introduction

Understanding and improving personal health behavior is a major challenge. Although advances in smart devices make it possible to capture fine-grained

This work was supported by the National Cancer Institute of the National Institutes of Health under award number R37CA276365. The content is solely the responsibility of the authors and does not necessarily represent the official views of the National Institutes of Health.

L. Cheng and F. Anwar (Eds.): SmartSP 2025, LNICST 699, pp. 283–293, 2027.
https://doi.org/10.1007/978-3-032-33701-6_17

medical, personal, and movement data about individuals, doing so as part of a medical study still presents numerous challenges. The resulting system must be inexpensive, automated, easy-to-use, reliable, and protect private patient data. This requires a carefully designed secure smartphone system.

General personalized health studies require multiple components. First, *movement* is a key indicator of fitness and activity, and its relationship to health outcomes is an important factor. As such, smart systems need to collect various high-frequency statistics, such as GPS location and tracking of wrist movement and heart rate through peripheral smart devices. Beyond just tracking, many health studies require *interventions*, where the smart app detects certain activities and prompts the study patient to perform a task. This task may also collect data like a survey.

To achieve these goals, the smartphone interface should be minimal and seamless to ensure that it is used and that participants only use the intended features. It should be implemented efficiently with only the necessary Bluetooth connections to peripherals and other storage costs, so the batteries of the equipment can last a full day without recharging.

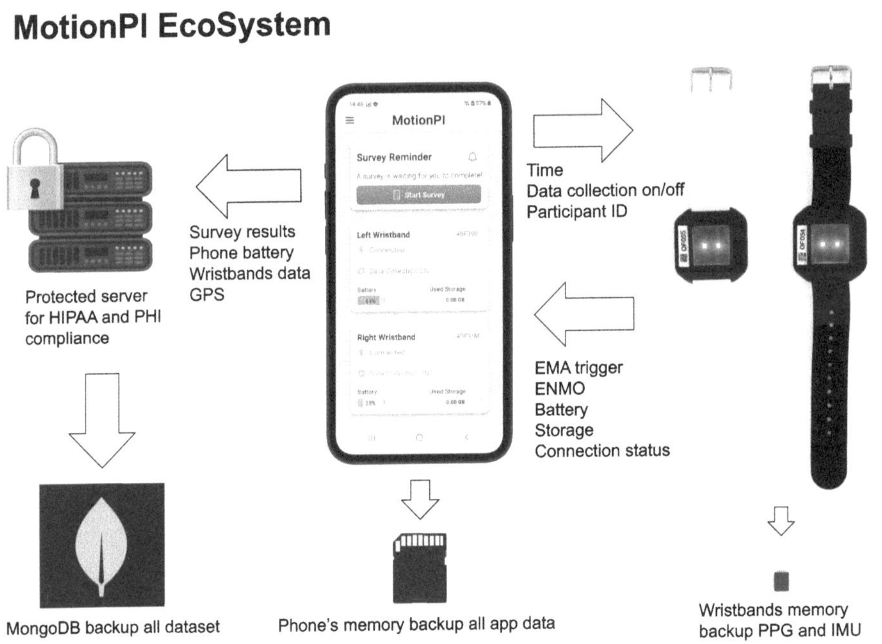

Fig. 1. Diagram of the MotionPI Ecosystem. The App plays a central role in coordinating the data collection from peripherals, high-frequency sensing, and EMAs, and its secure and distributed storage.

When dealing with patients' private health information, it must be secure. The equipment provided to study participants should not have residual data kept on the device of previous participants, and if it is there, it should be encrypted. The storage method should also be resilient and verifiably consistent. These studies need many participants, and it is a complex process to recruit them and convince them to actively participate in the procedures. If data is lost, it is a waste of time and expense.

Our Solution. We provide a smartphone system that stores data in multiple ways, both in the smartphone storage (with encryption) and in a secure cloud environment. This setup enables distributed, simultaneous, and secure uploads directly into a NoSQL (MongoDB) database. This structure, shown in Fig. 1, generates many advantages: (1) It is easy to monitor the data collection process and quality, (2) It enforces access control so that only authorized persons and all data analysts part of the project can access the data at any time, and (3) It enables verification that all the collected data has been successfully uploaded by comparing them with the locally stored files. To accomplish this, our proposed system, MotionPI, needs to make several critical design decisions. These include how the data are stored (both format and server environment), how to implement a secure container deployment, how to ensure data is eventually sent to the cloud when the smartphone's connectivity is sporadic, and it must ensure efficiency so it will not drain the smartphone battery too quickly. We document how we solve these issues in this report. Our system is currently being actively deployed in a large NIH-funded study.

2 Related Work

Several mobile health data collection platforms have been developed to support behavioral and physiological studies in the real world. Among the most widely used are **mCerebrum** [5], **Beiwe** [8], and **RADAR-base** [9]. Although mCerebrum is a widely used mobile health platform that supports sensor data collection and digital biomarkers, we encountered compatibility issues when trying to update and run the software on newer versions of Android.

The *mCerebrum* framework offers extensive sensing capabilities and supports high-frequency data collection, but its configuration requires technical expertise and often relies on continuous network connectivity. *Beiwe* provides strong privacy guarantees by encrypting data before upload, but is designed primarily for centralized studies and lacks support for edge-level computation or offline-triggered surveys. *RADAR-base* uses wearable devices and smartphones to stream data in real time, but its architecture assumes stable connectivity.

Other platforms, such as *AWARE* [4], allow sensor-based logging, but offer limited support for secure local storage or adaptive EMA logic.

In contrast to these systems, our proposed platform, **MotionPI**, is specifically designed for deployments with limited network availability, minimal participant interaction, and high privacy requirements. MotionPI enables encrypted local storage, robust background uploading to a secure cloud server, and EMA scheduling logic triggered by both time and sensor thresholds.

MotionPI combines a *dual storage* architecture (encrypted local and cloud redundancy) with *timed EMA triggers*—including BLE-based physical-activity detection (based on ENMO [1])—and device-scoped authentication for offline operation that tolerates intermittent connectivity; see Table 1. The remainder is necessary engineering integration (phone app + wristbands + backend + ops) that makes the system usable in real deployments while preserving confidentiality and availability under weak networks.

Table 1. Comparison of mobile data collection platforms. MotionPI supports offline-triggered surveys, BLE-based activity detection, and dual storage (local + cloud).

Platform	Timed EMA trigger	BLE activity trigger	Dual storage	Offline sign-in
mCerebrum [5]	yes	yes	no	no
Beiwe [8]	yes	no	yes	no
RADAR-base [9]	yes	no	no	no
AWARE [4]	yes	no	yes	via config URL
MotionPI	**yes**	**yes**	**yes**	**yes**

3 The Smartphone App

The MotionPI mobile application is a secure, resilient, and highly modular Flutter-based system developed to collect behavioral and physiological data in real-world health studies. It integrates passive (e.g., GPS and motion) and active assessments (surveys) through sensors and Bluetooth-connected wristbands. The app operates continuously with minimal user interaction and handles limited connectivity and low-power environments. It automatically operates in the background to handle continuous operation and geographically localizes each timestamp. Each participant is assigned an ID used as a unique identifier for their data and masking their identity; a study coordinator can maintain a list that maps these abstract IDs to participant names and information. Similarly, the data are marked with a phone ID using the Android advertising ID. The app then authenticates with the secure cloud server using JSON Web Tokens (JWT). If a token is missing, the app fetches a new one by signing up.

The user can select the name of the wristband on the settings page, and then the app connects simultaneously to two MotionSense [6] wristbands (left and right). It automatically discovers, connects, and resubscribes to wristbands using stored Media Access Control (MAC) addresses, and it monitors battery, charging status, storage usage, and motion using Euclidean Norm Minus One (ENMO) values [1]. The app displays real-time indicators for wristband connection status, battery status, and used storage on the home screen. It stores all data locally and sends them securely to the cloud server.

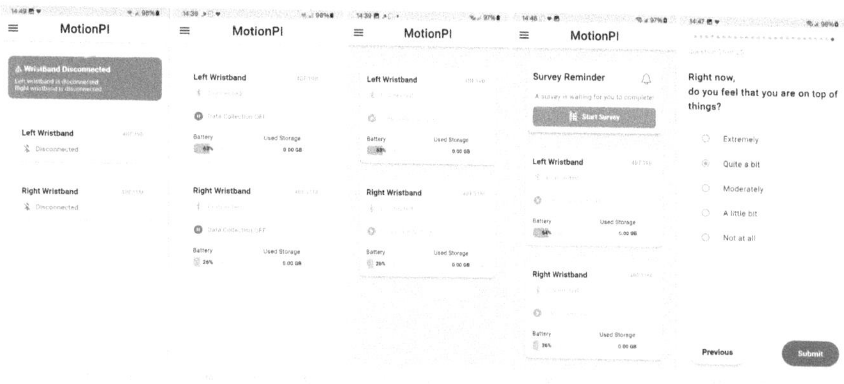

Fig. 2. Screenshots from the MotionPI App. The first (red) shows before the wristbands are connected, then after they are connected (yellow) but not activated, and in the middle, all are activated (green). The right two show when an EMA survey is triggered and available, and then within the EMA survey. (Color figure online)

The app schedules data collection by enabling from 7:30 AM to 9:30 PM daily. During this time, green LEDs on the wristbands and a status message on the home screen (the green screens in Fig. 2) confirm enacted data collection to the participant.

GPS coordinates are encrypted with AES-256 (CBC mode) before storage, as this information can reveal the identity of the participant (e.g., by inferring their home and work address).

The app delivers two types of EMA surveys via notification in a specific situation: Random Surveys; it is triggered three times daily at random times within morning, afternoon, and evening blocks. Activity Surveys; it is triggered upon detection of physical activity via the ENMO threshold of the wristband; see Fig. 2. Participants will be directed step by step to submit the survey. The submitted survey data is saved locally and securely transmitted to the cloud database.

All major app actions are logged and sent to the MongoDB backend and are easy to query in MongoDB Compass for deeper analysis. Not only does the system log the core data collection tasks, but also other critical events in the operation, such as when the participant turns Bluetooth on or off, when a wristband connects or disconnects from the app, and app state events, such as when data collection is enabled or disabled, when a wristband battery drops below 20%. Importantly, it records a variety of EMA survey-related events such as when an activity-triggered survey is initiated by wristband motion or otherwise, when an activity survey notification appears, when a participant declines the survey, and when a survey expires after 30 min without completion. These are important to assess how well a participant is following the study requirements and to calculate their monetary compensation for doing so. All of the above logs include participantID, phone ID, timestamp, wristband MAC, and local time.

3.1 Access Patterns for User Interface and Interaction

The app has different functionality for administrators (those running the study) and participants (the patients who are being monitored in the study).

The MotionPI app user interface is designed for clarity, accessibility and minimal burden for all types of users, while offering essential features for both participants and administrators. The homepage presents real-time information, including wristband connection status, battery and storage levels, data collection state, and survey reminders; again, see Fig. 2. If either wristband becomes disconnected, red banners and a short vibration appear to alert the participant immediately. The app will automatically connect whenever the wristbands return to connection distance or recharge.

The password-protected profile page allows users to set the participant ID (e.g., motionpi088), choose their dominant hand (left or right), and manually enable or disable data collection. These controls are critical for initial setup and troubleshooting.

Within the Settings page (also password protected), the admin can assign wristband labels with MAC addresses for wristband identification, update the app, and reset wristbands' internal memory. These settings are persistent, and allow for simple updates within large deployments.

4 Wristbands

The study uses wristband sensors extending MotionSenseHRV [6] to facilitate tracking and storing the levels of physical activity of the participants and provide triggers for the MotionPI application. The newly-designed wristbands support Bluetooth Low Energy (BLE) communication (Nordic Semiconductor nRF5340) with 4 GB on-board NAND flash (Micron Technology Inc. 4x MT29F8G01ADBFD12) for up to 30-day data recording capability with the sampling rate of 32 Hz and 64 Hz for IMU and PPG, respectively.

The onboard sensors consist of a 9-axis Inertial Measurement Unit (IMU) (TDK InvenSense ICM20948) and a photoplethysmography sensor (PPG) (Analog devices MAX86141) that measures blood flow using green and infrared wavelengths (OSRAM Inc. SFH701). The sensor enclosure is manufactured using the 3D printing technique (Stratasys, Ltd.), taking a dimension of $42 \times 44 \times 12$ mm, which is comparable to many commercially available wristbands. Additionally, the enclosure consists of optical barriers to mitigate ambient noise caused by variations in lighting conditions, improving the signal-to-noise ratio of the PPG signals. Finally, the intensity of the illumination is adapted to obtain PPG measurements that are agnostic to the participant-specific variations.

The device communicates with the MotionPI mobile application via a set of Bluetooth characteristics, which include commands to start or stop data collection, encode the participant ID, data collection time, and, when necessary, erase the onboard storage at the beginning of the study. To reduce communication overhead, only summary statistics of the activity state are transmitted via Bluetooth notifications. This notification includes the flag that indicates the detection of moderate to vigorous physical activity (MVPA) over an epoch of the past 7 min from the current time.

4.1 Physical Activity Triggers

The physical activity level is measured using accelerometry measurements. The IMU sensor measures wrist acceleration along with the effect of acceleration due to gravity. The IMU sensor also has a significant measurement bias. These imperfections in the sensor are addressed by constantly correcting for the bias error and compensating for acceleration due to gravity by subtracting the gravity vector. This quantity is referred to as Euclidean norm minus one (ENMO) [1], which is an approximation of the linear acceleration. ENMO is averaged over intervals of 15 s to obtain a measure of energy expenditure. We define a 15-s bout as MVPA if ENMO exceeds 0.1006 g (100.6 mG). We keep track of the MVPA levels over a 7-min epoch and declare the epoch as MVPA if there are 4.9 min (294 s) in the last 7 min of bouts that were declared as MVPA. The wristband notifies the MotionPI application if an epoch is detected as MVPA.

4.2 File-System Implementation

The sampled data, comprised of IMU and PPG measurements, is stored locally on the wristband using a FAT16 file system to organize the data. To improve performance and reliability, the file system was fitted with a custom-developed Flash Translation Layer (FTL), bridging the raw binary data into a mountable file system. Instead of storing all parts of the file system in a singular set of addresses like a conventional FTL, the custom FTL separates the file allocation table section and the data section on separate flash devices. Specifically, the file allocation table is stored on an onboard 8 MB NOR flash, while the data section is stored on the main 4 GB NAND flash. The file system was also modified to only support pre-allocated files, with timestamps and sizes of the file being marked only on file creation. This design for hardware separation of the file allocation table has several advantages - namely, it completely removes the need for file creation wear leveling on the NAND components, making it more durable (as those algorithms no longer need to run, thus eliminating the total number of write erase cycles needed for any file creation). While the system is slower during initial file creation (due to NOR being slower than NAND), writes to files themselves do not modify the file allocation table (due to the pre-allocation scheme), and due to this, the file system is faster than a traditional FTL when writing data for already opened files. Performance metrics and source code files for this FTL are available at [7].

Most importantly, this method offers data protection benefits, since in order for the data to be grabbed, attackers will need to have prerequisite knowledge of the physical layer file system separation, and extract all data from both the external NOR and NAND. Once this is done, the attacker would also need to figure out the file allocation table location and virtual addressing scheme on the NOR, which is non-trivial due to the idea that the file allocation table is mixed in with other miscellaneous runtime data on the external flash. The storage is made accessible by USB and can be viewed after collection via an administrator's computer. From a high level, the data is stored contiguously in 4 KB files, with a single file being created for both IMU and PPG, respectively. A graphical tool [2] is developed to download and extract onboard data to a human-readable format.

5 Secure, Robust Interaction with Cloud

The MotionPI mobile app communicates with a secure, resilient, cloud-hosted backend. The backend is implemented using the Express.js framework for the MotionPI data storage, authentication, and API management architecture. The cloud infrastructure ensures persistent, highly available storage and facilitates centralized data analysis, monitoring, and system scalability.

This secondary cloud storage is implemented using a Podman-managed MongoDB container that is running on a Rocky Linux virtual machine. The container is configured with authentication and persistent storage mounted via a specific dedicated local volume. All communication between the mobile app and backend is encrypted to ensure that personally identifiable and sensor data are not exposed during transmission.

The backend architecture is modular and RESTful. It includes user signup and token-based authentication. Each route is organized into its respective controller and router for maintainability and scalability. Data is validated using Mongoose schemas before being saved into MongoDB collections hosted on the cloud server. Incoming sign-in requests are parsed and validated via express.json() middleware, and routes are protected using JWT-based token authentication. The authMiddleware.js file ensures that only authenticated devices (smartphones) can access or push data to sensitive endpoints. For privacy, MotionPI uses JWTs for device-level access control. Each phone is registered with a unique token, stored on-device, and validated on each interaction with the backend. This design for the app from centralized login requirements enables secure offline sign-in. In the token authentication process, the device sends a signup or login request, and then the server verifies the device ID and issues a time-stamped JWT, and then the app stores and attaches this token to all future requests. All requests lacking a valid JWT are rejected with HTTP 401 responses.

Sensitive endpoints perform additional payload validation and format checking to prevent injection attacks or malformed data. This validation includes strict schema-based validation in Mongoose and type checking for arrays, timestamps, and Universally Unique Identifier (UUID). For example, the timestamp is validated to be a floating-point UNIX timestamp, and the phone ID and username fields are required for saving device data. These checks help ensure only valid data is stored. All data received is saved in MongoDB collections; it stores GPS coordinates, timestamps, phone IDs, device battery percentages, JSON-structured survey responses, and ENMO motion sensor data. Each record includes a timestamp, participant ID, and phone ID, allowing for structured, easy to query storage.

To ensure robustness even in cases of network interruption or app crashes, the app stores a file for unsent data using time-stamped files categorized by data type (e.g., ENMO, surveys), then, using retry mechanisms and scheduled background services, re-sends data when network connectivity is restored. These combined practices ensure both secure and reliable storage and transmission for our system. Through multiple tests, we have been able to verify that the data that is stored in the cloud database matches the data written directly (and encrypted) to the phone's memory, even when the internet connectivity of the phone had significant and varied interruptions.

All datasets from the MongoDB cloud database can be directly accessed for batch analysis and visualization via scripts or analytical tools (e.g., Python, R). As a result, this system design not only supports longitudinal studies with hundreds of participants, with unique JWTs per phone, but also online and complex analysis.

6 Ongoing Deployment and Conclusion

The MotionPI infrastructure is currently deployed and in-use as part of an NIH study. Each week (up to) 20 study participants are provided with a smartphone with the MotionPI software installed, along with 2 MotionSense wristbands as shown in Fig. 3.

In ongoing runs, even with continuous BLE connectivity, cellular data, and GPS enabled, the phone and wristbands sustains approximately 3% battery drain per hour over 14-h daily windows. This rate is lower than manufacturer endurance estimates for continuous screen-on phone activities such as internet use [3]. The reduced consumption is attributable to the app's predominantly screen-off, only event-focused participant interaction, and background data-collection design, which enables a full day of operation. Across participants, the system streams approximately 7.7 million data records per day to the cloud, sufficient for real-time monitoring and later batch analysis.

With minimal instruction, participants wear wristbands, carry the smartphone, and answer the triggered EMA surveys. The system has been successful in seamlessly and securely gathering all of the requisite data and storing it for easy monitoring and access in the cloud. This aligns with data more manually recovered from the phone's memory and wristbands.

We believe that the MotionPI system represents an easy-to-deploy smartphone-centered ecosystem that can facilitate various participatory data collection studies. It accommodates Bluetooth peripherals, triggered events, EMA surveys, and secure distributed data storage to facilitate simple monitoring and analysis. Critically, it has important safe-guards for data redundancy and privacy protection for personal protected health information.

Fig. 3. Package of items prepared for each study participant.

References

1. Bakrania, K., et al.: Intensity thresholds on raw acceleration data: Euclidean norm minus one (ENMO) and mean amplitude deviation (MAD) approaches. PLoS ONE **11**(10), e0164045 (2016)
2. Chang, Y., Mallory, D.: YAMS: yet another motionsense service utility (2025). https://github.com/SenSE-Lab-OSU/YAMS. Accessed 31 Jul 2025
3. Samsung Electronics: Galaxy A14 5G—specifications. https://www.samsung.com/latin_en/smartphones/galaxy-a/galaxy-a14-5g-black-128gb-sm-a146mzkgtpa/, battery: Internet Usage Time (LTE/Wi-Fi) Up to 22 h; Video Playback Up to 21 h; Capacity 5000 mAh
4. Ferreira, D., Kostakos, V., Dey, A.K.: AWARE: mobile context instrumentation framework. Front. ICT **2**, 6 (2015)
5. Hossain, S.M., et al.: mCerebrum: a mobile sensing software platform for development and validation of digital biomarkers and interventions. In: Proceedings of the 15th ACM Conference on Embedded Network Sensor Systems, pp. 1–14 (2017)
6. Kwon, S., et al.: The validity of MotionSense HRV in estimating sedentary behavior and physical activity under free-living and simulated activity settings. Sensors **21**(4), 1411 (2021)

7. Mallory, D.: MotionSenseHRV4 sensor software repository (2025). https://github.com/SenSE-Lab-OSU/MotionSenseHRV4Flash. Accessed 20 Oct 2025
8. Onnela, J.P., et al.: Beiwe: a data collection platform for high-throughput digital phenotyping. J. Open Source Softw. **6**(68), 3417 (2021)
9. Ranjan, Y., et al.: RADAR-base: open source mobile health platform for collecting, monitoring, and analyzing data using sensors, wearables, and mobile devices. JMIR mHealth uHealth **7**(8), e11734 (2019)

Adversarial Commercial Vehicle Datasets with Protocol Aware Annotation for Cybersecurity Research

Chandrima Ghatak(✉), Rik Chatterjee, and Jeremy Daily

Colorado State University, Fort Collins, CO 80523, USA
{chandrima.ghatak,rik.chatterjee,jeremy.daily}@colostate.edu

Abstract. Commercial vehicles are a vital part of freight transport and critical infrastructure, relying on SAE J1939 networks to coordinate safety systems, powertrain control, and fleet operations. While research into in-vehicle network security has advanced in the passenger vehicle domain, commercial vehicles remain critically underrepresented in public datasets, with detailed, frame-level attack labeling being even less common. Existing resources often lack semantic context, consistent labeling, or frame-level adversarial annotations, limiting their value for cybersecurity research.

We address this gap with four real-world, adversarially targeted J1939 datasets collected from a 2014 Kenworth T270 under controlled driving trials. Each dataset captures both normal and malicious traffic across multiple attack types and is annotated using a protocol-aware behavioral semantics schema. Implemented declaratively in YAML, this schema defines permissible transmitters, temporal constraints, and state-dependent behaviors, enabling automated, reproducible labeling of raw CAN logs with rich contextual metadata. This combination of datasets and a reusable annotation framework provides a standardized, scalable foundation for advancing cybersecurity research in the commercial vehicle domain.

Keywords: Commercial Vehicle Cybersecurity · Annotated Datasets · Protocol-Aware Labeling

1 Introduction

Commercial vehicles are a fundamental part of freight transport and critical infrastructure, operating daily over long distances to move goods, equipment, and essential resources. Their electronic control networks, dominated by the SAE (Society of Automotive Engineers) J1939 protocol [22], coordinate safety

This work was supported by the NSF PIVOT Project.
All datasets are publicly available at: https://github.com/SystemsCyber/J1939_Attack_Datasets.

L. Cheng and F. Anwar (Eds.): SmartSP 2025, LNICST 699, pp. 294–305, 2027.
https://doi.org/10.1007/978-3-032-33701-6_18

systems, powertrain control, and fleet telematics, enabling efficient and reliable operations. However, this same connectivity increases their exposure to cyber-physical threats, ranging from simple CAN (Controller Area Network) flooding to sophisticated, protocol-aware manipulations [3,12]. Given the rising frequency of known cyber-attacks on embedded systems and vehicles, and research suggesting different methods to tackle such risks [4,8–10,19], detecting and mitigating such threats, whether through statistical methods, machine learning, or hybrid approaches, requires access to large-scale, well-annotated datasets that capture realistic operational and adversarial conditions. While research into in-vehicle network security has matured in the passenger vehicle domain, commercial vehicles remain critically underrepresented in publicly available datasets, limiting the ability to evaluate detection methods and understand protocol behavior in this essential sector.

Recent public CAN intrusion datasets are largely passenger-vehicle-centric. The can-train-and-test dataset [14] offers multiple attack types but limited vehicle diversity. The HCRL dataset [13] contains short scripted attacks. ROAD [1] adds varied driving conditions but mostly captures stationary data. SynCAN dataset [11] provides both synthetic and real vehicle data. Dupont et al. [6], CAN-MIRGU [18], and CrySyS [7] address gaps through extended or specialized attack captures. Heavy-duty datasets are rare. The ORNL Driver Identification dataset [20] includes CAN, GPS, and biometrics under attack, but is limited to instrument cluster fuzzing. The University of Turku dataset [23] provides multi-session truck traces without contextual metadata. Across all, frame-level adversarial behaviors remain inconsistently labeled, semantic context is often missing, and commercial vehicle coverage is sparse, which limits their utility for large-scale automated analysis.

This gap creates two critical limitations. First, the absence of richly annotated real-world adversarial datasets for commercial vehicles hampers cybersecurity research in the area. Second, there is no standardized, software-driven process for generating such annotations at scale. Manual Subject Matter Expert (SME) labeling is infeasible for datasets containing millions of frames, and current approaches are often ad hoc, vehicle-specific, and lack protocol awareness.

We address these limitations with four real-world, adversarially targeted J1939 datasets collected from a 2014 Kenworth T270 Truck under controlled driving trials. Each is annotated using our protocol-aware behavioral semantics schema, which defines who may transmit which messages, when they may be sent, and under what operational conditions. Implemented declaratively in YAML, the schema powers an automated pipeline that ingests raw candump logs, decodes protocol metadata, evaluates message behavior across usage, temporal, and state dimensions, and outputs labeled CSV files with contextual metadata. This combination of dataset and reusable annotation framework enables reproducible, portable labeling of commercial vehicle CAN traffic, providing a foundation for advanced cybersecurity research.

2 Background

Commercial vehicles rely extensively on in-vehicle networks for control, diagnostics, and coordination between electronic control units (ECUs). The most common underlying data link is the Controller Area Network (CAN) [21], with higher-layer protocols such as SAE J1939 defining message semantics, network management, and transport mechanisms specific to the commercial vehicle domain.

Controller Area Network (CAN): CAN is a multi-master, broadcast serial bus designed for robust communication in noisy environments. Each CAN frame consists of an identifier (ID) and a data payload of up to 8 bytes in Classical CAN (or up to 64 bytes in CAN FD). The identifier also encodes arbitration priority, with lower numeric values winning bus access.

SAE J1939: SAE J1939 is a family of standards that specifies how CAN is used in commercial vehicles, defining message formats, parameter assignments, and network management procedures for heavy-duty applications. Messages use a 29-bit extended CAN identifier, from which the Parameter Group Number (PGN) is derived via the PDU Format and PDU Specific fields to identify the type of data or command. Depending on the PDU Format, messages are either PDU1 (destination-specific) or PDU2 (broadcast). Key fields include Priority (three-bit arbitration value, where lower numbers have higher priority), PGN (encodes the parameter group and meaning), Destination Address (DA) for PDU1 messages, Source Address (SA) of the transmitting ECU, and the Data Field, which carries up to 8 bytes per frame in Classical CAN as shown in Table 1.

Table 1. SAE J1939 29-bit Identifier Field Layout

Priority	Reserved	Data Page	PDU Format	PDU Specific	Source Address	Data Field
(3 bits)	(1 bit)	(1 bit)	(8 bits)	(8 bits)	(8 bits)	(8 bytes)

For messages exceeding 8 bytes, J1939 defines a Transport Protocol (TP) to segment and reassemble multi-packet messages using either BAM (Broadcast Announce Message) for broadcast transfers or RTS/CTS (Request to Send/-Clear to Send) for peer-to-peer communication. The standard also specifies an Address Claiming process in which ECUs announce and negotiate their 8-bit source addresses at startup or when new nodes join. Conflicts are resolved using the unique 64-bit NAME field, with the lower numerical value winning arbitration.

3 Threat Model

We assume an adversary capable of injecting, modifying, or replaying SAE J1939 messages on a commercial vehicle's CAN network. Access may be gained via the diagnostic connector or wiring harness [2], or through a compromised telematics or gateway device [12]. The attacker knows J1939 message formats, PGNs, and addressing schemes, enabling protocol-compliant malicious traffic. No cryptographic protections or authentication are assumed, consistent with current J1939 deployments.

The attack surface spans all J1939 layers. At the arbitration level, high-priority frames (e.g., CAN ID 0) can monopolize bus access, causing denial-of-service [15]. At the application layer, malicious PGN 0 torque control commands can override driver inputs or disable engine retarders [2]. At the network management layer, address claiming can be abused to evict ECUs or exhaust available addresses [17]. At the transport protocol layer, injecting abort messages can terminate multi-packet transfers, and flooding with diagnostic or request messages can overload ECUs [5].

4 Methodology

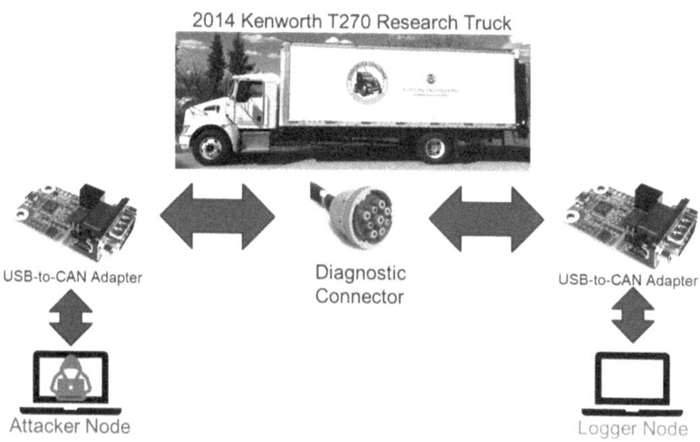

Fig. 1. Adversarial Data Collection Setup.

Data Collection: To replicate the previously documented adversarial behaviors described in the threat model, we carried out controlled, live driving tests on a PACCAR PX-7–powered 2014 Kenworth T270 at a closed airfield. The truck's SAE J1939 network operated at 250 kbps and included a Cummins 2350 engine control module (ECM), Allison RDS-2000 transmission controller, Bendix EC-60 brake controller, and a cab/body controller. Two Linux-based laptops equipped with USB-to-CAN adapters were connected to the vehicle's diagnostic connector. One acted as the *attacker node*, running the `can-utils` suite over SocketCAN to inject protocol-compliant malicious frames in real time. The second acted as the *logger node*, passively capturing all traffic using `candump` with millisecond-resolution timestamps as illustrated in Fig. 1.

The trial set covered four attack types:

1. **Network Flooding** via high-frequency, high-priority frames with PGN 0 to monopolize arbitration [15].
2. **Torque/Speed Control 1 (PGN 0) Command Injections** to command the engine and manipulate torque control values [2].
3. **Address Claiming** to evict active ECUs off the network by claiming its address with a lower NAME value [17].
4. **Request overloading** sending high-frequency low-priority request messages to saturate ECU processing resources [5].

All attacks were performed during normal driving conditions, ensuring realistic timing interactions between injected messages and legitimate traffic. Vulnerabilities exploited were drawn exclusively from prior research, and any platform-specific observations were reported through responsible disclosure channels.

Annotation Pipeline: Building on the threat model, our objective was to create an annotation system capable of detecting protocol-aware adversarial behaviors in large-scale commercial vehicle CAN datasets without requiring manual, frame-by-frame review. To accomplish this, we developed an automated pipeline that embeds SAE J1939 domain knowledge into a set of machine-executable labeling specifications. The pipeline ingests raw `candump`-format logs, extracts timestamped frames, and decodes protocol-level fields such as the Parameter Group Number (PGN), source and destination addresses, and arbitration priority.

A key departure from prior dataset labeling approaches, which often rely solely on static CAN IDs, time cutoffs, or script-based injection markers, is that our system evaluates each frame against semantic expectations of message behavior. These expectations are derived from both the SAE J1939 standard and empirical observations of legitimate ECU interactions. By formalizing these expectations, we separate the definition of anomalous behavior from the mechanism that applies these rules. This schema-driven design makes the labeling process reproducible and portable across vehicles, datasets, and attack scenarios, enabling consistent annotation in future research. In addition to attack labels, the pipeline appends metadata such as source/destination roles, decoded parameter values, and contextual state indicators to support richer downstream analysis.

Behavioral Semantics Categories and Justification: We classify anomalous behavior along three semantic axes, each corresponding to attack characteristics documented in prior work, including TruckSentry [16], which observed that all known J1939 attacks violate one or more of these dimensions corresponding to the SAE J1939 protocol:

- **Usage Semantics:** Captures violations of sender-role relationships or invalid PGN usage. This addresses attacks such as unauthorized torque control (PGN 0) commands from non-designated ECUs or spoofed identifiers with unsupported PGNs.
- **Temporal Semantics:** Detects hazardous transmission intervals, such as high-frequency flooding or arbitration monopolization, where messages are sent at sub-threshold inter-arrival times known to trigger denial-of-service conditions.
- **State Semantics:** Flags messages that are contextually invalid given the vehicle's operational state, such as address claims while in motion or torque control commands issued when ABS is inactive.

These categories are intentionally orthogonal. Usage semantics address *who* is transmitting *what*, temporal semantics address *when* it is transmitted, and state semantics address *under what conditions* it is valid. Together, they provide coverage for the known J1939 attack surface while remaining extensible for future threats. The declarative YAML schema operationalizes these semantics into reusable labeling rules that can be applied across datasets.

YAML Schema Design: Each annotation rule is expressed as a YAML object conforming to a structured schema (Listing 1.1). The schema formalizes annotation logic into five core components: (1) *Identifiers* (`name`, `type`, and `label`) that uniquely specify the rule and its output classification; (2) *Scope* defined by a `moi` (*message of interest*) filter that restricts matching to specific PGNs, source addresses, or other header fields; (3) *Context* definitions for state-dependent checks, enabling cross-message evaluation (e.g., correlating torque requests with vehicle speed); (4) *Parameters* specifying thresholds, comparators, or other quantitative constraints; and (5) optional *Metadata* fields describing severity, affected protocol layer, and a human-readable description.

Listing 1.1. YAML schema rule for detecting address claim messages issued while the vehicle is in motion.

```
rules:
  - name: Address Claim While Moving
    type: crule
    moi:
      pgn: 60928   # Address Claim
    context:
      pgn: 65265   # Vehicle Speed
      sa: 0
      offset: 1
      length: 2
      scale: 0.00390625
      comparator: ">"
      threshold: 1
```

```
  label: spoofed_address_claim
  metadata:
    severity: medium
    layer: network_management
    description: "Address claim issued while vehicle in motion."
```

This formalization supports *scalability*, rules can be applied to millions of frames with minimal runtime overhead, *Reproducibility*, datasets generated with the same schema remain directly comparable across experiments, and *portability*, adapting to a new vehicle typically requires modifying only the `moi` and `context` fields without altering the underlying detection logic.

The example in Listing 1.1 implements a *state semantics* rule targeting the SAE J1939 address claiming process. In nominal operation, address claims (PGN 60928) occur only during network initialization, typically when the vehicle is stationary. The rule specifies a `Message of Interest (moi)` filter to match address claim messages, then applies a `context` check by retrieving the most recent vehicle speed value (PGN 65265, scaled from raw bytes to km/h). If the speed exceeds 1 km/h at the time of the address claim, the frame is labeled as `spoofed_address_claim` and annotated with metadata indicating its severity, affected protocol layer, and a short description.

By combining a protocol-aware semantic model with a formally defined schema, the pipeline generates frame-level annotations that go beyond binary "attack" vs. "normal" labels.

5 Results and Evaluation

Results: Our labeling framework was applied to four adversarial scenarios captured during controlled tests on a 2014 Kenworth T270. Each scenario contains a mix of benign and malicious CAN traffic. Message labels are generated automatically via violations of usage, temporal, or state semantics.

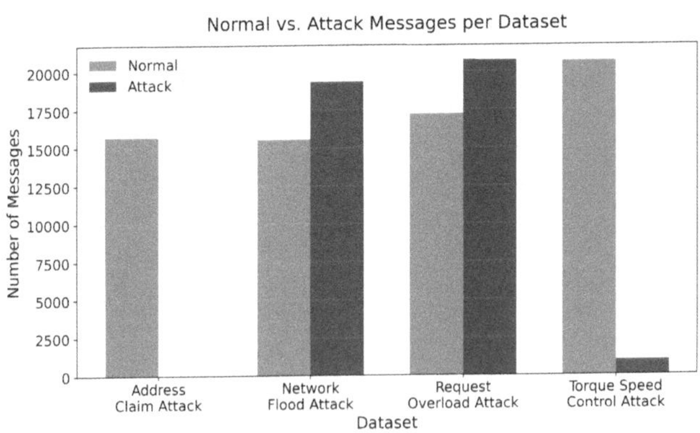

Fig. 2. Normal vs. attack message counts per dataset.

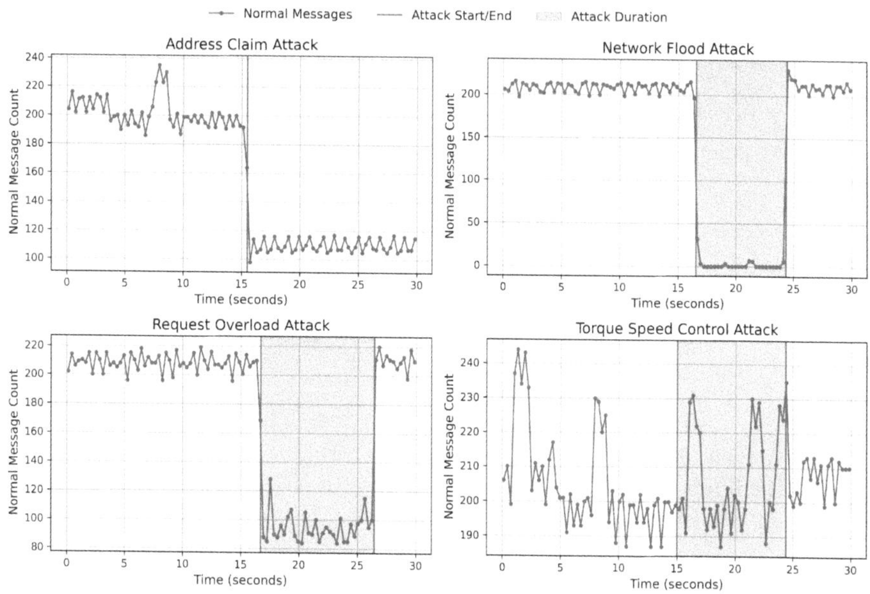

Fig. 3. Normal traffic over time by dataset with attack window.

All datasets are CSV files with one row per CAN frame and the following fields:

- timestamp, iface, can_id, dlc, data
- priority, pdu_format, pdu_specific, pdu_type
- pgn, pgn_label, destination, source
- label (normal or attack-type), rule_name, rule_type, semantics
- rule_severity, rule_layer, rule_description
- context_pgn, context_value

These fields support reproducible filtering, rule provenance, and downstream ML or statistical analysis.

Dataset Characterization: Each dataset is accompanied by a bar chart of normal vs. attack message counts and a time series plot showing normal traffic with the attack window highlighted. Figure 2 shows normal vs. attack message counts per dataset. This highlights class balance and attack intensity. Notably, the Address Claim Attack appears with no visible attack bar, as it consisted of only a single malicious frame—underscoring how even a single message can trigger significant network effects. Figure 3 plots normal message volume over time for each dataset, with the adversarial window shaded in gray and red lines marking start/end. This exposes burstiness and boundary effects.

Evaluation of Annotation Framework: We evaluated the accuracy of our automated annotation framework using four labeled datasets and the original raw *candump* style logs. Ground truth labels were derived from original logs where the exact timing, PGNs, and source addresses of malicious traffic were known.

Metrics: We calculated *precision*, *recall*, and *F1-score* per attack type as follows:

$$\text{Precision} = \frac{TP}{TP + FP}$$

$$\text{Recall} = \frac{TP}{TP + FN}$$

$$\text{F1} = 2 \times \frac{\text{Precision} \times \text{Recall}}{\text{Precision} + \text{Recall}}$$

where:

- **TP** = Attack messages correctly labeled as attack
- **FP** = Benign messages incorrectly labeled as attack
- **FN** = Attack messages not labeled as attack

Counts were obtained by comparing the framework's output labels to the ground truth per message (Fig. 2).

Table 2. Evaluation metrics for annotation framework by attack type

Attack Type	Precision	Recall	F1	Miss Reason
Address Claim Attack	0.500	1.000	0.6667	One legitimate "Cannot Claim" (254) message misclassified as attack
Network Flood Attack	1.000	1.000	1.000	No missed detections
Request Overload Attack	1.000	0.9993	0.99965	Some messages exceeded temporal gap threshold due to bus load
TSC1 Attack	1.000	1.000	1.000	No missed detections

Summary: The annotation framework achieved $\geq 99\%$ F1-score for most attack types. The few missed detections were entirely attributable to temporal threshold parameters in the YAML rule schema or to legitimate network management traffic being misclassified. In particular, one `Cannot Claim` message from source address 254 (NULL address) was incorrectly labeled as an address claim spoof. This occurred because the original rule schema did not differentiate between spoofed address claims and legitimate "Cannot Claim" messages. We have since updated the rule schema to correctly handle this case, ensuring that such legitimate messages are no longer marked as attacks. Temporal thresholds were retained as originally configured to avoid false positives in high-load environments.

6 Conclusion and Future Work

Commercial vehicles remain critically underrepresented in publicly available datasets, particularly those with detailed, frame-level attack labeling. In this data-driven world, the lack of representative, well-annotated datasets for commercial vehicles hampers progress across multiple domains, from design and evaluation of such systems to studying operational and forensic aspects of adversarial activity under realistic traffic conditions.

To address this gap, we presented four real-world J1939 datasets collected from a 2014 Kenworth T270 under controlled attack scenarios, annotated using a protocol-aware behavioral semantics schema. Each annotation is enriched with contextual metadata, enabling downstream tasks such as ML-based intrusion detection, temporal correlation analysis, and protocol compliance verification. This work provides both a reusable annotation framework and openly available datasets to support future research in commercial vehicle cybersecurity. All labeled datasets have been made publicly available (see footnote 1).

Our main limitation is the scope of data collection, as all datasets were captured from a single vehicle platform. In future work, we aim to broaden our coverage to multiple vehicle models and configurations and expand the annotation schema to additional domains. We also plan to provide richer contextual metadata, such as environmental conditions, operational states, and cross-domain sensor data, to further improve the utility of annotated datasets.

References

1. Bridges, R.: Real ORNL automotive dynamometer (ROAD) CAN intrusion dataset: a comprehensive guide to CAN IDS data and introduction of the ROAD dataset. Zenodo (2020). https://doi.org/10.5281/zenodo.10462796
2. Burakova, Y., Hass, B., Millar, L., Weimerskirch, A.: Truck hacking: an experimental analysis of the SAE J1939 standard. In: Proceedings of the 10th USENIX Conference on Offensive Technologies (WOOT 2016), pp. 211–220. USENIX Association, Austin, TX, USA (2016)
3. Chatterjee, R., Green, C., Daily, J.: Exploiting diagnostic protocol vulnerabilities on embedded networks in commercial vehicles. In: Symposium on Vehicles Security and Privacy (VehicleSec). VehicleSec Symposium, San Diego, CA, USA (2024). https://doi.org/10.14722/vehiclesec.2024.23046
4. Chatterjee, R., Karel, B., Baratto, R., Gordon, M., Daily, J.: Assured micropatching of race conditions in legacy real-time embedded systems. In: Proceedings of the Conference on Real-Time Embedded Systems (2024)
5. Chatterjee, R., Mukherjee, S., Daily, J.: Exploiting transport protocol vulnerabilities in sae j1939 networks. In: Proceedings of the Inaugural International Symposium on Vehicle Security & Privacy. Internet Society, San Diego, CA, USA (2023). https://doi.org/10.14722/vehiclesec.2023.23053
6. Dupont, G., Lekidis, A., den Hartog, J.J., Etalle, S.S.: Automotive controller area network (CAN) bus intrusion dataset v2. 4TU.ResearchData (2019). https://doi.org/10.4121/uuid:b74b4928-c377-4585-9432-2004dfa20a5d

7. Gazdag, A., Ferenc, R., Buttyán, L.: Crysys dataset of CAN traffic logs containing fabrication and masquerade attacks. Sci. Data **10**, 903 (2023). https://doi.org/10.1038/s41597-023-02716-9
8. Ghatak, C.: Toward robust embedded networks in heavy vehicles: machine learning strategies for fault tolerance. Master's thesis, Colorado State University (2024)
9. Ghatak, C., Chatterjee, R., Span, M.T., Daily, J.: A systems approach for designing open vehicle data archiving systems. In: Proceedings of the 2024 IEEE International Symposium on Systems Engineering (ISSE), pp. 1–8. IEEE (2024)
10. Ghatak, C., Jabeen, S., Shirazi, H., Ray, I.: Improving the resiliency of embedded networks in heavy vehicles - towards fault tolerance. In: Proceedings of Ninth Annual Industrial Control System Security (ICSS) Workshop. Annual Computer Security Applications Conference (ACSAC) (2023). https://www.acsac.org/2023/workshops/icss/chandrima-ghatak-paper.pdf
11. Hanselmann, M., Strauss, T., Dormann, K., Ulmer, H.: Canet: an unsupervised intrusion detection system for high dimensional can bus data. IEEE Access **8**, 58194–58205 (2020). https://doi.org/10.1109/ACCESS.2020.2982544
12. Jepson, J., Chatterjee, R., Daily, J.: Commercial vehicle electronic logging device security: unmasking the risk of truck-to-truck cyber worms. In: Symposium on Vehicles Security and Privacy (VehicleSec). VehicleSec Symposium, San Diego, CA, USA (2024). https://doi.org/10.14722/vehiclesec.2024.23047
13. Kang, H., Kwak, B.I., Lee, Y.H., Lee, H., Lee, H., Kim, H.K.: Car hacking: attack & defense challenge 2020 dataset (2021). https://doi.org/10.21227/qvr7-n418
14. Lampe, B., Meng, W.: can-train-and-test: a curated can dataset for automotive intrusion detection. Comput. Secur. **140**, 103777 (2024). https://www.sciencedirect.com/science/article/pii/S0167404824000786
15. Miller, C., Valasek, C.: Remote exploitation of an unaltered passenger vehicle. In: Black Hat USA, Black Hat Press, Las Vegas, NV, USA (2015)
16. Mukherjee, S., Chatterjee, R., Daily, J.: Trucksentry: context aware intrusion detection and prevention system for j1939 networks. IEEE Open J. Intell. Transp. Syst. **6**, 294–309 (2025). https://doi.org/10.1109/OJITS.2025.3545474
17. Murvay, P.S., Groza, B.: Security shortcomings and countermeasures for the SAE J1939 commercial vehicle bus protocol. IEEE Trans. Veh. Technol. **67**(5), 4325–4339 (2018). https://doi.org/10.1109/TVT.2018.2793239
18. Rajapaksha, S., Madzudzo, G., Kalutarage, H., Petrovski, A., Al-Kadri, M.O.: CAN-MIRGU: a comprehensive CAN bus attack dataset from moving vehicles for intrusion detection system evaluation. In: Proceedings of the Symposium on Vehicle Security and Privacy (VehicleSec) 2024. NDSS Symposium, San Diego, CA, USA (2024). https://doi.org/10.14722/vehiclesec.2024.23043
19. Ray, I., Sreedharan, S., Podder, R., Bashir, S.K., Ray, I.: Explainable ai for prioritizing and deploying defenses for cyber-physical system resiliency. In: Proceedings of the 2023 5th IEEE International Conference on Trust, Privacy and Security in Intelligent Systems and Applications (TPS-ISA), pp. 184–192. IEEE (2023)
20. Reid, E., Powers, S., Gallegos, E., Daily, J., Biggs, T., Lanigan, T.: ORNL driver identification dataset. Oak Ridge National Laboratory (2025). https://doi.org/10.13139/ORNLNCCS/2513388, dataset collected from 50 drivers operating a 2014 Kenworth T270 Class 6 truck, including CAN bus, GPS, IMU, and biometric data with an injected cyberattack scenario
21. Robert Bosch GmbH: CAN specification, version 2.0. Robert Bosch GmbH Standard (1991). https://www.bosch-semiconductors.com/media/ip_modules/pdf_1/can2spec.pdf. Accessed 12 Aug 2025

22. Society of Automotive Engineers: SAE J1939 Standards Collection. https://www.sae.org/standardsdev/groundvehicle/j1939a.htm. Accessed 12 Aug 2025
23. University of Turku: CAN bus dataset collected from a heavy-duty truck. https://doi.org/10.23729/3160254e-85e9-4268-a636-5b3e54091706 (2021), University of Turku

Demo

SPHERE CPS Enclave: A Reconfigurable Testbed for Industrial Control System Security Experimentation (Demo)

Jainta Paul[1], Brandon Jamjampour[4], Luis A. Garcia[1](✉), Jelena Mirkovic[2], David Balenson[2], Erik Kline[2], Yuri Pradkin[2], David Choffnes[3], Daniel Dubois[3], Terry Benzel[2], Srivatsan Ravi[2], Joseph Barnes[2], Geoff Lawler[2], Chris Tran[2], and Alba Regalado[2]

[1] University of Utah, Salt Lake City, UT, USA
{u1471999,la.garcia}@utah.edu
[2] USC Information Sciences Institute (USC-ISI), Marina del Rey, CA, USA
{mirkovic,balenson,kline,yuri,tbenzel,sravi,jdbarnes,glawler, ctran,alba}@isi.edu
[3] Northeastern University, Boston, MA, USA
choffnes@ccs.neu.edu, d.dubois@northeastern.edu
[4] California State University Long Beach, Long Beach, CA, USA
brandon.jamjampour01@student.csulb.edu

Abstract. We present a live demonstration of the SPHERE CPS enclave, a reconfigurable industrial-control experimentation environment built to make ICS security studies repeatable and shareable across research teams. The enclave combines PLC-based control, modular I/O, SCADA/HMI interaction, and an isolated, configurable network segment, with optional integration of simulated components to emulate larger process contexts. This demo walks attendees through an end-to-end workflow using a water-treatment scenario: provisioning the control and monitoring stack, running a baseline process, introducing representative faults or adversarial manipulations, and collecting synchronized controller, network, and process telemetry for replay and offline analysis. The goal is to support evaluations of detection and response techniques that depend on coupled cyber and physical behavior, including controller-logic attacks and network-mediated disruptions. We conclude by outlining planned extensions toward richer operator-in-the-loop studies (e.g., mixed-reality interfaces) and broader cross-domain interactions spanning water and energy-related infrastructure.

1 Introduction

Cybersecurity and privacy failures increasingly translate into real operational risk for critical infrastructure, including water, energy, and oil/gas. Well-known events such as the SolarWinds supply-chain compromise [6] and the Colonial Pipeline ransomware incident [9] illustrate how quickly cyber disruptions can cascade into real-world consequences. These systems are tightly coupled across

L. Cheng and F. Anwar (Eds.): SmartSP 2025, LNICST 699, pp. 309–313, 2027.
https://doi.org/10.1007/978-3-032-33701-6_19

software, networks, and physical processes, yet defenders and researchers often develop and evaluate protections in fragmented, ad hoc settings—making results hard to reproduce and easy for attackers to outpace [3,7,8]. Across the community, there is repeated demand for shared, representative infrastructure that enables repeatable experiments and cross-disciplinary collaboration [1,5].

The NSF-funded Security and Privacy Heterogeneous Environment for Reproducible Experimentation (SPHERE) [2] was created to meet this need by offering multiple coordinated experimental enclaves. Among them, a dedicated cyber-physical systems (CPS) enclave targets industrial control system (ICS) security by combining programmable logic controllers (PLCs), I/O modules, process instrumentation, SCADA/HMI functionality, and a configurable network substrate to support realistic cyber-physical studies.

In this demo, we showcase an initial water-treatment scenario implemented on the SPHERE CPS enclave [2]. The configuration captures core elements of a municipal-scale treatment workflow and is designed to support controlled observation of nominal behavior, structured fault/attack injection, and comparative evaluation of response strategies. While the present demo emphasizes baseline monitoring and repeatable perturbations, our longer-term direction is to incorporate AI agents that can observe system state, learn from prior runs, and coordinate with human operators to improve detection and recovery.

Overall, the SPHERE CPS enclave provides a modular and reconfigurable ICS environment—with remote access as a first-class capability—so that different research teams can run comparable experiments and transition emerging cyber-physical security ideas into more operationally grounded settings.

1.1 SPHERE Testbed

SPHERE [4] is a reconfigurable research infrastructure for cybersecurity experimentation that spans multiple hardware and workload classes. It includes: **General Compute Enclaves** (192 high-performance servers for application, system, and network security studies); **Machine Learning Enclaves** (10 GPU-enabled servers for security-oriented AI/ML); **Cyber-Physical Enclaves** (industrial control components such as PLCs and I/O modules for critical-infrastructure security); **Embedded Compute Enclaves** (912 edge platforms for IoT security, federated learning, and trusted execution environments); **IoT Enclaves** (500+ smart devices spanning home automation, medical, and industrial sensing); and **Programmable Network Enclaves** (SDN-capable components including Tofino switches and NetFPGA boards for network-security experimentation). These enclaves are connected through a dedicated, user-configurable network substrate intended to support realistic topologies and repeatable end-to-end studies. By pairing modern compute/virtualization with industrial automation components, SPHERE enables systematic evaluation of cyber-physical attack surfaces, defensive mechanisms, and resilience strategies.

1.2 CPS Experimental Capabilities

SPHERE supports controlled, high-fidelity experiments across a range of cybersecurity and privacy themes, including: (1) cyberattack emulation against industrial automation and other CPS-relevant deployments; (2) evaluation of anomaly detection, intrusion prevention, and response automation; (3) analysis of vulnerabilities in control protocols and IoT-integrated environments; (4) development and testing of secure-by-design approaches and resilient system architectures; and (5) exploration of digital-twin-enabled workflows for prediction, diagnosis, and security analysis.

The infrastructure is designed for both on-site and remote use, with integrated logging and tooling intended to make experiments repeatable and shareable. Depending on the study, runs may involve generating adversarial or potentially harmful traffic, taking measurements that interface with the public Internet, conducting human-subject interactions, or engaging with malicious external actors. To protect the broader Internet while enabling such research, SPHERE incorporates network security policies and operational safeguards aligned with safe experimentation.

Future expansions will add additional industry-relevant scenarios and incorporate emerging CPS threat models as the platform evolves.

Services and Community Building. SPHERE is designed to present a unified access experience across enclaves through a single interface. To support users with different expertise levels and workflows, SPHERE provides six portals: MAN (manual) for exploratory work, JUP (Jupyter) for mature computational workflows, GUI for novice users, EDU for education, AEC for artifact evaluation committees, and HUM for human-subject studies. These portals are intended to provide a consistent view of experiments while allowing users to transition between interaction modes as their needs change.

Beyond execution, SPHERE is intended to function as a shared substrate for high-quality artifact reuse and dissemination. The platform emphasizes reproducibility by supporting standardized ways to capture experiment topology, configuration, and workflow, coupled with extensive logging of user actions. The SPHERE team engages with research and education communities to identify experimentation and sharing needs, and works with conference and journal artifact-evaluation efforts to streamline hosting and evaluation on SPHERE. The project also plans open calls for mature artifacts to be deployed as representative environments, lowering the barrier for others to reproduce, extend, and compare results.

Demo Overview: SPHERE CPS Enclave The SPHERE CPS enclave [2] offers a remotely accessible, reconfigurable ICS environment for security experimentation. For this demonstration, the enclave is configured around a water-treatment slice that includes water-level sensing, flow regulation, and chemical dosing. The deployment integrates PLCs, sensor/actuator I/O modules, a SCADA/HMI interface, and an isolated network segment, with instrumentation aimed at capturing high-fidelity telemetry and supporting repeatable runs.

Demo Narrative:

1. *Scenario framing:* We introduce a concrete water-treatment security storyline (e.g., anomalous pump behavior arising from a simulated PLC logic modification) and identify the observable effects and success criteria.
2. *Environment setup:* Through the SPHERE portal, we instantiate the required PLC programs, I/O address mappings, network topology, and monitoring stack. Where needed, we include process-simulation components for subsystems that are not physically deployed.
3. *Execution under nominal and adversarial conditions:* We run baseline operation and then introduce controlled faults/attacks to illustrate how behavior changes across the controller, network, and process layers.
4. *Telemetry capture and replay:* We collect synchronized process variables, controller state, and network traces, enabling post-hoc analysis and replay-driven debugging.
5. *Artifact packaging and sharing:* We export the resulting configuration and data products as a reproducible bundle suitable for follow-on evaluation, algorithm development, or community sharing.

Demo Capabilities:

- Live visibility into process signals, PLC execution behavior, and operator-interface activity.
- Safe, controlled injection of faults and simulated attacks targeting PLC logic and/or process-network traffic.
- Built-in support for packaging experiments for reproducibility and collaborative analysis.
- Remote access via the SPHERE portal, with enforced security policies governing network interaction.

Future Directions: Although this demo highlights a baseline water-treatment workflow, the enclave's modular design enables rapid reconfiguration toward additional CPS domains (e.g., manufacturing or energy distribution). Next steps include extending the demo with AI-driven assistants that can detect anomalies, recommend mitigations, and coordinate with human operators—linking automated reasoning with human oversight for resilient critical-infrastructure operation.

Acknowledgements. The research reported in this paper was sponsored in part by the National Science Foundation (NSF) under awards FMitF-2425711 and 2330066. The views and conclusions contained in this document are those of the authors and should not be interpreted as representing the official policies, either expressed or implied, of the funding agencies.

References

1. Balenson, D., Mirkovic, J., Eide, E., Tinnel, L., Benzel, T., Emmerich, D., Johnson, D.: Cybersecurity artifacts workshop – report (2022). https://bit.ly/CyberArtifactsWkshp2022
2. Garcia, L., et al.: Sphere cps enclave: a reconfigurable testbed for industrial control system security experimentation. In: Proceedings of the ACM/IEEE 16th International Conference on Cyber-Physical Systems (with CPS-IoT Week 2025), pp. 1–2 (2025)
3. Government Technology: Hacktivism and DDOS Attacks Rise Dramatically in 2022. https://www.govtech.com/blogs/lohrmann-on-cybersecurity/hacktivism-and-ddos-attacks-rise-dramatically-in-2022
4. Mirkovic, J., et al.: Poster: security and privacy heterogeneous environment for reproducible experimentation (sphere). In: Proceedings of the 2024 on ACM SIGSAC Conference on Computer and Communications Security, pp. 5051–5053 (2024)
5. Mirkovic, J., Balenson, D., Ravi, S., Garcia, L., Benzel, T.: Cybersecurity Experimentation Workshop – 2022 – Report (2022). https://bit.ly/CyberExperWkshp2022
6. NPR: A 'Worst Nightmare' Cyberattack: The Untold Story of the SolarWinds Hack. https://www.npr.org/2021/04/16/985439655/a-worst-nightmare-cyberattack-the-untold-story-of-the-solarwinds-hack
7. Statista: Annual number of ransomware attacks worldwide from 2016 to first half 2022. https://www.statista.com/statistics/494947/ransomware-attacks-per-year-worldwide/
8. Sumeet Wadhwani, Spiceworks: Data Breaches Soared by 70% In Q3 2022 in an Otherwise Dull Year (2022). https://www.spiceworks.com/it-security/data-security/news/data-breach-report/
9. TechTarget.com: Colonial Pipeline hack explained: Everything you need to know. https://www.techtarget.com/whatis/feature/Colonial-Pipeline-hack-explained-Everything-you-need-to-know

Vulnerability Analysis on Multi-modal Sensor Fusion Under Physical Adversarial Attacks

Yi Zhu(✉)

Wayne State University, Detroit, MI 48202, USA
yzhu39@wayne.edu

Abstract. Multi-sensor fusion has been widely used by autonomous vehicles (AVs) to integrate the perception results from different sensing modalities including LiDAR, camera and radar. Recent studies have shown that physical adversarial attacks can compromise DNN-based multi-sensor fusion systems by simultaneously targeting all sensing modalities. Furthermore, our investigation shows that attackers can even manipulate a single modality to attack sensor fusion, revealing vulnerabilities in current fusion designs. These vulnerabilities pose significant safety risks for autonomous driving and may undermine public trust. In this poster, we propose a vulnerability analysis framework for multi-sensor fusion systems that can systematically identify the most vulnerable sensor modalities, providing developers with actionable insights to improve perception model robustness.

Keywords: Autonomous driving · multi-sensor fusion · adversarial attacks

1 Introduction

Recent years have witnessed the proliferation of autonomous vehicles (AVs). A fundamental function of AVs is perception, which enables the AV to understand its surrounding environment using onboard sensors. AV perception systems typically rely on sensor fusion, which aggregates the outputs from multiple sensing modalities, including LiDAR, camera, and radar. State-of-the-art multi-sensor fusion-based perception systems rely on Deep Neural Networks (DNNs).

However, DNNs have been previously found to be vulnerable to adversarial attacks where a small perturbation on DNNs input can significantly change the output predictions. To date, several studies have proposed physical adversarial attacks to individually attack DNNs in camera, LiDAR, and radar perception. Although sensor fusion is believed to be more robust than individual sensors, recent study [12] has demonstrate the possibility of attacking multi-sensor fusion systems. Our investigation shows that even attacking on a single sensor modality can compromise the overall sensor fusion output, revealing vulnerabilities in current fusion designs.

L. Cheng and F. Anwar (Eds.): SmartSP 2025, LNICST 699, pp. 314–318, 2027.
https://doi.org/10.1007/978-3-032-33701-6_20

In this poster, we develop a vulnerability analysis framework to estimate the susceptibility of each sensing modality under physical adversarial attacks. We first study the effective attack vectors for camera, LiDAR, and radar perception models. Building on this, our framework systematically identifies the sensor modalities that contribute most to the fusion output's vulnerability. Our proposed framework can provide valuable insights for developers to improve perception model robustness.

2 Attack Vectors Against Sensing Modalities

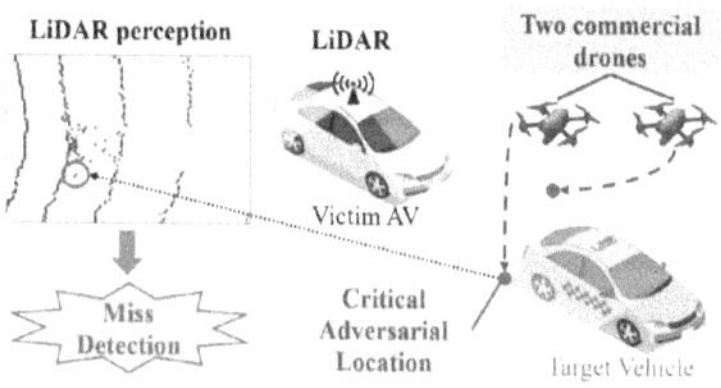

Fig. 1. LiDAR attack.

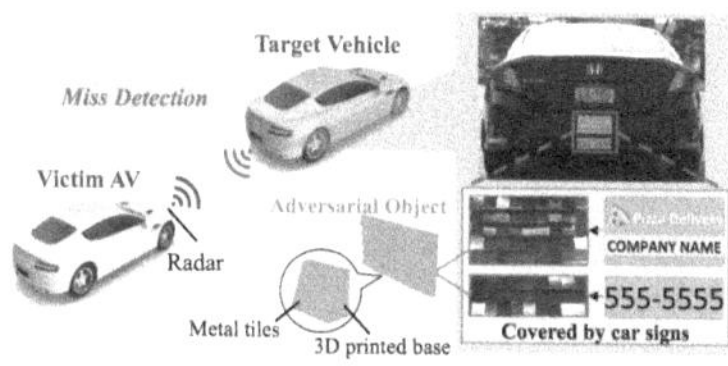

Fig. 2. Radar attack.

To perform physical adversarial attacks against DNNs in perception models, attackers need to manipulate the physical signals received by the sensors, such as image pixels, LiDAR point clouds, or radar signals. For camera perception, the attacker can use some stickers [6] or paintings [8] to change the input image pixel values to mislead the DNNs in camera perception. For LiDAR perception, our recent study [3, 10, 13] proposed to place arbitrary objects (e.g., drones) at some specific locations to attack the LiDAR perception, as shown in Fig. 1. In this attack, the drones themselves can reflect lasers, thus injecting points into the input LiDAR point cloud. By carefully choosing their locations, the attacker can significantly distort the learned features of the target vehicle, making the DNNs fail to the detect the target. For radar perception, our recent study [11] proposes to use some 3D printed objects, as shown in Fig. 2. These objects are designed with special geometric shape, which can generate malicious reflected signals. By sticking the objects on a target vehicle, these reflected signals introduce adversarial perturbations on the DNNs input to mislead the output, making the DNNs fail to detect the target.

Furthermore, we has investigated the possibility of using a single type of compositive adversarial objects to attack all three sensors through passive reflection [12]. As shown in Fig. 3, the adversarial object is a piece of cardboard attached by a color patch and a metal foil. According to [11], the metal surface on the object can attack radar perception. Its color patch can manipulate the input image pixel values to attack camera perception. The object can reflect lasers to attack LiDAR perception. By choosing appropriate number, size, color pattern of the objects and placing them at specific locations with specific orientations, the attacker can simultaneously attack all three types of sensors.

3 Vulnerability Analysis Framework

Building upon the identified effective attack vectors on LiDAR, camera and radar perception models, we now propose the vulnerability analysis framework. As discussed, the color pattern of an object affects the feature learning on camera perception while having no effect on LiDAR and radar perception. Injecting objects at specific locations mainly affects the LiDAR perception [13]. And the orientation of metal surfaces mainly affect the radar perception [11]. By systematically varying these attack vectors, we can selectively perturb the features learned by each perception model, LiDAR, radar, and camera, and analyze their influence on sensor fusion. The analysis framework works as follows: we first ran-

Fig. 3. Attack on sensor fusion.

domly select some samples in the dataset. For each sample, we perturb the attack vectors (object location, foil angle, and color pattern) and measure the resulting changes in fusion outputs. Specifically, we record the maximum change in detection confidence for each modality, denoted as V_{lidar}, V_{radar}, and V_{camera}. These values are then normalized within each scene and averaged across all scenes to yield $\hat{V}_{lidar}, \hat{V}_{radar}, \hat{V}_{camera}$. The normalized values quantify the relative impact of attacks on each modality. Higher value indicates that the sensor fusion is more vulnerable to the attacks on the corresponding sensor.

Table 1 summarizes the values of $\tilde{V}_{lidar}$, $\tilde{V}_{radar}$, and $\tilde{V}_{camera}$ for various sensor fusion systems, including BEVFusion [2], CRFNet [5], LFusion [1], Radarnet [9], RRPN [4], and HD-FPNet [7]. We conduct our experiments on 100 randomly sampled scenarios. We can find that the sensor fusion outputs can be significantly affected by attacking a specific sensing modality. This shows that these sensor fusion systems tend to rely on a single type of sensor and treat other sensors as auxiliaries. This highlights the need to develop more robust sensor fusion approaches that do not overly rely on or bias specific sensors. Our proposed vulnerability analysis framework serves as a tool to guide the development of such robust fusion models. In future work, we plan to evaluate more sensor fusion architectures using large-scale datasets.

Table 1. Vulnerability analysis on sensor fusion

Model	$\tilde{V}_{lidar}$	$\tilde{V}_{cam}$	$\tilde{V}_{radar}$
BEVFusion	**0.81**	0.19	0.00
CRFNet	0.0	**0.77**	0.23
Radarnet	**0.90**	0.00	0.10
LFusion	0.00	0.31	**0.69**
RRPN	0.00	0.01	**0.99**
HD-FPNet	0.19	**0.72**	0.09

References

1. Kim, J., Kim, Y., Kum, D.: Low-level sensor fusion network for 3D vehicle detection using radar range-azimuth heatmap and monocular image. In: Proceedings of the Asian Conference on Computer Vision (2020)
2. Liu, Z., et al.: Bevfusion: multi-task multi-sensor fusion with unified bird's-eye view representation. In: 2023 IEEE International Conference on Robotics and Automation (ICRA), pp. 2774–2781. IEEE (2023)
3. Lou, Y., et al.: A first physical-world trajectory prediction attack via lidar-induced deceptions in autonomous driving. In: 33rd USENIX Security Symposium, USENIX Security 24 (2024)
4. Nabati, R., Qi, H.: RRPN: radar region proposal network for object detection in autonomous vehicles. In: 2019 IEEE International Conference on Image Processing (ICIP), pp. 3093–3097. IEEE (2019)
5. Nobis, F., Geisslinger, M., Weber, M., Betz, J., Lienkamp, M.: A deep learning-based radar and camera sensor fusion architecture for object detection. In 2019 Sensor Data Fusion: Trends, Solutions, Applications (SDF), pp. 1–7. IEEE (2019)
6. Song, D., et al.: Physical adversarial examples for object detectors. In: 12th USENIX Workshop on Offensive Technologies (WOOT 18) (2018)
7. Wang, L., Chen, T., Anklam, C., Goldluecke, B.: High dimensional frustum point-net for 3D object detection from camera, lidar, and radar. In: 2020 IEEE Intelligent Vehicles Symposium (IV), pp. 1621–1628. IEEE (2020)
8. Xu, K., et al.: Adversarial T-shirt! Evading person detectors in a physical world. In: Vedaldi, A., Bischof, H., Brox, T., Frahm, J.-M. (eds.) ECCV 2020. LNCS, vol. 12350, pp. 665–681. Springer, Cham (2020). https://doi.org/10.1007/978-3-030-58558-7_39
9. Yang, B., Guo, R., Liang, M., Casas, S., Urtasun, R.: RadarNet: exploiting radar for robust perception of dynamic objects. In: Vedaldi, A., Bischof, H., Brox, T., Frahm, J.-M. (eds.) ECCV 2020. LNCS, vol. 12363, pp. 496–512. Springer, Cham (2020). https://doi.org/10.1007/978-3-030-58523-5_29
10. Zhu, Y., Miao, C., Hajiaghajani, F., Huai, M., Su, L., Qiao, C.: Adversarial attacks against lidar semantic segmentation in autonomous driving. In: Proceedings of the 19th ACM Conference on Embedded Networked Sensor Systems, pp. 329–342 (2021)
11. Zhu, Y., et al.: Tilemask: a passive-reflection-based attack against mmwave radar object detection in autonomous driving. In: Proceedings of the 2023 ACM SIGSAC Conference on Computer and Communications Security, pp. 1317–1331 (2023)

12. Zhu, Y., Miao, C., Xue, H., Yu, Y., Su, L., Qiao, C.: Malicious attacks against multi-sensor fusion in autonomous driving. In: Proceedings of the 30th Annual International Conference on Mobile Computing and Networking, pp. 436–451 (2024)
13. Zhu, Y., Miao, C., Zheng, T., Hajiaghajani, F., Su, L., Qiao, C.: Can we use arbitrary objects to attack lidar perception in autonomous driving? In: Proceedings of the 2021 ACM SIGSAC Conference on Computer and Communications Security, pp. 1945–1960 (2021)

Author Index

L. Cheng and F. Anwar (Eds.): SmartSP 2025, LNICST 699, pp. 319–320, 2027.
https://doi.org/10.1007/978-3-032-33701-6

Kolibri 360 GmbH
Ferdinand-Jühlke-Straße 7
99095 Erfurt, Deutschland
produktsicherheit@kolibri360.de